D0935613

# The Routledge Critics Series

GENERAL EDITOR: B. C. SOUTHAM, M.A., B.LITT. (OXON.)
*Formerly Department of English, Westfield College,
University of London*

# Lamb

## as Critic

*Edited by*

# Roy Park

*Fellow and Lecturer
Oxford University*

Routledge & Kegan Paul
London and Henley

First published in 1980
by Routledge & Kegan Paul Ltd
39 Store Street, London WC1E 7DD and
Broadway House, Newtown Road,
Henley-on-Thames, Oxon RG9 1EN
Printed in Great Britain by
Redwood Burn Ltd
Trowbridge & Esher

British Library Cataloguing in Publication Data
Lamb, Charles
    Lamb as critic.—(The Routledge critics series).
    1. English literature — History and criticism
    I. Title    II Park, Roy
    820'.9    PR403
    ISBN 0 7100 0376 5

*To Ian Jack*

# General editor's preface

The purpose of the Routledge Critics Series is to provide carefully chosen selections from the work of the most important British and American literary critics, the extracts headed by a considerable Introduction to the critic and his work, to the age in which he was writing, and to the influence and tradition to which his criticism has given rise.

Selections of a somewhat similar kind have always existed for the great critics, such as Johnson, Wordsworth, Arnold, Henry James, and the argument for their appearance in this series is that of reappraisal and re-selection: each age has its own particular needs and desiderata and looks in its especial own way at the writing of the past—at criticism as much as literature. And in the last twenty years or so there has also been a much more systematic and intelligent re-reading of other critics, particularly the lesser-known essayists and reviewers of the Victorian period, some of whose writing is now seen to be criticism of the highest order, not merely of historical interest, but valuable to us now in our present reading of nineteenth-century literature, and so informing us in our living experience of literature as well as throwing light upon the state of literature and criticism at particular moments in the past.

B.C.S.

# Contents

To write a few such things is perhaps as well as shining, a distinguish'd literary Character.

KEATS

Had he asked of me, what song the Sirens sang, or what name Achilles assumed when he hid himself among women, I might, with Sir Thomas Browne, have hazarded a "wide solution".

CHARLES LAMB

# Introduction

As a critic Charles Lamb has suffered both in comparison
with himself as an essayist, and with those professional
critics, Coleridge and Hazlitt, who were his friends and
contemporaries.  The comparison with Hazlitt, for example, was most damagingly expressed by Saintsbury when he
wrote:  'His love was ... "of the book," perhaps, rather
than, as in Hazlitt's case, "of literature." ... to Lamb
the book was a very little too much on a level with the
tea-pot ... he had a shade in excess of the collector's
feeling about him.' (1)   There are a number of implications in Saintsbury's wittily turned phrase.  First,
there is the suggestion of antiquarianism, of a love of
out-of-the-way authors, periods and genres.  Secondly,
there is more than a hint of amateurism, dilettantism and
even of later nineteenth-century aestheticism;  that,
somehow, for Lamb, there is a disconnection between literature and life.  But the most damaging implications are
that as a critic Lamb was what Hazlitt would have termed
'exclusive', and that, lacking a theoretical basis, his
critical writings cannot stand comparison with those of
the other early nineteenth-century critics.  It is primarily because of these two objections, his alleged 'exclusiveness' and an inadequate theoretical framework, that
Lamb has been shunted off into a side line of the English
critical tradition, and regarded merely as a rather quaint
and somewhat irrelevant figure.  Anyone wishing to reinstate him to a position in the mainstream of English criticism must meet and satisfy both charges.  The current
denial of his status as one of our greatest critics, although understandable, is unjustified.
   More than any other writer of his time, Lamb has suffered from the blanket appropriation of his life and

writings by the Victorians and Edwardians.  The Victorians, in particular, at least in relation to Lamb, appear
to have subscribed to Carlyle's view that the writings of
a man are important mainly as a means of providing a
greater understanding of the man himself.  The story of
his life had, for them, an irresistible appeal.  Born on
10 February 1775, the son of a clerk and servant to a
Bencher of the Inner Temple, Lamb attended Christ's Hospital until 1789 when he was fourteen.  Unlike Coleridge,
his near contemporary at school, he was denied a university education, partly perhaps because of a speech impediment, but more probably because of his family's limited
financial circumstances.  He worked as a clerk, first in
the office of Joseph Paice, then in the South Sea House
which also employed his elder brother John, and finally,
at the age of seventeen, entered the East India House in
1792 where he remained until his retirement in 1825.
During these early years he felt isolated and friendless,
and his meetings with Coleridge at 'The Salutation and
Cat' in 1794-5, which he remembered for the rest of his
life, only heightened these feelings once Coleridge had
left London for Bristol.  These early years of unsettled
adolescence culminated in a brief period of confinement in
a mental institution at the end of 1795.  His sister
Mary, ten years his senior, fared less well.  On 22 September 1796, Lamb returned home from work to find that his
sister, in a temporary fit of insanity, had attacked her
father with a knife and stabbed her mother to death.  In
spite of his brother's wish that she should be permanently
confined, Lamb, at the age of twenty-one, took upon himself the legal responsibility of caring for his sister, a
duty which he discharged until his death in 1834.  Now,
more than ever, Lamb felt himself to be a marked man:
poor, friendless, the subject of gossip, and working in a
dreary office with uncongenial colleagues.  The revelation of these events by George Henry Lewes and Thomas Noon
Talfourd after Mary's death in 1847, coupled with the Victorian bias for the personal and biographical, only resul-
ted in the dubious elevation of Lamb to the status of cul-
tural teddy-bear in the Victorian Establishment.  Between
1868 and 1876, five editions of his works were published.
Four further editions were issued between 1900 and 1908.
Yet the most remarkable feature of this period is less his
popularity as evinced by these successive editions, than
the century-long critical vacuum within which they were
published.  There are one or two exceptions, Pater,
Orage, Powys, but they are exceptions.  The works were
sunk in the man, and the man offered up as a sacrifice to
the Victorian ideal of heroic suffering and renunciation.

Paradoxically, however, Lamb's biography is relevant to
an assessment of his criticism on a number of counts.
C.S. Lewis once observed that a critical theory, for good
or ill, springs organically from the writer's whole attitude to life, and that if we wish to understand or to re-
fute it we must grub up its roots.    In Lamb's case there
are a number of pertinent biographical facts necessary to
rebut the charge that as a critic he is exclusive and
occult, that he likes the neglected by-ways of literature
only because they are neglected, and is hostile to greater
writers because of their very popularity.    It has even
been suggested that his admiration of Wordsworth and Coleridge among his contemporaries was only the result of personal friendship.    A distinction is necessary here.
When it is said that he is too exclusive this may mean
that the range of his critical sensibilities is limited.
Alternatively, we may mean that the range of his critical
writings is limited.    This is an obvious but crucial distinction too often forgotten by writers of literary history.    It cannot be denied that his critical output is
limited in quantity, and that much of what he did write
centred upon writers not of the first importance:   More,
Wither, Fuller, Temple, Vincent Bourne (but not Chaucer or
Spenser, Donne or Herbert).    But because the range of his
critical writings is limited, and many of his essays deal
with writers of minor importance, does not entail a corresponding limitation in the range of his critical sensibilities.    It is at this point that a knowledge of his
life, his letters, his opinions, his conversations, and
even his commonplace books, can be of the greatest importance.

Everyone knows that unlike his contemporaries - Wordsworth, Coleridge, Byron, Shelley, Keats, Hazlitt and De
Quincey - Lamb was an amateur, an amateur, moreover, as he
himself said, among professionals.    Working in an office
for thirty-five years, he did not have the same access to
editors, publishers, magazines or reviews.    Any writing
was executed before he went to the office, after his return in the evening, or during his brief periods of annual
leave.    Unlike many of his contemporaries, he had no private income;   the legacies and annuities so beneficial to
the early careers of Wordsworth and Coleridge played no
part in Lamb's life.    After 1809 when his salary was
greatly increased, there was not the same incentive to
write.    The years 1809 to 1820 are rather lean ones.
His 'Works', published in 1818, were collected and issued
at the request of friends.    The 'Specimens of English
Dramatic Poets', 1808, arose out of his practice of jot-
ting down favourite scenes in a commonplace book.    His

comments on the Garrick plays were contributed to William
Hone's 'Table Book' to help out the editor of the magazine.  His review of 'The Excursion' was the result of
personal pressures as were many of the articles for Leigh
Hunt's various periodicals.  Even the essays of Elia owe
their origin to the efforts of others on his behalf.  He
is primarily an occasional critic, responding to a variety
of pressures, personal, critical and financial.  In very
many cases the subject of an essay or letter is a writer
or artist who he feels has been neglected, maligned or
misunderstood: Shakespeare, Hogarth, Sidney, Spenser, the
Jacobean dramatists, Restoration comedy, and the early
seventeenth-century prose writers.  As his circle of
friends increased after 1800, he was compelled at times to
rent accommodation so that he might write without interruption.  These external considerations help to explain
the limitation in the range of his writings.  He is exclusive in this sense.  He does not write for his living.
He does not, as Hazlitt would say, have to 'coin his heart
for drachmas'.  Hazlitt's comprehensiveness is, after
all, very largely the result of an empty purse.  The difficulty occurs when the term 'exclusive' used descriptive-
ly, without praise or blame attached, is confused with the
normative use of the term, or is made the basis for extending its usage.  On the basis of his published criticism, there is a prima facie case for this conversion.
Limitation in the range of a writer's critical work would
be consistent with limited critical sympathies.  It is at
this point that the literary historian, in drawing his inferences, ignores what is generally known of Lamb's life.
The published criticism of Lamb is not the only extant
evidence.  His life at this point becomes relevant.  So
too do his correspondence, his jottings, the reported
conversations and commonplace books.  It becomes clear
that when we consider these additional sources of evidence
that his sympathies are not limited to the rather small
number of authors he wrote about.  From these we know of
his enjoyment of a host of other writers on whom he never
wrote: Chaucer, Spenser, Donne, Marvell, Milton, Dryden,
Pope, Richardson, Fielding, Smollett and many others.
Not to have written about them is a serious limitation,
but the omission can not be used as evidence for his exclusiveness as a critic.  His alleged repugnance to the
literature of the early nineteenth century is without
foundation.  He admired Wordsworth, revered Coleridge,
preferred the poetry of Keats to that of Shelley and
placed it second only to that of Wordsworth, and was impressed by the poetry of Blake and Clare.  He was silent
on the poetry of the most popular writers of the period:

Rogers, Campbell, Scott and Moore.   He was clearly unim-
pressed by the work of many of his friends such as
Southey, Leigh Hunt, Bernard Barton and Barry Cornwall.
He did not like Byron and alludes only in passing to the
novels of Scott.   Far from providing evidence of a res-
tricted critical range, these judgments suggest a strong
independent mind, contemptuous of critical fashions, and
with a penetrating insight into what is of permanent and
lasting value in literature.

Although the issue of Lamb's exclusiveness is important, it is far less so than the second of the objections:
that his criticism, little more than exclamatory and mar-
ginal jottings, lacks a theoretical framework. (2)   Unlike the earlier criticism, this raises the entire issue
of the nature and ultimate value of Lamb's critical
effort.   There is little point, however, in establishing
this to our own satisfaction only to have it circumscribed
immediately by the argument that after all he is far too
exclusive.   Thus, the question of the restriction of his
critical sympathies, though less important in a way, has a
logical primacy over the other, and as the arguments for
and against operate within fairly well-defined boundaries,
and can be dealt with reasonably summarily, it perhaps
deserves the chronological priority here given to it.
The second issue is much more like 'religion', which in
Lamb's view was a 'debateable land', a 'border-land' between the negative and affirmative.

Biographers and critics of Lamb have often pointed to
the curious anomaly that exists between his early interest
or 'sneaking kindness' for abstract speculation in the
late 1790s (p. 211) (3) and his subsequent rejection of
all theorising, philosophical or theological.   His early
interest in Necessitarianism and Unitarianism, his allusions to Priestley, Hartley, Reid, Price and Godwin are
regarded as discordant with the mature Lamb of the essays.
The latter, we are told, is not interested in the serious
issues of life, but takes refuge behind a persona, whimsical, playful, paradoxical and extravagant.   The intoler-
able pressure of events in his own life makes such a
flight from reality inevitable, if only for his own
sanity.   That the early Lamb had an adolescent and nas-
cent passion for philosophical theory is undeniable;   that
the later Lamb makes fun of it, avoids it, criticises it
in others, is equally incontrovertible.   As he expresses
it in the essay, Imperfect Sympathies, he has no wish for
Minerva in her full panoply.   Solutions, if there are
any, must be 'wide'.   There are two points that require
to be made here.   First, this radical shift is not peculiar to Lamb.   Wordsworth is, perhaps, the most famous

example, but Shelley, a generation later, is another.
Hazlitt began as a philosopher and, like Lamb, ended as an
essayist and critic.   Coleridge's greatest phase as a
poet, brief though it was, is accompanied by a diminishing
interest in English empirical philosophy.   In every instance the philosophy that was abandoned was an empirical
philosophy, one which, while it provided a platform for
liberalism in politics, religion, morals and social
theory, ran counter to the writers' deepest but unformula-
ted beliefs about the nature of poetry and of life.
There is little real difference between Wordsworth's abandonment of Godwin, Shelley's growing disenchantment with
empirical philosophers in general, and Lamb's subsequent
dismissal of philosophical abstraction.   Wordsworth and
Shelley, of course, were poets, and their main creative
effort occurred shortly afterwards.   In Lamb's case, the
medium was prose, and twenty years elapsed before his
changed attitude found its fullest expression in the
essays of Elia.   Although his early interest in philosophy is discordant with the work of the later writer, he is
far from being unique in this respect.   It is characteristic of the work of many of his contemporaries.

Secondly, although his early interest in philosophy and
theology is discordant with his later work, it is not discordant for the reasons usually put forward, namely, that
Lamb is trying to find refuge from a harsh reality.   It
is discordant because, in these early letters to Coleridge, his sense of life is expressed in terms of abstractions and abstract theories, whereas in the letters after
1800 and in his more mature work, it is expressed imaginatively as is the case with all great writers.   Coleridge
once wrote that

> a great Poet must be, implicitè if not explicitè, a
> profound Metaphysician.   He may not have it in logical
> coherence, in his Brain & Tongue;  but he must have it
> by *Tact* / for all sounds, & forms of human nature he
> must have the *ear* of a wild Arab listening in the
> silent Desart, the eye of a North American Indian
> tracing the footsteps of an Enemy upon the Leaves that
> strew the Forest - ;   the *Touch* of a Blind Man feeling
> the face of a darling Child -. (4)

The philosophical bases of Lamb's writings, as essayist
and as critic, are implicated in his work in the manner
Coleridge here suggests.   We read Lamb today for those
values which he, as reader, found in the literature of the
past.   His desertion of philosophy and theology was the
necessary abandonment that every artist, great or small,

must attempt, be he poet, dramatist, novelist or essayist.
Art is the expression, revelation, or in Lamb's own terms,
'apprehension' of what cannot be stated rationally, only
expressed imaginatively.   The high quality of some recent
criticism of Lamb as an essayist is due in large measure
to an increasing awareness of this fact.   It is this
recognition of the nature of art and its inextricable relation to life that is the key to his critical endeavour
as well.

The Romantic abandonment of abstraction for poetry -
and by poetry is meant the imaginative impulse common to
all men, and creative of art generally - is so widespread
that it is, perhaps, the most important feature of the
age.   For Hazlitt, the tension between the two constituted what he called 'the spirit of the age'.   The tension
itself can be expressed in a variety of more familiar
ways:   reason and imagination, understanding and feeling,
mechanism and dynamism.   The term 'abstraction', however,
is preferable if only because as readers and critics we
are concerned less with the faculty and more with the
work.   Moreover, 'reason' is such an ambiguous term that
we are forced to make distinctions between understanding,
commonsense, and reason in one or other of its various
manifestations:   scientific, practical, theoretical and
intuitive.   In any case, reason, however widely conceived, is hardly responsible as a whole for the sheer
inertia of human responsiveness and perception.   Abstraction, on the other hand, has two fairly clearly de-
fined aspects, both of which are of the greatest relevance
to Lamb.   First, as a process of generalisation, it is
obviously related to the formulation of theories, systems,
creeds, dogmas and solutions of one kind or another.   It
is clearly related to what might be called theoretical or
scientific abstraction.   Lamb's anti-scientific strain is
so well known as hardly to merit documentation.   He advised Coleridge in an early letter to omit all 'the scientific part' of Walton's 'Compleat Angler' (p. 259), and
six years later in 1802 he complained to the same correspondent that 'Science has succeeded to Poetry no less in
the little walks of Children than with Men' (p. 165).
In the essay, Detached Thoughts on Books and Reading, he
bracketed 'Scientific Treatises' with 'Court Calendars,
Directories, Pocket Books, Draught Boards bound and lettered at the back' as books 'which are no books' (p. 291).
In a letter towards the end of his life he apologised for
having 'a most unscientific head' but went on to affirm
that 'The March of Intellect, in respect of Science ... is
a Dead March' (p. 297).

The second aspect of abstraction, however, is even more

important. ⌈ This can be called familiar or mundane, as
opposed to scientific, abstraction, and characterises the
process whereby we become habituated to our daily world.
Life becomes so familiar, conventional, accustomed, habitual or automatic, that we cease to be aware of the wonder
and beauty of living itself. As Shelley says in his
essay, On Life, 'we live on, and in living we lose the
apprehension of life'. We see things only in general
terms; the living relationship between percipient and
object has been lost. Lamb describes this state perfectly in a very characteristic letter to Bernard Barton (p.
294):

> Do you know what it is to succumb under an insurmount-
> able day mare - a whoreson lethargy, Falstaff calls it
> - an indisposition to do any thing, or to be anything -
> a total deadness and distaste - a suspension of vital-
> ity - an indifference to locality - a numb soporifical
> good for nothingness - an ossification all over - an
> oysterlike insensibility to the passing events - a
> mind-stupor -

Stated in this way, the distinction does not appear worth
taking seriously. And yet this depressive note is one of
the most striking characteristics of his correspondence,
as indeed it is also of the letters of Keats. Lamb does
not hesitate even to borrow from Latin when he wishes to
ring the changes on what Terence had called 'the weariness
with everyday forms' (p. 334). Familiar or mundane abstraction is a perennial theme in the writings of Lamb and
of his contemporaries. Herein lies the importance of
childhood and of the memories of childhood. In his review of 'The Excursion' he writes of the child: 'how
apprehensive! how imaginative! how religious! (p. 199) and
of himself as a child in the essay, My First Play: 'I
knew nothing, understood nothing, discriminated nothing.
I felt all, loved all, wondered all -' (p. 288). The
very processes of living and growing up involve a progressive loss of wonder and relationship. The condition is
endemic in man and part of the toll of being a human being
where 'Custom lie[s] upon [us] with a weight,/Heavy as
frost, and deep almost as life!' As early as 1797 he had
written to Coleridge: 'To men, whose hearts are not quite
deadend by their commerce with the world, Innocence (no
longer familiar) becomes an awful idea.' (5) Taken together, these two aspects of abstraction become the domi-
nant image for Lamb of the fall of man. It is not so much
the loss of God or of Paradise, the imagery of which runs
throughout his writings, as a loss of what Wordsworth in

*loss of relationship + love.*

his preface to the 'Lyrical Ballads', 1800, called 'relationship and love'.   Perhaps more than other writers of this period Lamb, in his guise of Elia, gives the impression that he regrets the loss symbolised by childhood experience.   But as a man he clearly recognised that without the experience of the adult world, no great achievements were possible, that the fall was indeed fortunate. This is why, at the end of the letter to Bernard Barton cited previously, he can conclude:   'O for a vigorous fit of gout cholic tooth ache - an earwig in my auditory, a fly in my visual organs - pain is life - the sharper, the more evidence of life - but this apathy, t[his] death.' In the essay, New Year's Eve, he asserts that he would no more alter 'those untoward accidents and events' of his life than he would the incidents of a well-contrived novel (p. 285).   He clearly sees the ordinary, dull, familiar and routine world as essential to the achievement of a full life, and of great art.   The greatness of his many essays on the theme of childhood and the past derives from the fact that they could only have been written by someone whose eye, in Wordsworth's phrase 'hath kept watch o'er man's mortality'.

In spite, therefore, of the sophisticating medium of maturity as expressed by Lamb in the phrase 'Thou art sophisticated....   From what have I not fallen, if the child I remember was indeed myself' (p. 285), in spite of his repeated laments for that fall, Lamb at his best is still apprehensive, imaginative, religious.   Like his favourite actor, Munden, he can throw 'a preternatural interest over the commonest daily-life objects'.   Like Munden, he 'stands wondering, amid the common-place materials of life, like primaeval man with the sun and stars about him' (p. 74).   The imaginative quality of his later writings, while it has obvious parallels with the imaginative quality he attributes to childhood perception, is radically different from his adolescent passion for theological abstraction.   His attitude to life is no longer abstract, but poetic, imaginative, even religious. His interest in religious abstraction has been transformed and humanised, and is no longer in any meaningful way a dogma or creed.   He is 'religious' in what D.H. Lawrence called the 'natural' sense of the word, a sense requiring primarily a capacity for wonder.   Poetry, or in more general terms, art had become for Lamb the instrument of man's redemption.   This for Lamb is how we save our souls.   The abstract or fallen world of adult man is redeemed by establishing a new poetic or affective relationship with it.   This ascent is not an escape from the real world for as he points out in his essay on Hogarth, the

trouble with the ideal is that it takes away our attention
from the ordinary and the everyday, and as he had pointed
out to Wordsworth in 1801 poetry must spring 'from living
and daily circumstances' (p. 201).   He wants the ordinary
world of mortality, ruined·though it is;  he wants the
world of experience, however 'unpalatable' the 'draught of
mortality' might be (p. 286).   Without that world we cannot live;  and yet, to live only in that world is to cease
to be human in the fullest sense of the word.   Hence his
constant complaints about his office routine, his desk,
his colleagues at the East India House.   Hence his gratitude to Coleridge for 'rescuing' him (p. 215).   For Lamb,
the poet lives between divided worlds;  a Promethean figure, daily consumed and daily renewed, an Antaeus rising
stronger from his contact with the earth.   This oscilla-
tion between the abstract and poetic, evinced in his correspondence by the manic-depressive swing from one letter
to another, is both the power and the impotence, the grandeur and the agony of life and of art.   Keats called it a
world of half-seeing, of half-knowledge, a world of isolated verisimilitudes, a 'terra semi incognita of things un-
earthly'. (6)   But the imaginative perception of the
artist has not the stability of science, philosophy or religion.   It is transient, fleeting, elusive and impal-
pable, mysterious and insusceptible of rational explanation.   And it is not, nor does it involve, the perception
of another ideal or non-natural world as superimposed on
the ordinary and the everyday;  merely the ordinary and
the everyday glimpsed in a different way.

Keats's terminology in his formulation of 'negative
capability' is, of course, very familiar, and is usually
regarded as the classic expression.   In certain respects
it is.   But there is, in Lamb's essay, Imperfect Sympathies, a text just as good, if not better.   Its theoretical implications, however, have in general been overlooked
and the reason for this is not hard to find.   In this
passage Lamb is not discussing an abstract topic such as
the relationship between poetry and life, art and nature,
reason and imagination.   He seldom, if ever, does.   Instead, what we have is an apparently desultory and rambling essay;  personal, dramatic, charged with his customary
irony and replete with misleading circumstantial detail.
Largely because of this specific and personal emphasis,
the aesthetic implications of the essay have never been
acknowledged.   At first sight, Lamb appears to be discussing two types of men, two different nationalities.   But
the opposition which he establishes between the Caledonian
and Elian intellects far transcends this relatively minor
consideration.   We must not be misled by the author's

apologetic, self-mocking humour, for what he is in effect
doing is tracing the lines that divide not the perfect and
imperfect, the Scottish and the English intellect, but the
far more important gulf separating poetry and abstraction,
distinguishing between those who reach irritably after
fact and reason and those who are content to remain with
the 'uncertainties, Mysteries, doubts' of existence. (7)
This opposition is, perhaps, the central issue in the Romantic critical tradition, and Lamb's the fullest and most
potent expression of it in dramatic terms.  The quotation
is familiar, but as familiarity is one form of abstraction, we have tended to be blind to its more general significance (p. 158):

> The owners of the sort of faculties I allude to, [i.e.
> imperfect intellects] have minds rather suggestive than
> comprehensive.  They have no pretences to much clear-
> ness or precision in their ideas, or in their manner of
> expressing them.  Their intellectual wardrobe (to con-
> fess fairly) has few whole pieces in it.  They are
> content with fragments and scattered pieces of Truth.
> She presents no full front to them - a feature or side-
> face at the most.  Hints and glimpses, germs and crude
> essays at a system, is the utmost they pretend to....
> The light that lights them is not steady and polar, but
> mutable and shifting: waxing, and again waning....
> They are no systematizers, and would but err more by
> attempting it.

Lamb then proceeds to contrast the imperfect, or what
should be termed the poetic or imaginative mind with the
perfect or scientifically rational intellect, typified in
this essay by the nineteenth-century Scotsman.  The
essayist, however, subtly alters the pejorative context
within which he had previously considered the poetic intellect.  He no longer writes of 'Hints and glimpses,
germs and crude essays'.  Having considered ironically
the poetic from the standpoint of the abstract, he now
proceeds to reverse the perspective:  'crude essays' and
'germs' become 'half-intuitions', 'partial illuminations'
(p. 159):

> Surmises, guesses, misgivings, half-intuitions, semi-
> consciousnesses, partial illuminations, dim instincts,
> embryo conceptions, have no place in his brain, or vo-
> cabulary.  The twilight of dubiety never falls upon
> him....  Between the affirmative and the negative
> there is no border-land with him.  You cannot hover
> with him upon the confines of truth, or wander in the

maze of a probable argument.  He always keeps the
path....  He cannot compromise, or understand middle
actions.  There can be but a right and a wrong....
He stops a metaphor like a suspected person in an
enemy's country....  Above all, you must beware of indirect expressions before a Caledonian.  Clap an extinguisher upon your irony, if you are unhappily blest
with a vein of it.  Remember you are upon your oath.

If we compare this portrait of the 'perfect intellect'
with that by Keats of his friend and neighbour, Charles
Wentworth Dilke, we shall discover that both are the very
reverse of the poet who is negatively capable.  Dilke,
Keats tells us, belongs to that genus of 'stubborn argu-
ers' who 'never begin upon a subject they have not pre-
resolved on' and in Keats's view 'Dilke will never come at
a truth as long as he lives;  because he is always trying
at it'. (8)  In his essay, The Old and the New Schoolmaster,  Lamb, again in dramatic form, presents us with
just such a coach companion.  The essay, Imperfect Sympathies, however, is much more significant than these local
comparisons suggest.  If we can grasp the implications of
the essay, then we have in our hands the theoretical foundation underlying some of his finest critical essays:
Shakespeare, Hogarth, John Martin, and the Sanity of True
Genius.  The first of these is not a sport or a piece of
special pleading;  it needs no apology in the face of
modish derision.  The view expressed in it, after all, is
one shared by Hazlitt and Coleridge.
    All of these important essays, as well as a number of
others, operate on the basis of a similar opposition.  In
the essay on Shakespeare this is specifically the experience of reading as opposed to that of seeing the plays.
In the essay on Hogarth, Lamb's interpretation is set off
against the current one exemplified by Barry.  In the
Sanity of True Genius, Spenser is contrasted with the
fashionable late eighteenth-century novelists.  In the
essay on John Martin, Barrenness of the Imaginative Faculty in the Productions of Modern Art, Lamb uses Titian as a
model against which to measure the shortcomings of the
work of the modern painter.  But whether the representative chosen be Shakespeare, Hogarth, Spenser or Titian, in
each case he exemplifies the poetic, imaginative or 'imperfect' impulse which must not be compromised.  This
spirit or vision is neither empirical and natural on the
one hand, nor ideal and unconnected with ordinary life on
the other, but partakes of both.  The error of eighteenth-century art criticism for Lamb, as for the other
Romantic critics, is the false opposition which it sets up

between the ideal and the real.   Hogarth clearly did not
conform to the aesthetic theories of the ideal, and therefore Barry was compelled as a result to classify him as
realistic and comic, concerned only with the natural
world.    Lamb criticises both his assessment, and the
theory of the ideal giving rise to it.   In general terms,
however, the criticism is similar to his censure of the
stage representation of 'King Lear'.   The vision of the
artist and of the poet has been materialised.   This is
why he denies that Shakespeare's plays are based on the
'observation of life', and that his characters are
'natural'.

In the Shakespeare essay, as in the others, he is contending against the conversion of the poetic into the
abstract, the imitation into copy, art into reality, the
probable impossible (which he refers to specifically in
his criticism of Cooke's performance as Richard III) into
the impossible probable (p. 106).   In performing the role
of a character who in life would be unpleasant, the great
comic actor stresses the unreality of the impersonation by
entering into a 'tacit understanding', 'secret correspondence' with the audience by means of 'sub-insinuation',
'sub-reference', 'bye-intimation'. (9)   Likewise, the
poet and painter operate only by means of 'a wise falsification', 'a beautiful compromise'. (10).   Shakespeare's
characters are not real, natural, the result only of observation of empirical facts.   They do not belong to the
abstract world of the physical senses.   But whether the
tendency of the modern actor be to stress the naturalness
of the character and to 'avoid every turn which might tend
to unrealise' it (p. 66);   whether the modern novelist
depicts everyday life in fashionable circles alternating
'between Bath and Bond-street' (p. 157);   whether a modern
painter like Martin attempts to 'confine the illimitable'
(p. 348) in the 'grovelling fetters of externality' (p.
346) by the accumulation of minute, realistic detail;
whether Lamb criticises the stage performance of 'King
Lear' because it materialises a vision;   whether the modern audience invokes an 'insipid levelling morality' (p.
122) in its judgment of acted artificial drama, or Lamb
condemns a new illustrated edition of Bunyan's 'Pilgrim's
Progress' for its 'visual frippery' (p. 270), these and
many other critical insights are not scattered aperçus related only by the whimsical and paradoxical propensity of
their author.   They are, all of them, manifestations in
different ways of the principle embodied in the essay, Imperfect Sympathies.   They are to be found in places as
widely scattered as letters from the late 1790s to the
jottings on 'King Lear' published in 1834.   In a letter

of 1801 on the subject of Cooke's performance of Richard
III, Lamb praised Shakespeare for making the impossible
appear probable, and in a note to the Garrick Plays almost
thirty years later he praised the Elizabethan and Jacobean
dramatists for their ability to invest 'their bad characters with notions of good, which could by no possibility
have coexisted with their actions' (p. 140).  Then he
adds for good measure:  'It is not Nature's nature, but
Imagination's substituted nature, which does almost as
well in a fiction.'  This emphasis is clearly related to
the view expressed in Sanity of True Genius that where the
great poet 'seems most to recede from humanity, he will be
found the truest to it' (p. 156).  Contrary to most interpretations of his essay on Restoration Comedy, Lamb
throughout his criticism is insisting on the closest connection between literature and life.  But the relationship is not direct; it is not a one for one equation.
Neither literature nor painting must be made subject to
the criteria of the abstract world, of the world of the
'poor unassisted senses' (p. 97).  This is why in making his case against the stage representation of 'King
Lear' the imagery of physical sensation is so overpower-
ing.  His enthusiasm for Wordsworth's 'The Excursion' was
partly the result of his recognition that Wordsworth as a
poet was conducting the same kind of struggle against the
increasing dominance of this single-minded, not to say
simple-minded, Benthamite view of literature and life.
It would be a mistake, however, to see Lamb's creative and
critical endeavour as circumscribed by a limited historical perspective such as the term 'Benthamite' might suggest.  The tendency to abstraction, in either of its
aspects, theoretical or familiar, is endemic in human
nature.  And in all of these essays Lamb is criticising
actors, painters, critics, novelists, poets and dramatists
who have failed to achieve or even to be aware of the full
redemptive potential of literature and art.  His contri-
bution, like those of the other Romantics to this perennial issue, is of permanent value.

     If we accept C.S. Lewis's view that a writer's criti-
cism springs organically from his basic attitude to life,
then it is perhaps significant that the central text from
the essay, Imperfect Sympathies, is not a piece of literary theorising, or even of literary criticism.  We are
presented instead with a series of personal reflections on
the differences between two kinds of men in ordinary life.
His desire to keep alive the inspired condition of man, to
rescue him as he puts it in an early letter to Coleridge
'from the polluting spirit of the world' (p. 215), is
characteristic both of the man and of the writer.  Herein

lies the 'stamina of seriousness' that remained when the
vapours of early religious abstraction had evaporated (p.
293).   As in the case of Wordsworth, some of the best examples of this close relationship between life and art in
Lamb are to be found in his 'remembrance of things past'.
In childhood, in particular, he found the inspired condition, untrammelled and unsought for, free of the abstraction in both senses that we have made for ourselves.   The
very freedom of the child, however, imposes its own limitations, so that while the wonder, mysteriousness and ap-
prehensiveness of childhood is analogous to those modes of
seeing and feeling towards which the adult struggles, they
are not the same.   But whatever their limitations, Lamb
constantly strives to rescue them from adult indifference,
contempt and complacency.   In his review of 'The Excursion', for example, he characterised the poetic mind as
one in which 'call it strength or weakness - if weakness,
assuredly a fortunate one - the visible and audible things
of creation present, not dim symbols, or curious emblems,
which they have done at all times to those who have been
gifted with the poetical faculty;  but revelations and
quick insights into the life within us, the pledge of immortality'.   These, he adds, 'cannot be lasting:  it is
enough for the purpose of the poet, if they are felt' (p.
196).   The initial qualification, 'call it strength or
weakness', is a recognition of the tenuous hold that the
poetic vision, like childhood perception, has in the
esteem of the ordinary world.   In summing up the reasons
for Wordsworth's unpopularity he places the emphasis on
the adult contempt for the child (p. 199):

> If from ... a retrospect of his own mind when a child,
> he has gathered more reverential notions of that state
> than fall to the lot of ordinary observers, and, es-
> caping from the dissonant wranglings of men, has tuned
> his lyre ... to the milder utterance of that soft age,
> - his verses shall be censured as infantile by critics
> who confound poetry 'having children for its subject'
> with poetry that is 'childish,' and ... know not what
> the soul of a child is.

One of the functions of the Elian persona is to ward
off and remain impervious to adult criticism of his own
retrospective visions.   At the end of one such passage in
the essay, New Year's Eve, this is made quite explicit:
'That I am fond of indulging ... in such retrospection,
may be the symptom of some sickly idiosyncrasy....   If
these speculations seem fantastical to thee, reader - (a
busy man, perchance), if I tread out of the way of thy

sympathy, and am singularly-conceited only, I retire, impenetrable to ridicule, under the phantom cloud of Elia' (pp. 285-6). This, like the suppressed dedication to the 1823 'Essays' in which he tells the unsympathetic reader, 'you beat but on the case of ELIA' (p. 294), is a concrete instance of the conflict between the two kinds of intellect: the encroachments of the perfect intellect of the rational adult upon that of the imperfect creative writer, between the abstract and the poetic. The conflict remains the same throughout his writings, whether the subject be literature, painting, or life. At the end of the essay, The Old Benchers of the Inner Temple, an evocation of the old lawyers and their surroundings associated with his own early childhood, Lamb makes a quite specific connection between life, poetry and childhood:

> Fantastic forms, whither are ye fled? Or, if the like of you exist, why exist they no more for me? Ye inexplicable, half-understood appearances, why comes in reason to tear away the preternatural mist, bright or gloomy, that enshrouded you? Why make ye so sorry a figure in my relation, who made up to me - to my childish eyes - the mythology of the Temple? In those days I saw Gods, as 'old men covered with a mantle,' walking upon the earth. Let the dreams of classic idolatry perish, - extinct be the fairies and fairy trumpery of legendary fabling, - in the heart of childhood, there will, for ever, spring up a well of innocent or wholesome superstition - the seeds of exaggeration will be busy there, and vital - from every-day forms educing the unknown and the uncommon. In that little Goshen there will be light, when the grown world flounders about in the darkness of sense and materiality. While childhood, and while dreams, reducing childhood, shall be left, imagination shall not have spread her holy wings totally to fly the earth. (11)

Yet perhaps the most memorable expression of this perennial theme in his writings is to be found in the essay, The Old and the New Schoolmaster, when, unable to answer any of the interminable questions put to him by a type of the perfect intellect, Lamb reflects: 'Had he asked of me, what song the Sirens sang, or what name Achilles assumed when he hid himself among women, I might, with Sir Thomas Browne, have hazarded a "wide solution"' (p. 162).

## II THE DRAMATIC PRINCIPLE IN LITERATURE

Lamb's essay, On the Tragedies of Shakspeare, Considered
with Reference to their Fitness for Stage Representation,
exemplifies well the view that his critical response to
literature is a reflection of his more general response to
life.   This can best be illustrated by considering the
essay within two different but closely related contexts.
In the first instance it can be compared with the views of
Hazlitt and Coleridge on the same subject.   Lamb's own
demand for a 'dramatic morality' in literature provides
the second of these contexts.   If space permitted, the
essay could then be viewed against the more general back-
ground of early nineteenth-century discussions of painting
and literature, imagination and sight.   But, whatever the
context, it becomes quite clear that both the essay on
Shakspeare and that on Hogarth, written a few months earlier, are the direct consequence of firm convictions relative to the nature of man and moral experience.
    Like his essay, On the Artificial Comedy of the Last
Century, Lamb's essay on Shakespeare is in some respects a
special case.   Both embody critical themes and preoccupa-
tions which recur throughout his work, yet he seldom alludes or refers to the principal contention of either in
any of his other writings.   One or other of these, his
two most popular critical essays, has become the basis of
generally held but vaguely formulated beliefs as to the
nature of his critical writings as a whole.   In the essay
on Restoration Comedy he is said to view art, literature
or more specifically artificial comedy, as a fantasy world
which has no connection with life;  and in the other that
the plays of Shakespeare, or more specifically his tragedies, cannot be represented effectively on the stage.
Hence the notion has arisen that Lamb did not like the
theatre and entertained a bias against actors and acting.
This, however, is to ignore that two-thirds of his relatively small critical output is devoted to the criticism
of drama.   With his sister Mary, he was a constant
theatre-goer, and the stage exercised an influence upon
his critical writings no less important than the influence
of painting on those of Hazlitt.   It also played a more
important part in his social life than is the case with
Hazlitt.   He knew many of the greatest actors of his
time:  Liston, Munden, Elliston and Mathews;  he proposed
to the actress Fanny Kelly;  his many sketches of actors -
Bannister, Palmer, Suett, Dodd, Parsons, Emery, Bensley
and many others - are unsurpassed.   He wrote four plays,
as well as a number of prologues and epilogues to the
plays of others.   He was invited to draw up a descriptive

catalogue of the famous collection of theatrical paintings
owned by the comedian Charles Mathews.  His account of
the relationship of actor and audience, and of the effect
upon an audience of a well-acted play in the essay, Stage
Illusion, is the best in the language.  The term which
best characterises his general critical theory of literature is 'dramatic', and he is, with Hazlitt, the greatest
critic of the drama of his own or any other age in
England.

Nevertheless, in spite of his love of the theatre, Lamb
in his essay on Shakespeare, first published in Hunt's
'Reflector' in 1811, wrote of the stage (p. 93):

> I mean no disrespect to any actor, but the sort of
> pleasure which Shakspeare's plays give in the acting
> seems to me not at all to differ from that which the
> audience receive from those of other writers;  and,
> *they being in themselves essentially so different from
> all others*, I must conclude that there is something in
> the nature of acting which levels all distinctions.

His most serious charge occurs later in the essay, and it
is this passage which has been most widely quoted and most
frequently misinterpreted.  He writes of the acting of
the character of King Lear (p. 96):

> So to see Lear acted, - to see an old man tottering
> about the stage with a walking-stick, turned out of
> doors by his daughters in a rainy night, has nothing in
> it but what is painful and disgusting.  We want to
> take him into shelter and relieve him.  That is all
> the feeling which the acting of Lear ever produced in
> me.  But the Lear of Shakspeare cannot be acted.  The
> contemptible machinery by which they mimic the storm
> which he goes out in, is not more inadequate to repre-
> sent the horrors of the real elements, than any actor
> can be to represent Lear:  they might more easily pro-
> pose to personate the Satan of Milton upon a stage, or
> one of Michael Angelo's terrible figures.  The great-
> ness of Lear is not in corporal dimension, but in in-
> tellectual....  It is his mind which is laid bare.
> This case of flesh and blood seems too insignificant to
> be thought on....  On  the stage we see nothing but
> corporal infirmities and weakness ... while we read it,
> we see not Lear, but we are Lear....
> Lear is essentially impossible to be represented on
> a stage.

Few subsequent critics, for fear of committing some seri-

ous, albeit unspecified critical blunder, have dared to
support Lamb in a view that appears to impugn Shakespeare's mastery of stagecraft.   In the Victorian period,
Saintsbury was almost alone in his praise of the essay,
writing as he did of it as a 'magnificent paper', and admitting that 'I may be prejudiced in favour of this, by
caring myself infinitely to read the drama, and not caring
at all to see it acted;  but this objection could not be
made to Lamb'.   Lamb, he says, had 'come to that position
of the true critic ... that drama *may* be literature but is
not bound to be - that they are different things, and that
the points which drama need not have, and perhaps to which
it cannot do full justice, are in literature of the greatest importance.' (12)   In the early twentieth century,
Alfred Orage was equally outspoken in his praise:

> Lamb is at his best as a critic in his essay upon Gar-
> rick....   Lamb set himself to expressing what we all
> feel, the real inequality of the arts of acting and
> writing....   Lamb goes further, however, than to dis-
> sociate the two in value.   He would dissociate them
> altogether.   Though he was tolerant of acting, he much
> preferred the reading to the hearing of a great play.
> How much more subtly one can read a play of Shakespeare
> than anybody can speak it, or, still less, act it.   A
> thousand inflexions are made in the mind that cannot be
> conveyed either by voice or by gesture.   Voice and
> gesture at best must make a selection from the meanings
> the writer conveyed;  they are one interpretation
> only....   A popular representation of a great play is
> usually a misrepresentation. (13)

The attitude of most readers, however, is like Leigh
Hunt's towards the essay on Restoration Comedy when he
said that Lamb was playing tricks on his readers.   Percy
Fitzgerald, one of Lamb's Victorian editors, apologises
for his theories on acting as 'mere pleasant, fantastical
exercises'. (14)   But while some see the essay as mere
whimsy and paradox, others in attempting to defend it,
suggest a confusion between necessary and contingent arguments.   The essay, we are told, is not directed at the
intrinsic limitations of stage performance, but at the
obvious deficiencies of the early nineteenth-century stage
- its vast theatres, the star system, inadequate acting,
financial mismanagement, vociferous, inattentive and often
illiterate audiences, textual revisions and adaptations,
musical accompaniments, realistic sets, and ornate and
gaudy costumes.   With friends like these Lamb has no need
of enemies.   The impropriety of raising a normative argu-

ment purely on the basis of inferences drawn from contemporary theatrical conditions is too obvious for comment.

There are a number of possible interpretations of the
essay.   First, his argument is a normative one, independent of contemporary stage conditions, but capable of
being illustrated by it.   Secondly, Lamb assumes it to be
normative when it is only the result of his disgust with
contemporary productions.   His experience of unsatisfactory performances has led him to conclude that it is not
possible to stage a tragedy of Shakespeare without loss.
Thirdly, he is merely expressing a strong personal dissatisfaction with contemporary productions of Shakespeare's
tragedies.   Fitzgerald's 'whimsical' view of the essay
belongs to the second of these categories:   there is a
confusion between the normative and descriptive, but it is
wilful and deliberate.   Any interpretation of the essay
as 'special pleading' belongs to the same category except
that in this instance the confusion is unwitting.   Anyone
accepting the third explanation must, of necessity, interpret Lamb's use of the word 'essentially' in both the passages cited earlier as stylistic flourishes.   It also ignores his insistence earlier in the essay that the defect
of stage representation is 'inherent', and that it is
'not ... the fault of the actor (pp. 89, 89).   It also
fails to take into account Lamb's essay for the 'Examiner', 19 December 1813, in which he relates his experience of watching a performance of 'Richard III' in the
company of a blind man. (15)

Lamb was not the only critic to say so forcibly what
many felt but few dared to express.   'The Times' drama
critic, and later editor, Thomas Barnes is reported to
have said:   'And do I not know ... that you have written
about Shakspeare, and Shakspeare's own Lear, finer than
any one ever did in the world, and won't I let the world
know it?' (16)   More important, both Hazlitt and Coleridge were equally convinced of the validity of the argument.   Their views, however, were never embodied in a
single full-length essay with the result that Lamb has
attracted to himself all the odium for allegedly divorcing
drama from its performance on the stage.   Coleridge's
comments were never published in his own life time, and
even today lie buried in a patchwork of notes and lectures
pieced together under the title of 'Shakespearean Criticism'.   In one of his most popular works, 'Characters of
Shakespear's Plays', Hazlitt was content to say only that
'We do not like to see our author's plays acted, and least
of all, HAMLET' (vol. IV, p. 237). (17)   But in his
dramatic notices for the 'Examiner', later reprinted and
tucked away in one of the least read of his works, 'A View

of the English Stage', 1818, he was much more forthright.
To juxtapose Lamb's essay with quotations from both these
critics is to dispose of the view that the essay on
Shakespeare was an exercise in wilful paradox and whimsical eccentricity.   It also helps clarify the issue of
whether his argument is an aesthetic argument using, but
independent of, illustrations relating to the contemporary
stage, or an aesthetic argument dependent for its validity
on the evidence of the early nineteenth-century theatre.
    Hazlitt's comments occur in three articles written for
the 'Examiner' between March and July 1815, four years
after the appearance of Lamb's essay.   In the first, he
reviews the performance by Kean of Richard II (vol. V, pp.
221-2):

    We are not in the number of those who are anxious in
    recommending the getting-up of Shakespear's plays in
    general, as a duty which our stage-managers owe equally
    to the author, and the reader of those wonderful com-
    positions.   The representing the very finest of them
    on the stage, even by the best actors, is, we appre-
    hend, an abuse of the genius of the poet, and even in
    those of a second-rate class, the quantity of sentiment
    and imagery greatly outweighs the immediate impression
    of the situation and story.   Not only are the more re-
    fined poetical beauties and minuter strokes of charac-
    ter lost to the audience, but the most striking and
    impressive passages, those which having once read we
    can never forget, fail comparatively of their effect,
    except in one or two rare instances indeed.   It is
    only the *pantomime* part of tragedy, the exhibition of
    immediate and physical distress, that which gives the
    greatest opportunity for 'inexpressible dumb-show and
    noise,' which is sure to tell, and tell completely on
    the stage.   All the rest, all that appeals to our pro-
    founder feelings, to reflection and imagination, all
    that affects us most deeply in our closets, and in fact
    constitutes the glory of Shakespear, is little else
    than an interruption and a drag on the business of the
    stage....   We do not mean to say that there is less
    knowledge or display of mere stage-effect in Shakespear
    than in other writers, but that there is a much greater
    knowledge and display of other things, which divide the
    attention with it, and to which it is not possible to
    give an equal force in the representation.   Hence it
    is, that the reader of the plays of Shakespear is al-
    most always disappointed in seeing them acted;  and,
    for our own parts, we should never go to see them
    acted, if we could help it.

In June of the same year he returned to the subject in a review of Milton's 'Comus' (vol. V, p. 231):

> Every thing on the stage takes a literal, palpable shape, and is embodied to the sight.  So much is done by the senses, that the imagination is not prepared to eke out any deficiency that may occur....  The eye of the mind cannot penetrate through the glare of lights which surround it ... and the whole world of imagination fades into a dim and refined abstraction, compared with that part of it, which is brought out dressed, painted, moving, and breathing, a speaking pantomime before us.  Whatever is seen or done, is sure to tell: what is heard only, unless it relates to what is seen or done, has little or no effect.

Finally, in July 1815, a performance of Dryden's version of 'The Tempest' provoked the following outburst (vol. V, p. 234):

> ...we almost came to the resolution of never going to another representation of a play of Shakespear's as long as we lived;  and we certainly did come to this determination, that we never would go *by choice*.  To call it a representation, is indeed an abuse of language:  it is travestie, caricature, any thing you please, but a representation.  Even those daubs of pictures, formerly exhibited under the title of the Shakespear Gallery, had a less evident tendency to disturb and distort all the previous notions we had imbibed from reading Shakespear.

Like Lamb, Hazlitt points out that 'these same anomalous, unmeaning, vulgar, and ridiculous additions, are all that *take* in the present farcical representation of the Tempest....  The ears of the audience are not prepared to drink in the music of the poet' (vol. V, p. 235).

Coleridge's comments are more succinct, the result perhaps more of theory than of any great personal experience of stage performance, but no less dismissive of the view that drama is only fully drama when performed on the stage.  His first comment occurs in a lecture on 'The Tempest' (vol. I, p. 118):

> It addresses itself entirely to the imaginative faculty;  and although the illusion may be assisted by the effect on the senses of the complicated scenery and decorations of modern times yet this sort of assistance is dangerous.  For the principal and only genuine ex-

citement ought to come from within, - from the moved
and sympathetic imagination; whereas, where so much is
addressed to the mere external senses of seeing and
hearing, the spiritual vision is apt to languish, and
the attraction from without will withdraw the mind from
the proper and only legitimate interest which is intended to spring from within.

Elsewhere he comments on the same play, but with one significant addition relative to the nature of Elizabethan
acting (vol. II, p. 130):

> In this play Shakespeare has especially appealed to
> the imagination.... He did not appeal to any sensuous
> impression ... of time and place, but to the imagina-
> tion, and it is to be borne in mind, that of old, and
> as regards mere scenery, his works may be said to have
> been recited rather than acted - that is to say, des-
> cription and narration supplied the place of visual
> exhibition: the audience was told to fancy that they
> saw what they only heard described; the painting was
> not in colours, but in words.

Coleridge's comment occurs within a context where he is
rejecting the view that the characters of Shakespeare are
'portraits', an accumulation of observed detail. Like
Lamb, he insists that they represent a fusion of observation and meditation, which he, in turn, terms the 'ideal'.
The characters, he writes, do not 'strike us as portraits:
they have the union of reason perceiving, of judgment re-
cording, and of imagination diffusing over all a magic
glory' (vol. II, p. 130). Such unanimity among the three
greatest critics of the early nineteenth century, while it
does not give any more force to Lamb's argument, does suggest that it should be taken more seriously. For all of
them, Shakespearean tragedy is tragedy greater than it can
be acted.

In considering Lamb's essay on Shakespeare, it is important to distinguish fact from fiction, what Lamb says
from what he is often alleged to be saying, between statements and the implicit premises on which these statements
are said to hinge. Lamb does not say that Shakespeare's
tragedies cannot be acted: 'I am not arguing that Hamlet
should not be acted, but how much Hamlet is made another
thing by being acted' (p. 89). In this he differs from
Dr Johnson for whom a play read affects the mind like a
play acted. He nowhere impugns Shakespeare's mastery of
the stage, although unlike Hazlitt, he does not, perhaps,
take sufficient care to anticipate and deny the charge in

advance.   Nor does he divorce poetry from drama.   He
does not recommend closet drama, nor anywhere imply a
preference for it.   On the other hand, he does express a
preference for reading Shakespeare's tragedies to seeing
them acted on the stage.   He considers acting intrin-
sically incapable of reflecting or expressing adequately
the full moral complexity of felt and lived experience embodied in the greatest of the tragedies.   In the case of
the character of King Lear, he is prepared to argue that
the disproportion between reading and seeing the play
acted is such that he is 'essentially impossible to be
represented on a stage'.   Had Lamb sufficiently distinguished the dramatic principle in literature from stage
presentation or acted drama, much of the subsequent misunderstanding might have been avoided.   The former characterises all great works of literature irrespective of
genre.   It is a distinction, moreover, implicit in almost
everything he wrote, but is nowhere explicitly referred to
as such.   The most perfect embodiment of this principle
is to be found in the plays of Shakespeare, and more especially the tragedies.   This is why, in a letter to
William Hone introducing his selections from the Garrick
Plays he can say that 'above every other form of Poetry,
[I] have ever preferred the dramatic' (p. 139).   He is
not unique in this.   The preference of the seventeenth
and early eighteenth centuries for the epic gave way in
the latter part of the eighteenth to the emergence of the
drama as the greatest of the literary genres.   All the
Romantic poets aspired to write drama:   Scott, Wordsworth,
Coleridge, Byron, Shelley and Keats, and although their
effort was in the main unsuccessful, the dramatic criticism of the period is often of the highest quality.   But
their primary concern is less with acted drama, than with
the principle best illustrated by the genre itself.   In
his Preface to the 'Specimens of English Dramatic Poets',
1808, published three years before the essay on Shakespeare, Lamb had written (p. 112):

> The kind of extracts which I have sought after have
> been, not so much passages of wit and humour, though
> the old plays are rich in such, as scenes of passion,
> sometimes of the deepest quality, interesting situa-
> tions, serious descriptions.... The plays which I
> have made choice of have been, with few exceptions,
> those which treat of human life and manners, rather
> than masques and Arcadian pastorals, with their train
> of abstractions, unimpassioned deities, passionate mor-
> tals, Claius, and Medorus, and Amintas, and Amarillis.
> My leading design has been, to illustrate what may be

called the moral sense of our ancestors.  To shew in
what manner they felt, when they placed themselves by
the power of imagination in trying situations, in the
conflicts of duty and passion, or the strife of contending duties;  what sort of loves and enmities theirs
were;  how their griefs were tempered, and their full-
swoln joys abated:  how much of Shakspeare shines in
the great men his contemporaries.


In this context, the word 'dramatic' does not signify
'theatrical'.  The principle is present in novels, poems
and prose writings as well as plays.  It determines
Lamb's response not merely to Shakespeare or Elizabethan
and Jacobean drama, but to Wordsworth and Southey, Sir
Thomas Browne and Fuller, Addison and Hazlitt, and even
Gibbon and Hume.  Recommending Walton to Robert Lloyd in
February 1801 he wrote:  'The complete Angler is the only
Treatise written in Dialogues that is worth a halfpenny.'
In all the rest 'the Interlocutors are merely abstract
arguments personify'd;  not living dramatic characters, as
in Walton;  where *every thing* is *alive*;  the fishes are
absolutely *charactered*; - and birds and animals are as
interesting as men & women' (p. 260).  In writing to the
same correspondent on the subject of the prose writings of
Jeremy Taylor, he gives his preference to 'Holy Dying'
'because it contains better matter than the Holy Living,
which deals more in rules than illustrations' (p. 267).
The best general expression of the dramatic principle
occurs in the letter to Lloyd in which he replies to his
friend's proposal for an anthology of Taylor's prose writings.  It clearly indicates his general awareness of the
inadequacy of extracts, selections, specimens and anthol-
ogies of all kinds:  'It cannot be done, for who can disentangle and unthread the rich texture of Nature & Poetry
sewn so thick into a stout coat of theology, without
spoiling both *lace* & *coat*? how beggarly and how bald do
even Shakespeares Princely Pieces look, when thus violently divorced from *connexion* & *circumstance*!'  Without
their context, the famous speeches in Shakespeare's plays
are 'flat & have no power'.  You cannot, he insists, show
passages from poetry or prose in the same way that you
display minerals or pieces of rock:  'Every thing in
heaven & earth, in man and in story, in books & in fancy,
acts by Confederacy, by juxtaposition, by circumstance
& place' (pp. 268-9).  In his review of the first volume
of Hazlitt's 'Table-Talk', this principle becomes the
basis of his assessment of the success and failure of
eighteenth-century essay-writing:  'A series of Miscellan-

eous Essays, however well executed in the parts, if it
have not some pervading character to give a unity to it,
is ordinarily as tormenting to get through as a set of
aphorisms, or a jest-book' (p. 300). Plutarch, Montaigne
and Dr Johnson 'imparted their own personal peculiarities
to their themes', and 'By this balm are they preserved'.
Without some dramatic bond or union such collections present only a 'heterogenous mass'. Addison's greatest mistake, in Lamb's view, was his avoidance of 'perpetual
self-reference', with the result that 'The Spectator' is
'little more than bundles of Essays ... hanging together
with very slender principles of bond or union'. The
'mass of matter, spread through eight volumes, is really
somewhat too miscellaneous and diffuse, to hang together
for identity upon such a shade, such a tenuity' (p. 301).
His objection to abstractions in 1821 when he wrote this
review is just as strong as when he wrote the Preface to
the 'Specimens' in 1808 (pp. 301-2):

> Take up any one of the volumes of this description,
> published in the last century; - you will possibly
> alight upon two or three successive papers, depicting,
> with more or less gravity, sober views of life *as it is*
> - when - pop - you come upon a Vision, which you trem-
> bled at beforehand from a glimpse you caught at certain
> abstractions in Capitals, Fame, Riches, Long Life, Loss
> of Friends, Punishment by Exile - a set of denomina-
> tions part simple, part compounded - existing in
> single, double, and triple hypostases.  - You cannot
> think on their fantastic essences without giddiness, or
> describe them short of a solecism....  These Visions
> ... these heartless, bloodless literalities - these
> "thin consistencies", dependent for their personality
> upon Great Letters - for write them small, and the
> tender essences fade into abstractions - have at length
> happily melted away before the progress of good sense.

Hazlitt, in Lamb's view, 'is of the class of Essayists
first mentioned' (p. 302). The same principle is operative in his appreciation of the eighteenth-century historians. He prefers the work of a writer like Gilbert
Burnet who is implicated in the events described (p. 276):

> No palliatives, but all the stark wickedness, that ac-
> tually gives the momentum to national actors.  Quite
> the prattle of age & out lived importance.  Truth &
> sincerity staring out upon you perpetually....  None
> of the Damned Philosophical Humeian indifference, so
> cold & unnatural & unhuman.  None of the damned Gib-

bonian fine writing so fine & composite.... None of
Mr. Roscoe's sage remarks, all so apposite & coming in
so clever, lest the reader should have had the trouble
of drawing an inference.

Elsewhere, he lumps the work of the eighteenth-century
historians with government publications, scientific treatises and 'Draught Boards bound and lettered at the back'.
   In his role as drama critic, Lamb's insistence on a
dramatic principle is best expressed in his criticism of
the contemporary taste for domestic and sentimental drama,
and in particular, 'the notional beneficence and justice'
of modern comedy.  In a note to Middleton and Rowley's 'A
Fair Quarrel', he wrote (pp. 122-3):

   The insipid levelling morality to which the modern
   stage is tied down would not admit of such admirable
   passions as these scenes are filled with.  A puritanical obtuseness of sentiment, a stupid infantile goodness, is creeping among us, instead of the vigorous
   passions, and virtues clad in flesh and blood, with
   which the old dramatists present us.  Those noble and
   liberal casuists could discern in the differences, the
   quarrels, the animosities of man, a beauty and truth of
   moral feeling, no less than in the iterately inculcated
   duties of forgiveness and atonement.  With us all is
   hypocritical meekness.  A reconciliation scene (let
   the occasion be never so absurd or unnatural) is always
   sure of applause.  Our audiences come to the theatre
   to be complimented on their goodness.  They compare
   notes with the amiable characters in the play, and find
   a wonderful similarity of disposition between them.
   We have a common stock of dramatic morality out of
   which a writer may be supplied without the trouble of
   copying it from originals within his own breast.

The distinction between an abstract morality of stock
dramatic or theatrical commonplaces, and a morality that
is truly dramatic, is one which Lamb had first made as
early as 1799 in a letter to Robert Southey when he criticised the poet's tendency (p. 233)

   to conclude faintly, with some cold moral, as in the
   end of the Poem calld 'the Victory' ... a single common
   place line of comfort, which bears no proportion in
   weight or number to the many lines which describe suffering....  A Moral should be wrought into the body
   and soul, the matter and tendency, of a Poem, not taggd
   to the end, like 'A God send the good ship into har-

bour' at the conclusion of our bills of Lading....
Any dissenting minister may say & do as much.

In the first of his notes in the 'Specimens' he criticised
'Gorboduc' because the morality was separate from the life
of the play, and in the note immediately after his complaint against modern 'dramatic morality' he returned to
the theme of an abstract morality (pp. 123-4):

> The old play-writers are distinguished by an honest
> boldness of exhibition, they shew every thing without
> being ashamed.  If a reverse in fortune be the thing
> to be personified, they fairly bring us to the prison-
> grate and the alms-basket.  A poor man on our stage is
> always a gentleman, he may be known by a peculiar neat-
> ness of apparel, and by wearing black.  Our delicacy,
> in fact, forbids the dramatizing of Distress at all.
> It is never shewn in its essential properties;  it
> appears but as the adjunct to some virtue, as something
> which is to be relieved, from the approbation of which
> relief the spectators are to derive a certain soothing
> of self-referred satisfaction.  We turn away from the
> real essences of things to hunt after their relative
> shadows, moral duties:  whereas, if the truth of things
> were fairly represented, the relative duties might be
> safely trusted to themselves, and moral philosophy lose
> the name of a science.

When Wordsworth criticised 'The Ancient Mariner' in the
second edition of 'Lyrical Ballads' he met with a similar
response.  Lamb's defence of the poem is in terms of the
internal psychological and spiritual drama.  But Wordsworth's own poem, The Old Cumberland Beggar, is censured
precisely because the moral has not been dramatically
'wrought into the body and soul' of the verse:  'I will
just add that it appears to me a fault in the Beggar, that
the instructions conveyed in it are too direct and like a
lecture:  they dont slide into the mind of the reader,
while he is imagining no such matter. - An intelligent
reader finds a sort of insult in being told, I will teach
you how to think upon this subject' (p. 201).  More than
twenty years later he was still invoking the same principle.  Commenting in 1824 on the work of one of Bernard
Barton's friends, he wrote:  'It is only too stuft with
scripture, too Parsonish....  When I say it is too full
of Scripture, I mean it is too full of direct quotations;
no book can have too much of silent Scripture in it.  But
the natural power of a story is diminished when the uppermost purpose in the writer seems to be to recommend some-

thing else'. (18)    Even in the last year of his life, returning yet again to 'King Lear', he completed an article
on what might be termed the 'parenthetical principle' in
literature, whereby the explosive force of a situation is
only implicit.    Quoting the last scene of the play, he
concluded:

> This is the magnanimity of authorship, when a writer,
> having a topic presented to him, fruitful of beauties
> for common minds, waives his privilege, and trusts to
> the judicious few for understanding the reason  of his
> abstinence.    What a pudder would a common dramatist
> have raised here of a reconciliation scene, a perfect
> recognition, between the assumed Caius and his master!
> - to the suffusing of many fair eyes, and the moisten-
> ing of cambric handkerchiefs.  The old dying king par-
> tially catching at the truth, and immediately lapsing
> into obliviousness, with the high-minded carelessness
> of the other to have his services appreciated ... are
> among the most judicious, not to say heart-touching,
> strokes in Shakspeare. (19)

Continuing to cite examples where in a 'few but pregnant
words', the author 'rather intimates than reveals' the
significance, Lamb ends the article with a quotation from
the ballad Fair Rosamund:

> When good King Henry ruled this land,
>     The second of that name,
Now mark -
> (Besides the Queen) he dearly loved
>     A fair and comely dame.
There is great virtue in this *besides*.

Lamb's essay on Hogarth, published in Hunt's 'Reflector' only a few months before the essay on Shakespeare,
affords the clearest evidence that his demand for a dramatic principle or a dramatic morality is not confined to
the genre of drama.    He is critical of the current estimate of Hogarth's genius which regards the paintings and
engravings as the work of a comic realist, devoid of any
other purpose than amusement and entertainment.    The opposition which he establishes between Hogarth on the one
hand and Penny and Bunbury on the other, is similar to
that previously set up in the 'Specimens' between the
dramatists of the early seventeenth and those of the later
eighteenth centuries.    His criticism of modern dramatists
and audiences - 'We turn away from the real essences of
things to hunt after their relative shadows, moral duties'

- is here reiterated, extended, and made more explicit.
He no longer criticises in the general terms appropriate
to a note in an anthology.  His essay emphasises the
necessity of a moral complexity in any work of art that
affects to deal in a meaningful way with the nature of
human experience (p. 328):

> This then I suppose is the line of subjects in which
> Mr. Penny was so much superior to Hogarth.  I confess
> I am not of that opinion.  The relieving of poverty
> by the purse, and the restoring a young man to his
> parents by using the methods prescribed by the Humane
> Society, are doubtless very amiable subjects, pretty
> things to teach the first rudiments of humanity;  they
> amount to about as much instruction as the stories of
> good boys that give away their custards to poor beggar-
> boys in children's books.  But, good God! is this *milk
> for babes* to be set up in opposition to Hogarth's moral
> scenes, his *strong meat for men*?

Throughout the essay Lamb has switched from painting to
literature with the greatest ease.  The first few pages,
for example, are sustained by the analogy between Hogarth
and Shakespeare.  By this means he indicates his acceptance of the early nineteenth-century view of the unity of
all the arts as springing from the same creative impulse.
At the end of the passage just cited, he returns once
again to literature, emphasising the importance of the
dramatic principle in all great art (pp. 328-9):

> As well might we prefer the fulsome verses upon their
> own goodness, to which the gentlemen of the Literary
> Fund annually sit still with such shameless patience to
> listen, to the satires of Juvenal and Persius;  because
> the former are full of tender images of Worth relieved
> by Charity, and Charity stretching out her hand to
> rescue sinking Genius, and the theme of the latter is
> men's crimes and follies with their black consequences
> - forgetful meanwhile of those strains of moral pathos,
> those sublime heart-touches, which these poets (in *them*
> chiefly shewing themselves poets) are perpetually dart-
> ing across the otherwise appalling gloom of their sub-
> ject - consolatory remembrancers, when their pictures
> of guilty mankind have made us even to despair for our
> species, that there is such a thing as virtue and moral
> dignity in the world, that her unquenchable spark is
> not utterly out.

As in his review of Hazlitt's 'Table-Talk' where he had

criticised the dramatic vacuum and abstractness at the
centre of Addison's essays, he once again resorts to cap-
italised eighteenth-century personifications to make his
point that such a view of human nature is grossly over-
simplified.  Penny's paintings represent the same 'infantile goodness', the same complacent 'self-reference' he
had observed in modern drama and their audiences, the same
desire 'to be complimented on their goodness'.  No more
than Keats does Lamb believe in this kind of perfectibil-
ity.  At this crucial point of the essay, he introduces a
quotation from Marston (pp. 330-1):

> If they be bad things, then is satire and tragedy a bad
> thing;  let us proclaim at once an age of gold, and
> sink the existence of vice and misery in our specula-
> tions;  let us
>         —— wink, and shut our apprehensions up
>    From common sense of what men were and are:
> let us *make believe* with the children that every body
> is good and happy;  and, with Dr. Swift, write panegy-
> rics upon the world.

The witty, anguished tone, the depth of feeling, the contempt expressed in this passage are unusual in Lamb, but in
the essay on Shakespeare there occurs a similar quotation
in a comparable context (p. 100):

> Time would run back and fetch the age of gold,
> And speckled vanity
> Would sicken soon and die,
> And leprous Sin would melt from earthly mould;
> Yea Hell itself would pass away,
> And leave its dolorous mansions to the peering day.

When he compares Lillo's 'George Barnwell' with 'Othello',
it is in terms of a morality which is abstract, and a
dramatic morality which is ideal, achieved only by a difficult and subtle harmony of opposing forces:  of art and
life, subjective and objective, observation and meditation, reason and imagination, the abstract and the poetic.
In painting too it involves implication, suggestiveness,
the parenthetical principle.  When he praises Hogarth for
'extending ... the interest beyond the bounds of the subject', this he says 'could only have been conceived by a
great genius' (p. 320).  He quotes a passage from Shakespeare to illustrate his argument, and concludes:

> This he well calls *imaginary work*, where the specta-
> tor must meet the artist in his conceptions half way;

and it is peculiar to the confidence of high genius
alone to trust so much to spectators or readers.
Lesser artists shew every thing distinct and full, as
they require an object to be made out to themselves
before they can comprehend it.

In some respects, Lamb's essay on Shakespeare is the ob-
verse of the essay, Imperfect Sympathies.  In the latter,
a general essay, he expressed the central theoretical
basis of his critical theory;  the Shakespeare essay on
the other hand, specifically critical, is expressive of a
general attitude to life.  The intensity and vehemence
both of this essay and that on Hogarth, written a few
months earlier, derive in no small measure from his intense convictions as to the nature of moral experience
itself.  Coleridge is reported to have remarked that 'A
fall of some sort or other - the creation, as it were, of
the non-absolute - is the fundamental postulate of the
moral history of man'. (20)  Such a view in the eighteenth century was a commonplace.  Dr Johnson was not
alone when in his life of Milton he observed that we are
perpetually moralists, but geometricians only by chance,
and that what we had to learn was, how to do good, and
avoid evil.  The Augustan emphasis on original sin, however, is in marked contrast with the growing confidence
towards the end of the century in man's material and moral
progress.  Godwin, for example, dismissed Burke's insistence on the fallen nature of man as an old wives' tale,
and the growing optimism was reflected in a variety of
ways including the Pantisocratic schemes of Coleridge and
Southey.  Lamb, on the other hand, in spite of his
'sneaking kindness' for metaphysical speculation, appears
to have been unaffected by the millenerial opinions of
his contemporaries.  His earliest letters express moral
views that clearly belong to the Christian humanist tradition of the eighteenth century as represented by Johnson
and Burke.  The earliest letter to survive is dated 27
May 1796, and all seventeen letters of that year are addressed to Coleridge.  Between May and September they
deal in the main with literary projects, textual corrections, revisions and additions.  Following the murder of
his mother and his sister Mary's subsequent confinement,
the character of the letters changes in a number of important ways.  He becomes much more critical of Coleridge's
developing religious views.  He criticises 'a certain
freedom of expression, a certain air of mysticism, more
consonant to the conceits of pagan philosophy, than consistent with the humility of genuine piety' in Coleridge's

consolatory reflections on man's relationship with God (p. 211).   Lamb's own view is much more traditional (p. 212):

> Now, high as the human intellect comparatively will soar, and wide as its influence, malign or salutary, can extend, is there not, Coleridge, a distance between the Divine Mind and it, which makes such language blasphemy?...   Man, full of imperfections, at best, and subject to wants which momentarily remind him of dependence;   man, a weak and ignorant being, 'servile' from his birth 'to all the skiey influences,' with eyes sometimes open to discern the right path, but a head generally too dizzy to pursue it;   man, in the pride of speculation, forgetting his nature, and hailing in himself the future God, must make the angels laugh....   I only wish to *remind* you of that humility which best becometh the Christian character....   Let us learn to think humbly of ourselves, and rejoice in the appellation of 'dear children,' 'brethren,' and 'co-heirs with Christ of the promises,' seeking to know no further.

The echoes in this letter of Shakespeare, Milton and Pope are not accidental.   In another letter, 28 October 1796, only four days later, he again admonishes Coleridge for his 'mystical notions and the pride of metaphysics,' counselling him to 'attend to the proper business of human life, and talk a little together respecting our domestic concerns' (p. 213).   For Lamb, the proper study of mankind is man, but not in a theological or scientific manner.   Two or three more years were to elapse before all forms of abstraction were to be prohibited.   Man is a fallen creature, and he must recognise himself as such before there is any hope of redemption.   In the early letters this preoccupation is expressed in specifically Christian terms as in the letter in which he thanked Coleridge for rescuing him 'from the polluting spirit of the world - .   I might have been a worthless character without you - as it is, I do possess a certain improveable portion of devotional feelings - tho' when I view myself in the light of divine truth, and not according to the common measures of human judgment, I am altogether corrupt & sinful' (p. 215).   In other letters he complains that his colleagues at the East India Office do not share his religious and moral views:   'I have not one truly elevated character among my acquaintance:   not one Christian:   not one, but undervalues Christianity - singly what am I to do' (p. 292).   Throughout this early period his conception of the fall is in terms of the traditional dichotomy between Reason and Passion.

The specifically Christian element in Lamb's early letters, however, very rapidly diminished.  Even as early as
1801 in apologising to Walter Wilson, a friend and dissenter, he is clearly on the defensive (p. 293):

> I know that you think a very important difference in
> opinion with respect to some more serious subjects be-
> tween us makes me a dangerous companion;  but do not
> rashly infer, from some slight and light expressions
> which I may have made use of in a moment of levity in
> your presence, without sufficient regard to your feel-
> ings - do not conclude that I am an inveterate enemy to
> all religion.  I have had a time of seriousness, and I
> have known the importance and reality of a religious
> belief.  Latterly, I acknowledge, much of my serious-
> ness has gone off ... but I still retain at bottom a
> conviction of the truth, and a certainty of the useful-
> ness of religion....  I only want you to believe that
> I have *stamina* of seriousness within me.

This turn was not altogether unexpected, for as early as
December 1796 he had written to Coleridge lamenting that
he had only 'a taste for religion rather than a strong religious habit' (p. 214), and in a letter written a month
later the tone and phrasing are similar:  'I know, I am no
ways better in practice than my neighbors - but I have a
taste for religion, an occasional earnest aspiration after
perfection, which they have not.  I gain nothing by being
with such as myself - we encourage one another in mediocrity' (p. 292).  But although his religious convictions
altered, his conception of the nature of man remained constant.  The '*stamina* of seriousness' to which he refers
is now almost exclusively a moral stamina.  The change
can be seen as early as February 1800 when, in a letter to
Manning, he observes:  'I am determined to live a merry
Life in the midst of Sinners.  I try to consider all men
as such, and to pitch my expectations from human nature as
low as possible.  In this view, all unexpected virtues
are God-sends & beautiful exceptions' (p. 216).  Even in
his early stridently sectarian letters to Coleridge there
is invariably the Augustan emphasis on man as a social
animal:  less the relationship between the individual and
his God, as the companionship, conversation and intercourse with others.  He laments his lack of friends, his
isolation and loneliness (p. 214):

> few but laugh at me for reading my Testament - they
> talk a language I understand not:  I conceal sentiments
> that would be a puzzle to them.  I can only converse

with you by letter and with the dead in their books....
In our little range of duties and connexions, how few
sentiments can take place, without friends, with few
books....  We need some support, some leading-strings
to cheer and direct us.

Religious fellowship, he maintained at this period 'is the
true ba[lsam] of life', and quoting Wesley's saying that
'Religion is not a solitary thing' adds wistfully:  'Alas!
it necessarily is so with me' (p. 292).   This is why he
harps constantly on his meetings with Coleridge in 1795,
or his admiration for the works of another Unitarian,
Joseph Priestley:  'I am always longing to be with men
more excellent than myself.... I have just been reading,
Priestly on Philosophical necessity, in the thought that I
enjoy a kind of Communion, a kind of friendship even, with
the great & good.  Books are to me instead of friends'
(pp. 292-3).  A conception of the fall is still essential
after 1800, but its expression has altered.  His sense of
himself as a 'marked' man becomes less pressing after this
period.
     By 1808, when the 'Specimens' was published, Lamb had
progressed to a conception of human experience where the
two powerful antagonist forces were no longer Reason and
Passion, but Imagination and Reason, with Reason as the
faculty coordinating the operations of the senses.   Imagination, as with the other Romantics, has become the faculty operative in man's daily experience as well as the
source of all art.   The preface and notes, again and
again, set off imagination against the abstract.  His
desire now as he expresses it is for 'trying situations,
in the conflicts of duty and passion, or the strife of
contending duties;  what sort of loves and enmities theirs
were;  how their griefs were tempered, and their full-
swoln joys abated' (p. 112).   This is far removed from
his earlier sympathy with Sara's viewpoint in The Eolian
Harp, or his demand that Coleridge should produce a book
of evidences for Christianity.   It is Lamb's that is now
the 'unregenerate', imaginative or 'imperfect' mind.   The
openness to experience which he now demands is akin to
that of Keats when he said that what delighted the came-
lion poet shocked the virtuous philosopher.   For Lamb
too, the imagination 'enjoys light and shade;  it lives in
gusto, be it foul or fair, high or low, rich or poor, mean
or elevated'. (21)   He is no longer prepared to accept
traditional explanations of the nature of man, nor does he
wish to see them incorporated in works of the imagination.
His later comments on man and religion all stress the element of mystery, wonder, incomprehension, as when in reply

to a presentation copy of a medical treatise he wrote:   'I
have a most unscientific head, and can only *believe* that
we are wonderfully and fearfully made' (p. 297), or when
rebuking Southey for his dogmatic certainty, he observed:
'If men would honestly confess their misgivings (which few
men will) there are times when the strongest Christians of
us, I believe, have reeled under questionings of such
staggering obscurity' (p. 226).   In a letter to Bernard
Barton in 1825 he chided the poet for his certainty in the
resurrection in his poems on the deaths of children (p.
296):

> It is a natural thought, a sweet fallacy to the Survi-
> vors - but still a fallacy....   Epitaphs run upon this
> topic of consolation, till the very frequency induces a
> cheapness.   Tickets for admission into Paradise are
> sculptured out at a penny a letter, twopence a syl-
> lable &c.   It is all a mystery. ~~mystica~~

Why children die young, he adds, 'is among the obscurities
of providence'.   This is why he views religion after 1800
as a border-land, a middle ground or debateable land in-
volving the union of two notions.   Theological abstraction offered no solution to the trials of human life:
'Those metaphors solace me not, nor sweeten the unpalatable draught of mortality' (p. 286).

His sense of man's imperfection, and of the imperfection of the world, persisted to the end and the full range
of human strengths and weaknesses must be reflected in art.
Tragedy, for example, he tells us deals with the evils of
life as well as with man's highest aspirations after good.
He will not tolerate a work of literature, or the interpretation of a work of literature, that in any way diminishes the variety, complexity and diversity, the gradations of sense and virtue, whether like Southey's it is
religious and sectarian, like Godwin's scientific, or like
Barry's interpretation of Hogarth, merely humanitarian.
His demand is for *strong meat for men* not *milk for
babes*.   An emphasis merely on the darker aspects of
human life is equally false.   This is partly why he re-
jects the poetry of Byron(p. 238):

> he is great in so little a way - To be a Poet is to be
> The Man, the whole Man - not a petty portion of occa-
> sional low passion worked up into a permanent form of
> Humanity.   Shakspeare has thrust such rubbishly feel-
> ings into a corner, the dark dusty heart of Don John.

In the 'Specimens', he criticised some of the dramatists

for a similar imbalance:  'They torture and wound us abundantly.  They are economists only in delight' (p. 117).
In the last year of his life, it is his praise of Shakespeare that his plays contain so few revolting characters.
Hamlet's reflections on mortality in Act V are compared
unfavourably, as reflections, with those of Fuller in his
account of Wycliffe's exhumation (p. 265):

> Hamlet's tracing the body of Caesar to the clay that
> stops a beer-barrel, is a no less curious pursuit of
> 'ruined mortality;' but it is in an inverse ratio to
> this:  it degrades and saddens us, for one part of our
> nature at least;  but this expands the whole of our
> nature, and gives to the body a sort of ubiquity, - a
> diffusion, as far as the actions of its partner can
> have reach or influence.

This desire for what 'expands the whole of our nature' is
entirely characteristic.  On these grounds the poetry of
Byron is compared unfavourably with that of Wordsworth:
'Why, a line of Wordsworths is a lever to lift the immortal Spirit!  Byrons can only move the Spleen' (p. 239).
In his review of 'The Excursion' he made a similar point:
'the visible and audible things of creation present ...
revelations and quick insights into the life within us,
the pledge of immortality' (p. 196).  The prose of Walton
even inspired him with an 'immortal hunger' (p. 260).
    The simplest way of indicating the significance of
Lamb's general views of human nature for his literary
criticism is to return to the two verse quotations occur-
ring in the essays on Hogarth and Shakespeare.  In the
first he wrote:  'let us proclaim at once an age of gold,
and sink the existence of vice and misery in our speculations ... let us *make believe* with the children that every
body is good and happy' (pp. 330-1).  In the other, he
quotes from Milton's great ode:  'Time would run back and
fetch the age of gold.'  For Lamb, man is fallen and we
cannot 'wink, and shut our apprehensions up' from this
fact (p. 331).  Only in this way is redemption possible,
and it is possible in life and art only through the imagination.  As Shelley observed in the 'Defence of Poetry',
it is poetry itself that 'defeats the curse'. (22)  Imagination rescues man, as one twentieth-century writer has
it from his 'perishable activity', and sets him in the
light of his own 'imperishable consciousness'. (23)  When
a poet or painter does not succeed in achieving this, or
when a critic misinterprets a work that does, or an
audience confuses a play which does with one which does
not, then Lamb is inexorable in his judgment.  This is

Lamb's anti-Christ.   Failure to utilise the transforming
power of the imagination is to perpetuate man's inevitable
bondage to the familiar and the mundane, the theoretical
and the systematic.   But not so the greatest artists, for
as he says of Raphael's 'Building of the Ark' (p. 345):

> But not to the nautical preparations in the ship-yards
> of Civita Vecchia did Raphael look for instructions,
> when he imagined the Building of the Vessel that was to
> be conservatory of the wrecks of the species of drowned
> mankind.... There is the Patriarch, in calm fore-
> thought, and with holy prescience, giving directions.
> And there are his agents - the solitary but sufficient
> Three - hewing, sawing, every one with the might and
> earnestness of a Demiurgus;  under some instinctive
> rather than technical guidance;  giant-muscled;  every
> one a Hercules....  So work the workmen that should
> repair a world.

Here, in this short passage, is Lamb's most powerful metaphor of the role of the artist, contained in a criticism
of a particular work of art whose very subject is an ana-
logue of the original fall.   It contains within itself
the image of the artist, and the end to which that art is
dedicated.   The fall, which for Coleridge is a fundamental postulate of the moral history of man, and for Fried-
rich Schlegel a logically necessary concept, is for Lamb
an imaginative necessity.   Seen in this context, his
criticism of the theatrical presentation of Shakespeare's
tragedies has the profoundest implications.   It is the
greatest disservice to Lamb as a critic to suggest that he
is merely being whimsical and playful;  that the essay as
a whole is an exercise in special pleading.   The acting
of Shakespeare's greatest tragedies renders less than
wholly effective the imaginative impulse.   Far from re-
deeming man, from awakening him from what Wordsworth
called our 'sleep of death', (24) it initiates a second
fall, or reinforces the first.   It serves only to diminish the full imaginative force and potential of the work
itself.   Throughout his criticism, he is combatting the
loss of imaginative potential involved in inadequate interpretation, or in works of art which misconceive the
nature of their medium.   It is this sense of needless
loss, loss which is neither fortunate nor inevitable, but
self-inflicted and gratuitous, that both in his essays and
criticism, informs his characteristic imagery of a Paradise Lost.
   Lamb's conclusions with regard to the acting of 'King
Lear' are dependent on his view of the nature of the imag-

ination and its relation to the senses, the relationship
between poetry and painting, and his view of the moral
nature of man and the function of art.    Given these, his
conclusions could not have been any different.    They do
not in any important respect hinge on his lack of relish
for contemporary stage performances.    If we wish to deny
his argument, then either we must impugn his premises with
regard to the imagination, the nature of man, or the
nature of poetry;  or we must reject the application of
these principles to the specific case of acted drama.    If
we choose the former, we must re-assess our attitude to
the views of imagination, poetry and life expressed in the
early nineteenth century not merely by Lamb or Hazlitt or
Coleridge, but by the poets as well.    If we would deny
the application, then we must explain how the three greatest critics of the early nineteenth century all made the
same mistake independently of one another.

1 George Saintsbury, 'A History of English Criticism'
  (Edinburgh, 1911), p. 354.   Saintsbury greatly admired
  Lamb's writings:  'That Lamb is one of the most exquisite and delightful of critics, as of writers, is a
  proposition for which I will go to the stake' (p. 348).
2 See René Wellek, 'A History of Modern Criticism, 1750-
  1950' (London, 1955), ii, 193.
3 For the sake of convenience, references to passages reprinted in this edition are incorporated in the text of
  the introduction.   Lamb's formal criticism is to be
  found in the first two volumes of 'The Works of Charles
  and Mary Lamb', ed. E.V. Lucas (London, 1903-5), 7
  vols.   Volume 4 of this edition contains his notes on
  the Elizabethan and Jacobean dramatists.   References
  to his correspondence after October 1817 are to 'The
  Letters of Charles and Mary Lamb', ed. E.V. Lucas
  (London, 1935), 3 vols.   This edition, however, is now
  being superseded by 'The Letters of Charles and Mary
  Anne Lamb', ed. E.W. Marrs (Ithaca, NY, 1975), of which
  only three volumes have so far been published.
4 'Collected Letters of Samuel Taylor Coleridge', ed.
  E.L. Griggs (Oxford, 1956-71), ii, 810.   Other references are to 'Shakespearean Criticism', ed. T.M. Raysor
  (London, 1930, 1960), 2 vols; 'Biographia Literaria',
  ed. J. Shawcross (London, 1907), 2 vols.
5 'Letters', ed. Marrs, i, 22.
6 John Keats, 'Letters, 1814-1821', ed. H.E. Rollins
  (Cambridge, Mass., 1958), i, 255.   Like Shelley, Keats
  greatly admired Lamb.   He owned a copy of Lamb's
  'Specimens' (1808), and on p. 112 of his copy he com-
  mented on the criticism of Heywood's 'A Woman Killed
  with Kindness':

This is the most acute deep sighted and spiritual

piece of criticism ever penned.   It is almost
absurd to burden it with a notice in one's one [for
own] Book where it is ever safe:  but there is a
pleasure in unloading the mind by the pen's point
when such an incentive presents itself.   Besides it
is here in this scantly read book and this little
print almost buried and requires a 'hic vivet' - To
write a few such things is perhaps as well as shining, a distinguish'd literary Character.

For a full account of Keats's annotations, see Helen E.
Haworth, Keats's Copy of Lamb's 'Specimens of English
Dramatic Poets', 'Bulletin of the New York Public Lib-
rary', 74, 1970, 419-27.

7 Ibid., i, 193.
8 Ibid., ii, 213.
9 Lamb's various phrases, characterising the relation of
actor to audience, occur principally in the two essays,
Stage Illusion, and On Some of the Old Actors.
10 See pp. 343, 97.
11 'Works', ed. Lucas, ii, 90.
12 Saintsbury, op. cit., p. 351.
13 A.R. Orage, 'Selected Essays and Critical Writings',
ed. H. Read and D. Saurat (London, 1935), pp. 28-9.
14 Percy Fitzgerald, 'The Art of the Stage as set out in
Lamb's Dramatic Essays' (London, 1885), p. 259.
15 'Works', ed. Lucas, i, 158:

Having no drawback of sight to impair his sensibilities, he simply attended to the scene, and received
its unsophisticated impression.  *So much the rather
her celestial light shone inward*.   I was pleased
with an observation which he made, when I asked him
how he liked Kemble, who played *Richard*.   I should
have thought (said he) that that man had been reading something out of a book, if I had not known that
I was in a play-house.

16 E.V. Lucas, 'The Life of Charles Lamb' (London, 1905),
i, 320.
17 References to Hazlitt's writings are to 'The Complete
Works of William Hazlitt', ed. P.P. Howe (London, 1930-
4), 21 vols.   See also iv, 247-8 for similar comments
on 'A Midsummer Night's Dream'.
18 'Letters', ed. Lucas, iii, 415.
19 'Works', ed. Lucas, i, 346.
20 'Specimens of the Table Talk of the late Samuel Taylor
Coleridge' (London, 1835), 1 May 1830, i, 107.
21 Keats, 'Letters', i, 387.

22 Percy Bysshe Shelley, 'The Complete Works', ed. R.
   Ingpen and W.E. Peck (London, 1926-30), vii, 137.
23 Joseph Conrad, 'Notes on Life and Letters' (London,
   1921), Henry James:  An Appreciation.
24 Preface to 'The Excursion', ll. 60-1.

The texts of passages from the 'Specimens' (1808), the
'Essays' (1823) and the 'Last Essays' (1833) have been
transcribed from the original editions.    The essays on
Shakespeare, Hogarth, Fuller and Wither are taken from the
'Works' (1818).    Lamb's notes on the Garrick plays are
reproduced from the original articles in William Hone's
'Table Book' (1827).    The text of the earliest letters is
that of Edwin W. Marrs's new edition of 'The Letters of
Charles and Mary Anne Lamb' (Ithaca, NY, 1975).    Profes-
sor Marrs very generously corrected Lucas's transcription
of the letters.    I am indebted to the New York Public
Library, Berg Collection, for permission to print Lamb's
hitherto unpublished review of volume one of Hazlitt's
'Table-Talk' (1821).

ACKNOWLEDGMENTS

Many friends and colleagues have helped at various stages
of the work.  I am particularly indebted to Miss Jane
Aaron, Dr Colin Day, Mr Gavin Griffiths, Mrs Jan Orchard,
Dr Christopher Pelling and Professor Martin West.  Mr
Basil Savage, of the Charles Lamb Society, generously provided early editions at crucial stages of the work;  Miss
Margaret Weedon and Miss Eileen Davies, of the Oxford
English Faculty Library, were extremely helpful and understanding, while Professor Marrs's extraordinary kindness
in correcting Lucas's transcription of the letters, for
someone quite unknown to him, was an astonishing act of
academic altruism.  My wife, in her role of unpaid research assistant, read and re-read the finished text with
the greatest care, skill and patience.

# I Acting and Actors

# 1 Stage Illusion
## 1825, 1833

This essay first appeared in the 'London Magazine', August
1825 under the title Imperfect Dramatic Illusion.    Lamb
later reprinted it in the 'Last Essays' in 1833, altering
its title to Stage Illusion.

A PLAY is said to be well or ill acted in proportion to
the scenical illusion produced.    Whether such illusion
can in any case be perfect, is not the question.    The
nearest approach to it, we are told, is, when the actor
appears wholly unconscious of the presence of spectators.
In tragedy - in all which is to affect the feelings - this
undivided attention to his stage business, seems indispen-
sable.    Yet it is, in fact, dispensed with every day by
our cleverest tragedians;   and while these references to
an audience, in the shape of rant or sentiment, are not
too frequent or palpable, a sufficient quantity of illusion for the purposes of dramatic interest may be said to
be produced in spite of them.    But, tragedy apart, it
may be inquired whether, in certain characters in comedy,
especially those which are a little extravagant, or which
involve some notion repugnant to the moral sense, it is
not a proof of the highest skill in the comedian when,
without absolutely appealing to an audience, he keeps up a
tacit understanding with them;   and makes them, uncon-
sciously to themselves, a party in the scene.    The utmost
nicety is required in the mode of doing this;   but we
speak only of the great artists in the profession.
  The most mortifying infirmity in human nature, to feel
in ourselves, or to contemplate in another, is, perhaps,
cowardice.    To see a coward *done to the life* upon a stage
would produce anything but mirth.    Yet we most of us remember Jack Bannister's cowards.    Could any thing be more
agreeable, more pleasant?    We loved the rogues.    How was

this effected but by the exquisite art of the actor in a
perpetual sub-insinuation to us, the spectators, even in
the extremity of the shaking fit, that he was not half
such a coward as we took him for?   We saw all the common
symptoms of the malady upon him;   the quivering lip, the
cowering knees, the teeth chattering;   and could have
sworn "that man was frightened."   But we forgot all the
while - or kept it almost a secret to ourselves - that he
never once lost his self-possession;   that he let out by a
thousand droll looks and gestures - meant at *us*, and not
at all supposed to be visible to his fellows in the scene,
that his confidence in his own resources had never once
deserted him.   Was this a genuine picture of a coward? or
not rather a likeness, which the clever artist contrived
to palm upon us instead of an original;   while we secretly
connived at the delusion for the purpose of greater pleasure, than a more genuine counterfeiting of the imbecility,
helplessness, and utter self-desertion, which we know to
be concomitants of cowardice in real life, could have
given us?

Why are misers so hateful in the world, and so endurable on the stage, but because the skilful actor, by a
sort of sub-reference, rather than direct appeal to us,
disarms the character of a great deal of its odiousness,
by seeming to engage *our* compassion for the insecure
tenure by which he holds his money bags and parchments?
By this subtle vent half of the hatefulness of the character - the self-closeness with which in real life it coils
itself up from the sympathies of men - evaporates.   The
miser becomes sympathetic;   *i.e.* is no genuine miser.
Here again a diverting likeness is substituted for a very
disagreeable reality.

Spleen, irritability - the pitiable infirmities of old
men, which produce only pain to behold in the realities,
counterfeited upon a stage, divert not altogether for the
comic appendages to them, but in part from an inner conviction that they are *being acted* before us;   that a likeness only is going on, and not the thing itself.   They
please by being done under the life, or beside it;   not *to
the life*.   When Gatty acts an old man, is he angry
indeed? or only a pleasant counterfeit, just enough of a
likeness to recognise, without pressing upon us the uneasy
sense of reality?

Comedians, paradoxical as it may seem, may be too natural.   It was the case with a late actor.   Nothing could
be more earnest or true than the manner of Mr. Emery;
this told excellently in his Tyke, and characters of a
tragic cast.   But when he carried the same rigid exclusiveness of attention to the stage business, and wilful

blindness and oblivion of everything before the curtain
into his comedy, it produced a harsh and dissonant effect.
He was out of keeping with the rest of the *Personae
Dramatis*.   There was as little link between him and them
as betwixt himself and the audience.   He was a third
estate, dry, repulsive, and unsocial to all.   Individual-
ly considered, his execution was masterly.   But comedy is
not this unbending thing;   for this reason, that the same
degree of credibility is not required of it as to serious
scenes.   The degrees of credibility demanded to the two
things may be illustrated by the different sort of truth
which we expect when a man tells us a mournful or a merry
story.   If we suspect the former of falsehood in any one
tittle, we reject it altogether.   Our tears refuse to
flow at a suspected imposition.   But the teller of a
mirthful tale has latitude allowed him.   We are content
with less than absolute truth.   'Tis the same with dramatic illusion.   We confess we love in comedy to see an
audience naturalised behind the scenes, taken in into the
interest of the drama, welcomed as by-standers however.
There is something ungracious in a comic actor holding
himself aloof from all participation or concern with those
who are come to be diverted by him.   Macbeth must see the
dagger, and no ear but his own be told of it;   but an old
fool in farce may think he *sees something*, and by conscious words and looks express it, as plainly as he can
speak, to pit, box, and gallery.   When an impertinent in
tragedy, an Osric, for instance, breaks in upon the serious passions of the scene, we approve of the contempt with
which he is treated.   But when the pleasant impertinent
of comedy, in a piece purely meant to give delight, and
raise mirth out of whimsical perplexities, worries the
studious man with taking up his leisure, or making his
house his home, the same sort of contempt expressed (however *natural*) would destroy the balance of delight in the
spectators.   To make the intrusion comic, the actor who
plays the annoyed man must a little desert nature;   he
must, in short, be thinking of the audience, and express
only so much dissatisfaction and peevishness as is consistent with the pleasure of comedy.   In other words, his perplexity must seem half put on.   If he repel the intruder
with the sober set face of a man in earnest, and more especially if he deliver his expostulations in a tone which
in the world must necessarily provoke a duel;   his real-
life manner will destroy the whimsical and purely dramatic
existence of the other character (which to render it comic
demands an antagonist comicality on the part of the character opposed to it), and convert what was meant for
mirth, rather than belief, into a downright piece of im-

pertinence indeed, which would raise no diversion in us,
but rather stir pain, to see inflicted in earnest upon any
unworthy person.   A very judicious actor (in most of his
parts) seems to have fallen into an error of this sort in
his playing with Mr. Wrench in the farce of Free and Easy.

Many instances would be tedious;   these may suffice to
show that comic acting at least does not always demand
from the performer that strict abstraction from all reference to an audience, which is exacted of it;   but that
in some cases a sort of compromise may take place, and
all the purposes of dramatic delight be attained by a
judicious understanding, not too openly announced, between the ladies and gentlemen - on both sides of the
curtain.

The Old Actors was published as three articles in the
'London Magazine' for February, April and October 1822.
In reprinting them in the 'Essays' in the following year,
Lamb re-arranged them into the three essays now better
known as On Some of the Old Actors, On the Artificial
Comedy of the Last Century, and On the Acting of Munden.
In his edition of Lamb's 'Works', E.V. Lucas reprints the
original articles as an appendix to the first volume.

THE casual sight of an old Play Bill, which I picked up
the other day - I know not by what chance it was preserved
so long - tempts me to call to mind a few of the Players,
who make the principal figure in it.   It presents the
cast of parts in the Twelfth Night, at the old Drury-lane
Theatre two-and-thirty years ago.   There is something
very touching in these old remembrances.   They make us
think how we *once* used to read a Play Bill - not, as now
peradventure, singling out a favorite performer, and casting a negligent eye over the rest;   but spelling out every
name, down to the very mutes and servants of the scene; -
when it was a matter of no small moment to us whether
Whitfield, or Packer, took the part of Fabian;   when
Benson, and Burton, and Phillimore - names of small
account - had an importance, beyond what we can be content
to attribute now to the time's best actors. - "Orsino, by
Mr. Barrymore." - What a full Shakspearian sound it carries! how fresh to memory arise the image, and the manner,
of the gentle actor!
    Those who have only seen Mrs. Jordan within the last
ten or fifteen years, can have no adequate notion of her
performance of such parts as Ophelia;   Helena, in All's
Well that Ends Well;   and Viola in this play.   Her voice
had latterly acquired a coarseness, which suited well

enough with her Nells and Hoydens, but in those days it
sank, with her steady melting eye, into the heart.   Her
joyous parts - in which her memory now chiefly lives - in
her youth were outdone by her plaintive ones.   There is
no giving an account how she delivered the disguised story
of her love for Orsino.   It was no set speech, that she
had foreseen, so as to weave it into an harmonious period,
line necessarily following line, to make up the music -
yet I have heard it so spoken, or rather *read*, not without
its grace and beauty - but, when she had declared her sister's history to be a "blank," and that she "never told
her love," there was a pause, as if the story had ended -
and then the image of the "worm in the bud" came up as a
new suggestion - and the heightened image of "Patience"
still followed after that, as by some growing (and not
mechanical) process, thought springing up after thought, I
would almost say, as they were watered by her tears.   So
in those fine lines -

Write loyal cantos of contemned love -
Hollow your name to the reverberate hills - (1)

there was no preparation made in the foregoing image for
that which was to follow.   She used no rhetoric in her
passion;   or it was nature's own rhetoric, most legitimate
then, when it seemed altogether without rule or law.
Mrs. Powel (now Mrs. Rena[u]d), then in the pride of
her beauty, made an admirable Olivia.   She was particularly excellent in her unbending scenes in conversation
with the Clown.   I have seen some Olivias - and those
very sensible actresses too - who in these interlocutions
have seemed to set their wits at the jester, and to vie
conceits with him in downright emulation.   But she used
him for her sport, like what he was, to trifle a leisure
sentence or two with, and then to be dismissed, and she to
be the Great Lady still.   She touched the imperious fantastic humour of the character with nicety.   Her fine
spacious person filled the scene.
The part of Malvolio has in my judgment been so often
misunderstood, and the *general merits* of the actor, who
then played it, so unduly appreciated, that I shall hope
for pardon, if I am a little prolix upon these points.
Of all the actors who flourished in my time - a melancholy phrase if taken aright, reader - Bensley had most of
the swell of soul, was greatest in the delivery of heroic
conceptions, the emotions consequent upon the presentment
of a great idea to the fancy.   He had the true poetical
enthusiasm - the rarest faculty among players.   None that
I remember possessed even a portion of that fine madness

which he threw out in Hotspur's famous rant about
glory, (2) or the transports of the Venetian incendiary at
the vision of the fired city.  His voice had the disso-
nance, and at times the inspiriting effect of the trumpet.
His gait was uncouth and stiff, but no way embarrassed by
affectation;  and the thorough-bred gentleman was uppermost in every movement.  He seized the moment of passion
with the greatest truth;  like a faithful clock, never
striking before the time;  never anticipating or leading
you to anticipate.  He was totally destitute of trick and
artifice.  He seemed come upon the stage to do the poet's
message simply, and he did it with as genuine fidelity as
the nuncios in Homer deliver the errands of the gods.  He
let the passion or the sentiment do its own work without
prop or bolstering.  He would have scorned to mountebank
it;  and betrayed none of that *cleverness* which is the
bane of serious acting.  For this reason, his Iago was
the only endurable one which I remember to have seen.  No
spectator from his action could divine more of his artifice than Othello was supposed to do.  His confessions in
soliloquy alone put you in possession of the mystery.
There were no by-intimations to make the audience fancy
their own discernment so much greater than that of the
Moor - who commonly stands like a great helpless mark set
up for mine Ancient, and a quantity of barren spectators,
to shoot their bolts at.  The Iago of Bensley did not go
to work so grossly.  There was a triumphant tone about
the character, natural to a general consciousness of
power;  but none of that petty vanity which chuckles and
cannot contain itself upon any little successful stroke of
its knavery - as is common with your small villains, and
green probationers in mischief.  It did not clap or crow
before its time.  It was not a man setting his wits at a
child, and winking all the while at other children who are
mightily pleased at being let into the secret;  but a consummate villain entrapping a noble nature into toils,
against which no discernment was available, where the
manner was as fathomless as the purpose seemed dark, and
without motive.  The part of Malvolio, in the Twelfth
Night, was performed by Bensley, with a richness and a
dignity, of which (to judge from some recent castings of
that character) the very tradition must be worn out from
the stage.  No manager in those days would have dreamed
of giving it to Mr. Baddeley, or Mr. Parsons:  when Bensley was occasionally absent from the theatre, John Kemble
thought it no derogation to succeed to the part.  Malvolio is not essentially ludicrous.  He becomes comic but
by accident.  He is cold, austere, repelling;  but dignified, consistent, and, for what appears, rather of an

over-stretched morality.   Maria describes him as a sort
of Puritan;   and he might have worn his gold chain with
honour in one of our old round-head families, in the service of a Lambert, or a Lady Fairfax.   But his morality
and his manners are misplaced in Illyria.   He is opposed
to the proper *levities* of the piece, and falls in the unequal contest.   Still his pride, or his gravity, (call it
which you will) is inherent, and native to the man, not
mock or affected, which latter only are the fit objects to
excite laughter.   His quality is at the best unlovely,
but neither buffoon nor contemptible.   His bearing is
lofty, a little above his station, but probably not much
above his deserts.   We see no reason why he should not
have been brave, honourable, accomplished.   His careless
committal of the ring to the ground (which he was commissioned to restore to Cesario), bespeaks a generosity of
birth and feeling.   His dialect on all occasions is that
of a gentleman, and a man of education.   We must not confound him with the eternal old, low steward of comedy.
He is master of the household to a great Princess;   a dignity probably conferred upon him for other respects than
age or length of service.   Olivia, at the first indica-
tion of his supposed madness, declares that she "would not
have him miscarry for half of her dowry." (3)   Does this
look as if the character was meant to appear little or insignificant?   Once, indeed, she accuses him to his face -
of what? - of being "sick of self-love," - but with a
gentleness and considerateness which could not have been,
if she had not thought that this particular infirmity
shaded some virtues.   His rebuke to the knight, and his
sottish revellers, is sensible and spirited;   and when we
take into consideration the unprotected condition of his
mistress, and the strict regard with which her state of
real or dissembled mourning would draw the eyes of the
world upon her house-affairs, Malvolio might feel the
honour of the family in some sort in his keeping;   as it
appears not that Olivia had any more brothers, or kinsmen, to look to it - for Sir Toby had dropped all such
nice respects at the buttery hatch.   That Malvolio was
meant to be represented as possessing estimable qualities,
the expression of the Duke in his anxiety to have him rec-
onciled, almost infers.   "Pursue him, and entreat him to
a peace."   Even in his abused state of chains and darkness, a sort of greatness seems never to desert him.   He
argues highly and well with the supposed Sir Topas, and

*Clown. What is the opinion of Pythagoras concerning
wild fowl?

philosophises gallantly upon his straw*.   There must have
been some shadow of worth about the man; he must have
been something more than a mere vapour - a thing of straw,
or Jack in office - before Fabian and Maria could have
ventured sending him upon a courting-errand to Olivia.
There was some consonancy (as he would say) in the under-
taking, or the jest would have been too bold even for that
house of misrule.
   Bensley, accordingly, threw over the part an air of
Spanish loftiness.   He looked, spake, and moved like an
old Castilian.   He was starch, spruce, opinionated, but
his superstructure of pride seemed bottomed upon a sense
of worth.   There was something in it beyond the coxcomb.
It was big and swelling, but you could not be sure that it
was hollow.   You might wish to see it taken down, but you
felt that it was upon an elevation.   He was magnificent
from the outset; but when the decent sobrieties of the
character began to give way, and the poison of self-love,
in his conceit of the Countess's affection, gradually to
work, you would have thought that the hero of La
Mancha (4) in person stood before you.   How he went smiling to himself! with what ineffable carelessness would he
twirl his gold chain! what a dream it was! you were infected with the illusion, and did not wish that it should be
removed! you had no room for laughter! if an unseasonable
reflection of morality obtruded itself, it was a deep
sense of the pitiable infirmity of man's nature, that can
lay him open to such frenzies - but in truth you rather
admired than pitied the lunacy while it lasted - you felt
that an hour of such mistake was worth an age with the
eyes open.   Who would not wish to live but for a day in
the conceit of such a lady's love as Olivia?   Why, the
Duke would have given his principality but for a quarter
of a minute, sleeping or waking, to have been so deluded.
The man seemed to tread upon air, to taste manna, to walk
with his head in the clouds, to mate Hyperion.   O! shake
not the castles of his pride - endure yet for a season
bright moments of confidence - "stand still ye watches of
the element," (5) that Malvolio may be still in fancy fair
Olivia's lord - but fate and retribution say no - I hear
the mischievous titter of Maria - the witty taunts of Sir

   *Mal.* That the soul of our grandam might haply inhabit a
                                                    bird.
   *Clown.* What thinkest thou of his opinion?
   *Mal.* I think nobly of the soul, and no way approve of
                                              his opinion.

Toby - the still more insupportable triumph of the foolish
knight - the counterfeit Sir Topas is unmasked - and "thus
the whirligig of time," as the true clown hath it, "brings
in his revenges."   I confess that I never saw the catastrophe of this character, while Bensley played it, without
a kind of tragic interest.   There was good foolery too.
Few now remember Dodd.   What an Aguecheek the stage lost
in him!   Lovegrove, who came nearest to the old actors,
revived the character some few seasons ago, and made it
sufficiently grotesque; but Dodd was *it*, as it came out
of nature's hands.   It might be said to remain *in puris
naturalibus*. (6)   In expres[s]ing slowness of apprehension this actor surpassed all others.   You could see the
first dawn of an idea stealing slowly over his countenance, climbing up by little and little, with a painful
process, till it cleared up at last to the fulness of a
twilight conception - its highest meridian.   He seemed to
keep back his intellect, as some have had the power to re-
tard their pulsation.   The balloon takes less time in
filling, than it took to cover the expansion of his broad
moony face over all its quarters with expression.   A
glimmer of understanding would appear in a corner of his
eye, and for lack of fuel go out again.   A part of his
forehead would catch a little intelligence, and be a long
time in communicating it to the remainder.

I am ill at dates, but I think it is now better than
five and twenty years ago that walking in the gardens of
Gray's Inn - they were then far finer than they are now -
the accursed Verulam Buildings had not encroached upon all
the east side of them, cutting out delicate green crank-
les, and shouldering away one of two of the stately al-
coves of the terrace - the survivor stands gaping and re-
lationless as if it remembered its brother - they are
still the best gardens of any of the Inns of Court, my beloved Temple not forgotten - have the gravest character,
their aspect being altogether reverend and law-breathing -
Bacon has left the impress of his foot upon their gravel
walks - taking my afternoon solace on a summer day upon
the aforesaid terrace, a comely sad personage came towards
me, whom, from his grave air and deportment, I judged to
be one of the old Benchers of the Inn.   He had a serious
thoughtful forehead, and seemed to be in meditations of
mortality.   As I have an instinctive awe of old Benchers,
I was passing him with that sort of subindicative token of
respect which one is apt to demonstrate towards a venerable stranger, and which rather denotes an inclination to
greet him, than any positive motion of the body to that
effect - a species of humility and will-worship which I
observe, nine times out of ten, rather puzzles than

pleases the person it is offered to - when the face turning full upon me strangely identified itself with that of
Dodd.  Upon close inspection I was not mistaken.  But
could this sad thoughtful countenance be the same vacant
face of folly which I had hailed so often under circumstances of gaiety;  which I had never seen without a
smile, or recognised but as the usher of mirth;  that
looked out so formally flat in Foppington, so frothily
pert in Tattle, so impotently busy in Backbite;  so blank-
ly divested of all meaning, or resolutely expressive of
none, in Acres, in Fribble, and a thousand agreeable im-
pertinences?  Was this the face - full of thought and
carefulness - that had so often divested itself at will of
every trace of either to give me diversion, to clear my
cloudy face for two or three hours at least of its fur-
rows?  Was this the face - manly, sober, intelligent, -
which I had so often despised, made mocks at, made merry
with?  The remembrance of the freedoms which I had taken
with it came upon me with a reproach of insult.  I could
have asked it pardon.  I thought it looked upon me with a
sense of injury.  There is something strange as well as
sad in seeing actors - your pleasant fellows particularly
- subjected to and suffering the common lot - their fortunes, their casualties, their deaths, seem to belong to
the scene, their actions to be amenable to poetic justice
only.  We can hardly connect them with more awful respon-
sibilities.  The death of this fine actor took place
shortly after this meeting.  He had quitted the stage
some months;  and, as I learned afterwards, had been in
the habit of resorting daily to these gardens almost to
the day of his decease.  In these serious walks probably
he was divesting himself of many scenic and some real vanities - weaning himself from the frivolities of the lesser
and the greater theatre - doing gentle penance for a life
of no very reprehensible fooleries, - taking off by degrees the buffoon mask which he might feel he had worn too
long - and rehearsing for a more solemn cast of part.
Dying he "put on the weeds of Dominic*." (7)

    *Dodd was a man of reading, and left at his death a
choice collection of old English literature.  I should
judge him to have been a man of wit.  I know one instance of an impromptu which no length of study could
have bettered.  My merry friend, Jem White, (8) had
seen him one evening in Aguecheek, and recognising Dodd
the next day in Fleet Street, was irresistibly impelled
to take off his hat and salute him as the identical
Knight of the preceding evening with a "Save you, *Sir
Andrew*."  Dodd, not at all disconcerted at this unusual
address from a stranger, with a courteous half-rebuking
wave of the hand, put him off with an "Away, *Fool*."

If few can remember Dodd, many yet living will not
easily forget the pleasant creature, who in those days en-
acted the part of the Clown to Dodd's Sir Andrew. -
Richard, or rather Dicky Suett - for so in his life-time
he delighted to be called, and time hath ratified the appellation - lieth buried on the north side of the cemetery
of Holy Paul, to whose service his nonage and tender years
were dedicated.  There are who do yet remember him at
that period - his pipe clear and harmonious.  He would
often speak of his chorister days, when he was "cherub
Dicky."

What clipped his wings, or made it expedient that he
should exchange the holy for the profane state;  whether
he had lost his good voice (his best recommendation to
that office), like Sir John, "with hallooing and singing
of anthems;" (9)  or whether he was adjudged to lack something, even in those early years, of the gravity indispen-
sable to an occupation which professeth to "commerce with
the skies" (10) - I could never rightly learn;  but we
find him, after the probation of a twelvemonth or so, reverting to a secular condition, and become one of us.

I think he was not altogether of that timber, out of
which cathedral seats and sounding boards are hewed.  But
if a glad heart - kind and therefore glad - be any part of
sanctity, then might the robe of Motley, with which he invested himself with so much humility after his depriva-
tion, and which he wore so long with so much blameless
satisfaction to himself and to the public, be accepted for
a surplice - his white stole, and *albe*.

The first fruits of his secularization was an engage-
ment upon the boards of Old Drury, at which theatre he
commenced, as I have been told, with adopting the manner
of Parsons in old men's characters.  At the period in
which most of us knew him, he was no more an imitator than
he was in any true sense himself imitable.

He was the Robin Good-Fellow of the stage.  He came in
to trouble all things with a welcome perplexity, himself
no whit troubled for the matter.  He was known, like
Puck, by his note - *Ha! Ha! Ha!* - sometimes deepening to
*Ho! Ho! Ho!* with an irresistible accession, derived perhaps remotely from his ecclesiastical education, foreign
to his prototype of, - *O La!*  Thousands of hearts yet
respond to the chuckling *O La!* of Dicky Suett, brought
back to their remembrance by the faithful transcript of
his friend Mathews's mimicry.  The "force of nature could
no further go." (11)  He drolled upon the stock of these
two syllables richer than the cuckoo.

Care, that troubles all the world, was forgotten in his
composition.  Had he had but two grains (nay, half a

grain) of it, he could never have supported himself upon those two spider's strings, which served him (in the latter part of his unmixed existence) as legs.   A doubt or a scruple must have made him totter, a sigh have puffed him down;   the weight of a frown had staggered him, a wrinkle made him lose his balance.   But on he went, scrambling upon those airy stilts of his, with Robin Good-Fellow, "thorough brake, thorough briar," (12) reckless of a scratched face or a torn doublet.

Shakspeare foresaw him, when he framed his fools and jesters.   They have all the true Suett stamp, a loose and shambling gait, a slippery tongue, this last the ready midwife to a without-pain-delivered jest;   in words, light as air, venting truths deep as the centre;   with idlest rhymes tagging conceit when busiest, singing with Lear in the tempest, or Sir Toby at the buttery-hatch.

Jack Bannister and he had the fortune to be more of personal favourites with the town than any actors before or after.   The difference, I take it, was this: - Jack was more *beloved* for his sweet, good-natured, moral pretensions.   Dicky was more *liked* for his sweet, good-natured, no pretensions at all.   Your whole conscience stirred with Bannister's performance of Walter in the Children in the Wood - but Dicky seemed like a thing, as Shakspeare says of Love, too young to know what conscience is. (13)   He put us into Vesta's days.   Evil fled before him - not as from Jack, as from an antagonist, - but because it could not touch him, any more than a cannon-ball a fly.   He was delivered from the burthen of that death; and, when Death came himself, not in metaphor, to fetch Dicky, it is recorded of him by Robert Palmer, who kindly watched his exit, that he received the last stroke, neither varying his accustomed tranquillity, nor tune, with the simple exclamation, worthy to have been recorded in his epitaph - *O La! O La! Bobby!*

The elder Palmer (of stage-treading celebrity) commonly played Sir Toby in those days;   but there is a solidity of wit in the jests of that half-Falstaff which he did not quite fill out.   He was as much too showy as Moody (who sometimes took the part) was dry and sottish.   In sock or buskin there was an air of swaggering gentility about Jack Palmer.   He was a *gentleman* with a slight infusion of *the footman*.   His brother Bob (of recenter memory) who was his shadow in every thing while he lived, and dwindled into less than a shadow afterwards - was a *gentleman* with a little stronger infusion of the *latter ingredient*;   that was all.   It is amazing how a little of the more or less makes a difference in these things.   When you saw Bobby in the Duke's Servant*, you said, what a pity such a

*High Life Below Stairs.

pretty fellow was only a servant.   When you saw Jack fig-
uring in Captain Absolute, you thought you could trace his
promotion to some lady of quality who fancied the handsome
fellow in his top-knot, and had bought him a commission.
Therefore Jack in Dick Amlet was insuperable.

Jack had two voices, - both plausible, hypocritical,
and insinuating;  but his secondary or supplemental voice
still more decisively histrionic than his common one.   It
was reserved for the spectator;  and the dramatis personae
were supposed to know nothing at all about it.   The *lies*
of young Wilding, and the *sentiments* in Joseph Surface,
were thus marked out in a sort of italics to the audience.
This secret correspondence with the company before the
curtain (which is the bane and death of tragedy) has an
extremely happy effect in some kinds of comedy, in the
more highly artificial comedy of Congreve or of Sheridan
especially, where the absolute sense of reality (so indis-
pensable to scenes of interest) is not required, or would
rather interfere to diminish your pleasure.   The fact is,
you do not believe in such characters as Surface - the
villain of artificial comedy - even while you read or see
them.   If you did, they would shock and not divert you.
When Ben, in Love for Love, returns from sea, the following exquisite dialogue occurs at his first meeting with
his father -

*Sir Sampson*. Thou hast been many a weary league, Ben,
since I saw thee.
   *Ben*. Ey, ey, been!   Been far enough, an that be all. -
Well, father, and how do all at home? how does brother
Dick, and brother Val?
   *Sir Sampson*. Dick! body o' me, Dick has been dead these
two years.   I writ you word when you were at Leghorn.
   *Ben*. Mess, that's true; Marry, I had forgot.   Dick's
dead, as you say - Well, and how? - I have a many ques-
tions to ask you - (14)

Here is an instance of insensibility which in real life
would be revolting, or rather in real life could not have
co-existed with the warm-hearted temperament of the character.   But when you read it in the spirit with which
such playful selections and specious combinations rather
than strict *metaphrases* of nature should be taken, or when
you saw Bannister play it, it neither did, nor does wound
the moral sense at all.   For what is Ben - the pleasant
sailor which Bannister gives us - but a piece of satire -
a creation of Congreve's fancy - a dreamy combination of
all the accidents of a sailor's character - his contempt
of money - his credulity to women - with that necessary

estrangement from home which it is just within the verge
of credibility to suppose *might* produce such an hallucina-
tion as is here described.  We never think the worse of
Ben for it, or feel it as a stain upon his character.
But when an actor comes, and instead of the delightful
phantom - the creature dear to half-belief - which Bannister exhibited - displays before our eyes a downright
concretion of a Wapping sailor - a jolly warm-hearted
Jack Tar - and nothing else - when instead of investing it
with a delicious confusedness of the head, and a veering
undirected goodness of purpose - he gives to it a downright daylight understanding, and a full consciousness of
its actions;  thrusting forward the sensibilities of the
character with a pretence as if it stood upon nothing
else, and was to be judged by them alone - we feel the
discord of the thing;  the scene is disturbed;  a real man
has got in among the dramatis personae, and puts them out.
We want the sailor turned out.  We feel that his true
place is not behind the curtain but in the first or second
gallery.

3   On the Artificial Comedy of the Last Century
    1822, 1823

For bibliographical details see the headnote to the previous essay.

THE artificial Comedy, or Comedy of manners, is quite extinct on our stage.   Congreve and Farquhar show their
heads once in seven years only, to be exploded and put
down instantly.   The times cannot bear them.   Is it for
a few wild speeches, an occasional license of dialogue?
I think not altogether.   The business of their dramatic
characters will not stand the moral test.   We screw every
thing up to that.   Idle gallantry in a fiction, a dream,
the passing pageant of an evening, startles us in the same
way as the alarming indications of profligacy in a son or
ward in real life should startle a parent or guardian.
We have no such middle emotions as dramatic interests
left.   We see a stage libertine playing his loose pranks
of two hours' duration, and of no after consequence, with
the severe eyes which inspect real vices with their bearings upon two worlds.   We are spectators to a plot or
intrigue (not reducible in life to the point of strict
morality) and take it all for truth.   We substitute a
real for a dramatic person, and judge him accordingly.
We try him in our courts, from which there is no appeal to
the *dramatis personae*, his peers.   We have been spoiled
with - not sentimental comedy - but a tyrant far more per-
nicious to our pleasures which has succeeded to it, the
exclusive and all devouring drama of common life;   where
the moral point is every thing;   where, instead of the
fictitious half-believed personages of the stage (the
phantoms of old comedy) we recognise ourselves, our brothers, aunts, kinsfolk, allies, patrons, enemies, - the
same as in life, - with an interest in what is going on so
hearty and substantial, that we cannot afford our moral

judgment, in its deepest and most vital results, to compromise or slumber for a moment.   What is *there* transact-
ing, by no modification is made to affect us in any other
manner than the same events or characters would do in our
relationships of life.   We carry our fire-side concerns
to the theatre with us.   We do not go thither, like our
ancestors, to escape from the pressure of reality, so much
as to confirm our experience of it;  to make assurance
double, and take a bond of fate.   We must live our toil-
some lives twice over, as it was the mournful privilege of
Ulysses to descend twice to the shades. (15)   All that
neutral ground of character, which stood between vice and
virtue;  or which in fact was indifferent to neither,
where neither properly was called in question;  that happy
breathing-place from the burthen of a perpetual moral
questioning - the sanctuary and quiet Alsatia of hunted
casuistry (16) - is broken up and disfranchised, as injurious to the interests of society.   The privileges of
the place are taken away by law.   We dare not dally with
images, or names, of wrong.   We bark like foolish dogs at
shadows.   We dread infection from the scenic representation of disorder;  and fear a painted pustule.   In our
anxiety that our morality should not take cold, we wrap it
up in a great blanket surtout of precaution against the
breeze and sunshine.

I confess for myself that (with no great delinquencies
to answer for) I am glad for a season to take an airing
beyond the diocese of the strict conscience, - not to live
always in the precincts of the law-courts, - but now and
then, for a dream-while or so, to imagine a world with no
meddling restrictions - to get into recesses, whither the
hunter cannot follow me -

                          Secret shades
Of woody Ida's inmost grove,
While yet there was no fear of Jove - (17)

I come back to my cage and my restraint the fresher and
more healthy for it.   I wear my shackles more contentedly
for having respired the breath of an imaginary freedom.
I do not know how it is with others, but I feel the better
always for the perusal of one of Congreve's - nay, why
should I not add even of Wycherley's - comedies.   I am
the gayer at least for it;  and I could never connect
those sports of a witty fancy in any shape with any result
to be drawn from them to imitation in real life.   They
are a world of themselves almost as much as fairy-land.
Take one of their characters, male or female (with few exceptions they are alike), and place it in a modern play,

and my virtuous indignation shall rise against the profli-
gate wretch as warmly as the Catos of the pit could
desire;  because in a modern play I am to judge of the
right and the wrong.   The standard of *police* is the measure of *political justice*.   The atmosphere will blight it,
it cannot live here.   It has got into a moral world,
where it has no business, from which it must needs fall
headlong;  as dizzy, and incapable of making a stand, as a
Swedenborgian bad spirit that has wandered unawares into
the sphere of one of his Good Men, or Angels.   But in its
own world do we feel the creature is so very bad? – The
Fainalls and the Mirabels, the Dorimants and the Lady
Touchwoods, in their own sphere, do not offend my moral
sense;  in fact they do not appeal to it at all.   They
seem engaged in their proper element.   They break through
no laws, or conscientious restraints.   They know of none.
They have got out of Christendom into the land – what
shall I call it? – of cuckoldry – the Utopia of gallantry,
where pleasure is duty, and the manners perfect freedom.
It is altogether a speculative scene of things, which has
no reference whatever to the world that is.   No good
person can be justly offended as a spectator, because no
good person suffers on the stage.   Judged morally, every
character in these plays – the few exceptions only are
*mistakes* – is alike essentially vain and worthless.   The
great art of Congreve is especially shown in this, that he
has entirely excluded from his scenes, – some little generosities in the part of Angelica perhaps excepted, – not
only any thing like a faultless character, but any pretensions to goodness or good feelings whatsoever.   Whether
he did this designedly, or instinctively, the effect is as
happy, as the design (if design) was bold.   I used to
wonder at the strange power which his Way of the World in
particular possesses of interesting you all along in the
pursuits of characters, for whom you absolutely care
nothing – for you neither hate nor love his personages –
and I think it is owing to this very indifference for any,
that you endure the whole.   He has spread a privation of
moral light, I will call it, rather than by the ugly name
of palpable darkness, over his creations;  and his shadows
flit before you without distinction or preference.   Had
he introduced a good character, a single gush of moral
feeling, a revulsion of the judgment to actual life and
actual duties, the impertinent Goshen (18) would have only
lighted to the discovery of deformities, which now are
none, because we think them none.
    Translated into real life, the characters of his, and
his friend Wycherley's dramas, are profligates and strum-
pets, – the business of their brief existence, the undi-

vided pursuit of lawless gallantry.   No other spring of
action, or possible motive of conduct, is recognised;
principles which, universally acted upon, must reduce this
frame of things to a chaos.   But we do them wrong in so
translating them.   No such effects are produced in *their*
world.   When we are among them, we are amongst a chaotic
people.   We are not to judge them by our usages.   No
reverend institutions are insulted by their proceedings, -
for they have none among them.   No peace of families is
violated, - for no family ties exist among them.   No
purity of the marriage bed is stained, - for none is supposed to have a being.   No deep affections are disquieted, - no holy wedlock bands are snapped asunder, - for
affection's depth and wedded faith are not of the growth
of that soil.   There is neither right nor wrong, - gratitude or its opposite, - claim or duty, - paternity or
sonship.   Of what consequence is it to virtue, or how is
she at all concerned about it, whether Sir Simon, or
Dapperwit, steal away Miss Martha;   or who is the father
of Lord Froth's, or Sir Paul Pliant's children.

The whole is a passing pageant, where we should sit as
unconcerned at the issues, for life or death, as at a
battle of the frogs and mice.   But, like Don Quixote, we
take part against the puppets, and quite as impertinently.
We dare not contemplate an Atlantis, (19) a scheme, out of
which our coxcombical moral sense is for a little transitory ease excluded.   We have not the courage to imagine a
state of things for which there is neither reward nor
punishment.   We cling to the painful necessities of shame
and blame.   We would indict our very dreams.

Amidst the mortifying circumstances attendant upon
growing old, it is something to have seen the School for
Scandal in its glory.   This comedy grew out of Congreve
and Wycherley, but gathered some allays of the sentimental
comedy which followed theirs.   It is impossible that it
should be now *acted*, though it continues, at long intervals, to be announced in the bills.   Its hero, when
Palmer played it at least, was Joseph Surface.   When I
remember the gay boldness, the graceful solemn plausibility, the measured step, the insinuating voice - to express
it in a word - the downright *acted* villany of the part, so
different from the pressure of conscious actual wickedness, - the hypocritical assumption of hypocrisy, - which
made Jack so deservedly a favourite in that character, I
must needs conclude the present generation of play-goers
more virtuous than myself, or more dense.   I freely confess that he divided the palm with me with his better
brother;   that, in fact, I liked him quite as well.   Not
but there are passages, - like that, for instance, where

Joseph is made to refuse a pittance to a poor relation, -
incongruities which Sheridan was forced upon by the attempt to join the artificial with the sentimental comedy,
either of which must destroy the other - but over these
obstructions Jack's manner floated him so lightly, that a
refusal from him no more shocked you, than the easy compliance of Charles gave you in reality any pleasure;  you
got over the paltry question as quickly as you could, to
get back into the regions of pure comedy, where no cold
moral reigns.   The highly artificial manner of Palmer in
this character counteracted every disagreeable impression
which you might have received from the contrast, supposing
them real, between the two brothers.   You did not believe
in Joseph with the same faith with which you believed in
Charles.   The latter was a pleasant reality, the former a
no less pleasant poetical foil to it.   The comedy, I have
said, is incongruous;  a mixture of Congreve with sentimental incompatibilities:  the gaiety upon the whole is
buoyant;  but it required the consummate art of Palmer to
reconcile the discordant elements.

    A player with Jack's talents, if we had one now, would
not dare to do the part in the same manner.   He would instinctively avoid every turn which might tend to unrealise, and so to make the character fascinating.   He
must take his cue from his spectators, who would expect a
bad man and a good man as rigidly opposed to each other as
the death-beds of those geniuses are contrasted in the
prints, which I am sorry to say have disappeared from the
windows of my old friend Carrington Bowles, of St. Paul's
Church-yard memory (20) - (an exhibition as venerable as
the adjacent cathedral, and almost coeval) of the bad and
good man at the hour of death;  where the ghastly apprehensions of the former, - and truly the grim phantom with
his reality of a toasting fork is not to be despised, - so
finely contrast with the meek complacent kissing of the
rod, - taking it in like honey and butter, - with which
the latter submits to the scythe of the gentle bleeder,
Time, who wields his lancet with the apprehensive finger
of a popular young ladies' surgeon.   What flesh, like
loving grass, would not covet to meet half-way the stroke
of such a delicate mower? - John Palmer was twice an actor
in this exquisite part.   He was playing to you all the
while that he was playing upon Sir Peter and his lady.
You had the first intimation of a sentiment before it was
on his lips.   His altered voice was meant to you, and you
were to suppose that his fictitious co-flutterers on the
stage perceived nothing at all of it.   What was it to you
if that half-reality, the husband, was over-reached by the
puppetry - or the thin thing (Lady Teazle's reputation)

was persuaded it was dying of a plethory?   The fortunes
of Othello and Desdemona were not concerned in it.   Poor
Jack has past from the stage in good time, that he did not
live to this our age of seriousness.   The pleasant old
Teazle *King*, too, is gone in good time.   His manner would
scarce have past current in our day.   We must love or
hate - acquit or condemn - censure or pity - exert our de-
testable coxcombry of moral judgment upon every thing.
Joseph Surface, to go down now, must be a downright revolting villain - no compromise - his first appearance
must shock and give horror - his specious plausibilities,
which the pleasurable faculties of our fathers welcomed
with such hearty greetings, knowing that no harm (dramatic
harm even) could come, or was meant to come of them, must
inspire a cold and killing aversion.   Charles (the real
canting person of the scene - for the hypocrisy of Joseph
has its ulterior legitimate ends, but his brother's pro-
fessions of a good heart centre in downright self-satis-
faction) must be *loved*, and Joseph *hated*.   To balance one
disagreeable reality with another, Sir Peter Teazle must
be no longer the comic idea of a fretful old bachelor
bridegroom, whose teasings (while King acted it) were evidently as much played off at you, as they were meant to
concern any body on the stage, - he must be a real person,
capable in law of sustaining an injury - a person towards
whom duties are to be acknowledged - the genuine crim-con
antagonist of the villanous seducer Joseph.   To realise
him more, his sufferings under his unfortunate match must
have the downright pungency of life - must (or should)
make you not mirthful but uncomfortable, just as the same
predicament would move you in a neighbour or old friend.
The delicious scenes which give the play its name and
zest, must affect you in the same serious manner as if you
heard the reputation of a dear female friend attacked in
your real presence.   Crabtree, and Sir Benjamin - those
poor snakes that live but in the sunshine of your mirth -
must be ripened by this hot-bed process of realization
into asps or amphisbaenas;   and Mrs. Candour - O! frightful! become a hooded serpent.   Oh who that remembers
Parsons and Dodd - the wasp and butterfly of the School
for Scandal - in those two characters;   and charming natural Miss Pope, the perfect gentlewoman as distinguished
from the fine lady of comedy, in this latter part - would
forego the true scenic delight - the escape from life -
the oblivion of consequences - the holiday barring out of
the pedant Reflection - those Saturnalia of two or three
brief hours, well won from the world - to sit instead at
one of our modern plays - to have his coward conscience
(that forsooth must not be left for a moment) stimulated

with perpetual appeals - dulled rather, and blunted, as a
faculty without repose must be - and his moral vanity
pampered with images of notional justice, notional beneficence, lives saved without the spectators' risk, and
fortunes given away that cost the author nothing?

No piece was, perhaps, ever so completely cast in all
its parts as this *manager's comedy*.  Miss Farren had succeeded to Mrs. Abingdon in Lady Teazle;  and Smith, the
original Charles, had retired, when I first saw it.   The
rest of the characters, with very slight exceptions, remained.   I remember it was then the fashion to cry down
John Kemble, who took the part of Charles after Smith;
but, I thought, very unjustly.   Smith, I fancy, was more
airy, and took the eye with a certain gaiety of person.
He brought with him no sombre recollections of tragedy.
He had not to expiate the fault of having pleased beforehand in lofty declamation.   He had no sins of Hamlet or
of Richard to atone for.   His failure in these parts was
a passport to success in one of so opposite a tendency.
But, as far as I could judge, the weighty sense of Kemble
made up for more personal incapacity than he had to answer
for.   His harshest tones in this part came steeped and
dulcified in good humour.   He made his defects a grace.
His exact declamatory manner, as he managed it, only
served to convey the points of his dialogue with more precision.   It seemed to head the shafts to carry them
deeper.   Not one of his sparkling sentences was lost.   I
remember minutely how he delivered each in succession, and
cannot by any effort imagine how any of them could be altered for the better.   No man could deliver brilliant
dialogue - the dialogue of Congreve or of Wycherley - because none understood it - half so well as John Kemble.
His Valentine, in Love for Love, was, to my recollection,
faultless.   He flagged sometimes in the intervals of
tragic passion.   He would slumber over the level parts of
an heroic character.   His Macbeth has been known to nod.
But he always seemed to me to be particularly alive to
pointed and witty dialogue.   The relaxing levities of
tragedy have not been touched by any since him - the playful court-bred spirit in which he condescended to the
players in Hamlet - the sportive relief which he threw
into the darker shades of Richard - disappeared with him.
He had his sluggish moods, his torpors - but they were the
halting-stones and resting-places of his tragedy - politic
savings, and fetches of the breath - husbandry of the
lungs, where nature pointed him to be an economist -
rather, I think, than errors of the judgment.   They were,
at worst, less painful than the eternal tormenting unap-
peasable vigilance, the "lidless dragon eyes," (21) of
present fashionable tragedy.

From a letter to Robert Lloyd, 26 June.

Pierre & Jaffier are the best things in Otway. — Belvidere
is a poor Creature;  and has had more than her due fame —
Monimia is a little better, but she *whines*. - I like
Calista in the Fair Penitent better than either of Otway's
women — —.   Lee's Massacre of Paris is a noble play,
very chastely & finely written.   His Alexander is full of
that madness, "which rightly should possess a poet's
brain."   OEdipus is also a fine play, but less so than
these two.   It is a joint production of Lee & Dryden.
All for Love begins with uncommon Spirit, but soon flags,
and is of no worth upon the whole -.   The last scene of
Young's Revenge is sublime:  the rest of it not worth 1d-

# 5 Playhouse Memoranda
   1813, 1820

This paper was first published anonymously under the
general heading Table-Talk in the 'Examiner', 19 December
1813.   Although it was reprinted with the present title
in Leigh Hunt's 'Indicator', 13 December 1820, the text is
that of the 'Examiner'.

Take the play-house altogether, there is a less sum of
enjoyment than used to be.   Formerly you might see something like the effect of novelty upon a citizen, his wife
and daughters, in the Pit;   their curiosity upon every new
face that entered upon the stage.   The talk of how they
got in at the door, and how they were crowded upon some
former occasion, made a topic till the curtain drew up.
People go too often now-a-days to make their ingress or
egress of consequence.   Children of seven years of age
will talk as familiarly of the performers, aye and as
knowingly (according to the received opinion) as grown
persons;   more than the grown persons in my time.   Oh
when shall I forget first seeing a play, at the age of
five or six?   It was *Artaxerxes*.   Who played, or who
sang in it, I know not.   Such low ideas as actors' names,
or actors' merits, never entered my head.   The mystery of
delight was not cut open and dissipated for me by those
who took me there.   It was *Artaxerxes* and *Arbaces* and
*Mandane* that I saw, not Mr. Beard, or Mr. Leoni, or Mrs.
Kennedy.   It was all enchantment and a dream.   No such
pleasure has since visited me but in dreams.   I was in
Persia for the time, and the burning idol of their devotion in the Temple almost converted me into a worshipper.
I was awe-struck, and believed those significations to be
something more than elemental fires.   I was, with Uriel,
in the body of the sun. (22) - What should I have gained
by knowing (as I should have done, had I been born thirty

years later) that that solar representation was a mere
painted scene, that had neither fire nor light in itself,
and that the royal phantoms, which passed in review before
me, were but such common mortals as I could see every day
out of my father's window?   We crush the faculty of
delight and wonder in children, by explaining every thing.
We take them to the source of the Nile, and shew them the
scanty runnings, instead of letting the beginnings of that
seven fold stream remain in impenetrable darkness, a mysterious question of wonderment and delight to ages.

For bibliographical details see the headnote to 'On Some
of the Old Actors.'

NOT many nights ago I had come home from seeing this
extraordinary performer in Cockletop;   and when I retired
to my pillow, his whimsical image still stuck by me, in a
manner as to threaten sleep.   In vain I tried to divest
myself of it, by conjuring up the most opposite associations.   I resolved to be serious.   I raised up the
gravest topics of life;   private misery, public calamity.
All would not do.

————————There the antic sate
        Mocking our state - (23)

his queer visnomy - his bewildering costume - all the
strange things which he had raked together - his serpen-
tine rod, swagging about in his pocket - Cleopatra's tear,
and the rest of his relics - O'Keefe's wild farce, and *his*
wilder commentary - till the passion of laughter, like
grief in excess, relieved itself by its own weight, inviting the sleep which in the first instance it had driven
away.
    But I was not to escape so easily.   No sooner did I
fall into slumbers, than the same image, only more perplexing, assailed me in the shape of dreams.   Not one
Munden, but five hundred, were dancing before me, like the
faces which, whether you will or no, come when you have
been taking opium - all the strange combinations, which
this strangest of all strange mortals ever shot his proper
countenance into, from the day he came commissioned to dry
up the tears of the town for the loss of the now almost
forgotten Edwin.   O for the power of the pencil to have

fixed them when I awoke! A season or two since there was
exhibited a Hogarth gallery. I do not see why there
should not be a Munden gallery. In richness and variety
the latter would not fall far short of the former.

There is one face of Farley, one face of Knight, one
(but what a one it is!) of Liston; but Munden has none
that you can properly pin down, and call *his*. When you
think he has exhausted his battery of looks, in unaccountable warfare with your gravity, suddenly he sprouts out an
entirely new set of features, like Hydra. He is not one,
but legion. Not so much a comedian, as a company. If
his name could be multiplied like his countenance, it
might fill a play-bill. He, and he alone, literally
*makes faces*: applied to any other person, the phrase is a
mere figure, denoting certain modifications of the human
countenance. Out of some invisible wardrobe he dips for
faces, as his friend Suett used for wigs, and fetches them
out as easily. I should not be surprised to see him some
day put out the head of a river horse; or come forth a
pewitt, or lapwing, some feathered metamorphosis.

I have seen this gifted actor in Sir Christopher Curry
- in Old Dornton - diffuse a glow of sentiment which has
made the pulse of a crowded theatre beat like that of one
man; when he has come in aid of the pulpit, doing good to
the moral heart of a people. I have seen some faint
approaches to this sort of excellence in other players.
But in the grand grotesque of farce, Munden stands out as
single and unaccompanied as Hogarth. Hogarth, strange to
tell, had no followers. The school of Munden began, and
must end with himself.

Can any man *wonder*, like him? can any man *see ghosts*,
like him? or *fight with his own shadow* - "SESSA" (24) -
as he does in that strangely-neglected thing, the Cobbler
of Preston - where his alternations from the Cobbler to
the Magnifico, and from the Magnifico to the Cobbler, keep
the brain of the spectator in as wild a ferment, as if
some Arabian Night were being acted before him. Who like
him can throw, or ever attempted to throw, a preternatural
interest over the commonest daily-life objects? A table,
or a joint stool, in his conception, rises into a dignity
equivalent to Cassiopeia's chair. It is invested with
constellatory importance. You could not speak of it with
more deference, if it were mounted into the firmament. A
beggar in the hands of Michael Angelo, says Fuseli, (25)
rose the Patriarch of Poverty. So the gusto of Munden
antiquates and ennobles what it touches. His pots and
his ladles are as grand and primal as the seething-pots
and hooks seen in old prophetic vision. A tub of butter,
contemplated by him, amounts to a Platonic idea. He

understands a leg of mutton in its quiddity.   He stands
wondering, amid the common-place materials of life, like
primaeval man with the sun and stars about him.

1 Cf. 'Twelfth Night', I, v, 254, 256.   The other references in this paragraph are to Act II, Scene iv.
2 See '1 Henry IV', I, iii, 201-8.
3 'Twelfth Night', III, iv, 60-1.   The other references
  to the play in this passage are as follows:  I, v, 85;
  V, i, 366;  IV, ii, 49-54;  II, v, 118-19;  V, i, 363.
4 Don Quixote.
5 Cf. Marlowe, 'Edward II', V, i, 66.
6 'Quite naked'.
7 'Paradise Lost', III, 479.
8 Jem White (1775-1820), author of 'Falstaff's Letters',
  1796, was at school with Lamb and is commemorated in
  the essay, The Praise of Chimney-Sweepers.
9 '2 Henry IV', I, ii, 179-80.
10 Cf. Il Penseroso, l. 39.
11 Cf. Dryden, ['Lines on' Milton], l. 5.
12 Cf. 'A Midsummer Night's Dream', II, i, 3.
13 Sonnet 151.
14 Congreve, 'Love for Love', III, vi, 20-9.
15 Homer, 'Odyssey', XI.
16 A cant name for a precinct in Whitefriars which until
  1697 formed a sanctuary for debtors and criminals.
17 Il Penseroso, ll. 28-30.
18 See Exodus 8:22.
19 A fabulous island which, owing to the impiety of its
  inhabitants, was swallowed up by the sea.   The inhabitants of Bacon's Atlantis lived strictly according to
  moral laws.
20 Carrington Bowles, print publisher.
21 Coleridge, Ode to the Departing Year, l. 145.
22 See 'Paradise Lost', III, 648-50.
23 Cf. 'Richard II', III, ii, 162-3.
24 An exclamation of uncertain meaning used by Shakespeare.

25 Henry Fuseli (1741-1825), painter, writer and transla-
   tor.   Elected to the Royal Academy in 1790, he was its
   Professor of Painting from 1799 until 1803, 1810-25.

Lamb frequently refers in different places to actors, characters and plays, many of them relatively unknown to the modern reader. For the sake of convenience, and to avoid unnecessary duplication of notes and cross-references, separate lists of each are provided.

---

## ACTORS AND ACTRESSES

Abingdon, Mrs (1737-1815), made her first appearance at the Haymarket in 1755, and in 1764 returned to Drury Lane at Garrick's invitation. She was the original Lady Teazle in Sheridan's 'The School for Scandal', 1777.

Arnold, Samuel James (1774-1852), dramatist and manager of the Lyceum. He was also manager of Drury Lane, 1812-15, and produced many musical plays and foreign operas.

Baddeley, Robert (1733-94), comedian. He joined Drury Lane in 1763, and was the original Moses in Sheridan's 'The School for Scandal', 1777.

Bannister, John (1760-1836), popular comic actor at Drury Lane and a favourite with both Lamb and Hazlitt. He retired in 1815.

Barry, Spranger (1719-77), Garrick's greatest rival. He first appeared on the Dublin stage in 1744, and joined Drury Lane in 1746 where he remained until 1749-50 when he joined Covent Garden. He is buried in the cloisters of Westminster Abbey.

Beard, John (1716?-91), proprietor and manager of Covent Garden, and one of the most famous singers of the eighteenth century. Handel composed many of his tenor solos for him.

Bensley, Robert (1738?-1817), acted at Drury Lane and the Haymarket from 1775 until 1796.

Betterton, Thomas (1635?-1710), actor and dramatist.   He
   was greatly admired by his contemporaries.   He produced
   Congreve's 'Love for Love' in 1695.   Pepys called him
   'the best actor in the world'.   He was famous for his
   performance of Hamlet.
Betterton, Mrs (d. 1711), wife of Thomas Betterton, and
   the first notable actress on the English stage.
Cibber, Susannah Maria (1714-66), sister of Arne, the composer, and famous both as a singer and later as a tragic
   actress.   She first sang in opera at the Haymarket in
   1732, and was a favourite with Handel.   She first acted
   in tragedy in 1736, and joined Garrick's company at
   Drury Lane in 1753.
Cooke, George Frederick (1756-1811), Irish actor.   First
   appeared on the stage in 1776, and in London in 1778 at
   the Haymarket.   His last appearance in London was in
   1810.
Dodd, James William (1740?-96), first appeared at Drury
   Lane in 1765, and remained with the company until his
   retirement in 1796.
Dowton, William (1764-1851), made his first appearance at
   Drury Lane in 1796, and was with the company for thirty-
   six years.   A versatile actor, he was well known for
   his performances as Falstaff, and was considered the
   best actor of Malvolio.   He made his last appearance in
   1840.
Edwin, John, the Elder (1749-90), one of the great comic
   actors of his day, and for a long time the mainstay of
   the Haymarket.
Emery, John (1777-1822), one of the best actors of his
   time, especially well known for his rustic roles.   He
   acted at Covent Garden from 1801 until his death.   He
   also exhibited at the Royal Academy, 1801-17.
Farley, Charles (1771-1859), actor, manager, and stage
   manager, best known for his production of Covent Garden
   pantomimes, 1806-34.   He excelled as an actor in melo-
   dramas.
Farren, Elizabeth (1759?-1829), afterwards Countess of
   Derby, acted from 1777 until 1797.   She was famous for
   her performances of Lady Teazle which she acted for the
   last time in 1797.
Garrick, David (1717-79), the most famous of all English
   actors.   His career spanned the years 1741-76.
Gattie, Henry (1774-1844), appeared at Bath 1807-12, and a
   member of Drury Lane from 1813 until his retirement in
   1833.
Glover, Julia (1779-1850), made her debut in 1797.   She
   acted at Covent Garden 1797-1801, and frequently performed with Kean and Macready.   She was the original

Alhadra in Coleridge's 'Remorse', 1813.   She retired in
1850.   She was a better comic than tragic actress.

Johnston, Mrs (b. 1782), made her London debut in 1797.
She was the wife of Henry Erskine Johnston, the 'Scottish Roscius', and acted at Covent Garden and the Haymarket.

Jordan, Mrs (1762-1816), the greatest comic actress of her
time.   She made her debut at Drury Lane in 1785, and
retired from the stage in 1814.   She was painted by
Reynolds, Gainsborough, Hoppner and Romney.

Kean, Edmund (1787-1833), the greatest tragic actor of his
time, first appeared at Drury Lane in 1814 as Shylock.
See W. Hazlitt, 'Complete Works', ed. P.P. Howe (London,
1930-4), v. 179-80.   He does not appear to have been
greatly relished by Lamb.   He made his last appearance
in 1833 as Richard II at Drury Lane, and as Othello at
Covent Garden.

Kelly, Frances Maria (1790-1882), chiefly associated with
Drury Lane where she first appeared in 1798.   She refused an offer of marriage from Lamb in 1819.   She retired from the stage in 1835.

Kemble, John Philip (1757-1823), the foremost tragic actor
of his time, and brother of Mrs Siddons.   He first appeared in 1776, and at Drury Lane between 1783 and 1802
he played one hundred and twenty roles.   He last appeared at Covent Garden in 1817.

Kennedy, Mrs (d. 1793), formerly Mrs Farrell, singer.
She was taught by Arne, and first appeared at Covent
Garden in 1776.   Her greatest success was in male
parts.

King, Thomas (1730-1805), actor and dramatist, and manager
of Drury Lane.   He was engaged by Garrick for Drury
Lane in 1748, and was the original Sir Peter Teazle in
Sheridan's 'The School for Scandal', 1777.

Knight, Edward (1774-1826), comedian, popularly known as
'Little Knight'.   He was unequalled in the parts of
footmen, rustics and old men.

Leoni (d. 1797), tenor of great repute, and uncle and
teacher of the famous singer, John Braham.   His real
name was Myer Lyon.   His voice is said to have surpassed even that of his more famous nephew.   He made his
debut in 'Artaxerxes' in 1775.

Liston, John (1776?-1846), famous for his performance of
Lord Grizzle in Fielding's 'Tom Thumb'.   Hazlitt's
encomiums are numerous.   He acted at Covent Garden from
1808 until 1822, and retired in 1837.

Lovegrove, William (1778-1816), made his reputation at
Bath, and appeared in London in 1810.

Mathews, Charles (1776-1835), famous comic actor and impersonator, best known for his entertainments known as 'At Home'.   He played four hundred different roles. His famous collection of theatrical paintings was bought by the Garrick Club in 1836.

Mattocks, Isabella (1746-1826), comic actress and the chief support of Covent Garden where she acted an immense number of roles from 1761 until her retirement in 1808.   She was especially well known for her roles as chambermaid.

Munden, Joseph Shepherd (1758-1832), acted at Covent Garden almost continuously from 1790 until 1811, and at Drury Lane from 1813 until 1824.   He was the most famous comic actor of his day.

Oldfield, Anne (1683-1730), acted at Drury Lane in 1692, and was a member of the company from 1711 until 1730. She excelled in both tragedy and comedy.   The Narcissa of Pope's 'Moral Essays', she is buried in Westminster Abbey beneath Congreve's monument.

Macready, William Charles (1793-1873), first appeared on the stage in 1810, and was engaged by Covent Garden in 1816.   He was the leading actor at Drury Lane 1823-6, and at different times was manager of both theatres. He retired in 1851.

Packer, John Hayman (1730-1806), best known for his acting of old men.   He acted at Drury Lane under Garrick, and retired in 1805.

Palmer, John (1742?-98), one of the greatest eighteenth-century comic actors, popularly known as 'Plausible Jack'.   He was the original Joseph Surface, often considered his greatest role.   He died on stage at Liverpool.

Palmer, Robert (1757-1805), brother of the more famous John Palmer.   He excelled in rustic roles.

Parsons, William (1736-95), popularly known as the 'Comic Roscius'.   He joined Drury Lane in 1762 and remained with the company all his life.   He excelled in roles of old men, and was the original Crabtree in Sheridan's 'The School for Scandal', 1777.

Pearman, William (b. 1792), originally a seaman, became a popular tenor, making his debut at the English Opera House in 1817.

Pope, Jane (1742-1818), first appeared at Drury Lane in 1756, where she remained until her retirement in 1808. She excelled in the roles of soubrette, and was the original Mrs Candour in Sheridan's 'The School for Scandal', 1777.

Powell, Mrs (1761?-1831), previously Mrs Farmer, subsequently Mrs Renaud, first appeared in London around 1787, and acted at Drury Lane until 1811.   She was generally cast for 'heavy' parts, and retired from the stage in 1829.

Quin, James (1693-1766), the last of the old school of actors which gave way to that of Garrick.  He last appeared on the stage in 1753.

Russell, Samuel Thomas (1769?-1845), first appeared at Drury Lane as Charles Surface in 1795.  His most famous role was Jerry Sneak in Foote's 'The Mayor of Garratt', 1763.  He retired in 1842.

Saint Ledger, Mrs, made her debut in 1799.

Siddons, Mrs (1755-1831), probably the greatest English tragic actress.  She was engaged by Garrick at Drury Lane, 1775-6.  She acted at Covent Garden 1806-12, and was greatly admired by Byron, Lamb, Hazlitt and Hunt.

Smith, William (1730?-1819), known as 'Gentleman Smith', acted at Covent Garden for twenty-one years.  He appeared at Drury Lane in 1774 under Garrick as Richard III, and was the original Faulkland in Sheridan's 'The Rivals', 1775.  His greatest role was Charles Surface, and it was in this role in 1788 that he made his last appearance.

Suett, Richard (1755-1805), popular comic actor who first appeared at Drury Lane in 1780.  He was especially famous for his roles of Shakespeare's fools.

Wrench, Benjamin (1778-1843), made his first London appearance in 1809, and became a well-known comedian at various theatres.


## CHARACTERS

Absolute, Captain:  Sheridan's 'The Rivals', 1775.
Acres:  Sheridan's 'The Rivals', 1775.
Addleplot, Sir Simon:  Wycherley's 'Love in a Wood', 1671.
Amlet, Dick:  Vanbrugh's 'The Confederacy', 1705.
Angelica:  Congreve's 'Love for Love', 1695.
Backbite:  Sheridan's 'The School for Scandal', 1777.
Belvidera:  Otway's 'Venice Preserved', 1682.
Beverley, Mrs:  Moore's 'The Gamester', 1753.
Calista:  Rowe's 'The Fair Penitent', 1703.
Candour, Mrs:  Sheridan's 'The School for Scandal', 1777.
Cockletop:  O'Keeffe's 'Modern Antiques', 1791.
Curry, Sir Christopher:  Colman the Younger's 'Inkle and Yarico', 1787.
Dapperwit:  Wycherley's 'Love in a Wood', 1671.
Dorimant:  Etherege's 'The Man of Mode', 1676.
Dornton, Old:  Holcroft's 'The Road to Ruin', 1792.
Duke's Servant:  Garrick's 'High Life Below Stairs', 1759.
Euphrasia:  Murphy's 'The Grecian Daughter', 1772.

Fainall:   Congreve's 'The Way of the World', 1700.
Foppington:   Vanbrugh's 'The Relapse', 1696.
Foresight:   Congreve's 'Love for Love', 1695.
Fribble:   Garrick's 'Miss in her Teens', 1747.
Froth, Lord:   Congreve's 'The Double Dealer', 1693.
Frugal, Luke:   Massinger's 'The City Madam', 1632.
Glenalvon:   Home's 'Douglas', 1756.
Hoyden, Miss:   Vanbrugh's 'The Relapse', 1696.
Isabella:   Southerne's 'The Fatal Marriage', 1694.
Lubin Log:   Kenney's 'Love, Law, and Physic', 1812.
Martha, Mrs:   Wycherley's 'Love in a Wood', 1671.
Mirabel:   Farquhar's 'The Inconstant', 1702.
Monimia:   Otway's 'The Orphan', 1680.
Nell:   Coffey's 'The Devil to Pay', 1731.
Overreach, Sir Giles:   Massinger's 'A New Way to Pay Old
   Debts', 1633.
Phoebe:   Frances Brooke's 'Rosina', 1783.
Pierre:   Otway's 'Venice Preserved', 1682.
Pliant, Sir Paul:   Congreve's 'The Double Dealer', 1693.
Primrose, Dinah:   O'Keeffe's 'The Young Quaker', 1783.
Surface, Joseph:   Sheridan's 'The School for Scandal',
   1777.
Tattle:   Congreve's 'Love for Love', 1695.
Teazle, Sir Peter and Lady:   Sheridan's 'The School for
   Scandal', 1777.
Touchwood, Lady:   Congreve's 'The Double Dealer', 1693.
Yarico:   Colman the Younger's 'Inkle and Yarico', 1787.
Young Wilding:   Foote's 'The Liar', 1762.


PLAYS

Among the lesser-known plays mentioned by Lamb are the
following:
'Artaxerxes', 1762, by Thomas Augustus Arne (1710-78).
   Lamb saw this opera as a child on 1 December 1780.
'Children in the Wood, The', by Thomas Morton, 1793.
'Cobbler of Preston, The', by Charles Johnson, 1716.   It
   is based on 'The Taming of the Shrew'.
'Hypocrite, The'.   It is an adaptation by Cibber, Bicker-
   staffe and others of Molière's 'Tartuffe'.   In its
   operatic form, with music by Jolly, it was produced at
   the English Opera House in 1819.
'London Merchant, The: or The History of George Barn-
   well', by George Lillo, 1731.
'Modern Antiques: or The Merry Mourners', by John
   O'Keeffe, 1791.

# II Shakespeare

7   On the Tragedies of Shakspeare, considered with
    reference to their Fitness for Stage Representa⸱
    1812, 1818

---

Lamb's famous essay on Shakespeare's tragedies was first
published in the fourth number of Leigh Hunt's 'Reflector', 1812 under the heading *THEATRALIA. No. I. - On
Garrick, and Acting; and the Plays of Shakspeare, considered with reference to their fitness for Stage Representation.*   Lamb reprinted it in his 'Works', 1818.   In
the earlier version Lamb ended the essay thus:   'I have
hitherto confined my observation to the Tragic parts of
Shakespeare; in some future Number I propose to extend
this enquiry to the Comedies.'   The periodical, however,
ceased publication after the fourth issue.

---

TAKING a turn the other day in the Abbey, I was struck
with the affected attitude of a figure, which I do not
remember to have seen before, and which upon examination
proved to be a whole-length of the celebrated Mr. Garrick.
Though I would not go so far with some good catholics
abroad as to shut players altogether out of consecrated
ground, yet I own I was not a little scandalized at the *affectation*
introduction of theatrical airs and gestures into a place (5)
set apart to remind us of the saddest realities.   Going
nearer, I found inscribed under this harlequin figure the
following lines:-

                                    *made up, affected*
To paint fair Nature, by divine command,
Her magic pencil in his glowing hand,
A Shakspeare rose; then, to expand his fame
Wide o'er this breathing world, a Garrick came.
Though sunk in death the forms the Poet drew,
The Actor's genius bade them breathe anew; *renew old Poetic forms*
Though, like the bard himself, in night they lay,
Immortal Garrick call'd them back to day:
And till Eternity with pow'r sublime
                    *past / present / future.*

                *eternizing.*

Shall mark the mortal hour of hoary Time,
Shakspeare and Garrick like twin-stars shall shine,
And earth irradiate with a beam divine. (1)

It would be an insult to my readers' understandings to
attempt any thing like a criticism on this farrago of
false thoughts and nonsense.  But the reflection it led
me into was a kind of wonder, how, from the days of the
actor here celebrated to our own, it should have been the
fashion to compliment every performer in his turn, that
has had the luck to please the town in any of the great
characters of Shakspeare, with the notion of possessing a
*mind congenial with the poet's:* how people should come
thus unaccountably to confound the power of originating
poetical images and conceptions with the faculty of being
able to read or recite the same when put into words;*  or
what connection that absolute mastery over the heart and
soul of man, which a great dramatic poet possesses, has
with those low tricks upon the eye and ear, which a player
by observing a few general effects, which some common
passion, as grief, anger, &c. usually has upon the gestures and exterior, can so easily compass.  To know the
internal workings and movements of a great mind, of an
Othello or a Hamlet for instance, the *when* and the *why* and
the *how far* they should be moved;  to what pitch a passion
is becoming;  to give the reins and to pull in the curb
exactly at the moment when the drawing in or the slacken-
ing is most graceful;  seems to demand a reach of intellect of a vastly different extent from that which is employed upon the bare imitation of the signs of these passions in the countenance or gesture, which signs are
usually observed to be most lively and emphatic in the
weaker sort of minds, and which signs can after all but
indicate some passion, as I said before, anger, or grief,
generally;  but of the motives and grounds of the passion,
wherein it differs from the same passion in low and vulgar
natures, of these the actor can give no more idea by his
face or gesture than the eye (without a metaphor) can
speak, or the muscles utter intelligible sounds.  But

*It is observable that we fall into this confusion only
in *dramatic* recitations.  We never dream that the gentleman who reads Lucretius in public with great applause, is
therefore a great poet and philosopher;  nor do we find
that Tom Davies, the bookseller, who is recorded to have
recited the Paradise Lost better than any man in England
in his day (though I cannot help thinking there must be
some mistake in this tradition) was therefore, by his intimate friends, set upon a level with Milton.

such is the instantaneous nature of the impressions which
we take in at the eye and ear at a playhouse, compared
with the slow apprehension oftentimes of the understanding
in reading, that we are apt not only to sink the play-
writer in the consideration which we pay to the actor, but
even to identify in our minds in a perverse manner, the
actor with the character which he represents.   It is difficult for a frequent playgoer to disembarrass the idea of
Hamlet from the person and voice of Mr. K. (2)   We speak
of Lady Macbeth, while we are in reality thinking of Mrs.
S. (3)   Nor is this confusion incidental alone to unlettered persons, who, not possessing the advantage of
reading, are necessarily dependent upon the stage-player
for all the pleasure which they can receive from the
drama, and to whom the very idea of *what an author is*
cannot be made comprehensible without some pain and perplexity of mind:   the error is one from which persons
otherwise not meanly lettered, find it almost impossible
to extricate themselves.

Never let me be so ungrateful as to forget the very
high degree of satisfaction which I received some years
back from seeing for the first time a tragedy of Shakspeare performed, in which those two great performers sustained the principal parts.   It seemed to embody and
realize conceptions which had hitherto assumed no distinct
shape.   But dearly do we pay all our life after for this
juvenile pleasure, this sense of distinctness.   When the
novelty is past, we find to our cost that instead of
realizing an idea, we have only materialized and brought
down a fine vision to the standard of flesh and blood.
We have let go a dream, in quest of an unattainable substance.

How cruelly this operates upon the mind, to have its
free conceptions thus crampt and pressed down to the measure of a strait-lacing actuality, may be judged from that
delightful sensation of freshness, with which we turn to
those plays of Shakspeare which have escaped being performed, and to those passages in the acting plays of the
same writer which have happily been left out in the performance.   How far the very custom of hearing any thing
*spouted*, withers and blows upon a fine passage, may be
seen in those speeches from Henry the Fifth, &c. which are
current in the mouths of school-boys from their being to
be found in *Enfield Speakers*, (4) and such kind of books.
I confess myself utterly unable to appreciate that celebrated soliloquy in Hamlet, beginning "To be or not to
be," or to tell whether it be good, bad, or indifferent,
it has been so handled and pawed about by declamatory boys
and men, and torn so inhumanly from its living place and

principle of continuity in the play, till it is become to
me a perfect dead member.

It may seem a paradox, but I cannot help being of opinion that the plays of Shakspeare are less calculated for
performance on a stage, than those of almost any other
dramatist whatever.   Their distinguishing excellence is a
reason that they should be so.   There is so much in them,
which comes not under the province of acting, with which
eye, and tone, and gesture, have nothing to do.

The glory of the scenic art is to personate passion,
and the turns of passion; and the more coarse and palpable the passion is, the more hold upon the eyes and ears
of the spectators the performer obviously possesses.   For
this reason, scolding scenes, scenes where two persons
talk themselves into a fit of fury, and then in a surprising manner talk themselves out of it again, have always
been the most popular upon our stage.   And the reason is
plain, because the spectators are here most palpably ap-
pealed to, they are the proper judges in this war of
words, they are the legitimate ring that should be formed
round such "intellectual prize-fighters."   Talking is the
direct object of the imitation here.   But in all the best
dramas, and in Shakspeare above all, how obvious it is,
that the form of *speaking*, whether it be in soliloquy or
dialogue, is only a medium, and often a highly artificial
one, for putting the reader or spectator into possession
of that knowledge of the inner structure and workings of
mind in a character, which he could otherwise never have
arrived at *in that form of composition* by any gift short
of intuition.   We do here as we do with novels written in
the *epistolary form*.   How many improprieties, perfect
solecisms in letter-writing, do we put up with in Clarissa
and other books, for the sake of the delight which that
form upon the whole gives us.

But the practice of stage representation reduces every
thing to a controversy of elocution.   Every character,
from the boisterous blasphemings of Bajazet to the shrinking timidity of womanhood, must play the orator.   The
love-dialogues of Romeo and Juliet, those silver-sweet
sounds of lovers' tongues by night; the more intimate and
sacred sweetness of nuptial colloquy between an Othello or
a Posthumus with their married wives, all those delicacies
which are so delightful in the reading, as when we read of
those youthful dalliances in Paradise -

——————————————————————————As beseem'd
Fair couple link'd in happy nuptial league,
Alone: (5)

by the inherent fault of stage representation, how are
these things sullied and turned from their very nature by
being exposed to a large assembly;  when such speeches as
Imogen addresses to her lord, come drawling out of the
mouth of a hired actress, whose courtship, though nominal-
ly addressed to the personated Posthumus, is manifestly
aimed at the spectators, who are to judge of her endear-
ments and her returns of love.

   The character of Hamlet is perhaps that by which, since
the days of Betterton, a succession of popular performers
have had the greatest ambition to distinguish themselves.
The length of the part may be one of their reasons.  But
for the character itself, we find it in a play, and therefore we judge it a fit subject of dramatic representation.
The play itself abounds in maxims and reflexions beyond
any other, and therefore we consider it as a proper vehicle for conveying moral instruction.  But Hamlet himself
- what does he suffer meanwhile by being dragged forth as
the public schoolmaster, to give lectures to the crowd!
Why, nine parts in ten of what Hamlet does, are transactions between himself and his moral sense, they are the
effusions of his solitary musings, which he retires to
holes and corners and the most sequestered parts of the
palace to pour forth;  or rather, they are the silent
meditations with which his bosom is bursting, reduced to
*words* for the sake of the reader, who must else remain
ignorant of what is passing there.   These profound sorrows, these light-and-noise-abhorring ruminations, which
the tongue scarce dares utter to deaf walls and chambers,
how can they be represented by a gesticulating actor, who
comes and mouths them out before an audience, making four
hundred people his confidants at once[?]   I say not that
it is the fault of the actor so to do;  he must pronounce
them *ore rotundo*, (6) he must accompany them with his eye,
he must insinuate them into his auditory by some trick of
eye, tone, or gesture, or he fails.  *He must be thinking
all the while of his appearance, because he knows that all
the while the spectators are judging of it.*  And this is
the way to represent the shy, negligent, retiring Hamlet.

   It is true that there is no other mode of conveying a
vast quantity of thought and feeling to a great portion of
the audience, who otherwise would never earn it for themselves by reading, and the intellectual acquisition gained
this way may, for aught I know, be inestimable;  but I am
not arguing that Hamlet should not be acted, but how much
Hamlet is made another thing by being acted.   I have
heard much of the wonders which Garrick performed in this
part;  but as I never saw him, I must have leave to doubt
whether the representation of such a character came within

the province of his art.   Those who tell me of him, speak
of his eye, of the magic of his eye, and of his commanding
voice:   physical properties, vastly desirable in an actor,
and without which he can never insinuate meaning into an
auditory, - but what have they to do with Hamlet? what
have they to do with intellect?   In fact, the things
aimed at in theatrical representation, are to arrest the
spectator's eye upon the form and the gesture, and so to
gain a more favourable hearing to what is spoken:   it is
not what the character is, but how he looks;   not what he
says, but how he speaks it.   I see no reason to think
that if the play of Hamlet were written over again by some
such writer as Banks or Lillo, (7) retaining the process
of the story, but totally omitting all the poetry of it,
all the divine features of Shakspeare, his stupendous intellect;   and only taking care to give us enough of passionate dialogue, which Banks or Lillo were never at a
loss to furnish;   I see not how the effect could be much
different upon an audience, nor how the actor has it in
his power to represent Shakspeare to us differently from
his representation of Banks or Lillo.   Hamlet would still
be a youthful accomplished prince, and must be gracefully
personated;   he might be puzzled in his mind, wavering in
his conduct, seemingly-cruel to Ophelia, he might see a
ghost, and start at it, and address it kindly when he
found it to be his father;   all this in the poorest and
most homely language of the servilest creeper after nature
that ever consulted the palate of an audience;   without
troubling Shakspeare for the matter:   and I see not but
there would be room for all the power which an actor has,
to display itself.   All the passions and changes of passion might remain:   for those are much less difficult to
write or act than is thought, it is a trick easy to be
attained, it is but rising or falling a note or two in the
voice, a whisper with a significant foreboding look to
announce its approach, and so contagious the counterfeit
appearance of any emotion is, that let the words be what
they will, the look and tone shall carry it off and make
it pass for deep skill in the passions.

It is common for people to talk of Shakspeare's plays
being so natural;   that every body can understand him.
They are natural indeed, they are grounded deep in nature,
so deep that the depth of them lies out of the reach of
most of us.   You shall hear the same persons say that
George Barnwell is very natural, and Othello is very natural, that they are both very deep;   and to them they are
the same kind of thing.   At the one they sit and shed
tears, because a good sort of young man is tempted by a
naughty woman to commit a trifling peccadillo, the murder

of an uncle or so,* that is all, and so comes to an un-
timely end, which is so moving;  and at the other, because
a blackamoor in a fit of jealousy kills his innocent white
wife:  and the odds are that ninety-nine out of a hundred
would willingly behold the same catastrophe happen to both
the heroes, and have thought the rope more due to Othello
than to Barnwell.  For of the texture of Othello's mind,
the inward construction marvellously laid open with all
its strengths and weaknesses, its heroic confidences and
its human misgivings, its agonies of hate springing from
the depths of love, they see no more than the spectators
at a cheaper rate, who pay their pennies a-piece to look
through the man's telescope in Leicester-fields, see into
the inward plot and topography of the moon.  Some dim
thing or other they see, they see an actor personating a
passion, of grief, or anger, for instance, and they recog-
nize it as a copy of the usual external effects of such
passions;  or at least as being true to that symbol of the
emotion which passes current at the theatre for it, for it
is often no more than that:  but of the grounds of the
passion, its correspondence to a great or heroic nature,
which is the only worthy object of tragedy, - that common
auditors know any thing of this, or can have any such
notions dinned into them by the mere strength of an
actor's lungs, - that apprehensions foreign to them should
be thus infused into them by storm, I can neither believe,
nor understand how it can be possible.
     We talk of Shakspeare's admirable observation of life,
when we should feel, that not from a petty inquisition
into those cheap and every-day characters which surrounded
him, as they surround us, but from his own mind, which

*If this note could hope to meet the eye of any of the
Managers, I would intreat and beg of them, in the name of
both the Galleries, that this insult upon the morality of
the common people of London should cease to be eternally
repeated in the holiday weeks.  Why are the 'Prentices of
this famous and well-governed city, instead of an amusement, to be treated over and over again with a nauseous
sermon of George Barnwell?  Why at the end of their
vistoes are we to place the gallows?  Were I an uncle, I
should not much like a nephew of mine to have such an example placed before his eyes.  It is really making uncle-
murder too trivial to exhibit it as done upon such slight
motives;- it is attributing too much to such characters as
Millwood;- it is putting things into the heads of good
young men, which they would never otherwise have dreamed
of.  Uncles that think any thing of their lives, should
fairly petition the Chamberlain against it.

was, to borrow a phrase of Ben Jonson's, the very "sphere
of humanity," he fetched those images of virtue and of
knowledge, of which every one of us recognizing a part,
think we comprehend in our natures the whole; and oftentimes mistake the powers which he positively creates in
us, for nothing more than indigenous faculties of our own
minds, which only waited the application of corresponding
virtues in him to return a full and clear echo of the
same.

To return to Hamlet. - Among the distinguishing features of that wonderful character, one of the most interesting (yet painful) is that soreness of mind which makes
him treat the intrusions of Polonius with harshness, and
that asperity which he puts on in his interviews with
Ophelia. These tokens of an unhinged mind (if they be
not mixed in the latter case with a profound artifice of
love, to alienate Ophelia by affected discourtesies, so to
prepare her mind for the breaking off of that loving
intercourse, which can no longer find a place amidst business so serious as that which he has to do) are parts of
his character, which to reconcile with our admiration of
Hamlet, the most patient consideration of his situation is
no more than necessary; they are what we *forgive afterwards*, and explain by the whole of his character, but *at
the time* they are harsh and unpleasant. Yet such is the
actor's necessity of giving strong blows to the audience,
that I have never seen a player in this character, who did
not exaggerate and strain to the utmost these ambiguous
features, - these temporary deformities in the character.
They make him express a vulgar scorn at Polonius which
utterly degrades his gentility, and which no explanation
can render palateable; they make him shew contempt, and
curl up the nose at Ophelia's father, - contempt in its
very grossest and most hateful form; but they get applause by it: it is natural, people say; that is, the
words are scornful, and the actor expresses scorn, and
that they can judge of: but why so much scorn, and of
that sort, they never think of asking.

So to Ophelia. - All the Hamlets that I have ever seen,
rant and rave at her as if she had committed some great
crime, and the audience are highly pleased, because the
words of the part are satirical, and they are enforced by
the strongest expression of satirical indignation of which
the face and voice are capable. But then, whether Hamlet
is likely to have put on such brutal appearances to a lady
whom he loved so dearly, is never thought on. The truth
is, that in all such deep affections as had subsisted between Hamlet and Ophelia, there is a stock of *supereroga-
tory love*, (if I may venture to use the expression) which

*must be reasonable for audience rather than imaginative.*

in any great grief of heart, especially where that which
preys upon the mind cannot be communicated, confers a kind
of indulgence upon the grieved party to express itself,
even to its heart's dearest object, in the language of a
temporary alienation; but it is not alienation, it is a
distraction purely, and so it always makes itself to be
felt by that object: it is not anger, but grief assuming
the appearance of anger, - love awkwardly counterfeiting
hate, as sweet countenances when they try to frown: but
such sternness and fierce disgust as Hamlet is made to
shew, is no counterfeit, but the real face of absolute
aversion, - of irreconcileable alienation. It may be
said he puts on the madman; but then he should only so
far put on this counterfeit lunacy as his own real distraction will give him leave; that is, incompletely, im-
perfectly; not in that confirmed, practised way, like a
master of his art, or as Dame Quickly would say, "like one
of those harlotry players." (8)

I mean no disrespect to any actor, but the sort of
pleasure which Shakspeare's plays give in the acting seems
to me not at all to differ from that which the audience
receive from those of other writers; and, *they being in
themselves essentially so different from all others*, I
must conclude that there is something in the nature of
acting which levels all distinctions. And in fact, who
does not speak indifferently of the Gamester and of Macbeth as fine stage performances, and praise the Mrs.
Beverley in the same way as the Lady Macbeth of Mrs. S.?
Belvidera, and Calista, and Isabella, and Euphrasia, are
they less liked than Imogen, or than Juliet, or than
Desdemona? Are they not spoken of and remembered in the
same way? Is not the female performer as great (as they
call it) in one as in the other? Did not Garrick shine,
and was he not ambitious of shining in every drawling
tragedy that his wretched day produced, - the productions
of the Hills and the Murphys and the Browns, (9) - and
shall he have that honour to dwell in our minds for ever
as an inseparable concomitant with Shakspeare? A kindred
mind! O who can read that affecting sonnet of Shakspeare
which alludes to his profession as a player:-

Oh for my sake do you with Fortune chide,
The guilty goddess of my harmless deeds,
That did not better for my life provide
Than public means which public custom breeds -
Thence comes it that my name receives a brand;
And almost thence my nature is subdued
To what it works in, like the dyer's hand - (10)

Or that other confession:-

Alas! 'tis true, I have gone here and there,
And made myself a motly to thy view,
Gor'd mine own thoughts, sold cheap what is most dear -

Who can read these instances of jealous self-watchfulness
in our sweet Shakspeare, and dream of any congeniality between him and one that, by every tradition of him, appears
to have been as mere a player as ever existed; to have
had his mind tainted with the lowest players' vices, -
envy and jealousy, and miserable cravings after applause;
one who in the exercise of his profession was jealous even
of the women-performers that stood in his way; a manager
full of managerial tricks and stratagems and finesse:
that any resemblance should be dreamed of between him and
Shakspeare, - Shakspeare who, in the plenitude and consciousness of his own powers, could with that noble
modesty, which we can neither imitate nor appreciate, express himself thus of his own sense of his own defects:-

Wishing me like to one more rich in hope,
Featur'd like him, like him with friends possest;
Desiring *this man's art, and that man's scope.*

I am almost disposed to deny to Garrick the merit of
being an admirer of Shakspeare. A true lover of his excellencies he certainly was not; for would any true lover
of them have admitted into his matchless scenes such
ribald trash as Tate and Cibber, (11) and the rest of
them, that

With their darkness durst affront his light, (12)

have foisted into the acting plays of Shakspeare? I believe it impossible that he could have had a proper reverence for Shakspeare, and have condescended to go through
that interpolated scene in Richard the Third, in which
Richard tries to break his wife by telling her he
loves another woman, and says, "if she survives this she
is immortal." Yet I doubt not he delivered this vulgar
stuff with as much anxiety of emphasis as any of the genuine parts: and for acting, it is as well calculated as
any. But we have seen the part of Richard lately produce
great fame to an actor by his manner of playing it, and it
lets us into the secret of acting, and of popular judgments of Shakspeare derived from acting. Not one of the
spectators who have witnessed Mr. C.'s (13) exertions in
that part, but has come away with a proper conviction that

Richard is a very wicked man, and kills little children in
their beds, with something like the pleasure which the
giants and ogres in children's books are represented to
have taken in that practice;  moreover, that he is very
close and shrewd and devilish cunning, for you could see
that by his eye.

But is in fact this the impression we have in reading
the Richard of Shakspeare?  Do we feel any thing like
disgust, as we do at that butcher-like representation of
him that passes for him on the stage?  A horror at his
crimes blends with the effect which we feel, but how is it
qualified, how is it carried off, by the rich intellect
which he displays, his resources, his wit, his buoyant
spirits, his vast knowledge and insight into characters,
the poetry of his part, - not an atom of all which is made
perceivable in Mr. C.'s way of acting it.  Nothing but
his crimes, his actions, is visible;  they are prominent
and staring;  the murderer stands out, but where is the
lofty genius, the man of vast capacity, - the profound,
the witty, accomplished Richard?

The truth is, the Characters of Shakspeare are so much
the objects of meditation rather than of interest or curiosity as to their actions, that while we are reading any
of his great criminal characters, - Macbeth, Richard, even
Iago, - we think not so much of the crimes which they
commit, as of the ambition, the aspiring spirit, the intellectual activity, which prompts them to overleap those
moral fences.  Barnwell is a wretched murderer;  there is
a certain fitness between his neck and the rope;  he is
the legitimate heir to the gallows;  nobody who thinks at
all can think of any alleviating circumstances in his case
to make him a fit object of mercy.  Or to take an instance from the higher tragedy, what else but a mere
assassin is Glenalvon!  Do we think of any thing but of
the crime which he commits, and the rack which he deserves?  That is all which we really think about him.
Whereas in corresponding characters in Shakspeare so
little do the actions comparatively affect us, that while
the impulses, the inner mind in all its perverted greatness, solely seems real and is exclusively attended to,
the crime is comparatively nothing.  But when we see
these things represented, the acts which they do are comparatively every thing, their impulses nothing.  The
state of sublime emotion into which we are elevated by
those images of night and horror which Macbeth is made to
utter, that solemn prelude with which he entertains the
time till the bell shall strike which is to call him to
murder Duncan, - when we no longer read it in a book, when
we have given up that vantage-ground of abstraction which

reading possesses over seeing, and come to see a man in
his bodily shape before our eyes actually preparing to
commit a murder, if the acting be true and impressive, as
I have witnessed it in Mr. K.'s performance of that part,
the painful anxiety about the act, the natural longing to
prevent it while it yet seems unperpetrated, the too close
pressing semblance of reality, give a pain and an uneasi-
ness which totally destroy all the delight which the words
in the book convey, where the deed doing never presses
upon us with the painful sense of presence:  it rather
seems to belong to history, - to something past and inevitable, if it has any thing to do with time at all.
The sublime images, the poetry alone, is that which is
present to our minds in the reading.

So to see Lear acted, - to see an old man tottering
about the stage with a walking-stick, turned out of doors
by his daughters in a rainy night, has nothing in it but
what is painful and disgusting.  We want to take him into
shelter and relieve him.  That is all the feeling which
the acting of Lear ever produced in me.  But the Lear of
Shakspeare cannot be acted.  The contemptible machinery
by which they mimic the storm which he goes out in, is not
more inadequate to represent the horrors of the real elements, than any actor can be to represent Lear:  they
might more easily propose to personate the Satan of Milton
upon a stage, or one of Michael Angelo's terrible figures.
The greatness of Lear is not in corporal dimension, but in
intellectual: the explosions of his passion are terrible
as a volcano:  they are storms turning up and disclosing
to the bottom that sea, his mind, with all its vast
riches.  It is his mind which is laid bare.  This case
of flesh and blood seems too insignificant to be thought
on; even as he himself neglects it.  On the stage we see
nothing but corporal infirmities and weakness, the impotence of rage:  while we read it, we see not Lear, but we
are Lear, - we are in his mind, we are sustained by a
grandeur which baffles the malice of daughters and storms;
in the aberrations of his reason, we discover a mighty irregular power of reasoning, immethodized from the ordinary
purposes of life, but exerting its powers, as the wind
blows where it listeth, at will upon the corruptions and
abuses of mankind.  What have looks, or tones, to do with
that sublime identification of his age with that of the
heavens themselves, when in his reproaches to them for
conniving at the injustice of his children, he reminds
them that "they themselves are old." (14)   What gesture
shall we appropriate to this?   What has the voice or the
eye to do with such things?   But the play is beyond all
art, as the tamperings with it shew:  it is too hard and

stony; it must have love-scenes, and a happy ending. It
is not enough that Cordelia is a daughter, she must shine
as a lover too. Tate has put his hook in the nostrils of
this Leviathan, for Garrick and his followers, the showmen
of the scene, to draw the mighty beast about more easily.
A happy ending! - as if the living martyrdom that Lear had
gone through, - the flaying of his feelings alive, did not
make a fair dismissal from the stage of life the only
decorous thing for him. If he is to live and be happy
after, if he could sustain this world's burden after, why
all this pudder and preparation, - why torment us with all
this unnecessary sympathy? As if the childish pleasure
of getting his gilt robes and sceptre again could tempt
him to act over again his misused station, - as if at his
years, and with his experience, any thing was left but to
die.

Lear is essentially impossible to be represented on a
stage. But how many dramatic personages are there in
Shakspeare, which though more tractable and feasible (if I
may so speak) than Lear, yet from some circumstance, some
adjunct to their character, are improper to be shewn to
our bodily eye. Othello for instance. Nothing can be
more soothing, more flattering to the nobler parts of our
natures, than to read of a young Venetian lady of highest
extraction, through the force of love and from a sense of
merit in him whom she loved, laying aside every consideration of kindred, and country, and colour, and wedding with
a *coal-black Moor* - (for such he is represented, in the
imperfect state of knowledge respecting foreign countries
in those days, compared with our own, or in compliance
with popular notions, though the Moors are now well enough
known to be by many shades less unworthy of a white
woman's fancy) - it is the perfect triumph of virtue over
accidents, of the imagination over the senses. She sees
Othello's colour in his mind. But upon the stage, when
the imagination is no longer the ruling faculty, but we
are left to our poor unassisted senses, I appeal to every
one that has seen Othello played, whether he did not, on
the contrary, sink Othello's mind in his colour; whether
he did not find something extremely revolting in the
courtship and wedded caresses of Othello and Desdemona;
and whether the actual sight of the thing did not over-
weigh all that beautiful compromise which we make in reading; - and the reason it should do so is obvious, because
there is just so much reality presented to our senses as
to give a perception of disagreement, with not enough of
belief in the internal motives, - all that which is unseen, - to overpower and reconcile the first and obvious

prejudices.*   What we see upon a stage is body and bodily action;  what we are conscious of in reading is almost exclusively the mind, and its movements:  and this I think may sufficiently account for the very different sort of delight with which the same play so often affects us in the reading and the seeing.

It requires little reflection to perceive, that if those characters in Shakspeare which are within the precincts of nature, have yet something in them which appeals too exclusively to the imagination, to admit of their being made objects to the senses without suffering a change and a diminution, - that still stronger the objection must lie against representing another line of characters, which Shakspeare has introduced to give a wildness and a supernatural elevation to his scenes, as if to remove them still farther from that assimilation to common life in which their excellence is vulgarly supposed to consist.  When we read the incantations of those terrible beings the Witches in Macbeth, though some of the ingredients of their hellish composition savour of the grotesque, yet is the effect upon us other than the most serious and appalling that can be imagined?  Do we not feel spell-bound as Macbeth was?  Can any mirth accompany a sense of their presence?  We might as well laugh under a consciousness of the principle of Evil himself being truly and really present with us.  But attempt to bring these beings on to a stage, and you turn them instantly into so many old women, that men and children are to laugh at.  Contrary to the old saying, that "seeing is believing," the sight actually destroys the faith:  and the mirth in which we indulge at their expense, when we see these creatures upon a stage, seems to be a sort of indemnification which we make to ourselves for the terror which they put us in when reading made them an object of belief, - when we surrendered up our reason to the poet, as chil-

*The error of supposing that because Othello's colour does not offend us in the reading, it should also not offend us in the seeing, is just such a fallacy as supposing that an Adam and Eve in a picture shall affect us just as they do in the poem.  But in the poem we for a while have Paradisaical senses given us, which vanish when we see a man and his wife without clothes in the picture. The painters themselves feel this, as is apparent by the aukward shifts they have recourse to, to make them look not quite naked;  by a sort of prophetic anachronism, antedating the invention of fig-leaves.  So in the reading of the play, we see with Desdemona's eyes;  in the seeing of it, we are forced to look with our own.

dren to their nurses and their elders;   and we laugh at
our fears, as children who thought they saw something in
the dark, triumph when the bringing in of a candle discovers the vanity of their fears.   For this exposure of
supernatural agents upon a stage is truly bringing in a
candle to expose their own delusiveness.   It is the solitary taper and the book that generates a faith in these
terrors:   a ghost by chandelier light, and in good company, deceives no spectators, - a ghost that can be measured by the eye, and his human dimensions made out at
leisure.   The sight of a well-lighted house, and a well-
dressed audience, shall arm the most nervous child against
any apprehensions:   as Tom Brown says of the impenetrable
skin of Achilles with his impenetrable armour over it,
"Bully Dawson would have fought the devil with such advantages." (15)

Much has been said, and deservedly, in reprobation of
the vile mixture which Dryden has thrown into the Tempest: (16)   doubtless without some such vicious alloy, the
impure ears of that age would never have sate out to hear
so much innocence of love as is contained in the sweet
courtship of Ferdinand and Miranda.   But is the Tempest
of Shakspeare at all a subject for stage representation?
It is one thing to read of an enchanter, and to believe
the wondrous tale while we are reading it;   but to have a
conjuror brought before us in his conjuring-gown, with his
spirits about him, which none but himself and some hundred
of favoured spectators before the curtain are supposed to
see, involves such a quantity of the *hateful incredible*,
that all our reverence for the author cannot hinder us
from perceiving such gross attempts upon the senses to be
in the highest degree childish and inefficient.   Spirits
and fairies cannot be represented, they cannot even be
painted, - they can only be believed.   But the elaborate
and anxious provision of scenery, which the luxury of the
age demands, in these cases works a quite contrary effect
to what is intended.   That which in comedy, or plays of
familiar life, adds so much to the life of the imitation,
in plays which appeal to the higher faculties, positively
destroys the illusion which it is introduced to aid.   A
parlour or a drawing-room, - a library opening into a
garden, - a garden with an alcove in it, - a street, or
the piazza of Covent-garden, does well enough in a scene;
we are content to give as much credit to it as it demands;
or rather, we think little about it, - it is little more
than reading at the top of a page, "Scene, a Garden;"   we
do not imagine ourselves there, but we readily admit the
imitation of familiar objects.   But to think by the help
of painted trees and caverns, which we know to be painted,

to transport our minds to Prospero, and his island and his
lonely cell;*  or by the aid of a fiddle dexterously
thrown in, in an interval of speaking, to make us believe
that we hear those supernatural noises of which the isle
was full:- the Orrery Lecturer at the  Haymarket might as
well hope, by his musical glasses cleverly stationed out
of sight behind his apparatus, (17) to make us believe
that we do indeed hear the chrystal spheres ring out that
chime, which if it were to inwrap our fancy long, Milton
thinks,

> Time would run back and fetch the age of gold,
> And speckled vanity
> Would sicken soon and die,
> And leprous Sin would melt from earthly mould;
> Yea Hell itself would pass away,
> And leave its dolorous mansions to the peering
> > day. (18)

The Garden of Eden, with our first parents in it, is not
more impossible to be shewn on a stage, than the Enchanted
Isle, with its no less interesting and innocent first
settlers.

The subject of Scenery is closely connected with that
of the Dresses, which are so anxiously attended to on our
stage.   I remember the last time I saw Macbeth played,
the discrepancy I felt at the changes of garment which he
varied, - the shiftings and re-shiftings, like a Romish
priest at mass.   The luxury of stage-improvements, and
the importunity of the public eye, require this.   The
coronation robe of the Scottish monarch was fairly a
counterpart to that which our King wears when he goes to
the Parliament-house, - just so full and cumbersome, and
set out with ermine and pearls.   And if things must be
represented, I see not what to find fault with in this.
But in reading, what robe are we conscious of?   Some dim
images of royalty - a crown and sceptre, may float before
our eyes, but who shall describe the fashion of it?   Do
we see in our mind's eye what Webb or any other robe-maker
could pattern?   This is the inevitable consequence of
imitating every thing, to make all things natural.
Whereas the reading of a tragedy is a fine abstraction.

*It will be said these things are done in pictures.
But pictures and scenes are very different things.
Painting is a world of itself, but in scene-painting there
is the attempt to deceive;  and there is the discordancy,
never to be got over, between painted scenes and real
people.

It presents to the fancy just so much of external appearances as to make us feel that we are among flesh and
blood, while by far the greater and better part of our
imagination is employed upon the thoughts and internal
machinery of the character.  But in acting, scenery,
dress, the most contemptible things, call upon us to judge
of their naturalness.

Perhaps it would be no bad similitude, to liken the
pleasure which we take in seeing one of these fine plays
acted, compared with that quiet delight which we find in
the reading of it, to the different feelings with which a
reviewer, and a man that is not a reviewer, reads a fine
poem.  The accursed critical habit, - the being called
upon to judge and pronounce, must make it quite a different thing to the former.  In seeing these plays acted, we
are affected just as judges.  When Hamlet compares the
two pictures of Gertrude's first and second husband, who
wants to see the pictures?  But in the acting, a miniature must be lugged out; which we know not to be the picture, but only to shew how finely a miniature may be represented.  This shewing of every thing, levels all
things:  it makes tricks, bows, and curtesies, of importance.  Mrs. S. never got more fame by any thing than by
the manner in which she dismisses the guests in the
banquet-scene in Macbeth:  it is as much remembered as
any of her thrilling tones or impressive looks.  But does
such a trifle as this enter into the imaginations of the
readers of that wild and wonderful scene?  Does not the
mind dismiss the feasters as rapidly as it can?  Does it
care about the gracefulness of the doing it?  But by
acting, and judging of acting, all these non-essentials
are raised into an importance, injurious to the main interest of the play.

I have confined my observations to the tragic parts of
Shakspeare.  It would be no very difficult task to extend
the enquiry to his comedies;  and to shew why Falstaff,
Shallow, Sir Hugh Evans, and the rest, are equally incom-
patible with stage representation.  The length to which
this Essay has run, will make it, I am afraid, sufficiently distasteful to the Amateurs of the Theatre, without
going any deeper into the subject at present.

# 8  Cooke's Richard the Third

## (i) 1802

This review was published anonymously in the 'Morning Post', 4 January, and was first reprinted by J.D. Campbell in the 'Athenaeum', 4 August 1888.

Some few of us remember to have *seen*, and all of us have heard our fathers tell of Quin, and Garrick, and Barry, and some faint traditional notices are left us of their manner in particular scenes, and their stile of delivering certain emphatic sentences.  Hence our curiosity is excited, when a *new Hamlet* or a *new Richard* makes his appearance, in the first place, to inquire, how he acted in the *Closet scene*, in the *Tent scene*;  how he looked, and how he started, when the *Ghost* came on, and how he cried

Off with his head.  So much for Buckingham.

We do not reprehend this minute spirit of comparison. On the contrary, we consider it as a delightful artifice, by which we connect the recreations of the past with those of the present generation, what pleased our fathers with what pleases us.  We love to witness the obstinate attachments, the unconquerable prejudices (as they seem to us), of the old men, our seniors, the whimsical gratification they appear to derive from the very refusal to be gratified;  to hear them talk of the good *old* actors, whose race is for ever extinct.

With these impressions, we attended the first appearance of Mr. Cooke, in the character of *Richard the Third*, last winter.  We thought that he "bustled" through the scenes with at least as much spirit and effect as any of his predecessors whom we remember in the part, and was not deficient in the delivery of any of those rememberable speeches and exclamations, which old prescription hath set

102

up as *criteria* of comparison.   Now that the grace of
freshness is worn off, and Mr. Cooke is no longer a novi-
tiate candidate for public favour, we propose to enter
into the question - whether that popular actor is right or
wrong in his conception of the great outlines of the character;   those strong essential differences which separate
*Richard* from all the other creations of Shakespeare.   We
say *of Shakespeare*;   for though the Play, which passes for
*his* upon the *Stage*, materially differs from *that* which *he*
wrote under the same title, being in fact little better
than a compilation or a cento of passages extracted from
other of his Plays, and applied with gross violations of
propriety (as we are ready at any time to point out), besides some miserable additions, which *he* never could have
written;   all together producing an inevitable inconsistency of character, sufficient to puzzle and confound the
*best Actor*;   *yet*, in this chaos and perplexity, we are of
opinion, that it becomes an Actor to shew his taste, by
adhering, as much as possible, to the spirit and intention
of the original Author, and to consult his *safety* in
*steering* by the *Light*, which Shakespeare holds out to him,
as by a great *Leading Star*.   Upon these principles, we
presume to censure Mr. Cooke, while we are ready to acknowledge, that this Actor presents us with a very original
and very forcible portrait (if not of the *man Richard*,
whom Shakespeare drew, yet) of the *monster Richard*, as he
exists in the *popular idea*, in *his own exaggerated* and
*witty self-abuse*, in the overstrained representations of
the parties who were *sufferers* by his *ambition*;   and,
above all, in the impertinent and wretched *scenes*, so ab-
surdly foisted in by some, who have thought themselves
capable of adding to what *Shakespeare wrote*.

   But of Mr. Cooke's *Richard*:
   1st, *His predominant and masterly simulation.*
        He has a tongue can wheedle with the DEVIL.

It has been the policy of that antient and grey simulator,
in all ages, to hide his *horns* and *claws*.   The *Richard* of
Mr. Cooke perpetually obtrudes *his*.   We see the effect of
his deceit uniformly *successful*, but we do not comprehend
*how* it *succeeds*.   We can put ourselves, by a very common
fiction, into the place of the individuals upon whom it
acts, and say, that, in the like case, we should not have
been alike credulous.   The hypocrisy is too glaring and
visible.   It resembles more the shallow cunning of a mind
which is its own dupe, than the profound and practised art
of so powerful an intellect as *Richard's*.   It is too
obstreperous and loud, breaking out into *triumphs* and

*plaudits* at its own success, like an unexercised *noviciate* in *tricks*. It has none of the silent confidence, and steady self-command of the *experienced politician;* it possesses none of that *fine address*, which was necessary to have betrayed the heart of *Lady Anne*, or even to have imposed upon the duller wits of the *Lord Mayor* and *Citizens*.

2dly, *His habitual jocularity*, the effect of buoyant spirits, and an elastic mind, rejoicing in its own powers, and in the success of its machinations. This quality of unstrained mirth accompanies *Richard*, and is a prime feature in his character. It never leaves him; in plots, in stratagems, and in the midst of his bloody devices, it is perpetually driving him upon wit, and jests, and personal satire, fanciful allusions, and quaint felicities of phrase. It is one of the chief artifices by which the consummate master of dramatic effect has contrived to soften the horrors of the scene, and to make us contemplate a bloody and vicious character with delight. No where, in any of his plays, is to be found so much of sprightly colloquial dialogue, and soliloquies of genuine humour, as in *Richard*. This character of unlaboured mirth Mr. Cooke seems entirely to pass over, and substitutes in its stead the coarse, taunting humour, and clumsy merriment, of a low-minded assassin.

3dly, *His personal deformity*. - When the *Richard* of Mr. Cooke makes allusions to his own *form*, they seem accompanied with *unmixed distaste* and *pain*, like some obtrusive and *haunting* idea - But surely the *Richard* of Shakespeare mingles in these allusions a perpetual reference to his own powers and capacities, by which he is enabled to surmount these petty objections; and the joy of a defect *conquered*, or *turned* into an advantage, is one cause of these very allusions, and of the satisfaction, with which his mind recurs to them. These allusions themselves are made in an ironical and good humoured spirit of exaggeration - the most bitter of them are to be found in his self-congratulating soliloquy spoken in the very moment and crisis of joyful exultation on the success of his unheard of courtship.——No *partial excellence* can satisfy for this absence of a *just general conception* - otherwise we are inclined to admit, that, in the delivery of *single sentences*, in a *new* and often *felicitous* light thrown upon *old* and *hitherto misconstrued* passages, no actor that we have seen has gone beyond Mr. Cooke. He is always *alive* to the scene before him; and by the *fire* and *novelty* of his manner, he seems likely to infuse some *warm blood* into the *frozen declamatory stile*, into which our theatres have for some time past been degenerating.

## (ii)   1801

From a letter to Robert Lloyd, 26 June.

Cooke in Richard the Third is a perfect caricature.
He gives you the *monster* Richard, but not the *man*
Richard.   Shakespear's bloody character impresses you
with awe and deep admiration of his witty parts, his con-
sumate hypocrisy, and indefatigable prosecution of purpose.   You despise, detest, and loath the cunning,
vulgar, low and fierce Richard, which Cooke substitutes in
his place.   He gives you no other idea, than of a vulgar
villain, rejoycing in·his being able to over reach, and
not possessing that joy in *silent* consciousness, but be-
traying it, like a *poor* villain in sneers and distortions
of the face, like a droll at a country fair:   not to add
that cunning so self-betraying and manner so vulgar could
never have deceived the politic Buckingham, nor the soft
Lady Anne:   *both*, bred in courts, would have turned with
disgust from such a fellow. - Not but Cooke has *powers;*
but not of discrimination.   His manner is strong, coarse
& vigorous, and well adapted to some characters. - But the
lofty imagery and high sentiments and high passions of
*Poetry* come black & prose-smoked from his prose Lips. - I
have not seen him in *Over Reach*, but from what I remember
of the character, I think he could not have chosen one
more fit!   I thought the play a highly finished one, when
I read it sometime back.   I *remember* a most noble image.
Sir Giles drawing his sword in the last scene, says

> Some undone widow sits upon mine arm,
> And takes away the use on't. (19)

This is horribly fine, and I am not sure, that it did not
suggest to me my conclusion of Pride's Cure;  but my imitation is miserably inferior.

> This arm was busy in the day of Naseby:
> Tis paralytic now, & knows no use of weapons——(20)

... I am possessed with an Admiration of the genuine
Richard, his genius, and his mounting spirit, which no
consideration of his cruelties can depress..Shakespear has
not made Richard so black a Monster, as is supposed.
Whereever he is monstrous, it was to conform to vulgar
opinion.   But he is generally a Man.   Read his most exquisite address to the Widowed Queen to court her daughter
for him, the topics of maternal feeling, of a deep knowledge of the heart, are such as no monster could have

supplied.    Richard must have *felt*, before he could feign
so well;  tho' ambition choked the good seed.    I think it
the most finished piece of Eloquence in the world;  of
*persuasive* Oratory, far above Demosthenes, Burke, or any
man. - Far exceeding the courtship of Lady Anne. - *Her*
relenting is barely natural after all;  the more perhaps
S's merit to make *impossible* appear *probable*, but the
*Queen's consent* (taking in all the circumstances & topics,
*private* and *public*, with his angelic address, able to draw
the host of [piece cut out of letter] Lucifer,) is *probable;*  and [piece cut out of letter] resisted it. — —
This observation applies to many other parts.    All the
inconsistency is, that Shakespeares better Genius was
forced to struggle against the prejudices, which made a
monster of Richard.    He set out to paint a *monster*, but
his human sympathies produced a *Man* —
     Are you not tired with this *ingenious* criticism?    I
am....
     *Richard itself* is wholly metamorphosed in the wretched
*Acting play* of that name, which you will see:   altered by
*Cibber.* —

1 By Samuel Jackson Pratt (1749-1814).
2 John Philip Kemble.
3 Mrs Siddons.
4 A popular school anthology (1774), compiled by William Enfield.
5 Cf. 'Paradise Lost', IV, 338-40.
6 Horace, 'Ars Poetica', l. 323: 'With round, full voice.'
7 John Banks (c. 1650-c. 1700), minor Restoration dramatist; George Lillo (1693-1739), pioneer of eighteenth-century domestic tragedy.
8 Cf. '1 Henry IV', II, iv, 385.
9 John Hill (1716?-75), miscellaneous writer; Arthur Murphy (1727-1805), actor and playwright; John Brown (1715-66), minor dramatist.
10 The three sonnets quoted by Lamb in this passage are 111, 110, 29.
11 Nahum Tate (1652-1715), Poet Laureate, whose version of 'King Lear' (1681) was acted throughout the eighteenth and the early part of the nineteenth centuries; Colley Cibber (1671-1757), Poet Laureate, produced his version of 'Richard III' in 1700.
12 'Paradise Lost', I, 391.
13 George Frederick Cooke. For Lamb's criticism of Cooke's performance in the role of Richard III, see pp. 102-6.
14 Cf. 'King Lear', II, iv, 190-1.
15 'Observations on Virgil, Ovid and Homer', in 'The Works of Mr. Thomas Brown', 1707, i, 105.
16 First produced in 1670. For Hazlitt's criticism of this version, see 'Complete Works', ed. P.P. Howe (London, 1930-4), v, 234-5.
17 Lectures on astronomy were delivered during the winter at the Theatre Royal, Haymarket.

18 Cf. Hymn on the Morning of Christ's Nativity, 11.
   135-40.
19 Massinger, 'A New Way to Pay Old Debts', V, i.
20 This passage was later omitted by Lamb when the play
   was published in 1802 as 'John Woodvil'.

# III English Drama

9   Specimens of English Dramatic Poets, who lived about
    the time of Shakspeare: with notes
    1808, 1813, 1818

Lamb published the 'Specimens' in 1808.   Although a semi-
nal work, well reviewed and greatly admired by many other
writers, among them Wordsworth, Coleridge, Keats and Hazlitt, it never reached a second edition in Lamb's life-
time.   The Second Edition of 1813 consisted of the unsold
sheets of 1808 with the addition of a new imprint.   A
selection of the notes was reprinted in 'Works', 1818.
Working on the assumption that Lamb had seen the proof-
sheets of the 1835 'Specimens', E.V. Lucas chose that edition as the basis of what has now become the standard
text.   E.M.W. Tillyard in his anthology of Lamb's critical writings reverted to Lamb's own selection of the notes
in the 1818 'Works'.   The present text is that of 1808.
Exact references to the various scenes printed by Lamb are
provided where necessary.

## (i)   PREFACE

MORE than a third part of the following specimens are from
plays which are to be found only in the British Museum and
in some scarce private libraries.   The rest are from Dodsley's and Hawkins's collections, (1) and the works of
Jonson, Beaumont and Fletcher, and Massinger.
    I have chosen wherever I could to give entire scenes,
and in some instances successive scenes, rather than to
string together single passages and detached beauties,
which I have always found wearisome in the reading in selections of this nature.
    To every extract is prefixed an explanatory head, suf-
ficient to make it intelligible with the help of some
trifling omissions.   Where a line or more was obscure, as
having reference to something that had gone before, which
would have asked more time to explain than its consequence

in the scene seemed to deserve, I have had no hesitation
in leaving the line or passage out.  Sometimes where I
have met with a superfluous character, which seemed to
burthen without throwing any light upon the scene, I have
ventured to dismiss it altogether.  I have expunged without ceremony all that which the writers had better never
have written, that forms the objection so often repeated
to the promiscuous reading of Fletcher, Massinger, and
some others.

The kind of extracts which I have sought after have
been, not so much passages of wit and humour, though the
old plays are rich in such, as scenes of passion, sometimes of the deepest quality, interesting situations, serious descriptions, that which is more nearly allied to
poetry than to wit, and to tragic rather than to comic
poetry.  The plays which I have made choice of have been,
with few exceptions, those which treat of human life and
manners, rather than masques and Arcadian pastorals, with
their train of abstractions, unimpassioned deities, passionate mortals, Claius, and Medorus, and Amintas, and
Amarillis.  My leading design has been, to illustrate
what may be called the moral sense of our ancestors.  To
shew in what manner they felt, when they placed themselves
by the power of imagination in trying situations, in the
conflicts of duty and passion, or the strife of contending
duties;  what sort of loves and enmities theirs were;  how
their griefs were tempered, and their full-swoln joys
abated:  how much of Shakspeare shines in the great men
his contemporaries, and how far in his divine mind and
manners he surpassed them and all mankind.

Another object which I had in making these selections
was, to bring together the most admired scenes in Fletcher
and Massinger, in the estimation of the world the only
dramatic poets of that age who are entitled to be considered after Shakspeare, and to exhibit them in the same
volume with the more impressive scenes of old Marlowe,
Heywood, Tourneur, Webster, Ford, and others.  To shew
what we have slighted, while beyond all proportion we have
cried up one or two favourite names.

The specimens are not accompanied with any thing in the
shape of biographical notices.*  I had nothing of consequence to add to the slight sketches in Dodsley and the
Biographia Dramatica, (2) and I was unwilling to swell the
volume with mere transcription.  The reader will not fail
to observe from the frequent instances of two or more persons joining in the composition of the same play (the

*The few notes which are interspersed will be found to
be chiefly critical.

noble practice of those times), that of most of the writers contained in these selections it may be strictly
said, that they were contemporaries.  The whole period,
from the middle of Elizabeth's reign to the close of the
reign of Charles I., comprizes a space of little more than
half a century, within which time nearly all that we have
of excellence in serious dramatic composition was produced, if we except the Samson Agonistes of Milton.

---

### (ii)

GORBODUC, A TRAGEDY:  BY THOMAS SACKVILLE, LORD BUCKHURST,
AFTERWARDS EARL OF DORSET;  AND THOMAS NORTON.

The style of this old play is stiff and cumbersome,
like the dresses of its times.  There may be flesh and
blood underneath, but we cannot get at it.  Sir Philip
Sidney has praised it for its morality. (3)  One of its
authors might easily furnish that.  Norton was an associate to Hopkins, Sternhold, and Robert Wisdom, in the
Singing Psalms.  I am willing to believe that Lord Buckhurst supplied the more vital parts.  The chief beauty in
the extract is of a secret nature.  Marcella obscurely
intimates that the murdered prince Porrex and she had been
lovers.  [IV, ii.]

---

### (iii)

THE SPANISH TRAGEDY:  OR HIERONIMO IS MAD AGAIN.  A
TRAGEDY BY THOMAS KYD.

These scenes, which are the very salt of the old play
(which without them is but a caput mortuum, such another
piece of flatness as Locrine) (4) Hawkins, in his repub-
lication of this tragedy, has thrust out of the text into
the notes;  as omitted in the Second Edition "printed for
Ed. Allde, amended of such gross blunders as passed in the
first:" and thinks them to have been *foisted in by the
players*. - A late discovery at Dulwich College has ascertained that two sundry payments were made to Ben Jonson by
the Theatre for furnishing additions to Hieronimo.  See
Last Edition of Shakspeare by Reed.  There is nothing in
the undoubted plays of Jonson which would authorize us to
suppose that he could have supplied the scenes in question.  I should suspect the agency of some "more potent
spirit." (5)  Webster might have furnished them.  They

are full of that wild solemn preternatural cast of grief which bewilders us in the Duchess of Malfy.    [III, xi., xiia.]

---

(iv)

THE LOVE OF KING DAVID AND FAIR BETHSABE, WITH THE TRAGEDY OF ABSALOM:   BY GEORGE PEELE.

There is more of the same stuff, but I suppose the reader has a surfeit;  especially as this Canticle of David's has never been suspected to contain any pious sense couched underneath it, whatever his Son's may.— The Kingly bower "seated in hearing of a hundred streams" is the best of it.    [Scene I.]

---

(v)

LUSTS DOMINION, OR THE LASCIVIOUS QUEEN.    A TRAGEDY BY CHRISTOPHER MARLOWE. (6)

   Kit Marlowe, as old Isaac Walton assures us, made that *smooth song* which begins "Come live with me and be my love." (7)    The same romantic invitations "in folly ripe in reason rotten" (8) are given by the queen in the play, and the lover in the ditty.   He talks of "beds of roses, buckles of gold:"

   Thy silver dishes for thy meat,
   *As precious as the Gods do eat,*
   Shall on an ivory table be
   Prepar'd each day for thee and me.

The lines in the Extract have a luscious smoothness in them, and they were the most temperate which I could pick out of this Play.    The rest is in king Cambyses' vein; rape, and murder, and superlatives;  "huffing braggart puft" (9) lines* such as the play-writers anterior to Shakspeare are full of, and Pistol "but coldly imitates." (10) - *Blood* is made as light of in some of these old Dramas as *Money* in a modern Sentimental Comedy;   and

   [*In a note Lamb quotes as an example thirteen lines of the Moor's speech beginning 'Now Tragedy, thou minion of the night' (V, iii).]

as *this* is given away till it reminds us that it is
nothing but counters, so *that* is spilt till it affects us
no more than its representative  the paint of the prop-
erty-man in the theatre.   [I, i.]

---

### (vi)

TAMBURLAINE THE GREAT;   OR THE SCYTHIAN SHEPHERD.    IN TWO
PARTS. BY CHRISTOPHER MARLOWE. - PART THE FIRST.

I had the same difficulty (or rather much more) in
culling a few sane lines from this as from the preceding
Play.   The lunes of Tamburlaine are perfect "midsummer
madness." (11)   Nebuchadnazar's are mere modest pretensions compared with the thundering vaunts of this Scythian
Shepherd.   He comes in (in the Second Part) drawn by conquered kings, and reproaches these *pampered jades of Asia*
that they can *draw but twenty miles a day*.   Till I saw
this passáge with my own eyes, I never believed that it
was any thing more than a pleasant burlesque of Mine
Ancient's.   But I assure my readers that it is soberly
set down in a Play which their Ancestors took to be serious.   I have subjoined the genuine speech for their
amusement.   [Lamb here quotes the opening stage direction
from Act IV, scene iii., and the speech of Tamburlaine
beginning 'Holla  ye pamper'd jades of Asia'.]

---

### (vii)

EDWARD THE SECOND:   A TRAGEDY, BY CHRISTOPHER MARLOWE.

This tragedy is in a very different style from "mighty
Tamburlaine."   The reluctant pangs of abdicating Royalty
in Edward furnished hints which Shakspeare scarce improved
in his Richard the Second;   and the death-scene of Marlowe's king moves pity and terror beyond any scene ancient
or modern with which I am acquainted.   [V, i;  V, v.]

---

### (viii)

THE RICH JEW OF MALTA, A TRAGEDY:   BY CHRISTOPHER MARLOWE.

Marlowe's Jew does not approach so near to Shaks-

peare's, as his Edward II. does to Richard II.   Shylock
in the midst of his savage purpose is a man.   His
motives, feelings, resentments, have something human in
them.   "If you wrong us, shall we not revenge?" (12)
Barabas is a mere monster brought in with a large painted
nose to please the rabble.   He kills in sport, poisons
whole nunneries, invents infernal machines.   He is just
such an Exhibition as a century or two earlier might have
been played before the Londoners, *by the Royal Command*,
when a general pillage and massacre of the Hebrews had
been previously resolved on in the Cabinet.   It is curious to see a superstition wearing out.   The idea of a Jew
(which our pious ancestors contemplated with such horror)
has nothing in it now revolting.   We have tamed the claws
of the beast, and pared its nails, and now we take it to
our arms, fondle it, write plays to flatter it:   it is
visited by Princes, affects a taste, patronizes the arts,
and is the only liberal and gentlemanlike thing in Christendom.   [Act I.]

---

(ix)

THE TRAGICAL HISTORY OF THE LIFE AND DEATH OF DOCTOR
FAUSTUS:   BY CHRISTOPHER MARLOWE.

The growing horrors of Faustus are awfully marked by
the hours and half hours as they expire and bring him
nearer and nearer to the exactment of his dire compact.
It is indeed an agony and bloody sweat. (13)
Marlowe is said to have been tainted with atheistical
positions, to have denied God and the Trinity.   To such a
genius the History of Faustus must have been delectable
food:   to wander in fields where curiosity is forbidden to
go, to approach the dark gulf near enough to look in, to
be busied in speculations which are the rottenest part of
the core of the fruit that fell from the Tree of Knowledge.   Barabas the Jew, and Faustus the Conjuror, are
offsprings of a mind which at least delighted to dally
with interdicted subjects.   They both talk a language
which a believer would have been tender of putting into
the mouth of a character though but in fiction.   But the
holiest minds have sometimes not thought it blameable to
counterfeit impiety in the person of another, to bring
Vice in upon the stage speaking her own dialect, and,
themselves being armed with an Unction of self-confident
impunity, have not scrupled to handle and touch that familiarly, which would be death to others.   Milton in the

person of Satan has started speculations hardier than any
which the feeble armoury of the atheist ever furnished:
and the precise strait-laced Richardson has strengthened
Vice, from the mouth of Lovelace, with entangling sophis-
tries and abstruse pleas against her adversary Virtue
which Sedley, Villiers, and Rochester, wanted depth of
libertinism sufficient to have invented.   [V, ii;  V,
iii.]

---

## (x)

THE MERRY DEVIL OF EDMONTON.   AUTHOR UNCERTAIN.

This Scene has much of Shakspeare's manner in the
sweetness and goodnaturedness of it.   It seems written to
make the Reader happy.   Few of our dramatists or novelists have attended enough to this.   They torture and
wound us abundantly.   They are economists only in
delight.   Nothing can be finer, more gentlemanlike, and
noble, than the conversation and compliments of these
young men.   How delicious is Raymond Mounchensey's forgetting, in his fears, that Jerningham has a "Saint in
Essex";  and how sweetly his friend reminds him! - I wish
it could be ascertained that Michael Drayton was the
Author of this piece:  it would add a worthy appendage to
the renown of that Panegyrist of my native Earth;  who has
gone over her soil (in his Polyolbion) with the fidelity
of a herald, and the painful love of a son;  who has not
left a rivulet (so narrow that it may be stept over) without honorable mention;  and has animated Hills and Streams
with life and passion above the dreams of old mythology.
[I, iii.]

---

## (xi)

THE COMEDY OF OLD FORTUNATUS.   BY THOMAS DECKER.

The humour of a frantic Lover is here done to the life.
Orleans is as passionate an Inamorato as any which Shakspeare ever drew.   He is just such another adept in Love's
reasons.   The sober people of the world are with him

              a swarm of fools
   Crowding together to be counted wise. (14)

He talks "pure Biron and Romeo", he is almost as poetical as they, quite as philosophical, only a little
madder.   After all, Love's Sectaries are a "reason unto
themselves." (15)   We have gone retrograde in the noble
Heresy since the days when Sidney proselyted our nation to
this mixed health and disease; (16)   the kindliest symptom
yet the most alarming crisis in the ticklish state of
youth;   the nourisher and the destroyer of hopeful wits;
the mother of twin-births, wisdom and folly, valour and
weakness;   the servitude above freedom;   the gentle mind's
religion;   the liberal superstition.   [III, i.]

---

(xii)

THE SECOND PART OF THE HONEST WHORE.   BY THOMAS DECKER.

This simple picture of Honour and Shame, contrasted
without violence, and expressed without immodesty, is
worth all the *strong lines* against the Harlot's Profession, with which both Parts of this play are offensively
crowded.   A Satyrist is always to be suspected, who, to
make vice odious, dwells upon all its acts and minutest
circumstances with a sort of relish and retrospective
gust.   But so near are the boundaries of panegyric and
invective, that a worn out Sinner is sometimes found to
make the best Declaimer against Sin.   The same high-
seasoned descriptions which in his unregenerate state
served to inflame his appetites, in his new province of a
Moralist will serve him (a little turned) to expose the
enormity of those appetites in other men.   No one will
doubt, who reads Marston's Satires, that the Author in
some part of his life must have been something more than
a theorist in vice.   Have we never heard an old preacher
in the pulpit display such an insight into the mystery of
ungodliness, as made us wonder with reason how a good man
came by it?   When Cervantes with such proficiency of
fondness dwells upon the Don's library, who sees not that
he has been a great reader of books of Knight Errantry?
perhaps was at some time of his life in danger of falling
into those very extravagancies which he ridicules so happily in his Hero?   [IV, i.]

---

### (xiii)

SATIRO-MASTIX OR THE UNTRUSSING OF THE HUMOROUS POET, BY
THOMAS DECKER.

The beauty and force of this scene are much diminished
to the reader of the entire play, when he comes to find
that this solemn preparation is but a sham contrivance of
the father's, and the potion which Caelestina swallows
nothing more than a sleeping draught; from the effects of
which she is to awake in due time, to the surprise of her
husband, and the great mirth and edification of the King
and his courtiers.   As Hamlet says, they do but "poison
in jest." (17) - The sentiments are worthy of a real martyrdom, and an Appian sacrifice in earnest.   [V, i.]

---

### (xiv)

THE HISTORY OF ANTONIO AND MELLIDA.   THE FIRST PART.
BY JOHN MARSTON.

The situation of Andrugio and Lucio resembles that of
Lear and Kent, in that King's distresses.   Andrugio, like
Lear, manifests a kind of royal impatience, a turbulent
greatness, an affected resignation.   The Enemies which he
enters lists to combat, "Despair, and mighty Grief, and
sharp Impatience," and the Forces ("Cornets of Horse,"
&c.) (18) which he brings to vanquish them, are in the
boldest style of Allegory.   They are such a "race of
mourners" as "the infection of sorrows loud" in the intellect might beget on "some pregnant cloud" in the imagination. (19)   [III, i.]

---

### (xv)

ANTONIO'S REVENGE.   THE SECOND PART OF THE HISTORY OF
ANTONIO AND MELLIDA.   BY JOHN MARSTON.

This Prologue for its passionate earnestness, and for
the tragic note of preparation which it sounds, might have
preceded one of those old tales of Thebes, or Pelops'
line, which Milton has so highly commended, (20) as free
from the common error of the poets in his days, "of intermixing comic stuff with tragic sadness and gravity,
brought in without discretion corruptly to gratify the

people." (21) - It is as solemn a preparative as the
"warning voice which he who saw th' Apocalyps, heard
cry" - . (22)

---

(xvi)

WHAT YOU WILL: A COMEDY.   BY JOHN MARSTON.

   To judge of the liberality of these notions of dress we
must advert to the days of Gresham, and the consternation
which a Phenomenon habited like the Merchant here described would have excited among the flat round caps, and
cloth stockings, upon Change, when those "original arguments or tokens of a Citizen's vocation were in fashion
not more for thrift and usefulness than for distinction
and grace."   The blank uniformity to which all professional distinctions in apparel have been long hastening,
is one instance of the Decay of Symbols among us, which
whether it has contributed or not to make us a more intellectual, has certainly made us a less imaginative
people.   Shakspeare knew the force of signs:- "a malig-
nant and a turban'd Turk." (23)   "This meal-cap Miller"
says the Author of God's Revenge against Murder, (24) to
express his indignation at an atrocious outrage committed
by the miller Pierot upon the person of the fair Marieta.
[I, i.]

---

(xvii)

BYRON'S TRAGEDY.   BY GEO. CHAPMAN.

   The Selections which I have made from this Poet are
sufficient to give an idea of that "full and heightened
style" which Webster makes characteristic of Chapman. (25)
Of all the English Play-writers, Chapman perhaps approaches nearest to Shakspeare in the descriptive and didactic, in passages which are less purely dramatic.   Dramatic Imitation was not his talent.   He could not go out of
himself, as Shakspeare could shift at pleasure, to inform
and animate other existences, but in himself he had an eye
to perceive and a soul to embrace all forms.   He would
have made a great Epic Poet, if indeed he has not abundantly shewn himself to be one;   for his Homer is not so
properly a Translation as the Stories of Achilles and
Ulysses re-written.   The earnestness and passion which he

has put into every part of these poems would be incredible
to a reader of mere modern translations.   His almost
Greek zeal for the honor of his heroes is only paralleled
by that fierce spirit of Hebrew bigotry, with which
Milton, as if personating one of the Zealots of the old
law, clothed himself when he sate down to paint the acts
of Sampson against the Uncircumcised.   The great obstacle
to Chapman's Translations being read is their unconquerable
quaintness.   He pours out in the same breath the most
just and natural and the most violent and forced expressions.   He seems to grasp whatever words come first to
hand during the impetus of inspiration, as if all other
must be inadequate to the divine meaning.   But passion
(the all in all in Poetry) is every where present, raising
the low, dignifying the mean, and putting sense into the
absurd.   He makes his readers glow, weep, tremble, take
any affection which he pleases, be moved by words or in
spite of them, be disgusted and overcome their disgust.
I have often thought that the vulgar misconception of
Shakspeare, as of a wild irregular genius "in whom great
faults are compensated by great beauties," (26) would be
really true, applied to Chapman.   But there is no scale
by which to balance such disproportionate subjects as the
faults and beauties of a great genius.   To set off the
former with any fairness against the latter, the pain
which they give us should be in some proportion to the
pleasure which we receive from the other.   As these
transport us to the highest heaven, those should steep us
in agonies infernal.

---

### (xviii)

A WOMAN KILL'D WITH KINDNESS:   A TRAGEDY.   BY THOMAS
HEYWOOD.

Heywood is a sort of *prose* Shakspeare.   His scenes are
to the full as natural and affecting.   But we miss *the
Poet*, that which in Shakspeare always appears out and
above the surface of *the nature*.   Heywood's characters,
his Country Gentlemen, &c. are exactly what we see (but of
the best kind of what we see) in life.   Shakspeare makes
us believe, while we are among his lovely creations, that
they are nothing but what we are familiar with, as in
dreams new things seem old:   but we awake, and sigh for
the difference.

---

(xix)

THE ENGLISH TRAVELLER.   BY THOMAS HEYWOOD.

This piece of pleasant exaggeration (which for its life
and humour might have been told, or acted, by Petruchio
himself) gave rise to the title of Cowley's Latin Play,
Naufragium Joculare, and furnished the idea of the best
scene in it. - Heywood's Preface to this Play is interesting, as it shews the heroic indifference about posterity,
which some of these great writers seem to have felt.
There is a magnanimity in Authorship as in every thing
else.   [Lamb quotes seventeen lines of the preface.]
Of the 220 pieces which he here speaks of having been
concerned in, only 25, as enumerated by Dodsley, have come
down to us, for the reasons assigned in the preface.   The
rest have perished, exposed to the casualties of a
theatre.   Heywood's ambition seems to have been confined
to the pleasure of hearing the Players speak his lines
while he lived.   It does not appear that he ever contemplated the possibility of being read by after ages.   What
a slender pittance of fame was motive sufficient to the
production of such Plays as the English Traveller, the
Challenge for Beauty, and the Woman Killed with Kindness!
Posterity is bound to take care that a Writer loses nothing by such a noble modesty.   [II, i.]

------------------------------------------------------------

(xx)

A FAIR QUARREL:  A COMEDY.   BY THOMAS MIDDLETON AND WM.
ROWLEY.

The insipid levelling morality to which the modern
stage is tied down would not admit of such admirable passions as these scenes are filled with.   A puritanical
obtuseness of sentiment, a stupid infantile goodness, is
creeping among us, instead of the vigorous passions, and
virtues clad in flesh and blood, with which the old dramatists present us.   Those noble and liberal casuists
could discern in the differences, the quarrels, the animosities of man, a beauty and truth of moral feeling, no
less than in the iterately inculcated duties of forgiveness and atonement.   With us all is hypocritical meekness.   A reconciliation scene (let the occasion be never
so absurd or unnatural) is always sure of applause.   Our
audiences come to the theatre to be complimented on their
goodness.   They compare notes with the amiable characters

in the play, and find a wonderful similarity of disposition between them.   We have a common stock of dramatic
morality out of which a writer may be supplied without the
trouble of copying it from originals within his own
breast.   To know the boundaries of honor, to be judici-
ously valiant, to have a temperance which shall beget a
smoothness in the angry swellings of youth, to esteem life
as nothing when the sacred reputation of a parent is to be
defended, yet to shake and tremble under a pious cowardice
when that ark of an honest confidence is found to be frail
and tottering, to feel the true blows of a real disgrace
blunting that sword which the imaginary strokes of a supposed false imputation had put so keen an edge upon but
lately:  to do, or to imagine this done in a feigned
story, asks something more of a moral sense, somewhat a
greater delicacy of perception in questions of right and
wrong, than goes to the writing of two or three hackneyed
sentences about the laws of honor as opposed to the laws
of the land, or a common place against duelling.   Yet
such things would stand a writer now a days in far better
stead than Captain Ager and his conscientious honor;  and
he would be considered as a far better teacher of morality
than old Rowley or Middleton if they were living. (27)
[II, i;   III, i.]

---

(xxi)

A NEW WONDER:  A WOMAN NEVER VEXT.   A COMEDY.   BY WM.
ROWLEY.

The old play-writers are distinguished by an honest
boldness of exhibition, they shew every thing without
being ashamed.   If a reverse in fortune be the thing to
be personified, they fairly bring us to the prison-grate
and the alms-basket.   A poor man on our stage is always
a gentleman, he may be known by a peculiar neatness of
apparel, and by wearing black.   Our delicacy, in fact,
forbids the dramatizing of Distress at all.   It is never
shewn in its essential properties;*  it appears but as the
adjunct to some virtue, as something which is to be relieved, from the approbation of which relief the spectators are to derive a certain soothing of self-referred
satisfaction.   We turn away from the real essences of
things to hunt after their relative shadows, moral duties:

[*Lamb quotes extensively from Matheo Aleman's *The Rogue:
or, The Life of Guzman de Alfarache*, 1622, I, iii. l.]

whereas, if the truth of things were fairly represented, the relative duties might be safely trusted to themselves, and moral philosophy lose the name of a science.

---

(xxii)

WOMEN BEWARE WOMEN.   A TRAGEDY.   BY THOMAS MIDDLETON.

This is one of those scenes which has the air of being an immediate transcript from life.   Livia the "good neighbour" is as real a creature as one of Chaucer's characters.   She is such another jolly Housewife as the Wife of Bath.   [II, ii.]

---

(xxiii)

THE WITCH.   A TRAGI-COMEDY.   BY THOMAS MIDDLETON.

Though some resemblance may be traced between the Charms in Macbeth, and the Incantations in this Play, which is supposed to have preceded it, this coincidence will not detract much from the originality of Shakspeare. His Witches are distinguished from the Witches of Middleton by essential differences.   These are creatures to whom man or woman plotting some dire mischief might resort for occasional consultation.   Those originate deeds of blood, and begin bad impulses to men.   From the moment that their eyes first meet with Macbeth's, he is spellbound.   That meeting sways his destiny.   He can never break the fascination.   These Witches can hurt the body; those have power over the soul. - Hecate in Middleton has a Son, a low buffoon:   the hags of Shakspeare have neither child of their own, nor seem to be descended from any parent.   They are foul Anomalies, of whom we know not whence they are sprung, nor whether they have beginning or ending.   As they are without human passions, so they seem to be without human relations.   They come with thunder and lightning, and vanish to airy music.   This is all we know of them. - Except Hecate, they have no names;   which heightens their mysteriousness.   The names, and some of the properties, which Middleton has given to his Hags, excite smiles.   The Weird Sisters are serious things. Their presence cannot co-exist with mirth.   But, in a lesser degree, the Witches of Middleton are fine creations.   Their power too is, in some measure, over the mind.   They raise jars, jealousies, strifes, *like a thick scurf o'er life*. (28)

---

## (xxiv)

THE WITCH OF EDMONTON.   A TRAGI-COMEDY.   BY WILLIAM ROWLEY, THOMAS DECKER, JOHN FORD, &C.

Mother Sawyer differs from the hags of Middleton or Shakspeare.   She is the plain traditional old woman Witch of our ancestors;   poor, deformed, and ignorant;   the terror of villages, herself amenable to a justice.   That should be a hardy sheriff, with the power of the county at his heels, that would lay hands on the Weird Sisters. They are of another jurisdiction.   But upon the common and received opinion the author (or authors) have engrafted strong fancy.   There is something frightfully earnest in her invocations to the Familiar.

---

## (xxv)

THE ATHEIST'S TRAGEDY;   OR THE HONEST MAN'S REVENGE.   BY CYRIL TOURNEUR.

This way of description which seems unwilling ever to leave off, weaving parenthesis within parenthesis, was brought to its height by sir Philip Sidney.   He seems to have set the example to Shakspeare.   Many beautiful instances may be found all over the Arcadia.   These bountiful Wits always give full measure, pressed down and running over.   [II, i.]

---

## (xxvi)

THE REVENGER'S TRAGEDY.   BY CYRIL TOURNEUR.

The reality and life of this Dialogue passes any scenical illusion I ever felt.   I never read it but my ears tingle, and I feel a hot blush spread my cheeks, as if I were presently about to "proclaim" some such "malefactions" of myself, as the Brothers here rebuke in their unnatural parent;   in words more keen and dagger-like than those which Hamlet speaks to his mother.   Such power has the passion of shame truly personated, not only to "strike guilty creatures unto the soul" but to "appall" even those that are "free." (29)    [IV, iv.]

---

### (xxvii)

THE TRAGEDY OF THE DUCHESS OF MALFY.    BY JOHN WEBSTER.

All the several parts of the dreadful apparatus with which the Duchesses death is ushered in are not more remote from the conceptions of ordinary vengeance, than the strange character of suffering which they seem to bring upon their victim, is beyond the imagination of ordinary poets.    As they are not like inflictions *of this life*, so her language seems *not of this world*.    She has lived among horrors till she is become "native and endowed unto that element." (30)    She speaks the dialect of despair, her tongue has a smatch of Tartarus and the souls in bale. - What are "Luke's iron crown," the brazen bull of Perillus, (31) Procrustes' bed, to the waxen images which counterfeit death, to the wild masque of madmen, the tomb-maker, the bell-man, the living person's dirge, the mortification by degrees!    To move a horror skilfully, to touch a soul to the quick, to lay upon fear as much as it can bear, to wean and weary a life till it is ready to drop and then step in with mortal instruments to take its last forfeit:  this only a Webster can do.    Writers of an inferior genius may "upon horror's head horrors accumulate" (32) but they cannot do this.    They mistake quantity for quality, they "terrify babes with painted devils" (33) but they know not how a soul is capable of being moved;  their terrors want dignity, their affrightments are without decorum.    [I, i;   IV, i-ii.]

---

### (xxviii)

THE WHITE DEVIL:  OR, VITTORIA COROMBONA, A LADY OF VENICE.    A TRAGEDY .    BY JOHN WEBSTER.

The Author's Dedication to this Play is so modest, yet so conscious of self-merit withal, he speaks so frankly of the deservings of others, and by implication insinuates his own deserts so ingenuously, that I cannot forbear inserting it, as a specimen how a man may praise himself gracefully and commend others without suspicion of envy. [Lamb prints the preface as part of his note.]

This White Devil of Italy sets off a bad cause so spe-
ciously, and pleads with such an innocence-resembling
boldness, that we seem to see that matchless beauty of her
face which inspires such gay confidence into her; and are
ready to expect, when she has done her pleadings, that her
very judges, her accusers, the grave embassadors who sit
as spectators, and all the court, will rise and make proffer to defend her in spite of the utmost conviction of her
guilt; as the shepherds in Don Quixote make proffer to
follow the beautiful shepherdess Marcela "without reaping
any profit out of her manifest resolution made there in
their hearing." - (34)   [III, i.]

So sweet and lovely does she make the shame,
Which, like a canker in the fragrant rose,
Does spot the beauty of her budding name! (35)

I never saw any thing like this Dirge, except the Ditty
which reminds Ferdinand of his drowned Father in the Tempest. As that is of the water, watery; so this is of
the earth, earthy. Both have that intenseness of feeling, which seems to resolve itself into the elements which
it contemplates.   [V, iv.]

---

## (xxix)

THE LOVERS MELANCHOLY.   BY JOHN FORD.

This Story, which is originally to be met with in
Strada's Prolusions, has been paraphrased in rhyme by
Crashaw, Ambrose Phillips, and others: (36)  but none of
those versions can at all compare for harmony and grace
with this blank verse of Ford's: It is as fine as any
thing in Beaumont and Fletcher;  and almost equals the
strife which it celebrates.   [I, i.]

---

## (xxx)

TIS PITY SHE'S A WHORE: A TRAGEDY.   BY JOHN FORD.

The good Friar in this Play is evidently a Copy of
Friar Lawrence in Romeo and Juliet.  He is the same kind
Physician to the Souls of his young Charges; but he has
more desperate Patients to deal with.   [I, i.]

Sir Thomas Browne in the last Chapter of his Enquiries
into Vulgar and Common Errors, rebukes such Authors as
have chosen to relate prodigious and nameless Sins.    The
Chapter is entitled, *of some relations whose truth we
fear*.    His reasoning is solemn and fine.    [Lamb quotes
the lengthy passage beginning 'Lastly, as there are many
Relations whereto we cannot assent....'.]

---

(xxxi)

THE BROKEN HEART.    A TRAGEDY.    BY JOHN FORD.

I do not know where to find in any Play a catastrophe
so grand, so solemn, and so surprising as this.    This is
indeed, according to Milton, to "describe high passions
and high actions." (37)    The fortitude of the Spartan Boy
who let a beast gnaw out his bowels till he died without
expressing a groan, is a faint bodily image of this dilac-
eration of the spirit, and exenteration of the inmost
mind, which Calantha with a holy violence against her
nature keeps closely covered, till the last duties of a
Wife and a Queen are fulfilled.    Stories of martyrdom are
but of chains and the stake;   a little bodily suffering;
these torments

    On the purest spirits prey
    As on entrails, joints, and limbs,
    With answerable pains, but more intense. (38)

What a noble thing is the soul in it[s] strengths and in
its weaknesses! who would be less weak than Calantha? who
can be so strong? the expression of this transcendant
scene almost bears me in imagination to Calvary and the
Cross;   and I seem to perceive some analogy between the
scenical sufferings which I am here contemplating, and the
real agonies of that final completion to which I dare no
more than hint a reference. (39)
    Ford was of the first order of Poets.    He sought for
sublimity not by parcels in metaphors or visible images,
but directly where she has her full residence in the heart
of man;   in the actions and sufferings of the greatest
minds.    There is a grandeur of the soul above mountains,
seas, and the elements.    Even in the poor perverted
reason of Giovanni and Annabella (in the Play which pre-
cedes this) we discern traces of that fiery particle,
which in the irregular starting from out of the road of
beaten action, discovers something of a right line even in

obliquity, and shews hints of an improveable greatness in the lowest descents and degradations of our nature.   [V, iii.]

---

### (xxxii)

MUSTAPHA.   A TRAGEDY.   BY FULKE GREVILLE, LORD BROOKE.

These two Tragedies of Lord Brooke might with more propriety have been termed political treatises, than plays. Their author has strangely contrived to make passion, character, and interest, of the highest order, subservient to the expression of state dogmas and mysteries.   He is nine parts Machiavel and Tacitus for one part Sophocles or Seneca.   In this writer's estimate of the faculties of his own mind, the understanding must have held a most tyrannical pre-eminence.   Whether we look into his plays, or his most passionate love-poems, we shall find all frozen and made rigid with intellect.   The finest movements of the human heart, the utmost grandeur of which the soul is capable, are essentially comprized in the actions and speeches of Caelica and Camena.   Shakspeare, who seems to have had a peculiar delight in contemplating womanly perfection, whom for his many sweet images of female excellence all women are in an especial manner bound to love, has not raised the *ideal* of the female character higher than Lord Brooke in these two women has done.   But it requires a study equivalent to the learning of a new language to understand their meaning when they speak.   It is indeed hard to hit:

Much like thy riddle, Samson, in one day
Or seven though one should musing sit. (40)

It is as if a being of pure intellect should take upon him to express the emotions of our sensitive natures.   There would be all knowledge, but sympathetic expression would be wanting.

---

### (xxxiii)

THE CASE IS ALTERED.   A COMEDY.   BY BEN. JONSON.

The passion for wealth has worn out much of its grossness by tract of time.   Our ancestors certainly con-

ceived of money as able to confer a distinct gratification
in itself, not alone considered simply as a symbol of
wealth.   The old poets, when they introduce a miser, constantly make him address his gold as his mistress;   as
something to be seen, felt, and hugged;   as capable of
satisfying two of the senses at least.   The substitution
of a thin unsatisfying medium for the good old tangible
gold, has made avarice quite a Platonic affection in comparison with the seeing, touching, and handling-pleasures
of the old Chrysophilites.   A bank-note can no more
satisfy the touch of a true sensualist in this passion,
than Creusa could return her husband's embrace in the
shades.— See the Cave of Mammon in Spenser: (41)   Barabas's contemplation of his wealth, in the Jew of Malta;
Luke's raptures, in the City Madam, &c.   Above all hear
Guzman, in that excellent old Spanish Novel, The Rogue,
expatiate on the....   [Lamb quotes at length a passage
from Aleman's *The Rogue* (I, iii, 4) beginning 'ruddy
cheeks of your golden Ruddocks ...'.]

---

(xxxiv)

POETASTER:  OR, HIS ARRAIGNMENT.   A COMICAL SATYR.   BY
BEN. JONSON.

This Roman Play seems written to confute those enemies
of Ben. Jonson in his own days and ours, who have said
that he made a pedantical use of his learning.   He has
here revived the whole court of Augustus, by a learned
spell.   We are admitted to the society of the illustrious
dead.   Virgil, Horace, Ovid, Tibullus, converse in our
own tongue more finely and poetically than they expressed
themselves in their native Latin.— Nothing can be imagined more elegant, refined, and court-like, than the
scenes between this Lewis the Fourteenth of Antiquity and
his Literati. - The whole essence and secret of that kind
of intercourse is contained therein.   The economical
liberality by which greatness, seeming to wave some part
of its prerogative, takes care to lose none of the essentials;   the prudential liberties of an inferior which
flatter by commanded boldness and soothe with complimental
sincerity.

(xxxv)

THE NEW INN:   OR, THE LIGHT HEART.   A COMEDY.   BY BEN.
JONSON.

These and the preceding extracts may serve to shew the
poetical fancy and elegance of mind of the supposed rugged
old Bard.   A thousand beautiful passages might be adduced
from those numerous court masques and entertainments which
he was in the daily habit of furnishing, to prove the same
thing.   But they do not come within my plan.   That which
follows is a specimen of that talent for comic humour, and
the assemblage of ludicrous images, on which his reputation chiefly rests.   It may serve for a variety after so
many serious extracts.   [III, ii.]

---

(xxxvi)

THE ALCHEMIST.   A COMEDY.   BY BEN. JONSON.

The judgment is perfectly overwhelmed by the torrent of
images, words, and book-knowledge with which Mammon con-
founds and stuns his incredulous hearer.   They come pouring out like the successive strokes of Nilus.   They
"doubly redouble strokes upon the foe." (42)   Description
outstrides proof.   We are made to believe effects before
we have testimony for their causes:   as a lively description of the joys of heaven sometimes passes for an argument to prove the existence of such a place.   If there be
no one image which rises to the height of the sublime, yet
the confluence and assemblage of them all produces an
effect equal to the grandest poetry.   Zerxes' army that
drank up whole rivers from their numbers may stand for
single Achilles. - Epicure Mammon is the most determined
offspring of the author.   It has the whole "matter and
copy of the father, eye, nose, lip, the trick of his
frown:" (43)   It is just such a swaggerer as contemporaries have described old Ben to be.   Meercraft, Bobadil,
the Host of the New Inn, have all his "image and super-
scription:" (44)   but Mammon is arrogant pretension personified.   Sir Samson Legend, in Love for Love, is such
another lying overbearing character, but he does not come
up to Epicure Mammon.   What a "towring bravery" (45)
there is in his sensuality!   He affects no pleasure under
a Sultan.   It is as if "Egypt with Assyria strove in
luxury."   [II, i;  II, ii.] (46)

(xxxvii)

THE TRIUMPH OF LOVE:  BEING THE SECOND OF FOUR PLAYS, OR
MORAL REPRESENTATIONS, IN ONE.   BY FRANCIS BEAUMONT.

Violanta's prattle is so very pretty and so natural *in
her situation*, that I could not resist giving it a place.
Juno Lucina was never invoked with more elegance.   Pope
has been praised for giving dignity to a game at cards.
It required at least as much address to ennoble a lying-
in.   [Scene I.]

---

(xxxviii)

THE MAID'S TRAGEDY.   BY FRANCIS BEAUMONT, AND JOHN
FLETCHER.

One characteristic of the excellent old poets is their
being able to bestow grace upon subjects which naturally
do not seem susceptible of any.   I will mention two instances:  Zelmane in the Arcadia of Sidney, and Helena in
the All's Well that Ends Well of Shakspeare.   What can be
more unpromising at first sight than the idea of a young
man disguising himself in woman's attire, and passing himself off for a woman among women? and that too for a long
space of time? yet Sir Philip has preserved such a matchless decorum, that neither does Pyrocles' manhood suffer
any stain for the effeminacy of Zelmane, nor is the respect due to the princesses at all diminished when the de-
ception comes to be known.   In the sweetly constituted
mind of Sir Philip Sidney it seems as if no ugly thought
nor unhandsome meditation could find a harbour.   He
turned all that he touched into images of honour and
virtue.   Helena in Shakspeare, is a young woman seeking a
man in marriage.   The ordinary laws of courtship are reversed;  the habitual feelings are violated.   Yet with
such exquisite address this dangerous subject is handled,
that Helena's forwardness loses her no honour;  delicacy
dispenses with her laws in her favour, and Nature in her
single case seems content to suffer a sweet violation.
Aspatia in this Tragedy, is a character equally difficult with Helena of being managed with grace.   She too is
a slighted woman, refused by the man who had once engaged
to marry her.   Yet it is artfully contrived that while we
pity her, we respect her, and she descends without degradation.   So much true poetry and passion can do to confer
dignity upon subjects which do not seem capable of it.

But Aspatia must not be compared at all points with
Helena;  she does not so absolutely predominate over her
situation but she suffers some diminution, some abatement
of the full lustre of the female character;  which Helena
never does:  her character has many degrees of sweetness,
some of delicacy, but it has weakness which if we do not
despise, we are sorry for.   After all, Beaumont and
Fletcher were but an inferior sort of Shakspeares and
Sidneys. (47)

---

(xxxix)

PHILASTER;  OR, LOVE LIES A BLEEDING.   A TRAGI-COMEDY.
BY FRANCIS BEAUMONT AND JOHN FLETCHER.

The character of Bellario must have been extremely popular in its day.   For many years after the date of Philaster's first exhibition on the stage, scarce a play can
be found without one of these women pages in it, following
in the train of some pre-engaged lover, calling on the
gods to bless her happy rival (his mistress) whom no doubt
she secretly curses in her heart, giving rise to many
pretty *equivoques* by the way on the confusion of sex, and
either made happy at last by some surprising turn of fate,
or dismissed with the joint pity of the lovers and the
audience.   Our ancestors seem to have been wonderfully
delighted with these transformations of sex.   Women's
parts were then acted by young men.   What an odd double
confusion it must have made, to see a boy play a woman
playing a man:  one cannot disentangle the perplexity
without some violence to the imagination.
   Donne has a copy of verses addrest to his mistress,
dissuading her from a resolution, which she seems to have
taken up from some of these scenical representations, of
following him abroad as a page.   It is so earnest, so
weighty, so rich in poetry, in sense, in wit, and pathos,
that I have thought fit to insert it, as a solemn close
in future to all such sickly fancies as he there depre-
cates.   The Story of his romantic and unfortunate marriage with the Daughter of Sir George Moore, the Lady here
supposed to be addrest, may be read in Walton's Lives.
[Lamb quotes Elegy XVI, 'On his Mistress'.] (48)

## (xl)

THE FAITHFUL SHEPHERDESS.   BY JOHN FLETCHER.

If all the parts of this Play had been in unison with
these innocent scenes, and sweet lyric intermixtures, it
had been a Poem fit to vie with Comus or the Arcadia, to
have been put into the hands of boys and virgins, to have
made matter for young dreams like the loves of Hermia and
Lysander.   But a spot is on the face of this moon. –
Nothing short of infatuation could have driven Fletcher
upon mixing up with this blessedness such an ugly deformity as Cloe: the wanton shepherdess!   Coarse words do
but wound the ears; but a character of lewdness affronts
the mind.   Female lewdness at once shocks nature and
morality.   If Cloe was meant to set off Clorin by contrast, Fletcher should have known that such weeds by
juxta-position do not set off but kill sweet flowers.
[III, i.]

---

## (xli)

LOVE'S PILGRIMAGE.   A COMEDY.   BY JOHN FLETCHER.

This is one of the most pleasing if not the most shining scenes in Fletcher.   All is sweet, natural, and un-
forced.   It is a copy which we may suppose Massinger to
have profited by the studying.   [V, iv.]

---

## (xlii)

THIERRY AND THEODORET.   A TRAGEDY.   BY JOHN FLETCHER.

I have always considered this to be the finest scene in
Fletcher, and Ordella the most perfect idea of the female
heroic character, next to Calantha in the Broken Heart of
Ford, that has been embodied in fiction.   She is a piece
of sainted nature.   Yet noble as the whole scene is, it
must be confessed that the manner of it, compared with
Shakspeare's finest scenes, is slow and languid.   Its
motion is circular, not progressive.   Each line revolves
on itself in a sort of separate orbit.   They do not join
into one another like a running hand.   Every step that we
go we are stopped to admire some single object, like walking in beautiful scenery with a guide.   This slowness I

shall elsewhere have occasion to remark as characteristic
of Fletcher.  Another striking difference perceivable
between Fletcher and Shakspeare, is the fondness of the
former for unnatural and violent situations, like that in
the scene before us.  He seems to have thought that
nothing great could be produced in an ordinary way.  The
chief incidents in the Wife for a Month, in Cupid's Revenge, in the Double Marriage, and in many more of his
Tragedies, shew this.  Shakspeare had nothing of this
contortion in his mind, none of that craving after romantic incidents, and flights of strained and improbable
virtue, which I think always betrays an imperfect moral
sensibility.  [IV, i.]

---

### (xliii)

WIT WITHOUT MONEY.  A COMEDY.  BY JOHN FLETCHER.

The wit of Fletcher is excellent like his serious
scenes:  but there is something strained and far fetched
in both.  He is too mistrustful of Nature;  he always
goes a little on one side of her.  Shakspeare chose her
without a reserve:  and had riches, power, understanding,
and long life, with her, for a dowry.

---

### (xliv)

THE TWO NOBLE KINSMEN.  A TRAGEDY.  BY JOHN FLETCHER.

This scene bears indubitable marks of Fletcher:  the
two which precede it give strong countenance to the tradition that Shakspeare had a hand in this play.  The same
judgment may be formed of the death of Arcite, and some
other passages, not here given.  They have a luxuriance
in them which strongly resembles Shakspeare's manner in
those parts of his plays where, the progress of the interest being subordinate, the poet was at leisure for description.  I might fetch instances from Troilus and
Timon.  That Fletcher should have copied Shakspeare's
manner through so many entire scenes (which is the theory
of Mr. Steevens (49) is not very probable, that he could
have done it with such facility is to me not certain.
His ideas moved slow;  his versification, though sweet, is
tedious, it stops every moment;  he lays line upon line,
making up one after the other, adding image to image so

deliberately that we see where they join:  Shakspeare
mingles every thing, he runs line into line, embarrasses
sentences and metaphors;  before one idea has burst its
shell, another is hatched and clamorous for disclosure.
If Fletcher wrote some scenes in imitation, why did he
stop? or shall we say that Shakspeare wrote the other
scenes in imitation of Fletcher? that he gave Shakspeare
a curb and a bridle, and that Shakspeare gave him a pair
of spurs:  as Blackmore and Lucan are brought in exchang-
ing gifts in the Battle of the Books?   [II, ii.]

---

(xlv)

THE CITY MADAM.   A COMEDY.   BY PHILIP MASSINGER.

This bitter satire against the city women for aping the
fashions of the court ladies must have been peculiarly
gratifying to the females of the Herbert family and the
rest of Massinger's noble patrons and patronesses.   [IV,
iv.]

---

(xlvi)

THE PICTURE.   A TRAGI-COMEDY.   BY PHILIP MASSINGER.

The good sense, rational fondness, and chastised feeling, of this dialogue, make it more valuable than many of
those scenes in which this writer has attempted a deeper
passion and more tragical interest.   Massinger had not
the higher requisites of his art in any thing like the
degree in which they were possessed by Ford, Webster,
Tourneur, Heywood, and others.   He never shakes or dis-
turbs the mind with grief.   He is read with composure and
placid delight.   He wrote with that equability of all the
passions, which made his English style the purest and most
free from violent metaphors and harsh constructions, of
any of the dramatists who were his contemporaries.
[I, i.]

---

(xlvii)

THE VIRGIN MARTYR.   A TRAGEDY.   BY PHILIP MASSINGER AND
THOMAS DECKER.

This scene has beauties of so very high an order that,
with all my respect for Massinger, I do not think he had
poetical enthusiasm capable of furnishing them.   His associate Decker, who wrote Old Fortunatus, had poetry
enough for any thing.   The very impurities which obtrude
themselves among the sweet pieties of this play (like
Satan among the Sons of Heaven) and which the brief scope
of my plan fortunately enables me to leave out, have a
strength of contrast, a raciness, and a glow, in them,
which are above Massinger.   They set off the religion of
the rest, somehow as Caliban serves to shew Miranda.
[II, i.]

---

(xlviii)

THE OLD LAW.   A COMEDY.   BY PHILIP MASSINGER, THOMAS
MIDDLETON, AND WILLIAM ROWLEY.

There is an exquisiteness of moral sensibility, making
one to gush out tears of delight, and a poetical strange-
ness in all the improbable circumstances of this wild
play, which are unlike any thing in the dramas which Massinger wrote alone.   The pathos is of a subtler edge.
Middleton and Rowley, who assisted in this play, had both
of them finer geniuses than their associate.

---

(xlix)

THE MAID'S REVENGE.   A TRAGEDY.   BY JAMES SHIRLEY.

Shirley claims a place amongst the worthies of this
period, not so much for any transcendent genius in himself, as that he was the last of a great race, all of whom
spoke nearly the same language, and had a set of moral
feelings and notions in common.   A new language and quite
a new turn of tragic and comic interest came in with the
Restoration.

---

(1)

THE LADY OF PLEASURE.　A COMEDY.　BY JAMES SHIRLEY.

This dialogue is in the very spirit of the recriminat-
ing scenes between Lord and Lady Townley in the Provoked
Husband.　It is difficult to believe, but it must have
been Vanbrugh's prototype.　[I, i.]

Lamb's extracts and comments on the Garrick Plays were
contributed to William Hone's 'Table Book' throughout
1827.   They were later published with the 'Specimens' in
1835.   In a letter to the editor introducing the series
Lamb wrote:   'Imagine the luxury to one like me, who,
above every other form of Poetry, have ever preferred the
dramatic....   By those who remember the "Specimens,"
these must be considered as mere after-gleanings, supple-
mentary to that work, only comprising a longer period.'
Lamb once again supplied little or no bibliographical or
biographical details, his business, as he wrote, being
'with their poetry only.'

(i)

From "King John and Matilda," a Tragedy by Robert Daven-
port, acted in 1651.

Fitzwater:  son of water.   A striking instance of the
compatibility of the *serious pun* with the expression of
the profoundest sorrows.   Grief, as well as joy, finds
ease in thus playing with a word.   Old John of Gaunt in
Shakspeare thus descants on his *name:*  "Gaunt, and gaunt
indeed;" (50) to a long string of conceits, which no one
has ever yet felt as ridiculous.   The poet Wither thus,
in a mournful review of the declining estate of his
family, says with deepest nature:-

The very name of Wither shows decay. (51)

This scene has much passion and poetry in it, if I mis-

take not.   The last words of Fitzwater are an instance of
noble temperament;   but to understand him, the character
throughout of this mad, merry, feeling, insensible-seeming
lord, should be read.   That the venomous John could have
even counterfeited repentance so well, is out of nature;
but supposing the possibility, nothing is truer than the
way in which it is managed.   These old play-wrights invested their bad characters with notions of good, which
could by no possibility have coexisted with their actions.
Without a soul of goodness in himself, how could Shakspeare's Richard the Third have lit upon those sweet
phrases and inducements by which he attempts to win over
the dowager queen to let him wed her daughter[?]   It is
not Nature's nature, but Imagination's substituted nature,
which does almost as well in a fiction.   [V, iii.]

---

(ii)

From the "Parliament of Bees," a Masque, by John Day,
printed 1607.

   Whether this singular production, in which the Characters are all *Bees*, was ever acted, I have no information
to determine.   It is at least as capable of representation, as we can conceive the "Birds" of Aristophanes to
have been.

———————————— the doings,
   The births, the wars, the wooings,

of these pretty little winged creatures are with continued
liveliness portrayed throughout the whole of this curious
old Drama, in words which Bees would talk with, could they
talk;   the very air seems replete with humming and buzzing
melodies, while we read them.   Surely Bees were never so
be-rhymed before.

---

(iii)

From "Fortune by Land and Sea," a Comedy, by T. Heywood,
and W. Rowley, 1655.

   If I were to be consulted as to a Reprint of our Old
English Dramatists, I should advise to begin with the collected Plays of Heywood.   He was a fellow Actor, and

fellow Dramatist, with Shakspeare.   He possessed not the
imagination of the latter;  but in all those qualities
which gained for Shakspeare the attribute of *gentle*, he
was not inferior to him.   Generosity, courtesy, temperance in the depths of passion;  sweetness, in a word, and
gentleness;  Christianism;  and true hearty Anglicism of
feelings, shaping that Christianism;  shine throughout his
beautiful writings in a manner more conspicuous than in
those of Shakspeare, but only more conspicuous inasmuch as
in Heywood these qualities are primary, in the other subordinate to poetry.   I love them both equally, but Shakspeare has most of my wonder.   Heywood should be known to
his countrymen, as he deserves.  His plots are almost invariably English.   I am sometimes jealous, that Shakspeare laid so few of his scenes at home.   I laud Ben Jonson, for that in one instance having framed the first
draught of his Every Man in his Humour in Italy, he changed the scene, and Anglicised his characters.   The names
of them in the First Edition, may not be unamusing.  [Lamb
lists the original Italianate names of the characters.]

   How say you, Reader? do not Master Kitely, Mistress
Kitely, Master Knowell, Brainworm, &c. read better than
these Cisalpines?

---

(iv)

From "Tancred and Gismund," acted before the Court by the
Gentlemen of the Inner Temple, 1591.

   Nearly a century after the date of this Drama, Dryden
produced his admirable version of the same story from Boccacio.   The speech here extracted may be compared with
the corresponding passage in the Sigismonda and Guiscardo,
with no disadvantage to the elder performance.   It is
quite as weighty, as pointed, and as passionate. [V, ii.]

---

(v)

From the "Two Angry Women of Abingdon," a Comedy, by
Henry Porter, 1599.

   The pleasant Comedy, from which these Extracts are
taken, is contemporary with some of the earliest of Shakspeare's, and is no whit inferior to either the Comedy of
Errors, or the Taming of the Shrew, for instance.   It is
full of business, humour, and merry malice.   Its night-

scenes are peculiarly sprightly and wakeful.    The versification unencumbered, and rich with compound epithets.
Why do we go on with ever new Editions of Ford, and Massinger, and the thrice reprinted Selections of Dodsley?
what we want is as many volumes more, as these latter consist of, filled with plays (such as this), of which we
know comparatively nothing.    Not a third part of the
Treasures of old English Dramatic literature has been exhausted.    Are we afraid that the genius of Shakspeare
would suffer in our estimate by the disclosure?    He would
indeed be somewhat lessened as a miracle and a prodigy.
But he would lose no height by the confession.    When a
Giant is shown to us, does it detract from the curiosity
to be told that he has at home a gigantic brood of brethren, less only than himself?    Along *with* him, not *from*
him, sprang up the race of mighty Dramatists who, compared
with the Otways and Rowes that followed, were as Miltons
to a Young or an Akenside.    That he was their elder
Brother, not their Parent, is evident from the fact of the
very few direct imitations of him to be found in their
writings.    Webster, Decker, Heywood, and the rest of his
great contemporaries went on their own ways, and followed
their individual impulses, not blindly prescribing to
themselves his tract. Marlowe, the true (though imperfect)
Father of our *tragedy*, preceded him.    The *comedy* of
Fletcher is essentially unlike to that of his.    'Tis out
of no detracting spirit that I speak thus, for the Plays
of Shakspeare have been the strongest and the sweetest
food of my mind from infancy; but I resent the comparative obscurity in which some of his most valuable co-
operators remain, who were his dear intimates, his stage
and his chamber-fellows while he lived, and to whom his
gentle spirit doubtlessly then awarded the full portion
of their genius, as from them toward himself appears to
have been no grudging of his acknowledged excellence.

---

(vi)

From the "Fair Maid of the Exchange," a Comedy, by Thomas
Heywood, 1637.

The full title of this Play is "The Fair Maid of the
Exchange, with the humours of the Cripple of Fenchurch."
The above Satire against some Dramatic Plagiarists of the
time, is put into the mouth of the Cripple, who is an excellent fellow, and the Hero of the Comedy.    Of his
humour this extract is a sufficient specimen; but he is

described (albeit a tradesman, yet wealthy withal) with
heroic qualities of mind and body; the latter of which he
evinces by rescuing his Mistress (the Fair Maid) from
three robbers by the main force of one crutch lustily
applied; and the former by his foregoing the advantages
which this action gained him in her good opinion, and be-
stowing his wit and finesse in procuring for her a husband, in the person of his friend Golding, more worthy of
her beauty, than he could conceive his own maimed and
halting limbs to be. It would require some boldness in a
dramatist now-a-days to exhibit such a Character; and
some luck in finding a sufficient Actor, who would be willing to personate the infirmities, together with the virtues, of the Noble Cripple. [III, ii.]

After this Specimen of the pleasanter vein of Heywood,
I am tempted to extract some lines from his "Hierarchie of
Angels, 1634;" (52) not strictly as a Dramatic Poem, but
because the passage contains a string of names, all but
that of *Watson*, his contemporary Dramatists. He is com-
plaining in a mood half serious, half comic, of the disrespect which Poets in his own times meet with from the
world, compared with the honors paid them by Antiquity.
*Then* they could afford them three or four sonorous names,
and at full length; as to Ovid, the addition of Publius
Naso Sulmensis; to Seneca, that of Lucius Annaeas
Cordubensis; and the like.... [Lamb quotes from 'Our
modern Poets to that pass are driven' to 'And he's now but
Jack Ford, that once were John'.]
Possibly our Poet was a little sore, that this contemptuous curtailment of their Baptismal Names was chiefly
exercised upon his Poetical Brethren of the *Drama*. We
hear nothing about Sam Daniel, or Ned Spenser, in his
catalogue. The familiarity of common discourse might
probably take the greater liberties with the Dramatic
Poets, as conceiving of them as more upon a level with the
Stage Actors. Or did their greater publicity, and popularity in consequence, fasten these diminutives upon them
out of a feeling of love and kindness; as we say Harry
the Fifth, rather than Henry, when we would express good
will? - as himself says, in those reviving words put into
his mouth by Shakspeare, where he would comfort and confirm his doubting brothers:

Not Amurath an Amurath succeeds,
But Harry Harry! (53)

And doubtless Heywood had an indistinct conception of this
truth, when (coming to his own name), with that beautiful

*retracting* which is natural to one that, not Satirically given, has wandered a little out of his way into something recriminative, he goes on to say.... [Lamb quotes from 'Nor speak I this' to 'I hold he loves me best that calls me Tom'.]

---

### (vii)

From the "Guardian," a Comedy, by Abraham Cowley, 1650.

This was the first Draught of that which he published afterwards under the title of the "Cutter of Coleman Street;" and contains the character of a Foolish Poet, omitted in the latter. I give a few scraps of this character, both because the Edition is scarce, and as furnishing no unsuitable corollary to the Critical Admonitions in the preceding Extract. - The "Cutter" has always appeared to me the link between the Comedy of Fletcher and of Congreve. In the elegant passion of the Love Scenes it approaches the former; and Puny (the character substituted for the omitted Poet) is the Prototype of the half-witted Wits, the Brisks and Dapper Wits, of the latter.

---

### (viii)

From the "Brazen Age," an Historical Play, by Thomas Heywood, 1613.

I cannot take leave of this Drama without noticing a touch of the truest pathos, which the writer has put into the mouth of Meleager, as he is wasting away by the operation of the fatal brand, administered to him by his wretched Mother.

My flame encreaseth still - Oh father OEneus;
And you Althea, whom I would call Mother,
But that my genius prompts me thou'rt unkind:
*And yet farewell!*

What is the boasted "Forgive me, but forgive me!" of the dying wife of Shore in Rowe, compared with these three little words?

---

(ix)

From the "Battle of Alcazar," a Tragedy, 1594.

This address, for its barbaric splendor of conception, extravagant vein of promise, not to mention some idiomatic peculiarities, and the very structure of the verse, savours strongly of Marlowe;  but the real author, I believe, is unknown.   [II, iii.]

---

(x)

From "Two Tragedies in One," by Robert Yarrington, who wrote in the reign of Elizabeth.

The whole theory of the reason of our delight in Tragic Representations, which has cost so many elaborate chapters of Criticism, is condensed in these four last lines: *Aristotle quintessentialised*. (54)

It is curious, that this old Play comprises the distinct action of two Atrocities;  the one a vulgar murder, committed in our own Thames Street, with the names and incidents truly and historically set down;  the other a Murder in high life, supposed to be acting at the same time in Italy, the scenes alternating between that country and England:  the Story of the latter is *mutatis mutandis* no other than that of our own "Babes in the Wood," transferred to Italy, from delicacy no doubt to some of the family of the rich Wicked Uncle, who might yet be living. The treatment of the two differs as the romance-like narratives in "God's Revenge against Murder," (55) in which the Actors of the Murders (with the trifling exception that they *were Murderers*) are represented as most accomplished and every way amiable young Gentlefolks of either sex - as much as *that* differs from the honest unglossing pages of the homely Newgate Ordinary.

---

(xi)

From the "Arraignment of Paris," a Dramatic Pastoral, by George Peel, 1584.

TO MY ESTEEMED FRIEND, AND EXCELLENT MUSICIAN,
V.N., ESQ. (56)

DEAR SIR,
I conjure you in the name of all the Sylvan Deities,
and of the Muses, whom you honour, and they reciprocally
love and honour you, - rescue this old and passionate
*Ditty* (57) - the very flower of an old *forgotten Pastoral*,
which had it been in all parts equal, the Faithful Shepherdess of Fletcher had been but a second name in this
sort of Writing — rescue it from the profane hands of
every common Composer:  and in one of your tranquillest
moods, when you have most leisure from those sad thoughts,
which sometimes unworthily beset you;  yet a mood, in itself not unallied to the better sort of melancholy;  laying by for once the lofty Organ, with which you shake the
Temples;  attune, as to the Pipe of Paris himself, to some
milder and more love-according instrument, this pretty
Courtship between Paris and his (then-not as yet-forsaken)
OEnone.  Oblige me;  and all more knowing Judges of Music
and of Poesy;  by the adaptation of fit musical numbers,
which it only wants to be the rarest Love Dialogue in our
language.

Your Implorer,

C.L.

[I, v.]

---

(xii)

From Sir Richard Fanshaw's Translation of "Querer Por Solo
Querer" - "To love for love's sake" - a Romantic Drama,
written in Spanish by Mendoza:  1649.

To my taste this is fine, elegant, Queen-like raillery;
a second part of Love's Labours Lost, to which title this
extraordinary Play has still better pretensions than even
Shakspeare's:  for after leading three pair of Royal
Lovers thro' endless mazes of doubts, difficulties;  oppo-
sitions of dead fathers' wills;  a labyrinth of losings
and findings;  jealousies;  enchantments;  conflicts with
giants, and single-handed against armies;  to the exact
state in which all the Lovers might with the greatest propriety indulge their reciprocal wishes - when, the deuce
is in it, you think, but they must all be married now -
suddenly the three Ladies turn upon their Lovers;  and, as
an exemplification of the moral of the Play, "Loving for
loving's sake," and a hyper-platonic, truly Spanish proof
of their affections - demand that the Lovers shall consent
to their mistresses' taking upon them the vow of a single
life;  to which the Gallants with becoming refinement can

do [no] less than consent. - The fact is that it was a
Court Play, in which the Characters; males, giants, and
all; were played by females, and those of the highest
order of Grandeeship. No nobleman might be permitted
amongst them; and it was against the forms, that a great
Court Lady of Spain should consent to such an unrefined
[n]otion, as that of wedlock, though but in a play.

Appended to the Drama, the length of which may be
judged from its having taken nine days in the representation, and me three hours in the reading of it - hours well
wasted - is a poetical account of a fire, which broke out
in the Theatre on one of the nights of its acting, when
the whole Dramatis Personae were nearly burnt, because the
common people out of "base fear," and the Nobles out of
"pure respect," could not think of laying hands upon such
"great Donnas;" till the young King, breaking the etiquette, by snatching up his Queen, and bearing her through
the flames upon his back, the Grandees, (dilatory
AEneases), followed his example, and each saved one
(Anchises-fashion), till the whole Courtly Company of
Comedians were got off in tolerable safety. - Imagine
three or four stout London Fireman on such an occasion,
standing off in mere respect! [II.]

---

### (xiii)

From "Bussy D'Ambois," a Tragedy, by G. Chapman, 1613.

This calling upon Light and Darkness for information,
but, above all, the description of the Spirit - "Threw his
chang'd countenance headlong into clouds" - is tremendous,
to the curdling of the blood. - I know nothing in Poetry
like it. [V, iii.]

---

### (xiv)

From the "Devil's Law Case," a Tragi-Comedy, by John
Webster, 1623.

Webster was parish-clerk at St. Andrew's, Holborn.
The anxious recurrence to church-matters; sacrilege;
tomb-stones; with the frequent introduction of *dirges*;
in this, and his other tragedies, may be traced to his
professional sympathies.

(xv)

From the "Challenge to Beauty," a Tragi-comedy, by T.
Heywood, 1636.

The foundations of the English Drama were laid deep in
*tragedy* by Marlow, and others - Marlow especially - while
our *comedy* was yet in its lisping state.   To this tragic
preponderance (forgetting his own sweet Comedies, and
Shakspeare's), Heywood seems to refer with regret;   as in
the "Roscian Strain" he evidently alludes to Alleyn, (58)
who was great in the "Jew of Malta," as Heywood elsewhere
testifies, and in the principal tragic parts both of
Marlow and Shakspeare.   [Prologue.]

---

(xvi)

Dedications to Fletcher's "Faithful Shepherdess;"   without
date;   presumed to be the First Edition.

We can almost be not sorry for the ill dramatic success
of this Play, which brought out such spirited apologies;
in particular, the masterly definitions of Pastoral and
Tragi-Comedy in this Preface.

1 Robert Dodsley, 'Select Collection of Old Plays', 1744,
   12 vols; Thomas Hawkins, 'The Origin of English
   Drama', 1773, 3 vols.
2 'Biographia Dramatica', ed. Isaac Reed, 1782, 2 vols.
3 'An Apology for Poetry', 1595.
4 The authorship of 'Locrine' is unknown.   It is sometimes attributed to Peele.
5 Cf. 'Macbeth', IV, i, 76.
6 'Lust's Dominion' was not written by Marlowe.   It is
   sometimes attributed to Dekker, and was re-worked by
   Mrs Aphra Behn in 'Abdelazer', 1676.
7 'The Compleat Angler', chapter 4.
8 Raleigh, The Nymph's Reply to the Shepherd, l. 16.
9 Donne, 'Satires', IV, 164.
10 Cf. 'The Alchemist', II, ii, 45.
11 'Twelfth Night', III, iv, 53.
12 'The Merchant of Venice', III, i, 45-62.   In a letter
   to Southey, 29 October 1798, Lamb wrote:

> The Jew is a famous character, quite out of nature,
> but, when we consider the terrible Idea our simple
> ancestors had of a Jew, not more to be discommended
> for a certain discolouring ... than the witches &
> fairies of Marlow's mighty successor.   [Lamb quotes
> two passages:  II, iii, 174-98, 202-13.]
>     there is a mixture of the ludicrous & the ter-
> rible in these lines, brimful of genius and antique
> invention....   I need not tell *you*, that Marlow was
> author ... of the Tragedy of Edward 2d, in which are
> *certain lines* unequal'd in our English tongue -.

13 Lamb disliked Goethe's treatment of the Faust theme,
   comparing it unfavourably with Marlowe's.   See 'The
   Letters of Charles and Mary Lamb', ed. E.V. Lucas

(London, 1935), 3 vols, ii, 411;   'Henry Crabb Robinson on Books and Their Writers', ed. E.J. Morley (London, 1938), i, 45, 425.

14 Dekker, 'Old Fortunatus', III, i, 42-3.

15 Cf. Romans 2:14.

16 The reference is to Sidney's 'Arcadia'.

17 'Hamlet', III, ii, 229-30.

18 From the extract reprinted by Lamb.

19 Milton, Passion, 11. 54-6.

20 Il Penseroso, l. 99.

21 Milton's introduction to 'Samson Agonistes'.

22 'Paradise Lost', IV, 1-2.

23 'Othello', V, ii, 356.

24 John Reynolds, 'The Triumphs of God's Revenges Against ... Murther', 1621.

25 Webster's preface to 'The White Devil'.

26 A critical commonplace in eighteenth-century Shakespeare criticism.

27 Quoted in full by Hazlitt, 'Complete Works', ed. P.P. Howe (London, 1930-4), xviii, 213-14, and described as 'excellent criticism'.

28 From the extract reprinted by Lamb.   Quoted by Hazlitt in full in his 'Lectures on the Age of Elizabeth', 'Works', vi, 222-3.

29 Cf. 'Hamlet', II, ii, 584-8, 557.

30 'Hamlet', IV, vii, 180-1.

31 Goldsmith, 'The Traveller', l. 436.   The iron crown was a punishment devised for George Dosa, a sixteenth-century Hungarian revolutionary.   Luke, to whom Goldsmith alludes, was his brother.   The brazen bull was constructed by Perillus for Phalaris, tyrant of Acragas in Sicily.

32 'Othello', III, iii, 374.

33 'The White Devil', III, ii, 147.

34 'Don Quixote', II, chapter 6.

35 Cf. Shakespeare, sonnet 95.

36 Strada, 'Prolusiones Academicae', II, vi;   Crashaw, Music's Duel, the first poem of 'The Delights of the Muses';   Philips, Pastoral V.

37 Cf. 'Paradise Regained', IV, 266.

38 'Samson Agonistes', 11. 613-15.

39 This passage, when it was reprinted by Weber in his edition of Ford (1811), was severely censured by William Gifford in the 'Quarterly Review' (December 1811), and the editor criticised for polluting his pages with 'the blasphemies of a poor maniac'.   Hazlitt, although he considered the note as an 'impressive eulogy', remained unconvinced, 'Works', vi, 273.   In a letter to Wordsworth, 13 October 1804, Lamb maintained that Ford was 'the man' after Shakespeare.

40 'Samson Agonistes', ll. 1016-17.
41 'The Faerie Queene', II, vii.
42 Cf. 'Macbeth', I, ii, 39.
43 'The Winter's Tale', II, iii, 99-100.
44 Matthew 22:20.
45 Cf. 'Hamlet', V, ii, 79-80.
46 Cf. 'Paradise Lost', I, 721-2.
47 In a letter to Coleridge, 13 June 1796, Lamb copied out
   extracts from Beaumont and Fletcher's 'Wife for a
   Month' and 'Bonduca', and added:  '... only it just
   caught my eye in a little extract book I keep, which is
   full of quotations from B. and F. in particular, in
   which authors I can't help thinking there is a greater
   richness of poetical fancy than in any one, Shakspeare
   excepted.'  He adds a further passage from 'The Two
   Noble Kinsmen', commenting:  'I mean not to lay myself
   open by saying they exceed Milton, and perhaps Collins,
   in sublimity.  But don't you conceive all poets after
   Shakspeare yield to 'em in variety of genius?  Massinger treads close on their heels.'
48 Although there is little mention of Donne in Lamb's
   writings, he was, according to Hazlitt, one of Lamb's
   'favourite authors', 'Works', xii, 36.
49 George Steevens (1736-1800), Shakespeare editor.
50 'Richard II', II, i, 73-83.
51 Wither, To his Loving Friend and Cousin-German, Mr.
   William Wither, l. 14.
52 Published in 1635.
53 '2 Henry IV', V, ii, 48-9.
54 The lines, as quoted by Lamb, are:

       But though this sight bring surfeit to the eye,
       Delight your ears with pleasing harmony,
       That ears may countercheck your eyes, and say,
       "Why shed you tears? this deed is but a *Play*."

55 By John Reynolds.  See n. 24.
56 Vincent Novello (1781-1861), composer, conductor and
   organist.
57 'Fair, and fair, and twice so fair'.
58 Edward Alleyn (1566-1626), actor and partner of Philip
   Henslowe.  Quintus Roscius Gallus (d. 62 BC), the most
   famous comic actor of his day in Rome.

# IV Poetry

he wins his flight without self-loss through realms of
chaos "and old night." (3)   Or if, abandoning himself to
that severer chaos of a "human mind untuned," (4) he is
content awhile to be mad with Lear, or to hate mankind (a
sort of madness) with Timon, neither is that madness, nor
this misanthropy, so unchecked, but that, - never letting
the reins of reason wholly go, while most he seems to do
so, - he has his better genius still whispering at his
ear, with the good servant Kent suggesting saner counsels,
or with the honest steward Flavius recommending kindlier
resolutions.   Where he seems most to recede from humanity, he will be found the truest to it.   From beyond the
scope of Nature if he summon possible existences, he sub-
jugates them to the law of her consistency.   He is beautifully loyal to that sovereign directress, even when he
appears most to betray and desert her.   His ideal tribes
submit to policy;   his very monsters are tamed to his
hand, even as that wild sea-brood, shepherded by Proteus.
He tames, and he clothes them with attributes of flesh and
blood, till they wonder at themselves, like Indian Islan-
ders forced to submit to European vesture.   Caliban, the
Witches, are as true to the laws of their own nature (ours
with a difference), as Othello, Hamlet, and Macbeth.
Herein the great and the little wits are differenced;
that if the latter wander ever so little from nature or
actual existence, they lose themselves, and their readers.
Their phantoms are lawless;   their visions nightmares.
They do not create, which implies shaping and consistency.
Their imaginations are not active - for to be active is to
call something into act and form - but passive, as men in
sick dreams.   For the super-natural, or something super-
added to what we know of nature, they give you the plainly
non-natural.   And if this were all, and that these mental
hallucinations were discoverable only in the treatment of
subjects out of nature, or transcending it, the judgment
might with some plea be pardoned if it ran riot, and a
little wantonized:   but even in the describing of real and
every day life, that which is before their eyes, one of
these lesser wits shall more deviate from nature - show
more of that inconsequence, which has a natural alliance
with frenzy, - than a great genius in his "maddest
fits," (5) as Withers somewhere calls them.   We appeal to
any one that is acquainted with the common run of Lane's
novels, (6) - as they existed some twenty or thirty years
back, - those scanty intellectual viands of the whole
female reading public, till a happier genius arose, and
expelled for ever the innutritious phantoms, (7) - whether
he has not found his brain more "betossed," his memory
more puzzled, his sense of when and where more confounded,

among the improbable events, the incoherent incidents, th
inconsistent characters, or no-characters, of some third-
rate love intrigue - where the persons shall be a Lord
Glendamour and a Miss Rivers, and the scene only alternate
between Bath and Bond-street ᚬ a more bewildering dreami-
ness induced upon him, than he has felt wandering over all
the fairy grounds of Spenser.　In the productions we
refer to, nothing but names and places is familiar;　the
persons are neither of this world nor of any other con-
ceivable one;　an endless string of activities without
purpose, of purposes destitute of motive: - we meet phantoms in our known walks;　*fantasques* only christened.　In
the poet we have names which announce fiction;　and we
have absolutely no place at all, for the things and persons of the Fairy Queen prate not of their "whereabout." (8)　But in their inner nature, and the law of
their speech and actions, we are at home and upon acquainted ground.　The one turns life into a dream;　the other
to the wildest dreams gives the sobrieties of every day
occurences.　By what subtile art of tracing the mental
processes it is effected, we are not philosophers enough
to explain, but in that wonderful episode of the cave of
Mammon, (9) in which the Money God appears first in the
lowest form of a miser, is then a worker of metals, and
becomes the god of all the treasures of the world;　and
has a daughter, Ambition, before whom all the world kneels
for favours - with the Hesperian fruit, the waters of
Tantalus, with Pilate washing his hands vainly, but not
impertinently, in the same stream - that we should be at
one moment in the cave of an old hoarder of treasures, at
the next at the forge of the Cyclops, in a palace and yet
in hell, all at once, with the shifting mutations of the
most rambling dream, and our judgment yet all the time
awake, and neither able nor willing to detect the fallacy,
- is a proof of that hidden sanity which still guides the
poet in his widest seeming-aberrations.

It is not enough to say that the whole episode is a
copy of the mind's conceptions in sleep;　it is, in some
sort - but what a copy!　Let the most romantic of us,
that has been entertained all night with the spectacle of
some wild and magnificent vision, recombine it in the
morning, and try it by his waking judgment.　That which
appeared so shifting, and yet so coherent, while that
faculty was passive, when it comes under cool examination,
shall appear so reasonless and so unlinked, that we are
ashamed to have been so deluded;　and to have taken,
though but in sleep, a monster for a god.　But the trans-
itions in this episode are every whit as violent as in the
most extravagant dream, and yet the waking judgment rati-
fies them.

Lamb wrote this essay for the 'London Magazine' in August
1821, giving it the title Jews, Quakers, Scotchmen, and
other Imperfect Sympathies.   It is better known by the
abbreviated title under which it appeared when it was reprinted two years later in the 'Essays'.   The passage
printed below represents only about a quarter of the full
essay.

There is an order of imperfect intellects (under which
mine must be content to rank) which in its constitution is
essentially anti-Caledonian.   The owners of the sort of
faculties I allude to, have minds rather suggestive than
comprehensive.   They have no pretences to much clearness
or precision in their ideas, or in their manner of expressing them.   Their intellectual wardrobe (to confess
fairly) has few whole pieces in it.   They are content
with fragments and scattered pieces of Truth.   She presents no full front to them - a feature or side-face at
the most.   Hints and glimpses, germs and crude essays at
a system, is the utmost they pretend to.   They beat up a
little game peradventure - and leave it to knottier heads,
more robust constitutions, to run it down.   The light
that lights them is not steady and polar, but mutable and
shifting: waxing, and again waning.   Their conversation
is accordingly.   They will throw out a random word in or
out of season, and be content to let it pass for what it
is worth.   They cannot speak always as if they were upon
their oath - but must be understood, speaking or writing,
with some abatement.   They seldom wait to mature a proposition, but e'en bring it to market in the green ear.
They delight to impart their defective discoveries as they
arise, without waiting for their full development.   They
are no systematizers, and would but err more by attempting

it.    Their minds, as I said before, are suggestive
merely.    The brain of a true Caledonian (if I am not
taken) is constituted upon quite a different plan.    His
Minerva is born in panoply.    You are never admitted to
see his ideas in their growth - if, indeed, they do grow,
and are not rather put together upon principles of clock-
work.    You never catch his mind in an undress.    He never
hints or suggests any thing, but unlades his stock of
ideas in perfect order and completeness.    He brings his
total wealth into company, and gravely unpacks it.    His
riches are always about him.    He never stoops to catch a
glittering something in your presence, to share it with
you, before he quite knows whether it be true touch or
not.    You cannot cry *halves* to any thing that he finds.
He does not find, but bring.    You never witness his first
apprehension of a thing.    His understanding is always at
its meridian - you never see the first dawn, the early
streaks. - He has no falterings of self-suspicion.    Sur-
mises, guesses, misgivings, half-intuitions, semi-con-
sciousnesses, partial illuminations, dim instincts, embryo
conceptions, have no place in his brain, or vocabulary.
The twilight of dubiety never falls upon him.    Is he
orthodox - he has no doubts.    Is he an infidel - he has
none either.    Between the affirmative and the negative
there is no border-land with him.    You cannot hover with
him upon the confines of truth, or wander in the maze of a
probable argument.    He always keeps the path.    You cannot make excursions with him - for he sets you right.
His taste never fluctuates.    His morality never abates.
He cannot compromise, or understand middle actions.
There can be but a right and a wrong.    His conversation
is as a book.    His affirmations have the sanctity of an
oath.    You must speak upon the square with him.    He
stops a metaphor like a suspected person in an enemy's
country....    Above all, you must beware of indirect expressions before a Caledonian.    Clap an extinguisher upon
your irony, if you are unhappily blest with a vein of it.
Remember you are upon your oath....    Persons of this
nation are particularly fond of affirming a truth - which
nobody doubts.    They do not so properly affirm, as an-
nunciate it.

# 13 The Old and the New Schoolmaster
   1821, 1823

Written for the 'London Magazine' in May 1821, this essay, of which only half is reproduced here, was later included in the 'Essays'.

MY reading has been lamentably desultory and immethodical. Odd, out of the way, old English plays, and treatises, have supplied me with most of my notions, and ways of feeling. In every thing that relates to *science*, I am a whole Encyclopaedia behind the rest of the world. I should have scarcely cut a figure among the franklins, or country gentlemen, in king John's days. I know less geography than a school-boy of six weeks' standing. To me a map of old Ortelius is as authentic as Arrowsmith. (10) I do not know whereabout Africa merges into Asia; whether Ethiopia lie in one or other of those great divisions; nor can form the remotest conjecture of the position of New South Wales, or Van Diemen's Land. Yet do I hold a correspondence with a very dear friend in the first-named of these two Terrae Incognitae. I have no astronomy. I do not know where to look for the Bear, or Charles's Wain; the place of any star; or the name of any of them at sight. I guess at Venus only by her brightness - and if the sun on some portentous morn were to make his first appearance in the West, I verily believe, that, while all the world were gasping in apprehension about me, I alone should stand unterrified, from sheer incuriosity and want of observation. Of history and chronology I possess some vague points, such as one cannot help picking up in the course of miscellaneous study; but I never deliberately sat down to a chronicle, even of my own country. I have most dim apprehensions of the four great monarchies; and sometimes the Assyrian, sometimes the Persian, floats as *first* in my fancy. I make the widest conjectures con-

cerning Egypt, and her shepherd kings.   My friend
*M.*, (11) with great pains-taking, got me to think I
understood the first proposition in Euclid, but gave me
over in despair at the second.   I am entirely unacquainted with the modern languages;   and, like a better man
than myself, have "small Latin and less Greek." (12)   I
am a stranger to the shapes and texture of the commonest
trees, herbs, flowers - not from the circumstance of my
being town-born - for I should have brought the same in-
observant spirit into the world with me, had I first seen
it in "on Devon's leafy shores," (13) - and am no less at
a loss among purely town-objects, tools, engines, mechanic
processes. - Not that I affect ignorance - but my head has
not many mansions, nor spacious;   and I have been obliged
to fill it with such cabinet curiosities as it can hold
without aching.   I sometimes wonder, how I have passed my
probation with so little discredit in the world, as I have
done, upon so meagre a stock.   But the fact is, a man may
do very well with a very little knowledge, and scarce be
found out, in mixed company;   every body is so much more
ready to produce his own, than to call for a display of
your acquisitions.   But in a *tête-à-tête* there is no
shuffling.   The truth will out.   There is nothing which
I dread so much, as the being left alone for a quarter of
an hour with a sensible, well-informed man, that does not
know me.   I lately got into a dilemma of this sort.-
   In one of my daily jaunts between Bishopsgate and
Shacklewell, the coach stopped to take up a staid-looking
gentleman, about the wrong side of thirty, who was giving
his parting directions (while the steps were adjusting),
in a tone of mild authority, to a tall youth, who seemed
to be neither his clerk, his son, nor his servant, but
something partaking of all three.   The youth was dismissed, and we drove on.   As we were the sole passengers, he
naturally enough addressed his conversation to me;   and we
discussed the merits of the fare, the civility and punc-
tuality of the driver;   the circumstance of an opposition
coach having been lately set up, with the probabilities of
its success - to all which I was enabled to return pretty
satisfactory answers, having been drilled into this kind
of etiquette by some years' daily practice of riding to
and fro in the stage aforesaid - when he suddenly alarmed
me by a startling question, whether I had seen the show of
prize cattle that morning in Smithfield?   Now as I had
not seen it, and do not greatly care for such sort of exhibitions, I was obliged to return a cold negative.   He
seemed a little mortified, as well as astonished, at my
declaration, as (it appeared) he was just come fresh from
the sight, and doubtless had hoped to compare notes on the

subject.   However he assured me that I had lost a fine
treat, as it far exceeded the show of last year.   We were
now approaching Norton Falgate, when the sight of some
shop-goods *ticketed* freshened him up into a dissertation
upon the cheapness of cottons this spring.   I was now a
little in heart, as the nature of my morning avocations
had brought me into some sort of familiarity with the raw
material;   and I was surprised to find how eloquent I was
becoming on the state of the India market - when, presently, he dashed my incipient vanity to the earth at once, by
inquiring whether I had ever made any calculation as to
the value of the rental of all the retail shops in London.
Had he asked of me, what song the Sirens sang, or what
name Achilles assumed when he hid himself among women, I
might, with Sir Thomas Browne, have hazarded a "wide solution*." (14)   My companion saw my embarrassment, and, the
almshouses beyond Shoreditch just coming in view, with
great good-nature and dexterity shifted his conversation
to the subject of public charities;   which led to the comparative merits of provision for the poor in past and present times, with observations on the old monastic institutions, and charitable orders; - but, finding me rather
dimly impressed with some glimmering notions from old
poetic associations, than strongly fortified with any
speculations reducible to calculation on the subject, he
gave the matter up;   and, the country beginning to open
more and more upon us, as we approached the turnpike at
Kingsland (the destined termination of his journey), he
put a home thrust upon me, in the most unfortunate position he could have chosen, by advancing some queries relative to the North Pole Expedition.   While I was muttering
out something about the Panorama of those strange regions
(which I had actually seen), by way of parrying the question, the coach stopping relieved me from any further apprehensions.   My companion getting out, left me in the
comfortable possession of my ignorance;   and I heard him,
as he went off, putting questions to an outside passenger,
who had alighted with him, regarding an epidemic disorder,
that had been rife about Dalston;   and which, my friend
assured him, had gone through five or six schools in that
neighbourhood.   The truth now flashed upon me, that my
companion was a schoolmaster;   and that the youth, whom he
had parted from at our first acquaintance, must have been
one of the bigger boys, or the usher. - He was evidently a
kind-hearted man, who did not seem so much desirous of
provoking discussion by the questions which he put, as of
obtaining information at any rate.   It did not appear

* Urn Burial.

that he took any interest, either, in such kind of inquir-
ies, for their own sake; but that he was in some way
bound to seek for knowledge. A greenish-coloured coat,
which he had on, forbade me to surmise that he was a
clergyman. The adventure gave birth to some reflections
on the difference between persons of his profession in
past and present times....

The modern schoolmaster is expected to know a little of
every thing, because his pupil is required not to be entirely ignorant of any thing. He must be superficially,
if I may so say, omniscient. He is to know something of
pneumatics; of chemistry; of whatever is curious, or
proper to excite the attention of the youthful mind; an
insight into mechanics is desirable, with a touch of stat-
istics; the quality of soils, &c. botany, the constitution of his country, *cum multis aliis*. (15) You may get
a notion of some part of his expected duties by consulting
the famous Tractate on Education addressed to Mr. Hartlib.

All these things - these, or the desire of them - he is
expected to instil, not by set lessons from professors,
which he may charge in the bill, but at school-intervals,
as he walks the streets, or saunters through green fields
(those natural instructors), with his pupils. The least
part of what is expected from him, is to be done in
school-hours. He must insinuate knowledge at the *mollia
tempora fandi*. (16) He must seize every occasion - the
season of the year - the time of the day - a passing cloud
- a rainbow - a waggon of hay - a regiment of soldiers
going by - to inculcate something useful. He can receive
no pleasure from a casual glimpse of Nature, but must
catch at it as an object of instruction. He must interpret beauty into the picturesque. He cannot relish a
beggar-man, or a gipsy, for thinking of the suitable im-
provement. Nothing comes to him, not spoiled by the
sophisticating medium of moral uses. The Universe - that
Great Book, as it has been called - is to him indeed, to
all intents and purposes, a book, out of which he is
doomed to read tedious homilies to distasting school-
boys....

Boys are capital fellows in their own way, among their
mates; but they are unwholesome companions for grown
people. The restraint is felt no less on the one side,
than on the other. - Even a child, that "plaything for an
hour," (17) tires *always*. The noises of children, playing their own fancies - as I now hearken to them by fits,
sporting on the green before my window, while I am engaged
in these grave speculations at my neat suburban retreat at
Shacklewell - by distance made more sweet - inexpressibly
take from the labour of my task. It is like writing to

music.   They seem to modulate my periods.   They ought at
least to do so - for in the voice of that tender age there
is a kind of poetry, far unlike the harsh prose-accents of
man's conversation. - I should but spoil their sport, and
diminish my own sympathy for them, by mingling in their
pastime.

---

From a letter to Coleridge, 23 October.

---

Gcody Two Shoes is almost out of print.    Mrs. Barbauld['s] stuff has banished all the old classics of the
nursery;   & the Shopman at Newbery's hardly deign'd to
reach them off an old exploded corner of a shelf, when
Mary ask'd for them.    Mrs. B's & Mrs. Trimmer's nonsense
lay in piles about. (18)    Knowledge insignificant & vapid
as Mrs. B's books convey, it seems, must come to a child
in the *shape* of *knowledge*, & his empty noddle must be
turned with conceit of his own powers, when he has learnt,
that a Horse is an Animal, & Billy is better than a Horse,
& such like:   instead of that beautiful Interest in wild
tales, which made the child a man, while all the time he
suspected himself to be no bigger than a child.    Science
has succeeded to Poetry no less in the little walks of
Children than with Men.-:Is there no possibility of avert-
ing this sore evil?    Think what you would have been now,
if instead of being fed with Tales and old wives fables in
childhood, you had been crammed with Geography & Natural
History.?    Damn them.    I mean the cursed Barbauld Crew,
those Blights & Blasts of all that is Human in man &
child.

You masters of Logic ought to know - (Logic is nothing
more than a knowledge of *words*, as the Greek Etymon implys)
- that all words are no more to be taken in the literal
sense at all times, than a promise given to a Taylor. (19)
- When I exprest an apprehension that you were mortally
offended, I meant no more than by the application of a
certain formula of efficacious sounds, which had *done* in
similar cases before, to rouse a sense of decency in you,
and a remembrance of what was due to me!! - You Masters of
Logic should advert to this phenomenon in human speech,
before you arraign the usage of us Dramatic Geniuses - -.
Imagination is a good blood mare & goes well, but the mis-
fortune is she has too many paths before her. - Tis true,
I might have imaged to myself, that you had trundled your
frail carcase to Norfolk = I might also, and did imagine,
that you had *not* - but that you were lazy, or inventing
new properties in a triangle, and for that purpose mould-
ing and squeezing Landlord Crisp's 3 corner'd Beaver into
phantastic experimental forms; or that Archimedes was med-
itating to repulse the French, in case of a Cambridge In-
vasion, by a geometric hurling of Folios on their red
caps;  or peradventure that you were in extremities, in
great wants, & just set out for Trinity Bogs, when my
Letters came - .   In short, my Genius! (which is a short
word now adays for what-a-great-man-am-I!) was absolutely
stifled and overlaid with its own Riches. - Truth is one
and poor like the cruse of Elijah's Widow, Imagination is
the Baldface that multiplys its oil.; - and thou the old
crack'd *Salvy* pipkin that could not believe it could be
put to such purposes.-

This essay was first published in the 'London Magazine',
October 1821 and reprinted in the 'Essays' two years
later.   The passage reproduced is from the opening of the
essay.

WE are too hasty when we set down our ancestors in the
gross for fools, for the monstrous inconsistencies (as
they seem to us) involved in their creed of witchcraft.
In the relations of this visible world we find them to
have been as rational, and shrewd to detect an historic
anomaly, as ourselves.   But when once the invisible world
was supposed to be opened, and the lawless agency of bad
spirits assumed, what measures of probability, of decency,
of fitness, or proportion - of that which distinguishes
the likely from the palpable absurd - could they have to
guide them in the rejection or admission of any particular
testimony? - That maidens pined away, wasting inwardly as
their waxen images consumed before a fire - that corn was
lodged, and cattle lamed - that whirlwinds uptore in dia-
bolic revelry the oaks of the forest - or that spits and
kettles only danced a fearful-innocent vagary about some
rustic's kitchen when no wind was stirring - were all
equally probable where no law of agency was understood.
That the prince of the powers of darkness, passing by the
flower and pomp of the earth, should lay preposterous
seige to the weak fantasy of indigent eld - has neither
likelihood nor unlikelihood à *priori* to us, who have no
measure to guess at his policy, or standard to estimate
what rate those anile souls may fetch in the devil's market.   Nor, when the wicked are expressly symbolized by a
goat, was it to be wondered at so much, that *he* should
come sometimes in that body, and assert his metaphor. -
That the intercourse was opened at all between both worlds

was perhaps the mistake - but that once assumed, I see no
reason for disbelieving one attested story of this nature
more than another on the score of absurdity.   There is no
law to judge of the lawless, or canon by which a dream may
be criticised.

I have sometimes thought that I could not have existed
in the days of received witchcraft; that I could not have
slept in a village where one of those reputed hags dwelt.
Our ancestors were bolder or more obtuse.   Amidst the
universal belief that these wretches were in league with
the author of all evil, holding hell tributary to their
muttering, no simple Justice of the Peace seems to have
scrupled issuing, or silly Headborough serving, a warrant
upon them - as if they should subpoena Satan! - Prospero
in his boat, with his books and wand about him, suffers
himself to be conveyed away at the mercy of his enemies to
an unknown island.   He might have raised a storm or two,
we think, on the passage.   His acquiescence is in exact
analogy to the non-resistance of witches to the constituted powers. - What stops the Fiend in Spenser from tearing
Guyon to pieces (20) - or who had made it a condition of
his prey, that Guyon must take assay of the glorious bait
- we have no guess.   We do not know the laws of that
country.

From my childhood I was extremely inquisitive about
witches and witch-stories.   My maid, and more legendary
aunt, supplied me with good store.   But I shall mention
the accident which directed my curiosity originally into
this channel.   In my father's book-closet, the History of
the Bible, by Stackhouse, occupied a distinguished station.   The pictures with which it abounds - one of the
ark, in particular, and another of Solomon's temple, delineated with all the fidelity of ocular admeasurement, as
if the artist had been upon the spot - attracted my childish attention.   There was a picture, too, of the Witch
raising up Samuel, which I wish that I had never seen....
I have not met with the work from that time to this, but I
remember it consisted of Old Testament stories, orderly
set down, with the *objection* appended to each story, and
the *solution* of the objection regularly tacked to that.
The *objection* was a summary of whatever difficulties had
been opposed to the credibility of the history, by the
shrewdness of ancient or modern infidelity, drawn up with
an almost complimentary excess of candour.   The *solution*
was brief, modest, and satisfactory.   The bane and anti-
dote were both before you.   To doubts so put, and so
quashed, there seemed to be an end for ever.   The dragon
lay dead, for the foot of the veriest babe to trample on.
But - like as was rather feared than realised from that

slain monster in Spenser - from the womb of those crushed
errors young dragonets would creep, exceeding the prowess
of so tender a Saint George as myself to vanquish.    The
habit of expecting objections to every passage, set me
upon starting more objections, for the glory of finding a
solution of my own for them.    I became staggered and per-
plexed, a sceptic in long coats.    The pretty Bible
stories which I had read, or heard read in church, lost
their purity and sincerity of impression, and were turned
into so many historic or chronologic theses to be defended
against whatever impugners.    I was not to disbelieve
them, but - the next thing to that - I was to be quite
sure that some one or other would or had disbelieved them.
Next to making a child an infidel, is the letting him know
that there are infidels at all.    Credulity is the man's
weakness, but the child's strength.    O, how ugly sound
scriptural doubts from the mouth of a babe and a suckling!
- I should have lost myself in these mazes, and have pined
away, I think, with such unfit sustenance as these husks
afforded, but for a fortunate piece of ill-fortune, which
about this time befel me.    Turning over the picture of
the ark with too much haste, I unhappily made a breach in
its ingenious fabric - driving my inconsiderate fingers
right through the two larger quadrupeds - the elephant,
and the camel - that stare (as well they might) out of the
two last windows next the steerage in that unique piece of
naval architecture.    Stackhouse was henceforth locked up,
and became an interdicted treasure.    With the book, the
*objections* and *solutions* gradually cleared out of my head,
and have seldom returned since in any force to trouble me.

In his 'Lectures on the Age of Elizabeth', Hazlitt had
severely criticised Sidney's poetry and prose.   Lamb's
reply was published in the 'London Magazine' for September
1823 under the title Nugae Criticae....   Defence of the
Sonnets of Sir Philip Sydney.   The title was altered when
reprinted in the 'Last Essays'.

SYDNEY'S Sonnets - I speak of the best of them - are
among the very best of their sort.   They fall below the
plain moral dignity, the sanctity, and high yet modest
spirit of self-approval, of Milton, in his compositions of
a similar structure.   They are in truth what Milton, cen-
suring the Arcadia, says of that work (to which they are a
sort of after-tune or application), "vain and amatorious"
enough, yet the things in their kind (as he confesses to
be true of the romance) may be "full of worth and
wit." (21)   They savour of the Courtier, it must be allowed, and not of the Commonwealthsman.   But Milton was a
Courtier when he wrote the Masque at Ludlow Castle, and
still more a Courtier when he composed the Arcades.   When
the national struggle was to begin, he becomingly cast
these vanities behind him;   and if the order of time had
thrown Sir Philip upon the crisis which preceded the Revolution, there is no reason why he should not have acted
the same part in that emergency, which has glorified the
name of a later Sydney. (22)   He did not want for plainness or boldness of spirit.   His letter on the French
match may testify, he could speak his mind freely to
Princes. (23)   The times did not call him to the scaf-
fold.
   The Sonnets which we oftenest call to mind of Milton
were the compositions of his maturest years.   Those of
Sydney, which I am about to produce, were written in the

very hey-day of his blood. They are stuck full of amor-
ous fancies - far-fetched conceits, befitting his occupation; for True Love thinks no labour to send out Thoughts
upon the vast, and more than Indian voyages, to bring home
rich pearls, outlandish wealth, gums, jewels, spicery, to
sacrifice in self-depreciating similitudes, as shadows of
true amiabilities in the Beloved. We must be Lovers - or
at least the cooling touch of time, the *circum praecordia
frigus*, (24) must not have so damped our faculties, as to
take away our recollection that we were once so - before
we can duly appreciate the glorious vanities, and graceful
hyperboles, of the passion. The images which lie before
our feet (though by some accounted the only natural) are
least natural for the high Sydnean love to express its
fancies by. They may serve for the loves of Tibullus, or
the dear Author of the Schoolmistress; (25) for passions
that creep and whine in Elegies and Pastoral Ballads. I
am sure Milton never loved at this rate. I am afraid
some of his addresses (*ad Leonoram* I mean) have rather
erred on the farther side; and that the poet came not
much short of a religious indecorum, when he could thus
apostrophise a singing-girl:-

> Angelus unicuique suus (sic credite gentes)
>     Obtigit aetheriiis ales ab ordinibus.
> Quid mirum, Leonora, tibi si gloria major,
>     Nam tua praesentem vox sonat ipsa Deum?
> Aut Deus, aut vacui certè mens tertia coeli
>     Per tua secretò guttura serpit agens;
> Serpit agens, facilisque docet mortalia corda
>     Sensim immortali assuescere posse sono.
> QUOD SI CUNCTA QUIDEM DEUS EST, PER CUNCTA-
>         QUE FUSUS,
>     IN TE UNA LOQUITUR, CETERA MUTUS HABET. (26)

This is loving in a strange fashion; and it requires
some candour of construction (besides the slight darkening
of a dead language) to cast a veil over the ugly appearance of something very like blasphemy in the last two
verses. I think the Lover would have been staggered, if
he had gone about to express the same thought in English.
I am sure, Sydney has no flights like this. His extra-
vaganzas do not strike at the sky, though he takes leave
to adopt the pale Dian into a fellowship with his mortal
passions. [Lamb quotes Sonnet 31.]
     The last line of this poem is a little obscured by
transposition. He means, Do they call ungratefulness
there a virtue? [Lamb cites Sonnets 39, 23, 27, 41, 53,
64, 73, 74, 75, 103, 84.]

Of the foregoing, the first, the second, and the last
sonnet, are my favourites.   But the general beauty of
them all is, that they are so perfectly characteristical.
The spirit of "learning and of chivalry," - of which
union, Spenser has entitled Sydney to have been the
"president," (27) - shines through them.   I confess I can
see nothing of the "jejune" or "frigid" in them;   much
less of the "stiff" and "cumbrous" - which I have sometimes heard objected to the Arcadia. (28)   The verse runs
off swiftly and gallantly.   It might have been tuned to
the trumpet;   or tempered (as himself expresses it) to
"trampling horses' feet." (29)   They abound in felicitous
phrases -

O heav'nly Fool, thy most kiss-worthy face -

*8th Sonnet.*

————Sweet pillows, sweetest bed;
A chamber deaf to noise, and blind to light;
A rosy garland, and a weary head.

*2nd Sonnet.*

————That sweet enemy, - France -

*5th Sonnet.* (30)

But they are not rich in words only, in vague and un-
localised feelings - the failing too much of some poetry
of the present day - they are full, material, and circum-
stantiated.   Time and place appropriates every one of
them.   It is not a fever of passion wasting itself upon
a thin diet of dainty words, but a transcendent passion
pervading and illuminating action, pursuits, studies,
feats of arms, the opinions of contemporaries and his
judgment of them.   An historical thread runs through
them, which almost affixes a date to them;   marks the *when*
and *where* they were written.
I have dwelt the longer upon what I conceive the merit
of these poems, because I have been hurt by the wantonness
(I wish I could treat it by a gentler name) with which
W.H. takes every occasion of insulting the memory of Sir
Philip Sydney.   But the decisions of the Author of Table
Talk, &c., (most profound and subtle where they are, as
for the most part, just) are more safely to be relied
upon, on subjects and authors he has a partiality for,
than on such as he has conceived an accidental prejudice
against.   Milton wrote Sonnets, and was a king-hater;
and it was congenial perhaps to sacrifice a courtier to a
patriot.   But I was unwilling to lose a *fine idea* from my
mind.   The noble images, passions, sentiments, and poetical delicacies of character, scattered all over the Arcadia (spite of some stiffness and encumberment), justify to

me the character which his contemporaries have left us of
the writer.    I cannot think with the Critic, that Sir
Philip Sydney was that *opprobrious thing* which a foolish
nobleman in his insolent hostility chose to term him. (31)
I call to mind the epitaph made on him, to guide me to
juster thoughts of him;  and I repose upon the beautiful
lines in the "Friend's Passion for his Astrophel," printed
with the Elegies of Spenser and others.    [Lamb quotes
stanzas 15-18, 26-7 of Matthew Roydon's elegy.]

   Or let any one read the deeper sorrows (grief running
into rage) in the Poem, - the last in the collection ac-
companying the above, - which from internal testimony I
believe to be Lord Brooke's, - beginning with "Silence
augmenteth grief," (32) - and then seriously ask himself,
whether the subject of such absorbing and confounding regrets could have been *that thing* which Lord Oxford termed
him.

18 George Chapman
(i) 1802

---

From a letter to Coleridge, 23 October.

---

I have just finished Chapman's Homer.     Did you ever read
it? it has *most* the continuous power of interesting you
all along, like a rapid original, of any:   & in the uncommon excellence of the more finish'd parts goes beyond
Fairfax or any of 'em. - The Metre is 14 Syllables & capable of all sweetness & grandeur.     Cowper's damn'd blank
verse detains you every step with some heavy Miltonism. -
Chapman gallops off with you his own free pace. - Take a
simile for an example - The Council breaks up. - [Lamb
quotes from Chapman's translation of the 'Iliad', II, 70-
7.]    (what *Endless egression of phrases* the Dog com-
mands)!
Take another, Agamemnon wounded, bearing his wound heroi-
cally for the sake of the Army (look below) to a Woman in
Labor. - [Lamb quotes from Chapman's translation of the
'Iliad', XI, 228-39.]
    I will tell you more about Chapman & his peculiarities
my next.    I am much interes[ted] in him. -


(ii) 1824

---

From a letter to C.A. Elton, 11 August.

---

Your commendation of Master Chapman arrideth me.    Can any
one read the pert modern Frenchify'd notes &c. in Pope's
translation and contrast them with solemn weighty prefaces
of Chapman, writing in full faith, as he evidently does,
of the plenary inspiration of his author, worshipping his
meanest scraps and relics as divine, without one sceptical
misgiving of their authenticity - and doubt which was the

properest to expound Homer to their countrymen.   Reverend
Chapman!   You have read his hymn to Pan (the Homeric)
why, it is Miltons blank verse cloth'd with rhyme.   Paradise Lost could scarce lose, could it be so accoutred.   I
shall die in the belief that he has improved upon Homer in
the Odyssee particular, the disclosure of Ulysses of himself, to Alcinous, his previous behavior at the song of
the stern strife arising between Achilles and himself (how
it raises him above the Iliad Ulysses) -

19  Samuel Daniel
    1809

---

From a letter to Coleridge, 7 June.

---

I found 2 other volumes ... the Arcadia, & Daniel enriched
with MSS notes, I wish every book I have were so noted.
They have thoroughly converted me to relish Daniel, or to
say I relish him, for after all I believe I did relish
him.   You well call him sober-minded.   Your Notes are
excellent.

Coleridge first drew Lamb's attention to the poetry of
Wither in 1796.   In 1820, J.M. Gutch, a schoolfriend of
both, published a private edition of Wither in four volumes.   Lamb's marginalia on an interleaved copy of this
work provided the basis of the present article which first
appeared in 'Works', 1818.   It was never reprinted in
Lamb's lifetime.   His copy of Gutch's edition at one time
belonged to Swinburne and is described by him in 'Miscellanies', 1886.

THE poems of G. Wither are distinguished by a hearty homeliness of manner, and a plain moral speaking. (33)   He
seems to have passed his life in one continued act of an
innocent self-pleasing.   That which he calls his *Motto* is
a continued self-eulogy of two thousand lines, yet we read
it to the end without any feeling of distaste, almost
without a consciousness that we have been listening all
the while to a man praising himself.   There are none of
the cold particles in it, the hardness and self-ends which
render vanity and egotism hateful.   He seems to be praising another person, under the mask of self;   or rather we
feel that it was indifferent to him where he found the
virtue which he celebrates;   whether another's bosom, or
his own, were its chosen receptacle.   His poems are full,
and this in particular is one downright confession, of a
generous self-seeking.   But by self he sometimes means a
great deal, - his friends, his principles, his country,
the human race.
   Whoever expects to find in the satirical pieces of this
writer any of those peculiarities which pleased him in the
satires of Dryden or Pope, will be grievously disappointed.   Here are no high-finished characters, no nice
traits of individual nature, few or no personalities.

The game run down is coarse general vice, or folly as it
appears in classes.  A liar, a drunkard, a coxcomb, is
*stript and whipt*;  no Shaftesbury, no Villiers, or Whar-
ton, is curiously anatomized, and read upon.  But to a
well-natured mind there is a charm of moral sensibility
running through them which amply compensates the want of
those luxuries.  Wither seems every where bursting with a
love of goodness, and a hatred of all low and base
actions. - At this day it is hard to discover what parts
in the poem here particularly alluded to, *Abuses Stript
and Whipt*, could have occasioned the imprisonment of the
author.  Was Vice in High Places more suspicious than
now? had she more power;  or more leisure to listen after
ill reports?  That a man should be convicted of a libel
when he named no names but Hate, and Envy, and Lust, and
Avarice, is like one of the indictments in the Pilgrim's
Progress, where Faithful is arraigned for having "railed
on our noble Prince Beelzebub, and spoken contemptibly of
his honorable friends, the Lord Old Man, the Lord Carnal
Delight, and the Lord Luxurious." (34)  What unlucky
jealousy could have tempted the great men of those days to
appropriate such innocent abstractions to themselves!
    Wither seems to have contemplated to a degree of idol-
atry his own possible virtue.  He is for ever anticipating persecution and martyrdom;  fingering, as it were, the
flames, to try how he can bear them.  Perhaps his premature defiance sometimes made him obnoxious to censures,
which he would otherwise have slipped by.
    The homely versification of these Satires is not likely
to attract in the present day.  It is certainly not such
as we should expect from a poet "soaring in the high
region of his fancies with his garland and his singing
robes about him;"* (35)  nor is it such as he has shewn in
his *Philarete*, and in some parts of his *Shepherds Hunting*.
He seems to have adopted this dress with voluntary humility, as fittest for a moral teacher, as our divines chuse
sober grey or black;  but in their humility consists their
sweetness.  The deepest tone of moral feeling in them,
(though all throughout is weighty, earnest and passionate)
is in those pathetic injunctions against shedding of blood
in quarrels, in the chapter entitled *Revenge*.  The story
of his own forbearance, which follows, is highly interesting.  While the Christian sings his own victory over
Anger, the Man of Courage cannot help peeping out to let
you know, that it was some higher principle than *fear*
which counselled this forbearance.
    Whether encaged, or roaming at liberty, Wither never

*Milton.

seems to have abated a jot of that free spirit, which sets
its mark upon his writings, as much as a predominant feature of independence impresses every page of our late
glorious Burns;  but the elder poet wraps his proof-armour
closer about him, the other wears his too much outwards;
he is thinking too much of annoying the foe, to be quite
easy within;  the spiritual defences of Wither are a perpetual source of inward sunshine, the magnanimity of the
modern is not without its alloy of soreness, and a sense
of injustice, which seems perpetually to gall and irri-
tate.   Wither was better skilled in the "sweet uses of
adversity," he knew how to extract the "precious jewel"
from the head of the "toad," without drawing any of the
"ugly venom" along with it. —— The prison notes of Wither
are finer than the wood notes of most of his poetical
brethren.   The description in the Fourth Eglogue of his
*Shepherds Hunting* (which was composed during his imprisonment in the Marshalsea) of the power of the Muse to extract pleasure from common objects, has been oftener
quoted, and is more known, than any part of his writings.
Indeed the whole Eglogue is in a strain so much above not
only what himself, but almsot what any other poet has
written, that he himself could not help noticing it;  he
remarks, that his spirits had been raised higher than they
were wont "through the love of poesy." - The praises of
Poetry have been often sung in ancient and in modern
times;  strange powers have been ascribed to it of influence over animate and inanimate auditors;  its force over
fascinated crowds has been acknowledged;  but, before
Wither, no one ever celebrated its power *at home*, the
wealth and the strength which this divine gift confers
upon its possessor.   Fame, and that too after death, was
all which hitherto the poets had promised themselves from
their art.   It seems to have been left to Wither to discover, that poetry was a present possession, as well as a
rich reversion;  and that the Muse had promise of both
lives, of this, and of that which was to come.
  The *Mistress of Philarete* is in substance a panegyric
protracted through several thousand lines in the mouth of
a single speaker, but diversified, so as to produce an almost dramatic effect, by the artful introduction of some
ladies, who are rather auditors than interlocutors in the
scene;  and of a boy, whose singing furnishes pretence for
an occasional change of metre:  though the seven syllable
line, in which the main part of it is written, is that in
which Wither has shewn himself so great a master, that I
do not know that I am always thankful to him for the exchange.
  Wither has chosen to bestow upon the lady whom he com-

mends, the name of Arete, or Virtue;  and, assuming to
himself the character of Philarete, or Lover of Virtue,
there is a sort of propriety in that heaped measure of
perfections, which he attributes to this partly real,
partly allegorical, personage.   Drayton before him had
shadowed his mistress under the name of Idea, or Perfect
Pattern, (36) and some of the old Italian love-strains are
couched in such religious terms as to make it doubtful,
whether it be a mistress, or Divine Grace, which the poet
is addressing.

In this poem (full of beauties) there are two passages
of pre-eminent merit.   The first is where the lover,
after a flight of rapturous commendation, expresses his
wonder why all men that are about his mistress, even to
her very servants, do not view her with the same eyes that
he does.   [Lamb quotes lines 1835-62.]

The other is, where he has been comparing her beauties
to gold, and stars, and the most excellent things in
nature;  and, fearing to be accused of hyperbole, the
common charge against poets, vindicates himself by boldly
taking upon him, that these comparisons are no hyperboles;
but that the best things in nature do, in a lover's eye,
fall short of those excellencies which he adores in her.
[Lamb quotes lines 1979-90, 2025-32, 1947-50.]

To the measure in which these lines are written, the
wits of Queen Anne's days contemptuously gave the name of
Namby Pamby, in ridicule of Ambrose Philips, who has used
it in some instances, as in the lines on Cuzzoni, to my
feeling at least, very deliciously; (37)  but Wither,
whose darling measure it seems to have been, may shew,
that in skilful hands it is capable of expressing the sub-
tilest movements of passion.   So true it is, which Drayton seems to have felt, that it is the poet who modifies
the metre, not the metre the poet;  in his own words, that

>      It's possible to climb;
> To kindle, or to stake;
>      Altho' in Skelton's rhime.* (38)

*A long line is a line we are long repeating.   In the
*Shepherds's Hunting* take the following -

> If thy verse doth bravely tower,
> *As she makes wing, she gets power;*
> Yet the higher she doth soar,
> She's affronted still the more,
> 'Till she to the high'st hath past,
> Then she rests with fame at last.

what longer measure can go beyond the majesty of this!
what Alexandrine is half so long in pronouncing, or expresses *labor slowly but strongly surmounting difficulty*
with the life with which it is done in the second of these
lines? or what metre could go beyond these, from
*Philarete* -

> Her true beauty leaves behind
> Apprehensions in my mind
> Of more sweetness, than all art
> Or inventions can impart.
> *Thoughts too deep to be express'd,*
> *And too strong to be suppress'd.*

---

(ii) 1796

---

From a letter to Coleridge, 1 July.

---

Quarles I am as great a stranger [to as] I was to
Withers. (39)   I wish you would try & do something to
[bring] our elder bards into more general fame.   I writhe
with indignation, [whe]n in books of Criticism, where
common place quotation is heaped upon quotation, I find no
mention of such men as Massinger or B. & Fl. men with
whom succeeding Dramatic Writers (otway alone excepted)
can bear no manner of Comparison.   Stupid Knox hath noticed none of 'em among his extracts. (40)

---

(iii) 1798

---

From a letter to Southey, 8 November.

---

   I perfectly accord with your opinion of Old Wither.
Quarles is a wittier writer, but Wither lays more hold of
the heart.   Quarles thinks of his audience when he lectures;  Wither soliloquises in company with a full heart.
What wretched stuff are the 'Divine Fancies' of Quarles!
Religion appears to him no longer valuable than it furnishes matter for quibbles and riddles;  he turns God's
grace into wantonness.   Wither is like an old friend,
whose warm-heartedness and estimable qualities make us
wish he possessed more genius, but at the same time make
us willing to dispense with that want.   I always love W.,
and sometimes admire Q.   Still that portrait poem is a

fine one;   and the extract from 'The Shepherds' Hunting'
places him in a starry height far above Quarles.

21  Milton
    (i) 1802

From a letter to Coleridge, 4 November.  Lamb greatly
admired Milton's poetry, but never wrote on the subject at
any length.  Hazlitt, on a number of occasions, refers to
Lamb's critical opinions, but these and other contemporary
references, are insufficient in length and number to provide materials for a balanced assessment of Lamb's mature
judgment of Milton.  According to B.W. Proctor, he preferred 'Paradise Regained' to 'Paradise Lost'.

The first Defence is the greatest work among them, because
it is uniformly great, and such as is befitting the very
mouth of a great nation speaking for itself.  But the
second Defence, which is but a succession of splendid epi-
sodes slightly tied together, has one passage which if you
have not read, I conjure you to lose no time, but read it;
it is his consolations in his blindness, which had been
made a reproach to him.  It begins whimsically, with poetical flourishes about Tiresias and other blind worthies
(which still are mainly interesting as displaying his
singular mind, and in what degree poetry entered into his
daily soul, not by fits and impulses, but engrained and
innate);  but the concluding page, *i.e.* of *this passage*
(not of the *Defensio*) which you will easily find, divested
of all brags and flourishes, gives so rational, so true an
enumeration of his comforts, so human, that it cannot be
read without the deepest interest. (41)

(ii) 1822, 1833

---

From Detached Thoughts on Books and Reading, first published in the 'London Magazine', July 1822 and reprinted
in the 'Last Essays'.

---

Milton almost requires a solemn service of music to be
played before you enter upon him.  But he brings his
music, to which, who listens, had need bring docile
thoughts, and purged ears.

---

(iii) 1834

---

This note was contributed to the 'Athenaeum' in 1834 under
the general heading Table-Talk by the late Elia, and with
other brief comments was the first of the series, appearing on 4 January.

---

"We read the Paradise Lost as a task," says Dr. Johnson.  Nay, rather as a celestial recreation, of which the
dullard mind is not at all hours alike recipient.  "Nobody ever wished it longer"; - nor the moon rounder, he
might have added.  Why, 'tis the perfectness and completeness of it, which makes us imagine that not a line
could be added to it, or diminished from it, with advantage.  Would we have a cubit added to the stature of the
Medicean Venus?  Do we wish her taller?

---

From a letter to Coleridge, 10 January.   In 1852 J.M.
Gutch recalled that Cowley's prose essays were 'especial
favourites' with Charles and Mary Lamb.

---

In all our comparisons of taste, I do not know whether I
have ever heard your opinion of a poet, very dear to me,
the now out of fashion Cowley - favor me with your judgment of him - & tell me if his prose essays, in particular, as well as no inconsiderable part of his verse, be
not delicious.   I prefer the graceful rambling of his
essays, even to the courtly elegance & ease of Addison -
abstracting from this latter's exquisite humour.

From a letter to Thomas Manning, Mid-April?

   You may *perhaps* never have met with Percy's Relicks of
ancient English Poetry; (42)  if you have, and are acquainted with the following Poem, no harm is done; - if
not, I send you a treat; - that's all.——
   It is in Scotch, and a very old Balad, I anglicise it
as I write it, for my own convenience. —— [Lamb quotes
'Edward, Edward,' but having changed his mind transcribed
it 'in its own old Scottish shape'.]  By which I mean to
say, that Edward, Edward is the very first dramatic poem
in the English Language.-.  If you deny that, I'll make
you eat your words.——

## 24 William Cowper
### (i) 1796

From a letter to Coleridge, 5 December.

I have been reading the "task" with fresh delight.    I am
glad you love Cowper.    I could forgive a man for not enjoying Milton, but I would not call that man my friend,
who should be offended with the "divine chit-chat of
Cowper." (43)

### (ii) 1809

From a letter to Charles Lloyd, the elder, 31 July.

I find Cowper is a favourite with nobody. (44)   His injudicious use of the stately slow Miltonic verse in a subject so very different, has given a distaste.   Nothing
can be more unlike to my fancy than Homer and Milton.
Homer is perfect prattle, tho' exquisite prattle, compared
to the deep oracular voice of Milton.   In Milton you love
to stop, and saturate your mind with every great image or
sentiment;   in Homer you want to go on, to have more of
his agreeable narrative.   Cowper delays you as much,
walking over a Bowling Green, as the other does, travelling over steep Alpine heights, where the labour enters
into and makes a part of the pleasure....   I should
scarce think that (Pope having got the ground) a translation in Pope's Couplet versification would ever supersede
his to the public, however faithfuller or in some respects
better.

187

From a letter to Bernard Barton, 15 May.   In 'Charles
Lamb:  His Life Recorded by his Contemporaries', Edmund
Blunden reproduced the following entry from Crabb Robin-
son's diary:

> When, in 1810, I gave Lamb a copy of the Catalogue of
> the paintings exhibited in Carnaby Street, he was de-
> lighted, especially with the description of a painting
> afterwards engraved....   It was after the friends of
> Blake had circulated a subscription paper for an en-
> graving of his 'Canterbury Pilgrims,' that Stothard was
> made a party to an engraving of a painting of the same
> subject, by himself....   Stothard's work is well
> known;  Blake's is known by very few.   Lamb preferred
> the latter greatly, and declared that Blake's descrip-
> tion was the finest criticism he had ever read of
> Chaucer's poem.

Traces of Blake's influence are to be found in Lamb's
essay on Hogarth published in 1811.   See p. 324.

Blake is a real name, I assure you, and a most extraordinary man, if he be still living.   He is the Robert Blake,
whose wild designs accompany a splendid folio edition of
the Night Thoughts, which you may have seen, in one of
which he pictures the parting of soul and body by a solid
mass of human form floating off God knows how from a lum-
pish mass (fac simile to itself) left behin[d] on the
dying bed. (45)   He paints in water colours, marvellous
strange pictures, visions of his brain which he asserts
that he has seen.   They have great merit.   He has *seen*
the old Welsh bards on Snowdon - he has seen the Beauti-
fullest, the Strongest, and the Ugliest Man, left alone

from the Massacre of the Britons by the Romans, and has
painted them from memory (I have seen his paintings) and
asserts them to be as good as the figures of Raphael and
Angelo, but not better, as they had precisely the same
retro-visions and prophetic visions with themself.    The
painters in Oil (which he will have it that neither of
them practised) he affirms to have been the ruin of art,
and affirms that all the while he was engaged in his
water-paintings, Titian was disturbing him, Titian the Ill
Genius of Oil Painting.    His Pictures, one in particular
the Canterbury Pilgrims (far above Stothard's) have great
merit, but hard, dry, yet with grace.    He has written a
Catalogue of them, with a most spirited criticism on
Chaucer, but mystical and full of Vision.    His poems have
been sold hitherto only in Manuscript.    I never read
them, but a friend at my desire procured the Sweep Song.
There is one to a Tiger, which I have heard recited,
beginning

     Tiger Tiger burning bright
     Thro' the desarts of the night –

which is glorious.    But alas! I have not the Book, for
the man is flown, whither I know not, to Hades, or a Mad
House – but I must look on him as one of the most extraordinary persons of the age.

From a letter to Coleridge, 10 December.

Burns was the god of my idolatry, as Bowles of yours.    I
am jealous of your fraternising with Bowles, when I think
you relish him more than Burns or my old favourite,
Cowper.    But you conciliate matters when you talk of the
'divine chit-chat' of the latter:  by the expression I see
you thoroughly relish him.

(ii) 1821, 1823

From Imperfect Sympathies, first published in the 'London
Magazine', August 1821.    When the essay was reprinted in
the 'Essays' two years later, Lamb excluded the following
passage:  'I have a great mind to give up Burns.    There
is certainly a bragging spirit of generosity, a swaggering
assertion of independence, and *all that*, in his writings.'

In my early life I had a passionate fondness for the
poetry of Burns.    I have sometimes foolishly hoped to in-
gratiate myself with his countrymen by expressing it.
But I have always found that a true Scot resents your admiration of his compatriot, even more than he would your
contempt of him.    The latter he imputes to your "imperfect acquaintance with many of the words which he uses;"
and the same objection makes it a presumption in you to
suppose that you can admire him. - Thomson they seem to
have forgotten.    Smollett they have neither forgotten nor
forgiven for his delineation of Rory and his companion,
upon their first introduction to our metropolis. - Speak
of Smollett as a great genius, and they will retort upon

you Hume's History compared with *his* Continuation of it.
What if the historian had continued Humphrey Clinker?

27  William Lisle Bowles
    1796

---

From a letter to Coleridge, 14 November.

---

Coleridge,
   I love you for dedicating your poetry to Bowles. (46)
Genius of the sacred fountain of tears, it was he who led
you gently by the hand through all this valley of weeping,
showed you the dark green yew trees and the willow shades
where, by the fall of waters, you might indulge an uncom-
plaining melancholy, a delicious regret for the past, or
weave fine visions of that awful future.

Lamb's review of Wordsworth's 'The Excursion' was published in the October number of the 'Quarterly Review'.
According to Lamb it was considerably altered by the
editor.   Southey's attempt to rescue the manuscript, of
which Lamb had no copy, was unsuccessful, and when E.V.
Lucas at the turn of the century made a similar attempt,
he was informed that the manuscript no longer existed.
As the review is one of the very few that Lamb wrote on
the work of a major contemporary, and the only review he
ever wrote with which he was at all satisfied, its loss is
particularly unfortunate.

   While Lamb is an excellent critic of Wordsworth in his
early letters, he began, like Coleridge, to allow his
friendship to affect the expression of his real opinions.
The views recorded in Crabb Robinson's 'Diary' are much
more frank and rather sharper than those communicated to
Wordsworth himself.   Hazlitt was aware of Lamb's predicament in giving public expression to his views of Wordsworth's poetry:   'Hazlitt said ... that if Lamb in his
criticism had found but one fault with Wordsworth, he
would never have forgiven him.   But some truth there is
in the extravagant statement' (Lucas, 'Life', I, 354).
Unlike Hazlitt, however, Lamb in the review keeps his reservations to himself.   Such reservations as he did express in private led to an estrangement from De Quincey.
According to Richard Woodhouse, De Quincey was aware of
Lamb's admiration for Wordsworth's poetry and

   was induced to mention that poet's name, and to speak
   of him in high terms.   Lamb gave him praise, but
   rather more qualified than the Opium-Eater expected,
   who spoke with much warmth on the subject, and complained that Lamb did not do Wordsworth justice;   upon

which Lamb, in his dry, facetious way, observed, "If we
are to talk in this strain, we ought to have said grace
before we began our conversation" (Blunden, 'Charles
Lamb:  His Life Recorded by his Contemporaries', pp.
99-100).

---

THE volume before us, as we learn from the Preface, is 'a
detached portion of an unfinished poem, containing views
of man, nature, and society;'  to be called the Recluse,
as having for its principal subject the 'sensations and
opinions of a poet living in retirement;'  and to be preceded by a 'record in verse of the origin and progress of
the author's own powers, with reference to the fitness
which they may be supposed to have conferred for the
task.'  To the completion of this plan we look forward
with a confidence which the execution of the finished part
is well calculated to inspire. - Meanwhile, in what is
before us there is ample matter for entertainment:  for
the 'Excursion' is not a branch (as might have been suspected) prematurely plucked from the parent tree to gratify an overhasty appetite for applause;  but is, in itself,
a complete and legitimate production.

It opens with the meeting of the poet with an aged man
whom he had known from his school days;  in plain words, a
Scottish pedlar;  a man who, though of low origin, had received good learning and impressions of the strictest
piety from his stepfather, a minister and village schoolmaster.  Among the hills of Athol, the child is described
to have become familiar with the appearances of nature in
his occupation as a feeder of sheep;  and from her silent
influences to have derived a character, meditative,
tender, and poetical.  With an imagination and feelings
thus nourished - his intellect not unaided by books, but
those, few, and chiefly of a religious cast - the necessity of seeking a maintenance in riper years, had induced
him to make choice of a profession, the *appellation* for
which has been gradually declining into contempt, but
which formerly designated a class of men, who, journeying
in country places, when roads presented less facilities
for travelling, and the intercourse between towns and
villages was unfrequent and hazardous, became a sort of
link of neighbourhood to distant habitations;  resembling,
in some small measure, in the effects of their periodical
returns, the caravan which Thomson so feelingly describes
as blessing the cheerless Siberian in its annual visitation, with 'news of human kind.' (47)

In the solitude incident to this rambling life, power
had been given him to keep alive that devotedness to
nature which he had imbibed in his childhood, together

with the opportunity of gaining such notices of persons
and things from his intercourse with society, as qualified
him to become a 'teacher of moral wisdom.'  With this
man, then, in a hale old age, released from the burthen of
his occupation, yet retaining much of its active habits,
the poet meets, and is by him introduced to a second character - a sceptic - one who had been partially roused from
an overwhelming desolation, brought upon him by the loss
of wife and children, by the powerful incitement of hope
which the French Revolution in its commencement put forth,
but who, disgusted with the failure of all its promises,
had fallen back into a laxity of faith and conduct which
induced at length a total despondence as to the dignity
and final destination of his species.   In the language of
the poet, he

    ——broke faith with those whom he had laid
In earth's dark chambers.

Yet he describes himself as subject to compunctious
visitations from that silent quarter.

.  ——Feebly must they have felt,
  Who, in old time, attired with snakes and whips
  The vengeful Furies.   Beautiful regards
  Were turned on me - the face of her I loved;
  The wife and mother;  pitifully fixing
  Tender reproaches, insupportable! - p. 133.

The conversations with this person, in which the Wanderer asserts the consolatory side of the question against
the darker views of human life maintained by his friend,
and finally calls to his assistance the experience of a
village priest, the third, or rather fourth interlocutor,
(for the poet himself is one,) form the groundwork of the
'Excursion.'
It will be seen by this sketch that the poem is of a
didactic nature, and not a fable or story;  yet it is not
wanting in stories of the most interesting kind, - such as
the lovers of Cowper and Goldsmith will recognise as something familiar and congenial to them.   We might instance
the Ruined Cottage, and the Solitary's own story, in the
first half of the work;  and the second half, as being
almost a continued cluster of narration.   But the pre-
vailing charm of the poem is, perhaps, that, conversational as it is in its plan, the dialogue throughout is
carried on in the very heart of the most romantic scenery
which the poet's native hills could supply;  and which, by
the perpetual references made to it either in the way of

illustration or for variety and pleasurable description's
sake, is brought before us as we read.   We breathe in the
fresh air, as we do while reading Walton's Complete
Angler;   only the country about us is as much bolder than
Walton's, as the thoughts and speculations, which form the
matter of the poem, exceed the trifling pastime and low-
pitched conversation of his humble fishermen.   We give
the description of the 'two huge peaks,' which from some
other vale peered into that in which the Solitary is entertaining the poet and companion.   [Lamb quotes II, 694-
724.]

To a mind constituted like that of Mr. Wordsworth, the
stream, the torrent, and the stirring leaf - seem not
merely to suggest associations of deity, but to be a kind
of speaking communication with it.   He walks through
every forest, as through some Dodona;   and every bird that
flits among the leaves, like that miraculous one* in
Tasso, but in language more intelligent, reveals to him
far higher love-lays.   In his poetry nothing in Nature is
dead.   Motion is synonymous with life.   [Lamb quotes I,
484-90.]

To such a mind, we say - call it strength or weakness -
if weakness, assuredly a fortunate one - the visible and
audible things of creation present, not dim symbols, or
curious emblems, which they have done at all times to
those who have been gifted with the poetical faculty;   but
revelations and quick insights into the life within us,
the pledge of immortality.   [Lamb quotes IV, 1170-4;
1132-47.]

Sometimes this harmony is imaged to us by an echo;   and
in one instance, it is with such transcendant beauty set
forth by a shadow and its corresponding substance, that it
would be a sin to cheat our readers at once of so happy an
illustration of the poet's system, and so fair a proof of
his descriptive powers.   [Lamb quotes IX, 437-51.]

Combinations, it is confessed, 'like those reflected in
that quiet pool,' cannot be lasting:   it is enough for the
purpose of the poet, if they are felt. - They are at least
his system;   and his readers, if they reject them for
their creed, may receive them merely as poetry.   In him,
*faith*, in friendly alliance and conjunction with the religion of his country, appears to have grown up, fostered by
meditation and lonely communions with Nature - an internal
principle of lofty consciousness, which stamps upon his
opinions and sentiments (we were almost going to say) the
character of an expanded and generous Quakerism.

From such a creed we should expect unusual results;

*[Lamb quotes from Fairfax's translation, XVI, xii.]

and, when applied to the purposes of consolation, more touching considerations than from the mouth of common teachers. The finest speculation of this sort perhaps in the poem before us, is the notion of the thoughts which may sustain the spirit, while they crush the frame of the sufferer, who from loss of objects of love by death, is commonly supposed to pine away under a broken heart. [Lamb quotes IV, 165-85; 1058-77.] This is high poetry; though (as we have ventured to lay the basis of the author's sentiments in a sort of liberal Quakerism) from some parts of it, others may, with more plausibility, object to the appearance of a kind of Natural Methodism: we could have wished therefore that the tale of Margaret had been postponed, till the reader had been strengthened by some previous acquaintance with the author's theory, and not placed in the front of the poem, with a kind of ominous aspect, beautifully tender as it is. It is a tale of a cottage, and its female tenant, gradually decaying together, while she expected the return of one whom poverty and not unkindness had driven from her arms. We trust ourselves only with the conclusion. [Lamb quotes I, 872-916.]

The fourth book, entitled 'Despondency Corrected,' we consider as the most valuable portion of the poem. For moral grandeur; for wide scope of thought and a long train of lofty imagery; for tender personal appeals; and a *versification* which we feel we ought to notice, but feel it also so involved in the poetry, that we can hardly mention it as a distinct excellence; it stands without competition among our didactic and descriptive verse. The general tendency of the argument (which we might almost affirm to be the leading moral of the poem) is to abate the pride of the calculating *understanding*, and to reinstate the *imagination* and the *affections* in those seats from which modern philosophy has laboured but too successfully to expel them. [Lamb quotes IV, 611-21.]

In the same spirit, those illusions of the imaginative faculty to which the peasantry in solitary districts are peculiarly subject, are represented as the kindly ministers of *conscience*. [Lamb quotes IV, 837-41.]

Reverting to more distant ages of the world, the operation of that same faculty in producing the several fictions of Chaldean, Persian, and Grecian idolatry, is described with such seductive power, that the Solitary, in good earnest, seems alarmed at the tendency of his own argument. - Notwithstanding his fears, however, there is one thought so uncommonly fine, relative to the spirituality which lay hid beneath the gross material forms of Greek worship, in metal or stone, that we cannot resist

the allurement of transcribing it.    [Lamb quotes IV, 729-
62.]

In discourse like this the first day passes away. - The
second (for this almost dramatic poem takes up the action
of two summer days) is varied by the introduction of the
village priest; to whom the Wanderer resigns the office
of chief speaker, which had been yielded to his age and
experience on the first.   The conference is begun at the
gate of the church-yard;  and after some natural speculations concerning death and immortality - and the custom of
funereal and sepulchral observances, as deduced from a
feeling of immortality - certain doubts are proposed respecting the quantity of moral worth existing in the world,
and in that mountainous district in particular.   In the
resolution of these doubts, the priest enters upon a most
affecting and singular strain of narration, derived from
the graves around him.   Pointing to hillock after hillock, he gives short histories of their tenants, disclosing
their humble virtues, and touching with tender hand upon
their frailties.

Nothing can be conceived finer than the manner of introducing these tales.   With heaven above his head, and
the mouldering turf at his feet - standing betwixt life
and death - he seems to maintain that spiritual relation
which he bore to his living flock, in its undiminished
strength, even with their ashes;  and to be in his proper
cure, or diocese, among the dead.

We might extract powerful instances of pathos from
these tales - the story of Ellen in particular - but their
force is in combination, and in the circumstances under
which they are introduced.   The traditionary anecdote of
the Jacobite and Hanoverian, as less liable to suffer by
transplanting, and as affording an instance of that finer
species of humour, that thoughtful playfulness in which
the author more nearly perhaps than in any other quality
resembles Cowper, we shall lay (at least a part of it)
before our readers.   It is the story of a whig who,
having wasted a large estate in election contests, retired 'beneath a borrowed name' to a small town among
these northern mountains, where a Caledonian laird, a
follower of the house of Stuart, who had fled his country
after the overthrow at Culloden, returning with the return
of lenient times, had also fixed his residence.   [Lamb
quotes VI, 457-521.]

The causes which have prevented the poetry of Mr.
Wordsworth from attaining its full share of popularity are
to be found in the boldness and originality of his genius.
The times are past when a poet could securely follow the
direction of his own mind into whatever tracts it might

lead.   A writer, who would be popular, must timidly coast the shore of prescribed sentiment and sympathy.   He must have just as much more of the imaginative faculty than his readers, as will serve to keep their apprehensions from stagnating, but not so much as to alarm their jealousy. He must not think or feel too deeply.

If he has had the fortune to be bred in the midst of the most magnificent objects of creation, he must not have given away his heart to them; or if he have, he must conceal his love, or not carry his expressions of it beyond that point of rapture, which the occasional tourist thinks it not overstepping decorum to betray, or the limit which that gentlemanly spy upon Nature, the picturesque traveller, has vouchsafed to countenance.   He must do this, or be content to be thought an enthusiast.

If from living among simple mountaineers, from a daily intercourse with them, not upon the footing of a patron, but in the character of an equal, he has detected, or imagines that he has detected, through the cloudy medium of their unlettered discourse, thoughts and apprehensions not vulgar;   traits of patience and constancy, love un-wearied, and heroic endurance, not unfit (as he may judge) to be made the subject of verse, he will be deemed a man of perverted genius by the philanthropist who, conceiving of the peasantry of his country only as objects of a pec-uniary sympathy, starts at finding them elevated to a level of humanity with himself, having their own loves, enmities, cravings, aspirations, &c., as much beyond his faculty to believe, as his beneficence to supply.

If from a familiar observation of the ways of children, and much more from a retrospect of his own mind when a child, he has gathered more reverential notions of that state than fall to the lot of ordinary observers, and, escaping from the dissonant wranglings of men, has tuned his lyre, though but for occasional harmonies, to the milder utterance of that soft age, - his verses shall be censured as infantile by critics who confound poetry 'having children for its subject' with poetry that is 'childish,' and who, having themselves perhaps never been *children*, never having possessed the tenderness and docil-ity of that age, know not what the soul of a child is - how apprehensive! how imaginative! how religious!

We have touched upon some of the causes which we con-ceive to have been unfriendly to the author's former poems.   We think they do not apply in the same force to the one before us.   There is in it more of uniform ele-vation, a wider scope of subject, less of manner, and it contains none of those starts and imperfect shapings which in some of this author's smaller pieces offended the weak,

and gave scandal to the perverse.   It must indeed be approached with seriousness.   It has in it much of that
quality which 'draws the devout, deterring the profane.'
Those who hate the Paradise Lost will not love this poem.
The steps of the great master are discernible in it;   not
in direct imitation or injurious parody, but in the following of the spirit, in free homage and generous subjec-
tion.

One objection it is impossible not to foresee.   It
will be asked, why put such eloquent discourse in the
mouth of a pedlar?   It might be answered that Mr. Wordsworth's plan required a character in humble life to be the
organ of his philosophy.   It was in harmony with the
system and scenery of his poem.   We read Piers Plowman's
Creed, and the lowness of the teacher seems to add a
simple dignity to the doctrine.   Besides, the poet has
bestowed an unusual share of education upon him.   Is it
too much to suppose that the author, at some early period
of his life, may himself have known such a person, a man
endowed with sentiments above his situation, another
Burns;   and that the dignified strains which he has attributed to the Wanderer may be no more than recollections of
his conversation, heightened only by the amplification
natural to poetry, or the lustre which imagination flings
back upon the objects and companions of our youth?   After
all, if there should be found readers willing to admire
the poem, who yet feel scandalized at a *name*, we would
advise them, wherever it occurs, to substitute silently
the word *Palmer*, or *Pilgrim*, or any less offensive desig-
nation, which shall connect the notion of sobriety in
heart and manners with the experience and privileges which
a wayfaring life confers.

---

(ii) 1801

---

From a letter to Wordsworth, 30 January.

---

Thanks for your Letter and Present. (48) - I had already borrowed your second volume -.   What most please me
are, the Song of Lucy . . . . *Simon's sickly daughter* in
the Sexton made me *cry*. - Next to these are the description of the continuous Echoes in the story of Joanna's
laugh, where the mountains and all the scenery absolutely
seem alive - and that fine Shaksperian character of the
Happy Man, in the Brothers,

that creeps about the fields,

> Following his fancies by the hour, to bring
> Tears down his cheek, or solitary smiles
> Into his face, until the Setting Sun
> Write Fool upon his forehead. - (49)

I will mention one more:  the delicate and curious feeling
in the wish for the Cumberland Beggar, that he may ha[ve]
about him the melody of Birds, altho' he hear them not. -
Here the mind knowingly passes a fiction upon herself,
first substituting her own feelings for the Beggar's, and,
in the same breath detecting the fallacy, will not part
with the wish. - - The Poets Epitaph is disfigured, to my
taste by the vulgar satire upon parsons and lawyers in the
beginning, and the coarse epithet of pin point in the 6th
stanza. - All the rest is eminently good, and your own - .
I will just add that it appears to me a fault in the
Beggar, that the instructions conveyed in it are too
direct and like a lecture:  they dont slide into the mind
of the reader, while he is imagining no such matter. - An
intelligent reader finds a sort of insult in being told,
I will teach you how to think upon this subject.  This
fault, if I am right, is in a ten thousandth worse degree
to be found in Sterne and many many novelists & modern
poets, who continually put a sign post up to shew where
you are to feel.  They set out with assuming their readers to be stupid.  Very different from Robinson Crusoe,
the Vicar of Wakefie[l]d, Roderick Random, and other
beautiful bare narratives. - There is implied an unwritten
compact between Author and reader;  I will tell you a
story, and I suppose you will understand it....  I could,
too, have wished that The Critical preface had appeared in
a separate treatise. - All its dogmas are true and just
and most of them new, *as* criticism. - But they associate
a *diminishing* idea with the Poems which follow, as having
been written for Experiments on the public taste, more
than having sprung (as they must have done) from living
and daily circumstances....  Separate from the pleasure
of your company, I dont mu[ch] care if I never see a mountain in my life. - I have passed all my days in London,
until I have formed as many and intense local attachments,
as any of you Mountaineers can have done with dead
nature....
  My attachments are all local, purely local - ....
Your sun & moon and skys and hills & lakes affect me no
more ... than as a gilded room with tapestry and tapers,
where I might live with handsome visible objects. - I consider the clouds above me but as a roof beautifully painted, but unable to satisfy the mind, and at last, like the
pictures of the apartment of a Connoisseur, unable to
afford him any longer a pleasure....

Thank you for Liking my Play!  ! - (50)

---

(iii) 1801

---

From a letter to Robert Lloyd, 7 February.

---

Wordsworth has published a second vol. Lyrical Balads. -
Most of them very good - but not so good as first vol. -

---

(iv) 1801

---

From a letter to Thomas Manning, 15 February.

---

   I had need be cautious henceforward what opinion I give
of the Lyrical Balads. -  All the north of England are in
a turmoil.   Cumberland and Westmorland have already declared a state of war. -  I lately received from Wordsw. a
copy of the second volume, accompanied by. an acknowledgment of having received from me many months since a copy
of a certain Tragedy, with excuses for not having made any
acknowledgment sooner, it being owing to an "almost insur-
mountable aversion from Letter writing." -  This letter I
answered in due form and time ... adding, unfortunately,
that no single piece had moved me so forcibly as the
Ancient Marinere, the Mad Mother, or the Lines at Tintern
Abbey.   The Post did not sleep a moment.   I received
almost instantaneously a long letter of four sweating
pages from my reluctant Letterwriter, the purport of which
was, that he was sorry his 2d vol. had not given me more
pleasure (Devil a hint did I give that it had *not pleased
me*) and "was compelled to wish that my range of Sensibility was more extended, being obliged to believe that I
should receive large influxes of happiness & happy
Thoughts" (I suppose from the L.B. -) With a deal of stuff
about a certain "Union of Tenderness & Imagination, which
in the sense he used Imag. was not the characteristic of
Shakesp. but which Milton possessed in a degree far exceeding other Poets:  which Union, as the highest species
of Poetry, and chiefly deserving that name, He was most
proud to aspire to" - then illustrating the said Union by
two quotations from his own 2d vol. (which I had been so
unfortunate as to miss) - . 1st Specimen - A father addresses his Son -

                    When thou

First cams't into the world, as it befalls
To new born Infants, thou didst sleep away
Two days: *And Blessings from thy father's tongue
Then fell upon thee.* (51)

The lines were thus undermark'd & then followed "This
Passage as combining in an extraordinary degree that union
of Imagination & Tenderness, which I am speaking of, I
consider as one of the Best I ever wrote." ——
    2d Specimen. - A Youth after years of absence revisits
his native place, and thinks (as most people do) that
there has been strange alteration in his absence - -

And that the rocks
And Everlasting Hills themselves were chang'd —— (52)

You see both these are good Poetry:  but after one has
been reading Shaksp. twenty of the best years of one's
life, to have a fellow start up, and prate about some unknown quality, which Shakspere possess'd in a degree inferior to Milton and somebody else!  ! - - This was not
to be *all* my castigation. - Coleridge, who had not written to me some months before, starts up from his bed of
sickness, to reprove me for my hardy presumption:  four
long pages, equally sweaty, and more tedious, came from
him:  assuring me, that, when the works of a man of true
Genius, such as W. undoubtedly was, do not please me at
first sight, I should suspect the fault to lie "in me &
not in them" - &c. &c. &c. &c. &c. —— What am I to do
with such people? - I certainly shall write them a very
merry Letter. -. -. ——
    Writing to *you*, I (must) may say, that the 2d vol. has
no such pieces as the 3 I enumerated. - It is full of
original thinking and an observing mind, but it does not
often make you laugh or cry. - It too artfully aims at
simplicity of expression.  And you sometimes doubt if
simplicity be not a cover for Poverty.  The best Piece in
it I will send you, being *short* - I have grievously offended my friends in the North by declaring my undue preference.  But I need not fear you - [Lamb quotes 'She
dwelt among the untrodden ways'.]  This is choice and
genuine, and so are many many more.  But one does not
like to have 'em ramm'd down one's throat - "Pray take it
- its very good - let me help you - eat faster." -. -.

## (v) 1801

From a letter to Thomas Manning, 27? February.

So, you dont think there's a Word's-worth of good
Poetry in the Great L.B.! (53) - I dare'nt put the dreaded
Syllables at their just length, for my *Arse tickles red*
from the northern castigation - . I send you the Three
Letters, which I beg you to return along with those former
Letters (which I hope you are not going to print, by your
detention) - ....
By my new plan I shall be as airy, up 4 pair of stairs, as
in the country; & in a garden in the midst of enchanting
more than Mahometan paradise London, whose dirtiest drab-
frequented alley, and her lowest bowing Tradesman, I would
not exchange for Skiddaw, Helvellyin, James, Walter, and
the Parson in the bargain ———. O! her Lamps of a night!
her rich goldsmiths, print shops, toy shops, mercers,
hardwaremen, pastry cooks! - St. Paul's ch. yard, the
Strand! Exeter Change! - Charing Cross, with the man *upon*
a black horse! ——— These are thy Gods O London ———.
A'nt you mightily moped in the banks of the Cam.? ——— had
not you better come and set up here? - You ca'nt think
what a difference. All the streets and pavements are
pure gold, I warrant you. - At least I know an Alchymy
that turns her mud into that metal - a mind that loves to
be at home in Crowds ——— ....
Between you & me the L. Balads are but *drowsy performances.* -

## (vi) 1808

From a letter to Thomas Manning, 26 February.

Wordsworth the great poet is coming to town. He is to
have apartments in the Mansion House. He says he does
not see much difficulty in writing like Shakspeare, if he
had a mind to try it. It is clear then nothing is wanting but the mind. Even Coleridge a little checked at
this hardihood of assertion.

## (vii) 1809

From a letter to Coleridge, 30 October.

I believe I exprest my admiration of the Pamphlet. (54)
Its power over me was like that which Milton's pamphlets
must have had on his contemporaries who were tuned to
them. What a piece of prose. Do you hear if it is read
at all? I am out of the world [o]f readers. I hate all
that do read, for they read nothing but reviews & new
books. I gather myse[lf] up unto the old things.

## (viii) 1811

From Crabb Robinson's 'Diary', 8 January.

We spoke of Wordsworth and Coleridge. Lamb, to my
surprise, asserted Coleridge to be the greater man. He
preferred the *Mariner* to anything Wordsworth had written.
Wordsworth, he thought, is narrow and confined in his
views compared with [Coleridge]. He does not, like
Shakespeare, become everything he pleases, but forces the
reader to submit to his individual feelings. This, I
observed, lies very much in the lyrical character, and
Lamb concluded by expressing high admiration of Wordsworth. He had read many of his things with great pleasure indeed, especially the sonnets, which I had before
spoken of as my favourites. Lamb also spoke in high
praise of *Hart-leap Well* as one of Wordsworth's most exquisite pieces, but did not think highly of the *Leech-
gatherer*.

## (ix) 1812

From Crabb Robinson's 'Diary', 6 June.

With Charles Lamb. Lent him *Peter Bell*. To my surprise
he finds nothing in it good. He complains of the slowness of the narrative, as if that were not the *art* of the
poet. Wordsworth says he, has great thoughts, but *here*
are none of them. He has no interest in the ass. These
are to me inconceivable judgments from Charles Lamb, whose
taste in general I acquiesce in, and who is certainly an
enthusiast for Wordsworth.

(x) 1814

From a letter to Wordsworth, 9 August.

It is the noblest conversational poem I ever read.   A day
in heaven.   The part (or rather main body) which has left
the sweetest odour on my memory (a bad term for the remains of an impression so recent) is the Tales of the
Church yard. (55)   The only girl among seven brethren
born out of due time and not duly taken away again - the
deaf man and the blind man - the Jacobite and the Hanoverian whom antipathies reconcile - the Scarron-entry of the
rusticating parson upon his solitude - these were all new
to me too.   My having known the story of Margaret (at the
beginning) a very old acquaintance even as long back as I
saw you first at Stowey, did not make her reappearance
less fresh -.   I dont know what to pick out of this Best
of Books upon the best subjects for partial naming -
   that gorgeous Sunset is famous, (56) I think it must
have been the identical one we saw on Salisbury plain five
years ago, that drew Phillips from the card table where he
had sat from rise of that luminary to its unequall'd set,
but neither he nor I had gifted eyes to see those symbols
of common things glorified such as the prophets saw them,
in that sunset - the wheel - the potters clay - the wash-
pot - the winepress - the almond tree rod - the baskets of
figs - the fourfold visaged fo[u]r - the throne & him that
sat thereon....
   There is a deal of noble matter about mountain scenery,
yet not so much as to overpower & discountenance a poor
Londoner or Southcountry man entirely, though Mary seems
to have felt it occasionally a little too powerfully, for
it was her remark during reading it that by your system it
was doubtful whether a Liver in Towns had a Soul to be
Saved.   She almost trembled for that invisible part of us
in her.

(xi) 1814

From a letter to Wordsworth, 19 September.

   The unlucky reason of the detention of Excursion was,
Hazlit & we having a misunderstanding.   He blowed us up
about 6 months ago, since which the union hath snapt, but
M. Burney (57) borrowd it for him & after reiterated mes-

sages I only got it on friday.   His remarks had some
vigor in them, particularly something about an old ruin
being *too modern for your Primeval Nature, and about a
lichen*, but I forget the Passage, but the whole wore a
slovenly air of dispatch and disrespect.   That objection
which M Burney had imbibed from him about Voltaire, (58) I
explained to M.B. (or tried) exactly on your principle of
its being a characteristic speech.   That it was no settled comparative estimate of voltaire with any of his own
tribe of buffoons - no injustice, even if *you* spoke it,
for I dared say you never could relish Candide.   I know I
tried to get thro' it about a twelvemonth since &
could'nt for the Dullness.   Now I think I have a wider
range in buffoonery than you.   Too much toleration perhaps.

---

(xii) 1814

---

From Crabb Robinson's 'Diary', 21 November, and 19
December.

---

He loves in *The Excursion* the history of the Country
Parson who had been a courtier, more than any other.   In
this I agree with him.   But he dislikes the Magdalen,
which, he says, would be as good in prose, in which I do
not agree with him....
Flaxman took umbrage at some mystical expressions in the
fragment in the preface in which Wordsworth talks of
seeing *Jehovah* unalarmed.   'If my brother had written
that,' said Flaxman, 'I should say burn it.'   But he
admitted that Wordsworth could not mean anything impious
in it.   Indeed, I was unable, and am still, to explain
the passage.   And Lamb's explanation is unsatisfactory,
viz. that there are deeper sufferings in the mind of man
than in any imagined hell.   If Wordsworth means to say
that all notions of personality in God as well as locality
of hell are but attempts to individualise notions concerning the mind, he will be much more of a metaphysical
philosopher *nach Deutscher Art*, than I had any conception
of, and yet this otherwise glorious and magnificent fragment tends thitherwards as far as I can discern any tendency in it.

---

(xiii) 1815

---

From a letter to Wordsworth, 7 January.

---

    I told you my Review was a very imperfect one.  But
what you will see in the Quarterly is a spurious one which
Mr Baviad Gifford has palm'd upon it for mine.  I never
felt more vexd in my life than when I read it.  I cannot
give you an idea of what he has done to it out of spite at
me because he once sufferd me to be called a lunatic in
his Thing. (59)  The *language* he has altered throughout.
Whatever inadequateness it had to its subject, it was in
point of composition the prettiest piece of prose I ever
writ, & so my sister (to whom alone I read the MS) said.
That charm if it had any is all gone:  more than a third
of the substance is cut away & that not all from one
place, but *passim*, so as to make utter nonsense.  Every
warm expression is changed for a nasty cold one.

---

(xiv) 1819

---

From Crabb Robinson's 'Diary', 3, 11 May.

---

Wordsworth has set himself back ten years by the publication of this unfortunate work [*Peter Bell*]....
Lamb spoke of *Peter Bell*, which he considers as one of the
worst of Wordsworth's works.  The lyric narrative Lamb
has no taste for, he is disgusted by the introduction,
which he deems puerile, and the story he thinks ill told,
though he allows the idea to be good.

---

(xv) 1821

---

From Crabb Robinson's 'Diary', 19 December.

---

I went late to Lamb's....   read to Lamb some of Wordsworth's manuscripts;  he hardly seemed to relish them.

Although Lamb and Coleridge had both been at school together, corresponded frequently and at great length prior to
1798, and were friends until Coleridge's death in 1834,
Lamb never wrote on Coleridge at length.   In view of the
fact that he did write on Wordsworth, Keats and Hazlitt,
and, according to Crabb Robinson, considered Coleridge
greater than Wordsworth, this is perhaps surprising.   He
nowhere refers to the 'Biographia', although we know from
Miss Mitford's correspondence that he took the view that
as a result of its publication 'Mr. Wordsworth will never
speak to Mr. Coleridge again' (Blunden, 'Charles Lamb:
His Life Recorded by his Contemporaries', pp. 77-8).
Years after Lamb's death, J.F. Russell suggested that Lamb
preferred the poetry of Wordsworth:  'He had a very high
opinion of Wordsworth, saying, "He is a very noble
fellow."   I think he undervalued Coleridge's poetry.   He
esteemed the "Ancient Mariner" and "Christabel" his best
productions in verse' (Lucas, 'Life', II, 271).   Only a
very small selection of some of the more general comments
are here reproduced from the early correspondence with
Coleridge.

---

From a letter to Coleridge, 27 May.

---

   Your poems I shall procure forthwith.   There were
noble lines in what you inserted in one of your Numbers
from Religious musings, but I thought them elaborate. (60)
I am somewhat glad you have given up that Paper - it must

have been dry, unprofitable, & of "dissonant mood" (61) to
your disposition.    I wish you success in all your undertakings, & am glad to hear you are employed about the Evidences of Religion. (62)    There is need of multiplying
such books an hundred fold in this philosophical age to
*prevent* converts to Atheism, for they seem too tough dis-
putants to meddle with afterwards - ....
   Your conciones ad populum are the most eloquent politics that ever came in my way.

---

(ii) 1796

---

From a letter to Coleridge, 31 May.

---

   of your Watchman, the Review of Burke was the best
prose, (63) I augurd great things from the 1st number.
There is some exquisite poetry interspersed.   I have re-
read the extract from the Religious musings & retract
whatever invidious there was in my censure of it as elaborate.   There are times, when one is not in a disposition
thoroughly to relish good writing.   I have re-read it in
a more favorable moment & hesitate not to pronounce it
sublime.   If there be any thing in it approachg. to
tumidity (which I meant not to infer in elaborate (I meant
simply labord)) it is the Gigantic hyperbole by which you
describe the Evils of existing Society.   Snakes Lions
hyenas & behemoths is carrying your resentment beyond
bounds....   Wordsworth's poem I have hurried thro' not
without delight.... (64)    I have red all your Rel: Musings with uninterrupted feelings of profound admiration.
You may safely rest your fame on it.   The best remaing.
things are what I have before read, & they lose nothing by
my recollection of your manner of reciting 'em....   I
rather *wish* you had left the Monody on C. (65) concluding
as it did abruptly.   It had more of Unity. -   The conclusion of your R. Musings I fear will entitle you to the
reproof of your Beloved woman, who wisely will not suffer
your fancy to run riot, but bids you walk humbly with your
God....   of what is new to me among your poems next to
the Musings, that beginning "My pensive Sara" gave me most
pleasure: (66)   the lines in it I just alluded to are most
exquisite - they made my sister & self smile, as conveying
a pleasing picture of Mrs. C. checquing your wild wand-
rings, which we were so fond of hearing you indulge when
among us.   It has endeared us more than any thing to your
good Lady;   & your own self-reproof that follows delighted

us.   Tis a charming poem throughout (you have well re-
markd that "charming, admirable, exquisite" are words expressive of feelings, more than conveying of ideas, else I
might plead very [w]ell want of room in my paper as
ex[c]use for generalizing.).   I want room to tell you how
we are charmed with your verses in the Manner of Spencer -
&c. &c. &c. &c &c
    I am glad you resume the Watchman - change the Name,
leave out all articles of News & whatever things are peculiar to News Papers, & confine yourself to Ethics, verse,
criticism, or rather do not confine yourself - .   [L]et
your plan be as diffuse as the Spectator, & I'll answer
for it the work prospers.

---

(iii) 1796

---

From a letter to Coleridge, 29 June.

---

I am not sorry to find you (for all Sara) immersed in
clouds of smoke & metaphysic.   You know I had a sneaking
kindness for this last noble science, & you taught me some
smattering of it.   I look to become no mean proficient
under your tuition.

---

(iv) 1796

---

From a letter to Coleridge, 24 October.   On 22 September
Mary Lamb, in a fit of insanity, killed her mother and
wounded her father.   Coleridge's letters of condolence
were treasured by Lamb.

---

Coleridge,
    I feel myself much your debtor for that spirit of con-
fidence and friendship which dictated your last letter.
May your soul find peace at last in your cottage life!
I only wish you were *but* settled.   Do continue to write
to me.   I read your letters with my sister, and they give
us both abundance of delight.   Especially they please us
two, when you talk in a religious strain, - not but we are
offended occasionally with a certain freedom of expression, a certain air of mysticism, more consonant to the
conceits of pagan philosophy, than consistent with the
humility of genuine piety.   To instance now in your last

letter - you say, 'it is by the press, that God hath given
finite spirits both evil and good (I suppose you mean
*simply* bad men and good men) a portion as it were of His
Omnipresence!'   Now, high as the human intellect comparatively will soar, and wide as its influence, malign or
salutary, can extend, is there not, Coleridge, a distance
between the Divine Mind and it, which makes such language
blasphemy?   Again, in your first fine consolatory epistle
you say, 'you are a temporary sharer in human misery, that
you may be an eternal partaker of the Divine Nature.'
What more than this do those men say, who are for exalting
the man Christ Jesus into the second person of an unknown
Trinity, - men, whom you or I scruple not to call idola-
tors?   Man, full of imperfections, at best, and subject
to wants which momentarily remind him of dependence;   man,
a weak and ignorant being, 'servile' from his birth 'to
all the skiey influences,' (67) with eyes sometimes open
to discern the right path, but a head generally too dizzy
to pursue it;   man, in the pride of speculation, forgetting his nature, and hailing in himself the future God,
must make the angels laugh.   Be not angry with me, Coleridge;   I wish not to cavil;   I know I cannot *instruct*
you;   I only wish to *remind* you of that humility which
best becometh the Christian character.   God, in the New
Testament (*our best guide*), is represented to us in the
kind, condescending, amiable, familiar light of a *parent:*
and in my poor mind 'tis best for us so to consider of
Him, as our *heavenly* Father, and our *best Friend*, without
indulging too bold conceptions of His nature.   Let us
learn to think humbly of ourselves, and rejoice in the
appellation of 'dear children,' 'brethren,' and 'co-heirs
with Christ of the promises,' seeking to know no further.

---

(v)  1796

---

From a letter to Coleridge, 28 October.

---

My dear Friend,
   I am not ignorant that to be a partaker of the Divine
Nature is a phrase to be met with in Scripture:  I am only
apprehensive, lest we in these latter days, tinctured
(some of us perhaps pretty deeply) with mystical notions
and the pride of metaphysics, might be apt to affix to
such phrases a meaning, which the primitive users of them,
the simple fishermen of Galilee for instance, never intended to convey.   With that other part of your apology I am

not quite so well satisfied.    You seem to me to have been
straining your comparing faculties to bring together
things infinitely distant and unlike;   the feeble narrow-
sphered operations of the human intellect and the everywhere diffused mind of Deity, the peerless wisdom of
Jehovah.    Even the expression appears to me inaccurate -
portion of omnipresence - omnipresence is an attribute
whose very essence is unlimitedness.    How can omnipresence be affirmed of anything in part?    But enough of
this spirit of disputatiousness.    Let us attend to the
proper business of human life, and talk a little together
respecting our domestic concerns.

---

(vi) 1796

---

From a letter to Coleridge, 8 November.

---

I love them (68) as I love the Confessions of Rousseau,
and for the same reason:   the same frankness, the same
openness of heart, the same disclosure of all the most
hidden and delicate affections of the mind....
    Cultivate simplicity, Coleridge, or rather, I should
say, banish elaborateness;   for simplicity springs spon-
taneous from the heart, and carries into daylight its own
modest buds and genuine, sweet, and clear flowers of expression.    I allow no hot-beds in the gardens of Parnas-
sus.

---

(vii) 1796

---

From a letter to Coleridge, 1 December.

---

I have seen your last very beautiful poem in the Monthly
Magazine (69) - write thus, & you most generally have
written thus, & I shall never quarrel with you about simplicity - .

---

## (viii) 1796

From a letter to Coleridge, 10 December.

The music of poesy may charm for a while the importunate
teasing cares of life;  but the teased and troubled man is
not in a disposition to make that music....
Not a soul loves Bowles here;  scarce one has heard of
Burns;  few but laugh at me for reading my Testament -
they talk a language I understand not:  I conceal sentiments that would be a puzzle to them.   I can only converse with you by letter and with the dead in their
books....   In our little range of duties and connexions,
how few sentiments can take place, without friends, with
few books, with a taste for religion rather than a strong
religious habit!   We need some support, some leading-
strings to cheer and direct us.

## (ix) 1797

From a letter to Coleridge, 7 January.

Coleridge, I want you to write an Epic poem.   Nothing
short of it can satisfy the vast capacity of true poetic
genius.   Having one great End to direct all your poetical
faculties to, & on which to lay out your hopes, your ambition, will shew you to what you are equal.   By the sacred
energies of Milton, by the dainty sweet & soothing phan-
tasies of honey tongued Spencer, I adjure you to attempt
the Epic - .   Or do something, more ample, than the writing an occasional brief ode or sonnet....   You have
learning, you have fancy, you have enthusiasm - you have
strength & amplitude of wing enow for flights like those I
recommend ———

## (x) 1797

From a letter to Coleridge, 5 February.

Southey certainly has no pretensions to vie with you in
the Sublime of poetry, but he tells a plain tale better
than you....   I was reading your Religious Musings the

other day, & sincerely I think it the noblest poem in the
language, next after the Paradise lost, & even that was
not made the vehicle of such grand truths.   "There is one
Mind" &c down to "Almighty's Throne" are without a rival
in the whole compass of my poetical reading.... (70)   The
loftier walks of Pindus are your proper region.   There
you have no compeer, in modern tim[e]s.   Leave the low-
lands unenvied in possession of Such men as Cowper &
Southey....
     ... I have a dim recollection, that when in town you
were talking of the Origin of Evil as a most prolific subject for a Long Poem - why not adopt it, Coleridge? there
would be room for imagination.

(xi) 1797

From a letter to Coleridge, 13 June.

     Lloyd tells me that Sheridan put you upon writing your
tragedy. (71)   I hope you are only Coleridgeizing when
you talk of finishing it in a few days.   Shakspeare was a
more modest man;   but you best know your own power.

(xii) 1798

From a letter to Coleridge, 28 January.

     You have writ me Many kind letters, and I have answered
none of them - .  I do'nt deserve your attentions - an unnatural indifference has been creeping on me, since my
last misfortunes, or I should have seized the first opening of a correspondence with *you* - to you I owe much,
under God - in my brief acquaintance with you in London
your conversations won me to the better cause, and res-
cued me from the polluting spirit of the world - .   I
might have been a worthless character without you - as it
is, I do possess a certain improveable portion of devotional feelings - tho' when I view myself in the light of
divine truth, and not according to the common measures of
human judgment, I am altogether corrupt & sinful - this is
no cant - I am very sincere - - - -

(xiii) 1798

---

From a letter to Southey, 8 November.

---

If you wrote that review in 'Crit. Rev.,' (72) I am sorry
you are so sparing of praise to the 'Ancient Marinere;' -
so far from calling it, as you do, with some wit, but more
severity, 'A Dutch Attempt,' &c., I call it a right English attempt, and a successful one, to dethrone German
sublimity.   You have selected a passage fertile in unmeaning miracles, but have passed by fifty passages as
miraculous as the miracles they celebrate.   I never so
deeply felt the pathetic as in that part,

> A spring of love gush'd from my heart,
> And I bless'd them unaware -

It stung me into high pleasure through sufferings.   Lloyd
does not like it;  his head is too metaphysical, and your
taste too correct;  at least I must allege something
against you both, to excuse my own dotage -

> So lonely 'twas, that God himself
> Scarce seemèd there to be! - &c., &c.

But you allow some elaborate beauties - you should have
extracted 'em.   'The Ancient Marinere' plays more tricks
with the mind than that last poem, which is yet one of the
finest written.   But I am getting too dogmatical.

---

(xiv) 1800

---

From a letter to Thomas Manning, 8 February.

---

    I cannot but smile at Lloyd's beginning to find out,
that Col. can tell lyes.... As long as Lloyd or I have
known Col. so long have we known him in the daily & hourly
habit of quizzing the world by lyes most unaccountable &
most disinterested fictions.... To sum up my inferences
from the above facts, I am determined to live a merry Life
in the midst of Sinners.   I try to consider all men as
such, and to pitch my expectations from human nature as
low as possible.   In this view, all unexpected virtues
are Godsends & beautiful exceptions.   Only let Young Love
beware, when he sets out in his progress thro' life, how
he forms erroneous conceptions of finding all Saints! - -

---

(xv) 1800

---

From a letter to Coleridge, 6 August.

---

I have had the Anthology, and like only one thing in
it, (73) *Lewti;* but of that the last stanza is detest-
able, the rest most exquisite! - the epithet *enviable*
would dash the finest poem.   For God's sake (I never was
more serious), don't make me ridiculous any more by term-
ing me gentle-hearted in print, or do it in better
verses. (74)   It did well enough five years ago when I
came to see you, and was moral coxcomb enough at the time
you wrote the lines, to feed upon such epithets; but, besides that, the meaning of gentle is equivocal at best,
and almost always means poor-spirited, the very quality of
gentleness is abhorrent to such vile trumpetings.   My
*sentiment* is long since vanished.   I hope my *virtues* have
done *sucking*.   I can scarce think but you meant it in
joke.

---

(xvi) 1800

---

From a letter to Coleridge, 14 August.

---

In the next edition of the Anthology ... please to blot
out *gentle hearted*, and substitute drunken dog, ragged-
head, seld-shaven, odd-ey'd, stuttering, or any other epithet which truly and properly belongs to the Gentleman in
question.   And for Charles read Tom, or Bob, or Richard,
*for more delicacy.* - Damn you, I was beginning to forgive
you, & believe in earnest that the lugging in of my Proper
name was purely unintentional on your part, when looking
back for further conviction, stares me in the face
Charles Lamb of the *India House.   Now* I am convinced it
was all done in Malice, heaped, sack-upon-sack, congrega-
ted, studied Malice.   You Dog! - you[r] 141st Page shall
not save you.   I own I was just ready to acknowledge that
there is a something not unlike good poetry in that Page,
if you had not run into the unintelligible abstraction-fit
about the manner of the Deity's making Spirits perceive
his presence. (75)   God, nor created thing alive, can receive any honor from such thin, shew-box, attributes. ....
Now I do affirm, that Lewti is a very beautiful Poem.   I
*was* in earnest when I praised it.   It describes a silly
species of one not the wisest of passions.   *Therefore* it

cannot deeply affect a disenthralled mind. .   But such
imagery, such novelty, such delicacy, & such versification, never got into an Anthology before.   I am only
sorry that the cause of all the passionate complaint is
not greater, than the trifling circumstance of Lewti being
out of temper one day; . . . . .

----

(xvii) 1801

----

From a letter to Wordsworth, 30 January.

----

I am sorry that Coleridge has christened his Ancient Marinere "a poet's Reverie" (76) - it is as bad as Bottom the
Weaver's declaration that he is not a Lion but only the
scenical representation of a Lion.   What new idea is
gained by this Title, but one subversive of all credit,
which the Tale should force upon us, of its truth? - For
me, I was never so affected with any human Tale.   After
first reading it, I was totally possessed with it for many
days. - I dislike all the miraculous part of it, but the
feelings of the man under the operation of such scenery
dragged me along like Tom Piper's magic Whistle. - I totally differ from your idea that the Marinere should have
had a character and profession. - This is a Beauty in
Gulliver's Travels, where the mind is kept in a placid
state of little wonderments;  but the Ancient Marinere
undergoes such Trials, as overwhelm and bury all individuality or memory of what he was. - Like the state of a man
in a Bad dream, one terrible peculiarity of which is, that
all consciousness of personality is gone. - Your other observation is I think as well a little unfounded:  the Marinere from being conversant in supernatural events *has*
acquired a supernatural and strange cast of *phrase*, eye,
appearance &c. which frighten the wedding guest. - You
will excuse my remarks, because I am hurt and vexed that
you should think it necessary, with a prose apology, to
open they eyes of dead men that cannot see - - - .   To
sum up a general opinion of the second vol. - I do not
feel any one poem in it so forcibly as the Ancient Marinere, the Mad mother, and the Lines at Tintern Abbey in
the first. - -

----

(xviii) 1802

From a letter to Coleridge, 8 September.

I feel that I shall remember your mountains to the last
day I live.   They haunt me perpetually.   I am like a
man who has been falling in Love unknown to himself, which
he finds out when he leaves the Lady.   I do not remember
any very strong impression while they were present, but
being gone their Mementoes are shelved in my brain - .


(xix) 1802

From a letter to Thomas Manning, 24 September.

I set out with Mary to Keswick, without giving Coleridge
any notice, for my time being precious did not admit of
it;  he received us with all the hospitality in the world,
and gave up his time to shew us all the wonders of the
country....   Such an impression I never received from
objects of sight before, nor do I suppose that I can ever
again.   Glorious creatures, fine old fellows, Skiddaw &c.
I never shall forget ye, how ye lay about that night, like
an intrenchment, gone to bed as it seemed for the night,
but promising that ye were to be seen in the morning....
In fine I have satisfied myself, that there is such a
thing as that, which tourists call *romantic*, which I very
much suspected before:  they make such a spluttering about
it, and toss their splendid epithets around them, till
they give as dim a light, as four oClock next morning the
Lamps do after an illumination....   But I am returned
... & you cannot conceive the degradation I felt at first,
from being accustommed to wander free as air among mountains, & bathe in rivers without being controuled by any
one, to come home & *work*:  I felt very *little*.   I had
been dreaming I was a very great man.   But that is going
off, & I find I shall conform in time to that state of
Life, to which it has pleased God to call me.   Besides,
after all, Fleet Street & the Strand are better places to
live in for good & all than among Skiddaw:  Still, I turn
back to those great places, where I wandered about, par-
ticipating in their greatness.   After all I could not
*live* in Skiddaw:  I could spend a year, two, three years,
among them, but I must have a prospect of seeing Fleet
Street at the End of that time:  or I should mope & pine
away, I know.   Still Skiddaw is a fine Creature.

(xx) 1802

---

From a letter to Coleridge, 23 October.

---

I read daily your political Essays. (77)   I was particularly pleased with Once a Jacobin:  tho' the argument is
obvious enough, the style was less swelling than your
things sometimes are, and it was plausible ad populum.

---

(xxi) 1808

---

From a letter of Mary Lamb to Sarah Hazlitt, with a post-
script by Lamb, 9 December.

---

There came this morning a printed Prospectus from S T
Coleridge Grasmere of a Weekly Paper to be called *The
Friend*.   A flaming Prospectus, I have no time to give the
heads of it.   To commence first Saturdy. in Jany.   There
came also Notice of a Turkey from Mr Clarkson, which I am
more sanguine in expecting the accomplishment of than I am
of Coleridge's prophecy.

---

(xxii) 1810

---

From a letter to Robert Lloyd, 1 January.

---

Coleridge's friend is occasionally sublime -.   What do
you think of that De[s]cription of Luther in his Study in
one of the earlier numbers? (78)   The worst is, he is always promising something which never comes, it is now 18th
Number, and continues introductory, the 17th (that stupid
long letter) (79) was nothing better than a Prospectus &
ought to have preceded the 1st Number.   But I rejoice
that it lives. -

---

(xxiii) 1810

---

From a letter to Thomas Manning, 2 January.

---

Coleridge is bringing out a paper in weekly numbers,
called the 'Friend,' which I would send, if I could....
It is chiefly intended to puff off Wordsworth's poetry;
but there are some noble things in it by the by.

---

(xxiv) 1816

---

From a letter to Wordsworth, 26 April.

---

Coleridge is printing Xtabel by Ld. Byron's recommendation
to Murray, (80) with what he calls a vision Kubla Khan -
which said vision he repeats so enchantingly that it ir-
radiates & brings heaven & Elysian bowers into my parlour
while he sings or says it, but there is an observation
Never tell thy dreams, and I am almost afraid that Kubla
Khan is an owl that wont bear day light, I fear lest it
should be discovered by the lantern of typography & clear
reducting to letters, no better than nonsense or no
sense....   He is at present under the medical care of a
Mr Gilman (Killman?) a Highgate Apothecary, (81) where he
plays at leaving off Laud - m. - I think his essentials
not touched, he is very bad, but then he wonderfully picks
up another day, and his face when he repeats his verses
hath its ancient glory, an Arch angel a little damaged. -
   ... Coleridge is absent but 4 miles, & the neighborhood
of such a man is as exciting as the presence of 50 ordinary Persons.   Tis enough to be within the whiff & wind
of his genius, for us not to possess our souls in quiet.
If I lived with him or the *Author of the Excursion*, I
should in a very little time lose my own identity, & be
dragged along in the current of other peoples thoughts,
hampered in a net.   How cool I sit in this office, with
no possible interruption further than what I may term
*material;*   there is not as much metaphysics in 36 of the
people here as there is in the first page of Lockes treatise on the Human understanding, or as much poetry as in
any ten lines of the Pleasure  of Hope or more natural
Beggars Petition. (82)

---

(xxv) 1816

From a letter to Wordsworth, 23 September.

Have you read the review of Coleridges character, person,
physiognomy &c. in the Examiner, (83) - his features even
to his *nose* - O horrible license beyond the old Comedy - .
He is himself gone to the sea side with his favorite Apothecary, having left for publication as I hear a prodigious mass of composition for a Sermon to the middling
ranks of people to persuade them they are not so distres-
sed as is commonly supposed.   Methinks he should recite
it to a congregation of Bilston Colliers, - the fate of
Cinna the Poet would instantaneously be his.   God bless
him, but certain that rogue-Examiner has beset him in most
unmannerly strains.   Yet there is a kind of respect
shines thro' the disrespect that to those who know the
rare compound (that is the subject of it) almost balances
the reproof, but then those who know him but partially or
at a distance are so extremely apt to drop the qualifying
part thro' their fingers.

(xxvi) 1816, 1817

From Crabb Robinson's 'Diary', 2 November, and 29 January.

   We talked of Hazlitt's late ferocious attack on Coleridge, which Lamb thought fair enough, between the parties;  but he was half angry with Martin Burney for as-
serting the praise was greater than the abuse.   Nobody,
said Lamb, will care about or understand the 'taking up
the deep pauses of conversation between seraphs and car-
dinals,' but the satire will be universally felt.   Such
an article is like saluting a man:  'Sir, you are the
greatest man I ever saw,' and then pulling him by the
nose....   The conversation was on Hazlitt's attack on
Coleridge and Wordsworth.   Lamb spoke strongly in apology
for Hazlitt and *at* me.   He represented the praise of
Coleridge as an ample set-off, and he thought both Coleridge and Wordsworth had deserved this at his [Hazlitt's]
hands.   At the same time he declared he had quarrelled
with Hazlitt about it.   He had sent the article against
Coleridge to Wordsworth, who had written about it without
feeling, and he [Lamb] appeared to have been much offended
with Coleridge for not noticing as it deserved what Lamb

had related to him about Hazlitt, viz. that when he sat
down to write a critique on *The Excursion* he actually
cried because he was disappointed, and could not praise it
as it deserved.   To which Coleridge gave no answer, but
by going on with the sentiment that *The Excursion* was a
falling-off.

---

(xxvii) 1824

---

From a letter to Bernard Barton, 23 January.

---

Coleridgs book is good part printed, but sticks a
little for *more copy*.   It bears an unsaleable Title.
Extracts from Bishop Leighton, but I am confident there
will be plenty of good notes in it. more of Bishop Coleridge than Leighton, I hope, for what is Leighton? (84)

---

(xxviii) 1834

---

Lamb's obituary of Coleridge was written in the album of a
Mr  Keymer, a London bookseller at the request of John
Forster.   Forster first published it in his memorial article on Lamb for the 'New Monthly Magazine', February
1835.   Coleridge had died on 25 July 1834.

---

When I heard of the death of Coleridge, it was without
grief.   It seemed to me that he long had been on the confines of the next world, - that he had a hunger for eternity.   I grieved then that I could not grieve.   But
since, I feel how great a part he was of me.   His great
and dear spirit haunts me.   I cannot think a thought, I
cannot make a criticism on men or books, without an ineffectual turning and reference to him.   He was the proof
and touchstone of all my cogitations.   He was a Grecian
(or in the first form) at Christ's Hospital, where I was
deputy Grecian;  and the same subordination and deference
to him I have preserved through a life-long acquaintance.
Great in his writings, he was greatest in his conversation.   In him was disproved that old maxim, that we
should allow every one his share of talk.   He would talk
from morn to dewy eve, nor cease till far midnight, yet
who ever would interrupt him, - who would obstruct that
continuous flow of converse, fetched from Helicon or Zion?

He had the tact of making the unintelligible seem plain.
Many who read the abstruser parts of his "Friend" would
complain that his works did not answer to his spoken
wisdom.   They were identical.   But he had a tone in oral
delivery, which seemed to convey sense to those who were
otherwise imperfect recipients.   He was my fifty years
old friend without a dissension.   Never saw I his likeness, nor probably the world can see again.   I seem to
love the house he died at more passionately than when he
lived.   I love the faithful Gilmans more than while they
exercised their virtues towards him living.   What was his
mansion is consecrated to me a chapel.

---

Lamb's Letter of Elia to Robert Southey was published in
the 'London Magazine', October 1823.   It arose out of an
allusion to the 'Essays' of Elia in one of Southey's many
reviews for the 'Quarterly', and was the culmination of a
series of incidents in connection with that periodical
over a period of twelve years.   Although Lamb regretted
publishing the letter almost immediately after its appearance, it was praised by Coleridge, Hazlitt and Crabb Robinson who wrote in his diary:   'Nothing that Lamb has ever
written has impressed me more strongly with the sweetness
of his disposition, the strength of his affections' (I,
298).   The Letter is here reproduced in a slightly abrid-
ged form.

---

    SIR, - You have done me an unfriendly office, without
perhaps much considering what you were doing.   You have
given an ill name to my poor Lucubrations.   In a recent
Paper on Infidelity, you usher in a conditional commendation of them with an exception;   which, preceding the en-
comium, and taking up nearly the same space with it, must
impress your readers with the notion, that the objection-
able parts in them are at least equal in quantity to the
pardonable.   The censure is in fact the criticism;   the
praise - a concession merely.   Exceptions usually follow,
to qualify praise or blame.   But there stands your reproof, in the very front of your notice, in ugly characters, like some bugbear, to frighten all good Christians
from purchasing.   Through you I am become an object of
suspicion to preceptors of youth, and fathers of families.
*"A book, which wants only a sounder religious feeling to
be as delightful as it is original."*   With no further explanation, what must your readers conjecture, but that my

little volume is some vehicle for heresy or infidelity?
The quotation, which you honour me by subjoining, oddly
enough, is of a character, which bespeaks a temperament in
the writer the very reverse of *that* your reproof goes to
insinuate.   Had you been taxing me with superstition, the
passage would have been pertinent to the censure.   Was it
worth your while to go so far out of your way to affront
the feelings of an old friend, and commit yourself by an
irrelevant quotation, for the pleasure of reflecting upon
a poor child, an exile at Genoa? (85)

I am at a loss what particular Essay you had in view
(if my poor ramblings amount to that appellation) when you
were in such a hurry to thrust in your objection, like bad
news, foremost. -   Perhaps the Paper on "Saying Graces"
was the obnoxious feature.   I have endeavoured there to
rescue a voluntary duty - good in place, but never, as I
remember, literally commanded - from the charge of an un-
decent formality.   Rightly taken, Sir, that Paper was not
against Graces, but Want of Grace;   not against the ceremony, but the carelessness and slovenliness so often observed in the performance of it.

Or was it *that* on the "New Year" - in which I have described the feelings of the merely natural man, on a consideration of the amazing change, which is supposable to
take place on our removal from this fleshly scene? - If
men would honestly confess their misgivings (which few men
will) there are times when the strongest Christians of us,
I believe, have reeled under questionings of such staggering obscurity.   I do not accuse you of this weakness.
There are some who tremblingly reach out shaking hands to
the guidance of Faith - Others who stoutly venture into
the dark (their Human Confidence their leader, whom they
mistake for Faith);   and, investing themselves beforehand
with Cherubic wings, as they fancy, find their new robes
as familiar, and fitting to their supposed growth and
stature in godliness, as the coat they left off yesterday
- Some whose hope totters upon crutches - Others who stalk
into futurity upon stilts.

The contemplation of a Spiritual World, - which, without the addition of a misgiving conscience, is enough to
shake some natures to their foundation - is smoothly got
over by others, who shall float over the black billows, in
their little boat of No-Distrust, as unconcernedly as over
a summer sea.   The difference is chiefly constitutional.

One man shall love his friends and his friends' faces;
and, under the uncertainty of conversing with them again,
in the same manner and familiar circumstances of sight,
speech, &c. as upon earth - in a moment of no irreverent
weakness - for a dream-while - no more - would be almost

content, for a reward of a life of virtue (if he could as-
cribe such acceptance to his lame performances), to take
up his portion with those he loved, and was made to love,
in this good world, which he knows - which was created so
lovely, beyond his deservings.    Another, embracing a more
exalted vision - so that he might receive indefinite ad-
ditaments of power, knowledge, beauty, glory, &c. - is
ready to forego the recognition of humbler individualities
of earth, and the old familiar faces.    The shapings of
our heavens are the modifications of our constitution;
and Mr. Feeble Mind, or Mr. Great Heart, is born in every
one of us.

Some (and such have been accounted the safest divines)
have shrunk from pronouncing upon the final state of any
man;   nor dare they pronounce the case of Judas to be desperate.    Others (with stronger optics), as plainly as
with the eye of flesh, shall behold a *given king* in bliss,
and a *given chamberlain* in torment;  (86) even to the eter-
nising of a cast of the eye in the latter, his own self-
mocked and good-humouredly-borne deformity on earth, but
supposed to aggravate the uncouth and hideous expression
of his pangs in the other place.    That one man can presume so far, and that another would with shuddering dis-
claim such confidences, is, I believe, an effect of the
nerves purely.

If in either of these Papers, or elsewhere, I have been
betrayed into some levities - not affronting the sanctuary, but glancing perhaps at some of the out-skirts and
extreme edges, the debateable land between the holy and
the profane regions - (for the admixture of man's inventions, twisting themselves with the name of religion itself, has artfully made it difficult to touch even the
alloy, without, in some men's estimation, soiling the fine
gold) - if I have sported within the purlieus of serious
matter - it was, I dare say, a humour - be not startled,
Sir - which I have unwittingly derived from yourself.
You have all your life been making a jest of the Devil.
Not of the scriptural meaning of that dark essence - personal or allegorical;  for the nature is no where plainly
delivered.    I acquit you of intentional irreverence.
But indeed you have made wonderfully free with, and been
mighty pleasant upon, the popular idea and attributes of
him.    A noble Lord, (87) your brother Visionary, has
scarcely taken greater liberties with the material keys,
and merely Catholic notion of St. Peter. - You have flat-
tered him in prose:  you have chanted him in goodly odes.
You have been his Jester;  Volunteer Laureat, and self-
elected Court Poet to Beëlzebub.

You have never ridiculed, I believe, what you thought

to be religion, but you are always girding at what some
pious, but perhaps mistaken folks, think to be so.   For
this reason I am sorry to hear, that you are engaged upon
a life of George Fox.   I know you will fall into the
error of intermixing some comic stuff with your seriousness.   The Quakers tremble at the subject in your hands.
The Methodists are shy of you, upon account of *their* founder. (88)   But, above all, our Popish brethren are most
in your debt.   The errors of that church have proved a
fruitful source to your scoffing vein.   Their Legend has
been a Golden one to you.   And here, your friends, Sir,
have noticed a noteable inconsistency.   To the imposing
rites, the solemn penances, devout austerities of that
communion;   the affecting though erring piety of their
hermits;   the silence and solitude of the Chartreux -
their crossings, their holy waters - their Virgin, and
their saints - to these, they say, you have been indebted
for the best feelings, and the richest imagery, of your
Epic poetry.   You have drawn copious drafts upon Loretto.
We thought at one time you were going post to Rome - but
that in the facetious commentaries, which it is your
custom to append so plentifully, and (some say) injudi-
ciously, to your loftiest performances in this kind, you
spurn the uplifted toe, which you but just now seemed to
court;   leave his holiness in the lurch;   and show him a
fair pair of Protestant heels under your Romish vestment.
When we think you already at the wicket, suddenly a violent cross wind blows you transverse -

                                   ten thousand leagues awry.
                          Then might we see
Cowls, hoods, and habits, with their wearers, tost
And flutter'd into rags;   then reliques, beads,
Indulgences, dispenses, pardons, bulls,
The sport of winds. (89)

You pick up pence by showing the hallowed bones, shrine,
and crucifix;   and you take money a second time by exposing the trick of them afterwards.   You carry your verse
to Castle Angelo for sale in a morning;   and, swifter than
a pedlar can transmute his pack, you are at Canterbury
with your prose ware before night.
     Sir, is it that I dislike you in this merry vein?   The
very reverse.   No countenance becomes an intelligent jest
better than your own.   It is your grave aspect, when you
look awful upon your poor friends, which I would depre-
cate.
     In more than one place, if I mistake not, you have been
pleased to compliment me at the expence of my companions.

I cannot accept your compliment at such a price.  The up-
braiding a man's poverty naturally makes him look about
him, to see whether he be so poor indeed as he is presumed
to be.  You have put me upon counting my riches.  [Lamb
briefly enumerates his various friends: Wordsworth, Coleridge, Crabb Robinson, Talfourd, Allan Cunningham, Barry
Cornwall and others.]

I will come to the point at once.  I believe you will
not make many exceptions to my associates so far.  But I
have purposely omitted some intimacies, which I do not yet
repent of having contracted, with two gentlemen, diamet-
rically opposed to yourself in principles.  You will
understand me to allude to the authors of Rimini and of
the Table Talk.  And first, of the former. ⁓ (90)

It is an error more particularly incident to persons of
the correctest principles and habits, to seclude themselves from the rest of mankind, as from another species;
and form into knots and clubs.  The best people, herding
thus exclusively, are in danger of contracting a narrowness.  Heat and cold, dryness and moisture, in the natural world, do not fly asunder, to split the globe into
sectarian parts and separations;  but mingling, as they
best may, correct the malignity of any single predomi-
nance.  The analogy holds, I suppose, in the moral world.
If all the good people were to ship themselves off to
Terra Incognitas, what, in humanity's name, is to become
of the refuse?  If the persons, whom I have chiefly in
view, have not pushed matters to this extremity yet, they
carry them as far as they can go.  Instead of mixing with
the infidel and the freethinker - in the room of opening a
negociation, to try at least to find out at which gate the
error entered - they huddle close together, in a weak fear
of infection, like that pusillanimous underling in
Spenser -

This is the wandering wood, this Error's den;
A monster vile, whom God and man does hate:
Therefore, I reed, beware.  Fly, fly, quoth then
The fearful Dwarf. (91)

and, if they be writers in orthodox journals - addressing
themselves only to the irritable passions of the unbelie-
ver - they proceed in a safe system of strengthening the
strong hands, and confirming the valiant knees;  of converting the already converted, and proselyting their own
party.  I am the more convinced of this from a passage in
the very Treatise which occasioned this letter....  And
... this ... I think, warrants me in concluding that, when
you sit down to pen theology, you do not at all consider

your opponents; but have in your eye, merely and exclusively, readers of the same way of thinking with yourself,
and therefore have no occasion to trouble yourself with
the quality of the logic, to which you treat them....

I own I could never think so considerably of myself as
to decline the society of an agreeable or worthy man upon
difference of opinion only.   The impediments and the fac-
ilitations to a sound belief are various and inscrutable
as the heart of man.   Some believe upon weak principles.
Others cannot feel the efficacy of the strongest.   One of
the most candid, most upright, and single-meaning men, I
ever knew, was the late Thomas Holcroft. (92)   I believe
he never said one thing and meant another, in his life;
and, as near as I can guess, he never acted otherwise than
with the most scrupulous attention to conscience.   Ought
we to wish the character false, for the sake of a hollow
compliment to Christianity?

Accident introduced me to the acquaintance of Mr. L.H.
- and the experience of his many friendly qualities confirmed a friendship between us.   You, who have been mis-
represented yourself, I should hope, have not lent an idle
ear to the calumnies which have been spread abroad respecting this gentleman.   I was admitted to his household for
some years, and do most solemnly aver that I believe him
to be in his domestic relations as correct as any man.
He chose an ill-judged subject for a poem;   the peccant
humours of which have been visited on him tenfold
by the artful use, which his adversaries have made, of an
*equivocal term*.   The subject itself was started by Dante,
but better because brieflier treated of.   But the crime
of the Lovers, in the Italian and the English poet, with
its aggravated enormity of circumstance, is not of a kind
(as the critics of the latter well knew) with those con-
junctions, for which Nature herself has provided no excuse, because no temptation. - It has nothing in common
with the black horrors, sung by Ford and Massinger.   The
familiarising of it in tale or fable may be for that
reason incidentally more contagious.   In spite of Rimini,
I must look upon its author as a man of taste, and a poet.
He is better than so, he is one of the most cordial-minded
men I ever knew, and matchless as a fire-side companion.
I mean not to affront or wound your feelings when I say
that, in his more genial moods, he has often reminded me
of you.   There is the same air of mild dogmatism - the
same condescending to a boyish sportiveness - in both your
conversations....   L.H. is unfortunate in holding some
loose and not very definite speculations (for at times I
think he hardly knows whither his premises would carry
him) on marriage - the tenets, I conceive, of the Politi-

cal Justice, carried a little further.  For any thing I
could discover in his practice, they have reference, like
those, to some future possible condition of society, and
not to the present times.  But neither for these obliquities of thinking (upon which my own conclusions are as
distant as the poles asunder) - nor for his political as-
perities and petulancies, which are wearing out with the
heats and vanities of youth - did I select him for a
friend;  but for qualities which fitted him for that
relation....

From the *other gentleman* I neither expect nor desire
(as he is well assured) any such concessions as L.H. made
to C. (93)  What hath soured him, and made him to suspect
his friends of infidelity towards him, when there was no
such matter, I know not.  I stood well with him for fifteen years (the proudest of my life), and have ever spoke
my full mind of him to some, to whom his panegyric must
naturally be least tasteful.  I never in thought swerved
from him, I never betrayed him, I never slackened in my
admiration of him, I was the same to him (neither better
nor worse),though he could not see it, as in the days when
he thought fit to trust me.  At this instant, he may be
preparing for me some compliment, above my deserts, as he
has sprinkled many such among his admirable books, for
which I rest his debtor;  or, for any thing I know, or can
guess to the contrary, he may be about to read a lecture
on my weaknesses.  He is welcome to them (as he was to my
humble hearth), if they can divert a spleen, or ventilate
a fit of sullenness.  I wish he would not quarrel with
the world at the rate he does;  but the reconciliation
must be effected by himself, and I despair of living to
see that day.  But, protesting against much that he has
written, and some things which he chooses to do;  judging
him by his conversation which I enjoyed so long, and relished so deeply;  or by his books, in those places where
no clouding passion intervenes - I should belie my own
conscience, if I said less, than that I think W.H. to be,
in his natural and healthy state, one of the wisest and
finest spirits breathing.  So far from being ashamed of
that intimacy, which was betwixt us, it is my boast that I
was able for so many years to have preserved it entire;
and I think I shall go to my grave without finding, or expecting to find, such another companion.  But I forget my
manners - you will pardon me, Sir - I return to the correspondence. -

Sir, you were pleased (you know where) to invite me to
a compliance with the wholesome forms and doctrines of the
Church of England.  I take your advice with as much kindness, as it was meant.  But I must think the invitation

rather more kind than seasonable. I am a Dissenter.
The last sect, with which you can remember me to have made
common profession, were the Unitarians. You would think
it not very pertinent, if (fearing that all was not well
with you), I were gravely to invite you (for a remedy) to
attend with me a course of Mr. Belsham's Lectures at Hackney. (94) Perhaps I have scruples to some of your forms
and doctrines. But if I come, am I secure of civil
treatment? - The last time I was in any of your places of
worship was on Easter Sunday last. I had the satisfaction of listening to a very sensible sermon of an argumentative turn, delivered with great propriety, by one of
your bishops. The place was Westminster Abbey. As such
religion, as I have, has always acted on me more by way of
sentiment than argumentative process, I was not unwilling,
after sermon ended, by no unbecoming transition, to pass
over to some serious feelings, impossible to be disconnected from the sight of those old tombs, &c. But, by whose
order I know not, I was debarred that privilege even for
so short a space as a few minutes; and turned, like a dog
or some profane person, out into the common street; with
feelings, which I could not help, but not very genial to
the day or the discourse. I do not know that I shall
ever venture myself again into one of your Churches....

---

(ii) 1796

---

From a letter to Coleridge, 8 June.

---

With Joan of Arc I have been delighted, amazed. (95)
I had not presumed to expect any thing of such excellence
from Southey. Why the poem is alone sufficient to redeem
the character of the age we live in from the imputation of
degenerating in Poetry, were there no such beings extant
as Burns & Bowles, Cowper & ———— fill up the blank how
you please, I say nothing. The subject is well chosen.
It opens well.... I am delighted with the very many passages of simple pathos abounding throughout the poem -
passages which the author of "Crazy Kate" might have written. (96) - Has not Master Southey spoke very slightingly
in his preface & disparagingly of Cowper's Homer? (97) -
what makes him reluctant to give Cowper his fame? And
does not Southey use too often the expletives "did" &
"does"? they have a good effect at times, but are too inconsiderable or rather become blemishes, when they mark a
style. On the whole, I expect Southey one day to rival

Milton.   I already deem him equal to Cowper, & superior
to all living Poets Besides. what says Coleridge?

---

(iii) 1796

---

From a letter to Coleridge, 13 June.

---

My second thoughts entirely coincide with your comments on
'Joan of Arc,' and I can only wonder at my childish judgment which over-looked the 1st book and could prefer the
9th:   not that I was insensible to the soberer beauties of
the former, but the latter caught me with its glare of
magic, - the former, however, left a more pleasing general
recollection in my mind.   Let me add, the 1st book was
the favourite of my sister....   I must not pass over
without acknowledging my obligations to your full and satisfactory account of personifications.   I have read it
again and ,again, and it will be a guide to my future
taste.   Perhaps I had estimated Southey's merits too much
by number, weight, and measure.   I now agree completely
and entirely in your opinion of the genius of Southey.

---

(iv) 1799

---

From a letter to Southey, 15 March.

---

I think you are too apt to conclude faintly, with some
cold moral, as in the end of the Poem calld "the Victory" (98) - "Be thou her comforter, who art the widow's
friend" - a single common place line of comfort, which
bears no proportion in weight or number to the many lines
which describe suffering - - .   This is to convert Religion into mediocre feelings, which should burn & glow &
tremble. - .   A Moral should be wrought into the body and
soul, the matter and tendency, of a Poem, not taggd to the
end, like "A God send the good ship into harbour" at the
conclusion of our bills of Lading. . . - - The finishing
of the "Sailor" is also imperfect.   Any dissenting minister may say & do as much -
    These remarks, I know, are crude & unwrought, but I do
not lay claim to much accurate thinking - I never judge
system-wise of things, but fasten upon particulars - - -.

(v) 1811

From Crabb Robinson's 'Diary', 8 January.

He had just read *The Curse of Kehama*. (99)   He liked it
better, he said, than any of Southey's long poems.   The
descriptions he deemed beautiful, particularly the finding
of Kailyal by Ereenia;   he liked the opening and part of
the description of hell, but, after all, he was not made
happier by reading the poem.   There is too much trick in
it.   The three statues and the vacant space for Kehama
resembles a pantomime scene and the love is very ill managed.   But Charles Lamb deems the poem infinitely superior to *Thalaba*.

(vi) 1815

From a letter to Southey, 6 May.

I have received from Longman a copy of Roderick with
the Authors Compts, for which I much thank you....   The
storey of the brave Maccabee was already, you may be sure,
familiar to me in all its parts.   I have since the receit
of your present read it quite through again, and with no
diminished pleasure.   I dont know whether I ought to say
that it has given me more pleasure than any of your long
poems.   Kehama is doubtless more powerful, but I dont
feel that firm footing in it that I do in Roderick, my
imagination goes sinking and floundering in the vast
spaces of unopened-before systems & faiths, I am put out
of the pale of my old sympathies, my moral sense i[s] almost outraged, I cant believe or with horror am made to
believe such desperate chances against omnipotence, such
disturbances of faith to the centre -.   The more potent
the more painful the spell -.   Jove and his brotherhood
of gods tottering with the giant assailings I can bear,
for the soul's hopes are not struck at in such contests,
but your Oriental Almighties are too much types of the in-
tangible prototype to be meddled with without shuddering -.   One never connects what are call'd The attributes
with Jupiter -.   I mention only what diminishes my delight at the wonderworkings of Kehama, not what impeaches
its power which I confess with trembling -
but Roderick is a comfortable poem -.   It reminds me
of the delight I took in the first reading of the Joan of

Arc -.    It is maturer & better than *that*, though not
better to me now than that was then.    It suits me better
than Madoc.    I am at home in Spain & Xtendom.    I have a
timid imagination I am afraid.    I do not willingly admit
of strange beliefs or out of the way creeds or places.    I
never read books of travels, at least not farther than
Paris, or Rome.    I can just endure Moors because of their
connection as foes with Xtians, but Abyssinians, Ethiops,
Esquumaux, Dervises & all that tribe I hate.    I believe I
fear them in some manner.    A Mahometan turban on the
stage, tho' enveloping some well known face (Mr. Cooke or
Mr Maddox whom I see another day good Christn. & English
waiters, innkeepers &c) does not give me pleasure unal-
loyed.    I am a Christian, Englishman, Londoner, *Templar* -
God help me when I come to put off these snug relations &
to get abroad into the world to come -.

31   Walter Savage Landor
     1799

From a letter to Southey, 31 October.

I have but just got your letter, being returned from
Herts, where I have passed a few red-letter days with much
pleasure.   I would describe the county to you, as you
have done by Devonshire, but alas! I am a poor pen at that
same.   I could tell you of an old house with a tapestry
bed-room, the 'judgment of Solomon' composing one pannel,
and 'Actaeon spying Diana naked' the other.   I could tell
of an old marble hall, with Hogarth's prints and the Roman
Caesars in marble hung round.   I could tell of a *wilderness*, and of a village church, and where the bones of my
honoured grandam lie;   but there are feelings which refuse
to be translated, sulky aborigines, which will not be nat-
uralized in another soil.   Of this nature are old family
faces and scenes of infancy.
    ... I have seen Gebor! (100)   Gebor aptly so denomina-
ted from Geborish, *quasi* Gibberish.   But Gebor hath some
lucid intervals.   I remember darkly one beautiful simile
veiled in uncouth phrases about the youngest daughter of
the Ark.

From a letter to Bernard Barton, 11 September.   In 'My
Friends and Acquaintance', P.G. Patmore noted that al‐
though Lamb liked Barton, he did not value him highly as a
poet:   'Bernard Barton was mentioned, and Lamb said that
he did not write nonsense, at any rate - which all the
rest of them did (meaning the Magazine poets of the day).
He was dull enough;  but not nonsensical.   "He writes
English, too," said Lamb, "which they do not."'   According to Thomas Westwood, Lamb's next door neighbour, Barton's presentation copies were among those thrown over the
garden wall.

You have misapprehended me sadly, if you suppose that I
meant to impute any inconsistency (in your writing poetry)
with you[r] religious profession. (101)   I do not remember what I said, but it was spoken sportively, I am sure.
One of my levities, which you are not so used to as my
older friends.   I probably was thinking of the light in
which your so indulging yourself would appear to *Quakers*,
and put their objection in my own foolish mouth.   I would
eat my words (provided they should be written on not very
coarse paper) rather than I would throw cold water upon
your, and my once, harmless occupation.   I have read
Napoleon and the rest with delight.   I like them for what
they are, and for what they are not.   I have sickened on
the modern rhodomontade & Byronism, and your plain Quakerish Beauty has captivated me.   It is all wholesome
cates, aye, and toothsome too, and withal Quakerish.   If
I were George Fox, and George Fox Licenser of the Press,
they should have my absolute Imprimatur.

33  Byron
    (i) 1820

From a letter to Joseph Cottle, 26 May.    T.N. Talfourd,
Lamb's first editor, observed that he

> could find nothing to revere or love in the poetry of
> that extraordinary but most uncomfortable poet;  except
> the apostrophe to Parnassus, in which he exults in the
> sight of the real mountain instead of the mere poetic
> image.   All the Laras, and Giaours, and Childe Har-
> olds, were to him but 'unreal mockeries,' - the phan-
> tasms of a feverish dream, - forms which did not appeal
> to the sympathies of mankind, and never can find root
> among them (Lucas, 'Life', II, 307).

J.F. Russell also recalled that Lamb once said that 'Byron
had written only one good-natured thing, and that was the
"Vision of Judgment"' (Ibid., II, 270).

It was quite a mistake that I could dislike anything
you should write against Ld Byron, for I have a thorough
aversion to his character, and a very moderate admiration
of his genius - he is great in so little a way - To be a
Poet is to be The Man, the whole Man - not a petty portion
of occasional low passion worked up into a permanent form
of Humanity.   Shakspeare has thrust such rubbishly feelings into a corner, the dark dusty heart of Don John in
the much Ado - The fact is - I have not yet seen your poem
to him.

## (ii) 1823

From Crabb Robinson's 'Diary', 8 January.

He reprobated the persecution of *The Vision of Judgment*,
by Lord Byron.    Southey's *Vision of Judgment* is more
worthy of punishment - for his is an arrogance beyond endurance.    Lord Byron's satire is one of the most good-
natured description - no malevolence!

## (iii) 1824

From a letter to Bernard Barton, 23 January.

Do you trouble yourself about Libel cases?    The Decision
against Hunt (102) for the "Vision of Judgment" made me
sick.    What is to become of the old talk about our good
old King - his personal virtues saving us from a revolution &c. &c.    Why, none that think it can utter it now.
It must stink.    And the Vision is really, as to-Him-ward
such a tolerant good humour'd thing.    What a wretched
thing a Lord Chief Justice is, always was, & will be! -

## (iv) 1824

From a letter to Bernard Barton, 15 May.

So we have lost another Poet.    I never much relished his
Lordship's mind, and shall be sorry if the Greeks have
cause to miss him.    He was to me offensive, and I never
can make out his great *power*, which his admirers talk of.
Why, a line of Wordsworths is a lever to lift the immortal
Spirit!    Byrons can only move the Spleen.    He was at
best a Satyrist - in any other way he was mean enough.    I
dare say I do him injustice, but I cannot love him, nor
squeeze a tear to his memory.    He did not like the world,
and he has left it, as Alderman Curtis advised the Radi-
cals, "if they dont like their country, damn 'em let 'em
leave it" - they possessing no rood of Ground in England,
and he 10000 acres. (103)    Byron was better than many
Curtises -

From a letter to Bernard Barton, 9 October.   According to
Talfourd,

> Shelley's poetry ... was icy cold to him;   except one
> or two of the minor poems, in which he could not help
> admiring the exquisite beauty of the expression;   and
> the 'Cenci,' in which, notwithstanding the painful
> nature of the subject, there is a warmth and passion,
> and a correspondent simplicity of diction, which prove
> how mighty a poet the author would have become had he
> lived long enough for his feelings to have free dis-
> course with his creative power.   Responding only to
> the touch of human affection, he could not bear poetry
> which, instead of making the whole world kin, renders
> our own passions and frailties and virtues strange to
> us;   presents them at distance in splendid masquerade;
> exalts them into new and unauthorized mythology, and
> crystallises all our freshest loves and mantling joys
> into clusters of radiant fancies (Lucas, 'Life', II,
> 307).

Lamb also liked 'Rosalind and Helen'.

> Shelly I saw once.   His voice was the most obnoxious
> squeak I ever was tormented with, ten thousand times worse
> than the Laureat's, who[se] voice is the worst part about
> him, except his Laureatcy.   Lord Byron opens upon him on
> Monday in a Parody (I suppose) of the Vision of Judgment,
> in which latter the Poet I think did not much show *his*.
> To award his Heaven and his Hell in the presumptuous
> manner he has done, was a piece of immodesty as bad as
> Shelleyism. -

(ii) 1824

---

From a letter to Bernard Barton, ?17 August.

---

I can no more understand Shelly than you can.   His
poetry is "thin sewn with profit or delight." (104)   Yet
I must point to your notice a sonnet conceiv'd and expressed with a witty delicacy.   It is that addressd to one
who hated him, but who could not persuade him to hate *him*
again. (105)   His coyness to the others passion (for hate
demands a return as much as Love, and starves without it)
is most arch and pleasant.   Pray, like it very much -
For his theories and nostrums they are oracular enough,
but I either comprehend 'em not or there is miching malice
and mischief in 'em....   But for the most part ringing
with their own emptiness.   Hazlitt said well of 'em -
Many are wiser and better for reading Shakspeare, but nobody was ever wiser or better for reading Sh——y (106)

35　John Clare
　　1822

---

---

　　I thank you heartily for your present... (107) I am an
inveterate old Londoner, but while I am among your choice
collections, I seem to be native to them, and free of the
country.　The quantity of your observation has astonished
me.　What have most pleased me have been Recollections
after a Ramble, and those Grongar Hill (108) kind of
pieces in eight syllable lines, my favourite measure, such
as Cowper Hill and Solitude.　In some of your story telling Ballads the provincial phrases sometimes startle me.
I think you are too profuse with them.　In poetry *slang*
of every kind is to be avoided.　There is a rustick
Cockneyism, as little pleasing as our's of London.
Transplant Arcadia to Helpstone.　The true rustic style,
the Arcadian English, I think is to be found in Shen-
stones.　Would his Schoolmistress, the prettiest of
poems, have been better, if he had used quite the Goody's
own language?　Now and then a home-rusticism is fresh and
startling, but where nothing is gained in expression, it
is out of tenor.　It may make folks smile and stare, but
the ungenial coalition of barbarous with refined phrases
will prevent you in the end from being so generally tas-
ted, as you deserve to be.　Excuse my freedom, and take
the same liberty with my *puns*.

---

Lamb reviewed the work of only two major contemporary
poets, Wordsworth and Keats.  His review of 'Lamia, Isabella, The Eve of Saint Agnes, and other poems' was published anonymously in the 'New Times', 19 July.  Two days
after its appearance, the newspaper printed further extracts from Keats's final volume of poems:  To Autumn, and
parts of To a Nightingale, and Hyperion.  E.V. Lucas has
suggested that these had been omitted from the original
article.  According to Crabb Robinson, Lamb considered
Keats the greatest of the contemporary poets after Wordsworth.  Thomas Hood recalled that in a conversation with
Wordsworth, Lamb had chosen Keats as the poet among the
younger generation most likely to endure, while Wordsworth
had chosen Shelley.  The review opens with a quotation of
four stanzas from The Eve of St. Agnes beginning 'A case-
ment high and triple-arch'd there was.'

---

Such is the description which Mr. Keats has given us,
with a delicacy worthy of Christabel, of a high-born damsel, in one of the apartments of an baronial castle, laying herself down devoutly to dream, on the charmed Eve of
St. Agnes;  and like the radiance, which comes from those
old windows upon the limbs and garments of the damsel, is
the almost Chaucer-like painting, with which this poet il-
lumes every subject he touches.  We have scarcely any
thing like it in modern description.  It brings us back
to ancient days, and

*Beauty making-beautiful old rhymes.* (109)

The finest thing in the volume is the paraphrase of
Boccacio's story of the Pot of Basil.  Two Florentines,
merchants, discovering that their sister Isabella has

placed her affections upon Lorenzo, a young factor in
their employ, when they had hopes of procuring for her a
noble match, decoy Lorenzo, under pretence of a ride, into
a wood, where they suddenly stab and bury him.   The anticipation of the assassination is wonderfully conceived in
one epithet, in the narration of the ride -

> So the two brothers, and their *murder'd* man,
>     Rode past fair Florence, to where Arno's stream
> Gurgles ——

Returning to their sister, they delude her with a story of
their having sent Lorenzo abroad to look after their mer-
chandises;  but the spirit of her lover appears to Isabella in a dream, and discovers how and where he was stabbed,
and the spot where they have buried him.   To ascertain
the truth of the vision, she sets out to the place, accompanied by her old nurse, ignorant as yet of her wild purpose.   Her arrival at it, and digging for the body, is
described in the following stanzas, than which there is
nothing more awfully simple in diction, more nakedly grand
and moving in sentiment, in Dante, in Chaucer, or in
Spenser:- [Lamb quotes stanzas 46-8.]
    To pursue the story in prose. - They find the body, and
with their joint strengths sever from it the head, which
Isabella takes home, and wrapping it in a silken scarf,
entombs it in a garden-pot, covers it with mould, and over
it she plants sweet basil, which, watered with her tears,
thrives so that no other basil tufts in all Florence
throve like her basil.   How her brothers, suspecting
something mysterious in this herb, which she watched day
and night, at length discover the head, and secretly convey the basil from her;  and how from the day that she
loses her basil she pines away, and at last dies, we must
refer our readers to the poem, or to the divine germ of it
in Boccacio.   It is a great while ago since we read the
original;  and in this affecting revival of it we do but

> *Weep again a long-forgotten woe.* (110)

More exuberantly rich in imagery and painting is the
story of the Lamia.   It is of as gorgeous stuff as ever
romance was composed of.   Her first appearance in serpen-
tine form -

> —— a beauteous wreath with melancholy eyes ——

her dialogue with Hermes, the *Star of Lethe,* as he is
called by one of those prodigal phrases which Mr. Keats

abounds in, which are each a poem in a word, and which in
this instance lays open to us at once, like a picture, all
the dim regions and their inhabitants, and the sudden
coming of a celestial among them;   the charming of her
into woman's shape again by the God;   her marriage with
the beautiful Lycius;   her magic palace, which those who
knew the street, and remembered it complete from childhood, never remembered to have seen before;   the few Persian mutes, her attendants,

> ———— ———— ———— who that same year
> Were seen about the markets:   none knew where
> They could inhabit;-

the high-wrought splendours of the nuptial bower, with the
fading of the whole pageantry, Lamia, and all, away, before the glance of Apollonius, - are all that fairy land
can do for us.   They are for younger impressibili-
ties. (111)   To *us* an ounce of feeling is worth a pound
of fancy;   and therefore we recur again, with a warmer
gratitude, to the story of Isabella and the pot of basil,
and those never-cloying stanzas which we have cited, and
which we think should disarm criticism, if it be not in
its nature cruel;   if it would not deny to honey its
sweetness, nor to roses redness, nor light to the stars in
Heaven;   if it would not bay the moon out of the skies,
rather than acknowledge she is fair.

1 Cf. Dryden, Absalom and Achitophel, 11. 163-4.
2 Cowley, Ode on the Death of Mr. William Hervey, stanza 13.
3 'Paradise Lost', I, 296.
4 Cf. 'King Lear', IV, vii, 16-17.
5 Wither, 'The Shepherd's Hunting', Eclogue 4, 1. 409.
6 William Lane (d. 1814), novel publisher and instrumental in establishing circulating libraries. The novels of the Minerva Press began appearing around 1790.
7 Sir Walter Scott is probably the novelist alluded to.
8 Cf. 'Macbeth', II, i, 58.
9 'The Faerie Queene', II, vii.
10 Abraham Ortelius (1527-98), Dutch geographer and author of 'Theatrum Orbis Terrarum', 1570. Aaron Arrowsmith (1750-1823), well-known contemporary cartographer.
11 Thomas Manning, Lamb's friend and Cambridge mathematics tutor.
12 Jonson, To the Memory of My Beloved, the Author, Mr. William Shakespeare, 1. 31.
13 'The Excursion', III, 518.
14 Sir Thomas Browne, 'Urn Burial', chapter 5.
15 'With many others.'
16 Cf. Virgil, 'Aeneid', IV, 293-4; 'The most favourable times for speaking.'
17 Parental Recollections, 1. 1. The poem was published in Charles and Mary Lamb's 'Poetry for Children', 1809.
18 John Newbery (1713-67), publisher, bookseller and author of books for children; Mrs Barbauld (1743-1825) was the author of 'Hymns in Prose for Children', 1781; Mrs Sarah Trimmer (1741-1810), author of many books for children of an exemplary and educational nature.

19 When Manning returned to Cambridge in late February
   1801 he found three letters from Lamb, in one of which
   Lamb had asked if Manning were mortally offended in
   some way.  In his reply, Manning had written:

> How could you think I should refuse to write to
> you?  Had you no easier way of solving the
> Phaenomenon?  You *Dramatic Writers* are very expert
> in *framing* Incidents to *produce* strange effects -
> tis very odd then when strange things *do* really
> take place, that you can't *fit them* with proper
> incidents for their causes (25 February).

   Lamb's letter, reprinted here, is in reply to this.
20 'The Faerie Queene', II, vii, 64.
21 'Eikonoklastes', I.
22 Algernon Sidney (1622-83), grand-nephew of Sir Philip
   Sidney, was executed after the discovery of the Rye
   House Plot.
23 In 1580 Sidney wrote a treatise protesting against the
   Queen's proposed marriage with the Duke of Anjou.
24 'Dry chill at the heart.'
25 By William Shenstone (1714-63).
26 'Ad Leonoram Romae canentem.'
27 Cf. Spenser's dedication of 'The Shepheards Calender'
   to Sidney.
28 Hazlitt, 'Complete Works', ed. P.P. Howe (London,
   1930-4), vi, 318-26.  Hazlitt is later referred to as
   W.H.
29 Sonnet 84.
30 Sonnets 73, 39, 41.
31 The Earl of Oxford is alleged to have called Sidney a
   'puppy'.
32 Seven elegies on the death of Sidney were printed at
   the end of Spenser's 'Colin Clout's Come Home Again',
   1595.
33 George Wither (1588-1667).  The works of Wither referred to in this essay are:  'Abuses Stript and
   Whipt', 1613;  'The Shepherd's Hunting', 1615;
   'Wither's Motto', 1621;  'Fair-Virtue, The Mistress of
   Phil'arete', 1622.
34 Pickthank's testimony in the Vanity-Fair episode.
35 'The Reason for Church Government', II, introduction.
36 Drayton, 'Idea', 1593.
37 Ambrose Philips (1674-1749), author of 'Pastorals',
   1710.
38 To Himself, and the Harp, ll. 93-5.
39 Francis Quarles (1592-1644), chiefly remembered for
   his 'Emblems', 1635, the most popular book of verse in
   the seventeenth century.

40 Vicesimus Knox (1752-1821), editor of 'Elegant
   Extracts'.
41 Lamb quotes from the 'Defensio Secunda' the passage
   beginning 'Et sane haud ultima Dei cura caeci ...
   ductor autem viae ero tibi ego'.
42 Percy's 'Reliques', 1765.
43 Coleridge's own description of Cowper's poetry.
44 Cowper's 'Homer', 1791.
45 The reference here should be to Blake's designs for
   Blair's 'Grave'.
46 Coleridge's 'Poems', 1797, were dedicated to his
   brother George, and contained a sonnet to Bowles.
47 'The Seasons', Winter, ll. 799-809.
48 Wordsworth's present was a copy of 'Lyrical Ballads',
   1800.
49 The Brothers, ll. 108-12.
50 Lamb had sent Wordsworth a copy of 'Pride's Cure',
   which was published in 1802 as 'John Woodvil'.
51 Michael, ll. 339-43.
52 The Brothers, ll. 98-9.
53 In his reply, 25 February 1801, to Lamb's earlier
   letter, Manning had written:

> I have not time to give you my opinion of the 2d
> Vol of Lyl Ballads, except that I think tis utterly
> absurd from one end to the other. *You* tell me tis
> good poetry - if you mean that there is nothing
> puerile, nothing bombast or conceited, or any thing
> else that is so often found to disfigure *poetry*, I
> agree, but will you read it over & over again?
> Answer me that, Master Lamb.... I had rather sit
> spinning all day than prosing over such uninterest-
> ing accounts of uninteresting things.

54 Wordsworth's pamphlet, 'Concerning ... the Convention
   of Cintra', was published in 1809.
55 'The Excursion', VI, VII.
56 Ibid., II, 852-81.
57 Martin Burney (1788-1842), grandson of Dr  Burney, and
   a close friend to whom Lamb dedicated his 'Works',
   1818, vol. 2.
58 Hazlitt reviewed Wordsworth's poem in the 'Examiner',
   21, 28 August, 2 October, 1814.  In Book II the Wanderer had described 'Candide' as the 'dull product of
   a scoffer's pen'.
59 William Gifford (1756-1826), editor of the 'Quarterly
   Review', and author of 'The Baviad', 1794, and 'The
   Maeviad', 1795.  See p. 150, n. 39.
60 Coleridge quoted from Religious Musings, in the second

and fourth numbers of 'The Watchman', 'Works', ii, 64-
7, 131.   Lamb is here referring to the first.   In a
letter to Coleridge, 8 June 1796, Lamb wrote:  'I dare
not *criticise* the Relig. Musings, I like not to *select*
any part where all is excellent.   I can only admire;
& I thank you for it in the name of Christian, as well
as a Lover of good Poetry.'   In the same letter he
wrote of the 'Conciones ad populum', 1795:  'They are
not unfrequently sublime, & I think you could not do
better than to turn 'em into verse.'
61 'Samson Agonistes', 1. 662.
62 This projected work was never written.
63 'The Watchman', no. I., 'Works', ii, 29-39.
64 Lucas suggests that the poem in question was Guilt and
   Sorrow.
65 Monody on the Death of Chatterton.
66 The Eolian Harp, 11. 49-64.
67 'Measure for Measure', III, i, 9.
68 Lamb is probably referring here to a number of sonnets
   on the birth of Hartley Coleridge.
69 Reflections on Having Left a Place of Retirement.
70 Religious Musings, 11. 105-16.
71 'Osorio', rejected by Sheridan, was altered, performed
   and published in 1813 as 'Remorse'.
72 'Critical Review', October 1798.   Southey had written
   that, in the Ancient Mariner genius 'has here been employed in producing a poem of little merit'.
73 'The Annual Anthology', ed. Southey, 1799-1800.
74 This Lime-tree bower my Prison.   Coleridge refers to
   Lamb on three occasions in this poem as 'my gentle-
   hearted Charles'.
75 Ibid., 11. 32-43.
76 The sub-title of the poem to which Lamb is objecting
   was added when 'Lyrical Ballads' was published in a
   second edition in 1800.   In a note to the poem Wordsworth had written:

> The Poem of my Friend has indeed great defects;
> first, that the principal person has no distinct
> character, either in his profession of Mariner, or
> as a human being who having been long under the
> controul of supernatural impressions might be sup-
> posed himself to partake of something supernatural:
> secondly, that he does not act, but is continually
> acted upon:  thirdly, that the events having no
> necessary connection do not produce each other;
> and lastly, that the imagery is somewhat too labor-
> iously accumulated.

77 In the 'Morning Post'.

78 'The Friend', ii, 111-21.

79 Ibid., ii, 222-9.

80 Fanny Godwin, reporting Lamb's opinion of Christabel,
   wrote to Mary Shelley, 29 July 1816:  'Lamb says it
   ought never to have been published;  that no one
   understands it;  and "Kubla Khan" ... is nonsense',
   Dowden, 'Life of Shelley', 1886, ii, 41.

81 James Gillman, Highgate doctor with whom Coleridge
   lived as a patient from 1816 until his death.   His
   biography of Coleridge, of which one volume was published in 1838, was never completed.

82 By Thomas Campbell, and Thomas Moss, respectively.
   Lamb, of course, intended Petition.

83 Hazlitt, 'Works', vii, 114-18.   Commenting on Cole-
   ridge's infirmity of purpose, Hazlitt had written:
   'Mr. Shandy would have settled the question at once:
   "You have little or no nose, Sir."'

84 'Aids to Reflection', 1825.

85 Thornton Hunt, son of Leigh Hunt, to whom Lamb had alluded in his essay, Witches, and other Night Fears.

86 In Southey's 'A Vision of Judgement', 1821.

87 Byron travestied Southey's funeral ode on George III
   in 'The Vision of Judgement', 1822.

88 Southey's 'Life of Wesley', 1820.   Although Southey
   collected materials for a life of George Fox, the work
   was never written.

89 'Paradise Lost', III, 488-93.

90 Leigh Hunt (1784-1859);  William Hazlitt (1778-1830).
   They are referred to later as L.H. and W.H.   Hunt's
   'The Story of Rimini', 1816, is based on the Paolo
   and Francesca episode in Dante's 'Inferno'.

91 'The Faerie Queene', I, i, 13.

92 Thomas Holcroft (1745-1809), playwright and radical.

93 Before his departure for Italy, Leigh Hunt had introduced himself to Coleridge and apologised for earlier
   adverse criticisms.

94 Thomas Belsham (1750-1829), Unitarian minister,
   writer, and Hazlitt's teacher at Hackney College.

95 'Joan of Arc', 1796.   Coleridge contributed to Book
   II.

96 Cowper, The Sofa, in 'The Task'.

97 Commenting on English translations of Homer, Southey
   had written in his preface:  'Pope has disguised him
   in fop-finery, and Cowper has stripped him naked.'

98 Lamb is commenting on the second volume of Southey's
   'Poems', 1797-99.

99 The poems of Southey referred to in the correspondence
   are:  'Thalaba the Destroyer', 1801;  'Madoc', 1805;

'The Curse of Kehama', 1810; 'Roderick, the Last of the Goths', 1814.

100 Landor, 'Gebir', 1798. Landor was an admirer of Lamb's essays.

101 Bernard Barton (1784-1849), Quaker poet and bank clerk. Lamb concluded this letter by saying that in feelings and matters not dogmatical, he hoped he was half a Quaker himself. Barton had just published 'Napoleon and Other Poems', 1822.

102 John Hunt, brother of Leigh Hunt, and publisher of 'The Liberal' in which Byron's 'The Vision of Judgement' was published in 1822, was fined £100 for the libel on the late king contained in the poem.

103 Sir William Curtis (1752-1829), Tory MP.

104 Cf. 'Paradise Regained', IV, 345.

105 Lines to a Reviewer is a short poem of only thirteen lines. Shelley admired the writings of Lamb. In a letter to Hunt, c. 20 August 1819, he wrote:

> What a lovely thing is his Rosamund Gray, how much knowledge of the sweetest & the deepest part of our nature [is] in it! When I think of such a mind as Lamb's, when I see how unnoticed remain things of such exquisite & complete perfection what should I hope for myself if I had not higher objects in view than fame. -

106 Hazlitt, On People of Sense, in 'The Plain Speaker', 'Works', xii, 245-6.

107 Clare had sent Lamb a copy of his 'Poems Descriptive of Rural Life and Scenery', 1820, and 'The Village Minstrel', 1821.

108 By John Dyer (1699-1758).

109 Cf. Shakespeare, sonnet 106.

110 Cf. Ibid., sonnet 30.

111 Cf. Hazlitt: 'The reading of Mr. Keats's Eve of Saint Agnes lately made me regret that I was not young again.... I know how I should have felt at one time in reading such passages', 'Works', xii, 225.

# V  Prose

Lamb's selection of passages from the writings of Sir
Thomas More appeared anonymously in Hunt's 'Indicator',
20 December 1820, and was first reprinted by E.V. Lucas in
his edition of Lamb.

Of the writings of this distinguished character little
is remembered at present beyond his *Eutopia*, and some Epi-
grams.   But there is extant a massive folio of his Theological Works in English, partly Practical Divinity, but
for the greater part Polemi[c], against the grand Lutheran
Heresy, just then beginning to flower.   From these I many
years ago made some extracts, rejecting only the antiquated orthography, (they being intended only for my own
amusement) except in some instances of proper names, &c.
I send them you as I find them, thinking that some of your
readers may consider them as curious.   The first is from
a Tract against Tyndale, called the *Confutation of Tyndale's Answer*.* (1)   The author of *Religio Medici*
somewhere says, "his conscience would give him the lye, if
she should say that he absolutely detested or hated any
essence *but the Devil*." (2)   Whether Browne was not out
in his metaphysics, when he supposed himself capable of
hating, that is, *entertaining a personal aversion to*, a
being so abstracted, or such a Concrete of all irreconcileable abstractions rather, as usually passes for the
meaning of that name, I contend not;   but that the same
hatred in kind, which he professed against our great
spiritual enemy, was in downright earnest cultivated and
defended by More against that portentous phenomenon in
those times, a *Heretic*, from his speeches against Luther

*To some foregone Tract of More's, of which I have lost
 the title.

and Tyndale cannot for a moment be doubted.   His account
of poor Hytton which follows (a reformado priest of the
day) is penned with a wit and malice hyper-satanic.   It
is infinitely diverting in the midst of its diabolism, if
it be not rather, what Coleridge calls,

> Too wicked for a smile, too foolish for a tear. (3)

[Lamb quotes from the preface to the *Confutation*, Pt.
I, pp. 13-14.]
What follows (from the same Tract) is *mildened* a little
by the introduction of the name of Erasmus, More's intimate friend;   though by the sting in the rear of it, it is
easy to see, that it was to a little temporising only, and
to some thin politic partitions from these Reformers, that
Erasmus owed his exemption from the bitter anathemas More
had in store for them.   The *love* almost make[s] the *hate*
more shocking by the contrast!
[Lamb quotes from the *Confutation*, II, ii, Pt. I, p.
177.]
The next extract is from a "Dialogue concerning Heresies," and has always struck me as a master-piece of eloquent logic, and something in the manner of Burke, when he
is stripping a sophism *sophistically;*   as he treats
Paine, (4) and others *passim*.
[Lamb quotes from the *Dialogue*, I, ii.]
I subjoin from the same "Dialogue" More's cunning defence of Miracles done at Saints' shrines, on Pilgrimages,
&c. all which he defends, as he was bound by holy church
to do, most stoutly.   The *manner* of it is arch and surprising, and the narration infinitely naive;   the *matter*
is the old fallacy of confounding miracles (things happen-
ing out of nature) with natural things, the grounds of
which we cannot explain.   In this sense every thing is a
miracle, and nothing is.
[Lamb quotes from the *Dialogue*, I, x.]
Diabolical Possession was a rag of the old abomination,
which this Contunder of Heresies thought himself obliged
no less to wrap tightly about the loins of his faith, than
any of the *splendiores panni* (5) of the old red Harlot.
But (read with allowance for the belief of the times) the
narrative will be found affecting, particularly in what
relates to the parents of the damsel, "rich, and sore
abashed."
[Lamb quotes from the *Dialogue*, I, xvi.]
I shall trouble you with one Excerpt more, from a "Dialogue of Comfort against Tribulation;"   because the style
of it is solemn and weighty;   and because it was written
by More in his last imprisonment in the Tower, preparatory

to his sentence.   After witnessing his treatment of Sir
John Hytton, and his brethren, we shall be inclined to
mitigate some of our remorse, that More should have suffered death himself *for conscience sake*.   The reader will
not do this passage justice, if he do not read it as part
of a sermon;   and as putting himself into the feelings of
an auditory of More's Creed and Times.

[Lamb quotes from the *Dialogue*, I, xviii.]

---

Lamb's note on Montaigne first appeared in a paper for the
'Examiner', 18 July 1813, and was reprinted by Leigh Hunt
in the 'Indicator', 13 December 1820, with the title Books
with One Idea in Them.

---

What could Pope mean by that line, - "sage Montaigne, or
more sage Charron?" (6)   Montaigne is an immense trea-
sure-house of observation, anticipating all the discoveries of succeeding essayists.   You cannot dip in him
without being struck with the aphorism, that there is
nothing new under the sun.   All the writers on common
life since him have done nothing but echo him.   You cannot open him without detecting a Spectator, or starting a
Rambler;   besides that his own character pervades the
whole, and binds it sweetly together.   Charron is a mere
piece of formality, scholastic dry bones, without sinew or
living flesh.

39  Izaak Walton
    (i) 1796

---

From a letter to Coleridge, 8 June.

---

I have just been reading a book, which I may be too partial to as it was the delight of my childhood, but I will
recommend it to you. - it is Isaac Walton's complete
Angler!"   All the scientific part you may omit in reading.   The dialogue is very simple, full of pastoral beauties & will charm you.   Many pretty old verses are interspersed.

---

(ii) 1796

---

From a letter to Coleridge, 28 October.

---

Among all your quaint readings did you ever light upon
Walton's 'Complete Angler?'   I asked you the question
once before;   it breathes the very spirit of innocence,
purity, and simplicity of heart;   there are many choice
old verses interspersed in it;   it would sweeten a man's
temper at any time to read it;   it would Christianise
every discordant angry passion;   pray make yourself acquainted with it.

---

(iii) 1801

---

From a letter to Robert Lloyd, 7 February.

---

    I shall expect you to bring me a brimful account of the
pleasure which Walton has given you, when you come to
town. - It must square with your mind.   The delightful
innocence and healthfulness of the Anglers mind will have
blown upon yours like a Zephyr. - Dont you already feel
your spirit *filled* with the scenes? - the banks of rivers
- the cowslip beds - the pastoral scenes - the neat ale-
houses - and hostesses and milkmaids, as far exceeding
Virgil and Pope, as the Holy Living (7) is beyond Thomas a
Kempis. - Are not the eating and drinking joys painted to
the Life? - do they not inspire you with an immortal hunger? - -   Are not you ambitious of being made an Angler? -
What edition have you got? is it Hawkins's with plates of
Piscator &c?   That sells very dear.   I have only been
able to purchase the last Edition without the old Plates,
which pleased my childhood; - the plates being worn out, &
the old Edition difficult & expensive to procure. - - (The
complete Angler is the only Treatise written in Dialogues
that is worth a halfpenny. - Many elegant dialogues have
been written (such as Bishop Berkley's Minute philosopher) (8) but in all of them the Interlocutors are merely
abstract arguments personify'd;   not living dramatic characters, as in Walton;   where *every thing* is *alive*;   the
fishes are absolutely *charactered*; - and birds and animals
are as interesting as men· & women.) - -

---

This passage is from the opening of Lamb's essay Imperfect
Sympathies, which first appeared in the 'London Magazine',
August 1821, and was reprinted in 'Essays', 1823.   Although references to the writings of Browne and many other
contemporary prose writers abound in the letters and
essays, Lamb never wrote on any of them at length.   John
Mitford recalled after Lamb's death that in prose 'he appeared to know more or less of most of our great authors
of Elizabeth and James's time.   Fuller, Burton, Sir T.
Browne, Feltham, were his favourites' (Lucas, 'Life', II,
168).   Blunden in his valuable anthology reprinted an
account of an interview with Lamb in which the discussion
ranged over Burton, Sidney, Jeremy Taylor, Barrow, Bos-
well's Life, Cowper's letters, Cudworth's 'Intellectual
System', Dryden and Goldsmith (pp. 191-2).

---

I am of a constitution so general, that it consorts and
sympathizeth with all things, I have no antipathy, or
rather idiosyncracy in any thing.   Those national repug-
nancies do not touch me, nor do I behold with prejudice
the French, Italian, Spaniard, or Dutch. - *Religio
Medici*. (9)

THAT the author of the Religio Medici, mounted upon the
airy stilts of abstraction, conversant about notional and
conjectural essences;  in whose categories of Being the
possible took the upper hand of the actual;  should have
overlooked the impertinent individualities of such poor
concretions as mankind, is not much to be admired.   It is
rather to be wondered at, that in the genus of animals he
should have condescended to distinguish that species at
all.

---

Lamb's selection from Fuller was first published by Leigh
Hunt in the fourth number of the 'Reflector', 1812, and
was included by Lamb in the 1818 'Works'.  In order to
make sense of Lamb's comments some of the passages from
Fuller are also reproduced, although Lamb's transcrip-
tions, here as elsewhere, are not exact..

---

THE writings of Fuller (10) are usually designated by the
title of quaint, and with sufficient reason;  for such was
his natural bias to conceits, that I doubt not upon most
occasions it would have been going out of his way to have
expressed himself out of them.  But his wit is not always
a *lumen siccum*, (11) a dry faculty of surprising;  on the
contrary, his conceits are oftentimes deeply steeped in
human feeling and passion.  Above all, his way of telling
a story, for its eager liveliness, and the perpetual running commentary of the narrator happily blended with the
narration, is perhaps unequalled.

   As his works are now scarcely perused but by antiqua-
ries, I thought it might not be unacceptable to my readers
to present them with some specimens of his manner, in
single thoughts and phrases;  and in some few passages of
greater length, chiefly of a narrative description.  I
shall arrange them as I casually find them in my book of
extracts, without being solicitous to specify the particular work from which they are taken.

   [Lamb quotes a number of short passages, often of only
a sentence or two, under a variety of subject headings.]

   *Text of St Paul.*- "St. Paul saith, let not the sun go
down on your wrath, to carry news to the antipodes in
another world of thy revengeful nature.  Yet let us take
the Apostle's meaning rather than his words, with all possible speed to depose our passion;  not understanding him

so literally, that we may take leave to be angry till
sunset:  then might our wrath lengthen with the days;
and men in Greenland, where the day lasts above a quarter
of a year, have plentiful scope for revenge."* (12)
[Lamb quotes a number of passages without comment.]
  *Henry de Essex.* - "He is too well known in our English
Chronicles, being Baron of Raleigh, in Essex, and Hereditary Standard Bearer of England.  It happened in the
reign of this king [Henry II.] there was a fierce battle
fought in Flintshire, at Coleshall, between the English
and Welsh, wherein this Henry de Essex *animum et signum
simul abjecit*, betwixt traitor and coward, cast away both
his courage and banner together, occasioning a great overthrow of English.  But he that had the baseness to do,
had the boldness to deny the doing of so foul a fact;
until he was challenged in combat by Robert de Momford, a
knight, eye-witness thereof, and by him overcome in a
duel.  Whereupon his large inheritance was confiscated to
the king, and he himself, *partly thrust, partly going into
a convent, hid his head in a cowl, under which, betwixt
shame and sanctity, he blushed out the remainder* of his
life."** - Worthies.  Article, Bedfordshire.

  *This whimsical prevention of a consequence which no one
would have thought of deducing, - setting up an absurdum
on purpose to hunt it down, - placing guards as it were at
the very outposts of possibility, - gravely giving out
laws to insanity and prescribing moral fences to distem-
pered intellects, could never have entered into a head
less entertainingly constructed than that of Fuller, or
Sir Thomas Browne, the very air of whose style the conclusion of this passage most aptly imitates.

  **The fine imagination of Fuller has done what might have
been pronounced impossible:  it has given an interest, and
a holy character, to coward infamy.  Nothing can be more
beautiful than the concluding account of the last days,
and expiatory retirement, of poor Henry de Essex.  The address with which the whole of this little story is told is
most consummate:  the charm of it seems to consist in a
perpetual balance of antitheses not too violently opposed,
and the consequent activity of mind in which the reader is
kept: - "Betwixt traitor and coward" - "baseness to do,
boldness to deny" - "partly thrust, partly going, into a
convent" - "betwixt shame and sanctity."  The reader by
this artifice is taken into a kind of partnership with the
writer, - his judgment is exercised in settling the preponderance, - he feels as if he were consulted as to the
issue.  But the modern historian flings at once the dead
weight of his own judgment into the scale, and settles the
matter.

*Sir Edward Harwood, Knt.* - "I have read of a bird,
which hath a face like, and yet will prey upon, a man;
who coming to the water to drink, and finding there by
reflection, that he had killed one like himself, pineth
away by degrees, and never afterwards enjoyeth
itself."* (13)   [Lamb quotes the rest of the passage, and
two further extracts without comment.]

*Burning of Wickliffe's Body by Order of the Council of
Constance.* - "Hitherto [A.D. 1428] the corpse of John
Wickliffe had quietly slept in his grave about forty-one
years after his death, till his body was reduced to bones,
and his bones almost to dust.   For though the earth in
the chancel of Lutterworth, in Leicestershire, where he
was interred, hath not so quick a digestion with the earth
of Aceldama, to consume  flesh in twenty-four hours, yet
such the appetite thereof, and all other English graves,
to leave small reversions of a body after so many years.
But now such the spleen of the Council of Constance, as
they not only cursed his memory as dying an obstinate
heretic, but ordered that his bones (with this charitable
caution, - if it may be discerned from the bodies of other
faithful people) to be taken out of the ground, and thrown
far off from any Christian burial.   In obedience here-
unto, Rich. Fleming, Bishop of Lincoln, Diocesan of Lutterworth, sent his officers (vultures with a quick sight,
scent, at a dead carcase) to ungrave him.   Accordingly to
Lutterworth they come, Sumner, Commissary, Official, Chan-
cellor, Proctors, Doctors, and their servants (so that the
remnant of the body would not hold out a bone amongst so
many hands), take what was left out of the grave, and

*I do not know where Fuller read of this bird;  but a
more awful and affecting story, and moralizing of a story,
in Natural History, or rather in that Fabulous Natural
History, where poets and mythologists found the Phoenix
and the Unicorn, and "other strange fowl," is no where extant.   It is a fable which Sir Thomas Browne, if he had
heard of it, would have exploded among his Vulgar Errors;
but the delight which he would have taken in the discussing of its probabilities, would have shewn that the *truth
of the fact*, though the avowed object of his search, was
not so much the motive which put him upon the investiga-
tion, as those hidden affinities and poetical analogies, -
those *essential verities* in the application of strange
fable, which made him linger with such reluctant delay
among the last fading lights of popular tradition;  and
not seldom to conjure up a superstition, that had been
long extinct, from its dusty grave, to inter it himself
with greater ceremonies and solemnities of burial.

burnt them to ashes, and cast them into Swift, a neigh-
bouring brook, running hard by.  *Thus this brook has conveyed his ashes into Avon, Avon into Severn, Severn into
the narrow seas, they into the main ocean;  and thus the
ashes of Wickliffe are the emblem of his doctrine, which
now is dispersed all the world over.*"* - Church History. (14)

*The concluding period of this most lively narrative I
will not call a conceit:  it is one of the grandest conceptions I ever met with.   One feels the ashes of Wickliffe gliding away out of the reach of the Sumners, Com-
missaries, Officials, Proctors, Doctors, and all the pud-
dering rout of executioners of the impotent rage of the
baffled Council:  from Swift into Avon, from Avon into
Severn, from Severn into the narrow seas, from the narrow
seas into the main ocean, where they become the emblem of
his doctrine, "dispersed all the world over."   Hamlet's
tracing the body of Caesar to the clay that stops a beer-
barrel, is a no less curious pursuit of "ruined mortality;" (15) but it is in an inverse ratio to this:  it degrades and saddens us, for one part of our nature at
least;  but this expands the whole of our nature, and
gives to the body a sort of ubiquity, - a diffusion, as
far as the actions of its partner can have reach or influence.
   I have seen this passage smiled at, and set down as a
quaint conceit of old Fuller.   But what is not a conceit
to those who read it in a temper different from that in
which the writer composed it?   The most pathetic parts of
poetry to cold tempers seem and are nonsense, as divinity
was to the Greeks foolishness.   When Richard II., medi-
tating on his own utter annihilation as to royalty, cries
out,

     "O that I were a mockery king of snow,
     To melt before the sun of Bolingbroke," (16)

if we have been going on pace for pace with the passion
before, this sudden conversion of a strong-felt metaphor
into something to be actually realized in nature, like
that of Jeremiah, "Oh! that my head were waters, and mine
eyes a fountain of tears," (17) is strictly and strikingly
natural;  but come unprepared upon it, and it is a conceit:  and so is a "head" turned into "waters." (18)

From a letter to Robert Lloyd, 16 April.   As late as 1831
Lamb is reported to have said that he always read Jeremy
Taylor 'with much delight.   He was one of the greatest
giants of the olden time.   His profusion of illustration,
his richness and variety of imagery, always astonish me;
and his copiousness and magnificence of expression ever
afford me interest and pleasure.'   In the same conversation, he said of Barrow:   'He is dry, and often tedious,
but what energy and felicity of language, what force of
argument, what clearness and power of thought, what rich
diversified illustrations!   I wish all would read Barrow'
(Blunden, p. 191).

If by the work of Bishop Taylor, whose Title you have not
given correctly, you mean his Contemplations on the State
of Man in this Life and that which is to come;   I dare
hope you will join with me in believing it to be spurious.
·The suspicious circumstance of its being a posthumous
work, with the total dissimilarity in style to the genuine
works, I think evince that it never was the work of Doctor
Jeremy Taylor Late Lord Bishop of Down & Connor in Ireland
and Administrator of the See of Dromore;   such are the
Titles which his Sounding title pages give him, & I love
the man, and I love his paraphernalia, and I like to name
him with all his attributions and additions - .  If you are
yet but lightly acquainted with his real manner, take up
and read the whole first chapter of the Holy *Dying*;   in
particular turn to the first paragraph of the 2 sect. of
that chapter for a simile of a rose, or more truly many
similes within simile, for such were the riches of his
fancy, that when a beauteous image offered, before he
could stay to expand it into all its capacities, throngs
of new coming images came up, and justled out the first,

or blended in disorder with it, which imitates the order
of every rapid mind.   But read all the first chapter by
my advice; & I know I need not advise you, when you have
read it, to read the second. . - or for another specimen,
(where so many beauties crowd, the judgment has yet vanity
enough to think it can discern a handsomest, till a second
judgment and a third ad infinitum start up to disallow
their elder brother's pretensions) turn to the Story of
the Ephesian Matron in the second section of the 5th Chapter of the same Holy *Dying* (I still refer to the *Dying*
part, because it contains better matter than the Holy
Living, which deals more in rules than illustrations, I
mean in comparison with the other only, else it has more &
more beautiful illustrations than any prose book besides)
- read it yourself and shew it to Plumstead (with my Love,
& bid him write to me) and ask him if Willy himself has
ever told a story with more circumstances of fancy &
humour.   The paragraph begins "But that which is to be
faulted," & the story not long after follows. - - Make
these references, while P. is with you, that you may stir
him up to the Love of Jeremy Taylor, & make a convertite
of him. - - Coleridge was the man who first solemnly ex-
horted me to "study" the works of Dr. Jeremy Taylor, and I
have had reason to bless the hour in which he did it. -
Read as many of his works as you can get....
    Bp. Taylor has more, & more beautiful, imagery, and
(what is more to a Lover of Willy) more knowledge & description of human life and manners, than any prose book in
the language.: - he has more delicacy, & sweetness, than
any mortal, the "gentle" Shakespear hardly excepted, -
his similes and allusions are taken, as the bees take
honey, from all the youngest, greenest, exquisitest parts
of nature, from plants, & flowers, & fruit, young boys &
virgins, from little children perpetually, from sucking
infants, babies' smiles, roses, gardens, - his imagination
was a spatious Garden where no vile insectoe could crawl
in, his apprehension a "Court" where no foul thoughts kept
"leets & holydays." - (19)

    Snail & worm give no offence, -
        Newt nor blind worm be not seen, -
    Come not near our fairy queen — (20)

You must read Bishop Taylor with allowances for the subjects on which he wrote, and the age *in* which. - You may
skip or patiently endure his tedious discourses on rites &
ceremonies, Baptism & the Eucharist, the Clerical function, and the antiquity of Episcopacy, a good deal of
which are inserted in works not purely controversial - his

polemical works you may skip altogether, unless you have a
taste for the exertions of vigorous reason & subtle distinguishing on uninteresting topics. - Such of his works
as you should begin with, to get a taste for him (after
which your Love will lead you to his Polemical and drier
works, as Love led Leander "over boots" knee-deep thro'
the Hellespont,) - but read first the Holy Living & Dying,
his Life of Christ & *Sermons* both in folio.- And above
all try to get a beautiful little tract on the measures
and offices of Friendship, printed with his *opuscula* duo-
decimo, & also at the end of his Polemical Discourses in
folio. - - Another thing you will observe in Bp. Taylor,
without which consideration you will do him injustice.
He wrote to different classes of people.  His Holy Living
& Dying & Life of X't were designed and have been used as
popular books of family Devotion, and have been thumbed by
old women, and laid about in the window seats of old
houses in great families, like the Bible, and the "Queene-
like-Closet or rare boke of Recipes in medicine & cookery,
fitted to all capacities" - - .  Accordingly in these *the
fancy* is perpetually applied to;  any slight conceit; allusion, or analogy, any "prettiness," a story true or
false, serves for an argument, adapted to women & young
persons & "incompetent judgments" - whereas the Liberty of
Prophecy (a book in your father's book-case) is a series
of severe & masterly reasoning, fitted to great Clerks &
learned Fathers, with no more of Fancy, than is subordinate & ornamental. - Such various powers had the Bishop of
Down & Connor, Administrator of the See of Dromore!  My
theme and my glory! -

---

(ii) 1801

---

From a letter to Robert Lloyd, 18 November.

---

To your enquiry respecting a selection from B'p Taylor
I answer - it cannot be done, & if it could it would not
*take* with John Bull. - It cannot be done, for who can disentangle and unthread the rich texture of Nature & Poetry
sewn so thick into a stout coat of theology, without
spoiling both *lace* & *coat*? how beggarly and how bald do
even Shakespeares Princely Pieces look, when thus violently divorced from *connexion* & *circumstance*! when we meet
with To be or not to be - or Jacques's moralizings upon
the Deer - or Brutus and Cassius' quarrel & reconciliation
- in an Enfield speaker or in Elegant Extracts - how we

stare & will scarcely acknowledge to ourselves (what we are conscious we feel) that they are flat & have no power. Something exactly like this have I experienced when I have picked out similes & stars from Holy Dying and shewn them per se, as you'd shew specimens of minerals or pieces of rock - . Compare the grand effect of the Star-paved fir- mament - & imagine a boy capable of picking out those pretty twinklers one by one & playing at chuck farthing with them. - Every thing in heaven & earth, in man and in story, in books & in fancy, acts by Confederacy, by jux- taposition, by circumstance & place - .

43  John Bunyan
    1828

From a letter to Bernard Barton, 11 October.

A splendid edition of Bunyan's Pilgrim - why the
thought is enough to turn ones moral stomach. (21)   His
cockle hat and staff transformed to a smart cockd beaver,
and a jemmy cane, his amice gray to the last Regent Street
cut, and his painful Palmer's pace to the modern swagger.
Stop thy friends sacriligious hand.   Nothing can be done
for B. but to reprint the old cuts in as homely but good a
style as possible.   The Vanity Fair and the pilgrims
there - the silly soothness in his setting out countenances the Christian idiocy (in a good sense) of his admiration of the Shepherds on the Delectable Mountains, the
Lions so truly Allegorical and remote from any similitude
to Pidcocks (22) - The great head (the author's) capacious
of dreams and similitudes dreaming in the dungeon.   Perhaps you dont know *my* edition, what I had when a child -
if you do, can you bear new designs from - Martin, enameld
into copper or silver plate by - Heath, (23) - accompaned
with verses from Mrs Heman's pen - O how unlike his own -
[Lamb quotes Bunyan's 'Author's Apology for his Book'.]
Shew me such poetry in any of the 15 forthcoming combination of show and emptiness, yclept Annuals.   Let me whisper in you ear that wholesome sacramental bread is not
more nutritious than papistical wafer stuff, than these
(to head and heart) exceed the visual frippery - of Mit-
fords Salamander God, baking himself up to the work of
creation in a solar oven, not yet by the terms of the context itself existing.   Blake's ravings made genteel.

This essay, first published in March 1826, was one of a
series written that year for the 'New Monthly Magazine'
under the heading Popular Fallacies.   The fallacy in this
case, of which the essay was illustrative, was That my
Lord Shaftesbury and Sir William Temple are models of the
Genteel Style in Writing.   This cumbersome title was altered to The Genteel Style in Writing when the essay was
reprinted in 'Last Essays', 1833.

IT is an ordinary criticism, that my Lord Shaftesbury,
and Sir William Temple, are models of the genteel style in
writing. (24)   We should prefer saying - of the lordly,
and the gentlemanly.   Nothing can be more unlike than the
inflated finical rhapsodies of Shaftesbury, and the plain
natural chit-chat of Temple.   The man of rank is discernible in both writers;  but in the one it is only insinuated gracefully, in the other it stands out offensively.
The peer seems to have written with his coronet on, and
his Earl's mantle before him;  the commoner in his elbow
chair and undress. - What can be more pleasant than the
way in which the retired statesman peeps out in the
essays, penned by the latter in his delightful retreat at
Shene?   They scent of Nimeguen, and the Hague.   Scarce
an authority is quoted under an ambassador.   Don Francis-
co de Melo, a "Portugal Envoy in England," tells him it
was frequent in his country for men, spent with age or
other decays, so as they could not hope for above a year
or two of life, to ship themselves away in a Brazil fleet,
and after their arrival there to go on a great length,
sometimes of twenty or thirty years, or more, by the force
of that vigour they recovered with that remove.   "Whether
such an effect (Temple beautifully adds) might grow from
the air, or the fruits of that climate, or by approaching

nearer the sun, which is the fountain of light and heat,
when their natural heat was so far decayed:  or whether
the piecing out of an old man's life were worth the pains;
I cannot tell:  perhaps the play is not worth the candle."
- Monsieur Pompone, "French Ambassador in his (Sir William's) time at the Hague," certifies him, that in his
life he had never heard of any man in France that arrived
at a hundred years of age;  a limitation of life which
the old gentleman imputes to the excellence of their climate, giving them such a liveliness of temper and humour,
as disposes them to more pleasures of all kinds than in
other countries;  and moralises upon the matter very sensibly.  The "late Robert Earl of Leicester" furnishes him
with a story of a Countess of Desmond, married out of England in Edward the Fourth's time, and who lived far in
King James's reign.  The "same noble person" gives him an
account, how such a year, in the same reign, there went
about the country a set of morrice-dancers, composed of
ten men who danced, a Maid Marian, and a tabor and pipe;
and how these twelve, one with another, made up twelve
hundred years.  "It was not so much (says Temple) that so
many in one small county (Herefordshire) should live to
that age, as that they should be in vigour and in humour
to travel and to dance."  Monsieur Zulichem, one of his
"colleagues at the Hague," informs him of a cure for the
gout;  which is confirmed by another "Envoy," Monsieur
Serinchamps, in that town, who had tried it. - Old Prince
Maurice of Nassau recommends to him the use of hammocks in
that complaint;  having been allured to sleep, while suffering under it himself, by the "constant motion or swing-
ing of those airy beds."  Count Egmont, and the Rhine-
grave who "was killed last summer before Maestricht," impart to him their experiences.

But the rank of the writer is never more innocently
disclosed, than where he takes for granted the compliments
paid by foreigners to his fruit-trees.  For the taste and
perfection of what we esteem the best, he can truly say,
that the French, who have eaten his peaches and grapes at
Shene in no very ill year, have generally concluded that
the last are as good as any they have eaten in France on
this side Fontainbleau;  and the first as good as any
they have eat in Gascony.  Italians have agreed his white
figs to be as good as any of that sort in Italy, which is
the earlier kind of white fig there;  for in the later
kind and the blue, we cannot come near the warm climates,
no more than in the Frontignac or Muscat grape.  His
orange-trees too, are as large as any he saw when he was
young in France, except those of Fontainbleau, or what he
has seen since in the Low Countries;  except some very old

ones of the Prince of Orange's.   Of grapes he had the
honour of bringing over four sorts into England, which he
enumerates, and supposes that they are all by this time
pretty common among some gardeners in his neighbourhood,
as well as several persons of quality;   for he ever
thought all things of this kind "the commoner they are
made the better."   The garden pedantry with which he asserts that 'tis to little purpose to plant any of the best
fruits, as peaches or grapes, hardly, he doubts, beyond
Northamptonshire at the furthest northwards;   and praises
the "Bishop of Munster at Cosevelt," for attempting nothing beyond cherries in that cold climate;   is equally
pleasant and in character.   "I may perhaps" (he thus ends
his sweet Garden Essay with a passage worthy of
Cowley) (25) "be allowed to know something of this trade,
since I have so long allowed myself to be good for nothing
else, which few men will do, or enjoy their gardens, without often looking abroad to see how other matters play,
what motions in the state, and what invitations they may
hope for into other scenes.   For my own part, as the
country life, and this part of it more particularly, were
the inclination of my youth itself, so they are the pleasure of my age;   and I can truly say that, among many great
employments that have fallen to my share, I have never
asked or sought for any of them, but have often endeavoured to escape from them, into the ease and freedom of a
private scene, where a man may go his own way and his own
pace, in the common paths and circles of life.   The measure of choosing well is whether a man likes what he has
chosen, which I thank God has befallen me;   and though
among the follies of my life, building and planting have
not been the least, and have cost me more than I have the
confidence to own;   yet they have been fully recompensed
by the sweetness and satisfaction of this retreat, where,
since my resolution taken of never entering again into any
public employments, I have passed five years without ever
once going to town, though I am almost in sight of it, and
have a house there always ready to receive me.   Nor has
this been any sort of affectation, as some have thought
it, but a mere want of desire or humour to make so small a
remove;   for when I am in this corner, I can truly say
with Horace, *Me quoties reficit, &c.*" [Lamb quotes from
Horace's 'Epistles', I, xviii, 104-12.]
     The writings of Temple are, in general, after this easy
copy.   On one occasion, indeed, his wit, which was mostly
subordinate to nature and tenderness, has seduced him into
a string of felicitous antitheses;   which, it is obvious
to remark, have been a model to Addison and succeeding
essayists.   "Who would not be covetous, and with reason,"

he says, "if health could be purchased with gold? who not
ambitious, if it were at the command of power, or restored
by honour? but, alas! a white staff will not help gouty
feet to walk better than a common cane;  nor a blue riband
bind up a wound so well as a fillet.   The glitter of
gold, or of diamonds, will but hurt sore eyes instead of
curing them;  and an aching head will be no more eased by
wearing a crown, than a common night-cap."   In a far
better style, and more accordant with his own humour of
plainness, are the concluding sentences of his "Discourse
upon Poetry."   Temple took a part in the controversy
about the ancient and the modern learning;  and, with that
partiality so natural and so graceful in an old man, whose
state engagements had left him little leisure to look into
modern productions, while his retirement gave him occasion
to look back upon the classic studies of his youth - decided in favour of the latter.   "Certain it is," he says,
"that, whether the fierceness of the Gothic humours, or
noise of their perpetual wars, frighted it away, or that
the unequal mixture of the modern languages would not bear
it - the great heights and excellency both of poetry and
music fell with the Roman learning and empire, and have
never since recovered the admiration and applauses that
before attended them.   Yet, such as they are amongst us,
they must be confessed to be the softest and sweetest, the
most general and most innocent amusements of common time
and life.   They still find room in the courts of princes,
and the cottages of shepherds.   They serve to revive and
animate the dead calm of poor and idle lives, and to allay
or divert the violent passions and perturbations of the
greatest and the busiest men.   And both these effects are
of equal use to human life;  for the mind of man is like
the sea, which is neither agreeable to the beholder nor
the voyager, in a calm or in a storm, but is so to both
when a little agitated by gentle gales;  and so the mind,
when moved by soft and easy passions or affections.    I
know very well that many who pretend to be wise by the
forms of being grave, are apt to despise both poetry and
music, as toys and trifles too light for the use or entertainment of serious men.   But whoever find themselves
wholly insensible to their charms, would, I think, do well
to keep their own counsel, for fear of reproaching their
own temper, and bringing the goodness of their natures, if
not of their understandings, into question.   While this
world lasts, I doubt not but the pleasure and request of
these two entertainments will do so too;  and happy those
that content themselves with these, or any other so easy
and so innocent, and do not trouble the world or other
men, because they cannot be quiet themselves, though

nobody hurts them." "When all is done (he concludes), human life is at the greatest and the best but líke a froward child, that must be played with, and humoured a little, to keep it quiet, till it falls asleep, and then the care is over."

From a letter to Thomas Manning, 1 March.

My private goings on are orderly as the movements of the
spheres, and stale as their music to angel's ears.   Public affairs - except as they touch upon me, & so turn into
private - I cannot whip my mind up to feel any interest
in. - - I grieve indeed that War and Nature & Mr. Pitt
that hangs up in Lloyd's best parlour, should have conspired to call up three necessaries, simple commoners as
our fathers knew them, into the upper house of Luxuries -
- .   Bread, and Beer, and Coals, Manning. - But as to
France and Frenchman, And the Abbe Sieyes & his constitutions, (26) I cannot make these present times present to
me.   I read histories of the past, and I live in them;
altho' to abstract senses they are far less momentous,
than the noises which keep Europe awake.   I am reading
Burnet's Own Times. (27) - Did you ever read that garru-
lous, pleasant history?   He tells his story like an old
man, past political service, bragging to his sons, on
winter evenings, of the part he took in public transactions, when "his old cap was new."   Full of scandal,
which all true history is.   No palliatives, but all the
stark wickedness, that actually gives the momentum to
national actors.   Quite the prattle of age & out lived
importance.   Truth & sincerity staring out upon you perpetually in alto relievo. (28) - Himself a party man, he
makes you a party man.   None of the Damned Philosophical
Humeian indifference, so cold & unnatural & unhuman.
None of the damned Gibbonian fine writing so fine & composite.   None of Mr. Robertson's periods with three members.   None of Mr. Roscoe's sage remarks, (29) all so
apposite & coming in so clever, lest the reader should
have had the trouble of drawing an inference.   Burnet's

good old prattle I can bring present to my mind;  I can
make the revolution present to me - . the French Revolution, by a converse perversity in my nature, I fling as
far *from* me.——

From a letter to Walter Wilson, 16 December.  Walter
Wilson, who worked for a time with Lamb in the East India
House, published his 'Memoirs of the Life and Times of
Daniel Defoe' in 1830.  Although the eighteenth-century
English novelists were among Lamb's favourite reading and
a frequent topic of his conversation, with the exception
of Defoe, he never wrote on any of them.  Wilson, in this
instance, provided a stimulus lacking in the case of
Richardson, Fielding and Smollett.  Lamb disliked the
majority of modern novels.  Wilson reprinted the part of
this letter enclosed within quotation marks in the third
volume of his 'Memoirs'.

I have nothing of Defoe's but two or three Novels, and
the Plague History.  I can give you no information about
him.  As a slight general character of what I remember of
them (for I have not look'd into them latterly) I would
say that "in the appearance of *truth* in all the incidents
and conversations that occur in them, they exceed any
works of fiction I am acquainted with.  It is perfect illusion.  The *Author* never appears in these self-narra-
tives (for so they ought to be called or rather Auto-bio-
graphies) but the *Narrator* chains us down to an implicit
belief in every thing he says.  There is all the minute
detail of a log-book in it.  Dates are painfully pressed
upon the memory.  Facts are repeated over and over in
varying phrases, till you cannot chuse but believe them.
It is like reading Evidence given in a Court of Justice.
So anxious the Story-teller seems, that the truth should
be clearly comprehended, that when he has told us a matter
of fact, or a motive, in a line or two farther down he *repeats* it with his favorite figure of speech "I say" so and
so, - though he had made it abundantly plain before.

This is in imitation of the common people's way of speaking, or rather of the way in which they are addressed by a master or mistress, who wishes to impress some thing upon their memories; and has a wonderful effect upon matter-of-fact readers. Indeed it is to such principally that he writes. His style is elsewhere beautiful, but plain & *homely*. Robinson Crusoe is delightful to all ranks and classes but it is easy to see that it is a written in phraseology peculiarly adapted to the lower conditions of readers; hence it is an especial favorite with sea-faring men, poor boys, servant maids &c. His novels are capital Kitchen-reading, while they are worthy from their deep interest to find a shelf in the Libraries of the wealthiest, and the most learned. His passion for *matter of fact narrative* sometimes betrayed him into a long relation of common incidents which might happen to any man, and have no interest but the intense appearance of truth in them, to recommend them. The whole latter half, or two thirds of, Colonel Jack is of this description. The beginning of Colonel Jack is the most affecting natural picture of a young thief that was ever drawn. His losing the stolen money in the hollow of a tree, and finding it again when he was in despair, and then being in equal distress at not knowing how to dispose of it, and several similar touches in the early history of the Colonel, evince a deep knowledge of human nature; and, putting out of question the superior *romantic* interest of the latter, in my mind very much exceed Crusoe. Roxana (1st Edition) is the next in Interest, though he left out the best part of it in subsequent Editions from a foolish hyper-criticism of his friend Southerne. (30) But Moll Flanders, the accot of the Plague &c. &c. are all of one family, and have the same stamp of character." -

---

(ii) 1823

---

From a letter to Walter Wilson, 24 February.

---

I do not prefer Col. Jack to either Rob. Cr. or Roxana - I only spoke of the beginning of it, his childish history. The rest is poor.... I do not know that Swift mentions him. Pope does. I forget if D'Israeli has. Dunlop I think has nothing of him. (31) He is quite new ground, and scarce known beyond Crusoe.... Do you know the Paper in the "Englishman" by Sir Rd. Steele, giving an accot of Selkirk? (32) It is admirable, and has all the germs of Crusoe. You must quote it entire.

---

(iii) 1830

---

This short essay was published by Walter Wilson in the
third volume of his 'Memoirs'.   The similarities between
this and Lamb's letter eight years earlier surprised the
author greatly.

---

It has happened not seldom that one work of some author
has so transcendantly surpassed in execution the rest of
his compositions, that the world has agreed to pass a sentence of dismissal upon the latter, and to consign them to
total neglect and oblivion.   It has done wisely in this,
not to suffer the contemplation of excellencies of a lower
standard to abate, or stand in the way of the pleasure it
has agreed to receive from the master-piece.
Again it has happened, that from no inferior merit of
execution in the rest, but from superior good fortune in
the choice of its subject, some single work shall have
been suffered to eclipse, and cast into shade the deserts
of its less fortunate brethren.   This has been done with
more or less injustice in the case of the popular allegory
of Bunyan, in which the beautiful and scriptural image of
a pilgrim or wayfarer (we are all such upon earth), addressing itself intelligibly and feelingly to the bosoms
of all, has silenced, and made almost to be forgotten, the
more awful and scarcely less tender beauties of the "Holy
War made by Shaddai upon Diabolus," of the same author;   a
romance less happy in its subject, but surely well worthy
of a secondary immortality.   But in no instance has this
excluding partiality been exerted with more unfairness
than against what may be termed the secondary novels or
romances of De Foe.
While all ages and descriptions of people hang delighted over the 'Adventures of Robinson Crusoe,' and shall
continue to do so we trust while the world lasts, how few
comparatively will bear to be told, that there exist other
fictitious narratives by the same writer - four of them at
least of no inferior interest, except what results from a
less felicitous choice of situation.   Roxana - Singleton
- Moll Flanders - Colonel Jack - are all genuine offspring
of the same father.   They bear the veritable impress of
De Foe.   An unpractised midwife that would not swear to
the nose, lip, forehead, and eye, of every one of them!
They are in their way as full of incident, and some of
them every bit as romantic;   only they want the uninhabi-
ted Island, and the charm that has bewitched the world, of
the striking solitary situation.
But are there no solitudes out of the cave and the

desert? or cannot the heart in the midst of crowds feel
frightfully alone?   Singleton, on the world of waters,
prowling about with pirates less merciful than the creatures of any howling wilderness;  is he not alone, with
the faces of men about him, but without a guide that can
conduct him through the mists of educational and habitual
ignorance;  or a fellow-heart that can interpret to him
the new-born yearnings and aspirations of unpractised
penitence?   Or when the boy Colonel Jack, in the loneliness of the heart (the worst solitude), goes to hide his
ill-purchased treasure in the hollow tree by night, and
miraculously loses, and miraculously finds it again - whom
hath he there to sympathise with him? or of what sort are
his associates?

The narrative manner of De Foe has a naturalness about
it, beyond that of any other novel or romance writer.
His fictions have all the air of true stories.   It is impossible to believe, while you are reading them, that a
real person is not narrating to you every where nothing
but what really happened to himself.   To this, the extreme *homeliness* of their style mainly contributes.   We
use the word in its best and heartiest sense - that which
comes *home* to the reader.   The narrators everywhere are
chosen from low life, or have had their origin in it;
therefore they tell their own tales, (Mr. Coleridge has
anticipated us in this remark,) (33) as persons in their
degree are observed to do, with infinite repetition, and
an overacted exactness, lest the hearer should not have
minded, or have forgotten, some things that had been told
before.   Hence the emphatic sentences marked in the good
old (but deserted) Italic type;  and hence, too, the frequent interposition of the reminding old colloquial parenthesis, "I say" - "mind" - and the like, when the story-
teller repeats what, to a practised reader, might appear
to have been sufficiently insisted upon before:  which
made an ingenious critic observe, that his works, in this
kind, were excellent reading for the kitchen.   And, in
truth, the heroes and heroines of De Foe, can never again
hope to be popular with a much higher class of readers,
than that of the servant-maid or the sailor.   Crusoe
keeps its rank only by tough prescription;  Singleton, the
pirate - Colonel Jack, the thief - Moll Flanders, both
thief and harlot - Roxana, harlot and something worse -
would be startling ingredients in the bill of fare of
modern literary delicacies.   But, then, what pirates,
what thieves, and what harlots is *the thief, the harlot,*
and *the pirate* of De Foe?   We would not hesitate to say,
that in no other book of fiction, where the lives of such
characters are described, is guilt and delinquency made

less seductive, or the suffering made more closely to
follow the commission, or the penitence more earnest or
more bleeding, or the intervening flashes of religious
visitation, upon the rude and uninstructed soul, more
meltingly and fearfully painted.   They, in this, come
near to the tenderness of Bunyan;   while the livelier pictures and incidents in them, as in Hogarth or in Fielding,
tend to diminish that "fastidiousness to the concerns and
pursuits of common life, which an unrestrained passion
for the ideal and the sentimental is in danger of producing." (34)

**47**  Joseph Priestley
(i) 1796

---

From a letter to Coleridge, 30, 31 May.

---

I *have* seen priestly. (35)   I love to see his name repeated in your writings.   I love & honor him almost pro-
fanely.   You would be charmed with his *sermons*, if you
never read em, - You have doubtless read his books, illustrative of the doctrine of Necessity.   Prefixed to a late
work of his, in answer to Paine there is a preface given
an account of the Man & his services to Men, written by
Lindsey, his dearest friend, - well worth your reading -

---

(ii) 1797

---

From a letter to Coleridge, 2 January.

---

I am at present re-re-reading Priestly's examinat:  of the
Scotch Drs: (36)  how the Rogue strings 'em up, three
together!   You have no doubt read that clear, strong,
humorous, most entertain'g piece of reasoning.   If not,
procure it, & be exquisitely amused.   I wish I could get
more of Priestly's works.

Oxford in the Vacation from which this passage has been
taken, first appeared in the 'London Magazine' for October
1820, and was reprinted in the 'Essays'.

Antiquity! thou wondrous charm, what art thou? that,
being nothing, art every thing!   When thou *wert*, thou
wert not antiquity - then thou wert nothing, but hadst a
remoter *antiquity*, as thou called'st it, to look back to
with blind veneration;   thou thyself being to thyself
flat, jejune, *modern!*   What mystery lurks in this retro-
version? or what half Januses* are we, that cannot look
forward with the same idolatry with which we for ever
revert!   The mighty future is as nothing, being every
thing! the past is every thing, being nothing!

(ii) 1821, 1823

New Year's Eve was published in the 'London Magazine',
January 1821 and was included in the 'Essays'.

Of all sound of all bells - (bells, the music nighest
bordering upon heaven) - most solemn and touching is the
peal which rings out the Old Year.   I never hear it without a gathering-up of my mind to a concentration of all
the images that have been diffused over the past twelvemonth;   all I have done or suffered, performed or neglected - in that regretted time.   I begin to know its worth,
as when a person dies.   It takes a personal colour;   nor

* Januses of one face. - SIR THOMAS BROWNE. (37)

was it a poetical flight in a contemporary, when he ex-
claimed

I saw the skirts of the departing Year. (38)

It is no more than what in sober sadness every one of
us seems to be conscious of, in that awful leave-
taking....   But I am none of those who -

Welcome the coming, speed the parting guest. (39)

I am naturally, beforehand, shy of novelties;   new
books, new faces, new years, - from some mental twist
which makes it difficult in me to face the prospective.
I have almost ceased to hope;   and am sanguine only in the
prospects of other (former) years.   I plunge into foregone visions and conclusions.   I encounter pell-mell with
past disappointments.   I am armour-proof against old dis-
couragements.   I forgive, or overcome in fancy, old adversaries.   I play over again *for love*, as the gamesters
phrase it, games, for which I once paid so dear.   I
would scarce now have any of those untoward accidents and
events of my life reversed.   I would no more alter them
than the incidents of some well-contrived novel....
In a degree beneath manhood, it is my infirmity to look
back upon those early days.   Do I advance a paradox, when
I say, that, skipping over the intervention of forty
years, a man may have leave to love *himself*, without the
imputation of self-love?
If I know aught of myself, no one whose mind is intro-
spective - and mine is painfully so - can have a less respect for his present identity.   ...but for the child
Elia - that "other me," there, in the back-ground - I
must take leave to cherish the remembrance of that young
master - with as little reference, I protest, to this
stupid changeling of five-and-forty, as if it had been a
child of some other house, and not of my parents....   God
help thee, Elia, how art thou changed!   Thou art sophisticated. - I know how honest, how courageous (for a weak-
ling) it was - how religious, how imaginative, how hopeful!   From what have I not fallen, if the child I remember was indeed myself, - and not some dissembling guardian, presenting a false identity, to give the rule to my
unpractised steps, and regulate the tone of my moral
being!
That I am fond of indulging, beyond a hope of sympathy,
in such retrospection, may be the symptom of some sickly
idiosyncrasy.   Or is it owing to another cause;   simply,
that being without wife or family, I have not learned to

project myself enough out of myself;  and having no offspring of my own to dally with, I turn back upon memory,
and adopt my own early idea, as my heir and favorite?   If
these speculations seem fantastical to thee, reader - (a
busy man, perchance), if I tread out of the way of thy
sympathy, and am singularly-conceited only, I retire, impenetrable to ridicule, under the phantom cloud of Elia.

...Not childhood alone, but the young man till thirty,
never feels practically that he is mortal.  He knows it
indeed, and, if need were, he could preach a homily on the
fragility of life;  but he brings it not home to himself,
any more than in a hot June we can appropriate to our imagination the freezing days of December.  But now, shall
I confess a truth? - I feel these audits but too powerfully.  I begin to count the probabilities of my duration, and to grudge at the expenditure of moments and
shortest periods, like miser's farthings.  In proportion
as the years both lessen and shorten, I set more count
upon their periods, and would fain lay my ineffectual
finger upon the spoke of the great wheel.  I am not content to pass away "like a weaver's shuttle."  Those metaphors solace me not, nor sweeten the unpalatable draught
of mortality.  I care not to be carried with the tide,
that smoothly bears human life to eternity;  and reluct at
the inevitable course of destiny.  I am in love with this
green earth;  the face of town and country;  the unspeak-
able rural solitudes, and the sweet security of streets.
I would set up my tabernacle here....   I do not want to
be weaned by age;  or drop, like mellow fruit, as they
say, into the grave. - Any alteration, on this earth of
mine, in diet or in lodging, puzzles and discomposes me.
My household-gods plant a terrible fixed foot, and are not
rooted up without blood.  They do not willingly seek Lav-
inian shores.  A new state of being staggers me.

Sun, and sky, and breeze, and solitary walks, and
summer holidays, and the greenness of fields, and the delicious juices of meats and fishes, and society, and the
cheerful glass, and candle-light, and fire-side conversations, and innocent vanities, and jests, and *irony itself*
- do these things go out with life?

(iii) 1821, 1823

---

Mackery End, in Hertfordshire was published in the 'London
Magazine', July 1821 and reprinted two years later in the
'Essays'.

---

We are both great readers in different directions.   While
I am hanging over (for the thousandth time) some passage
in old Burton, or one of his strange contemporaries, she
is abstracted in some modern tale, or adventure, whereof
our common reading-table is daily fed with assiduously
fresh supplies.   Narrative teazes me.   I have little
concern in the progress of events.   She must have a story
- well, ill, or indifferently told - so there be life
stirring in it, and plenty of good or evil accidents.
The fluctuations of fortune in fiction - and almost in
real life - have ceased to interest, or operate but dully
upon me.   Out-of-the-way humours and opinions - heads
with some diverting twist in them - the oddities of authorship please me most.   My cousin (40) has a native dis-
relish of any thing that sounds odd or bizarre.   Nothing
goes down with her, that is quaint, irregular, or out of
the road of common sympathy.   She "holds Nature more
clever." (41)   I can pardon her blindness to the beautiful obliquities of the Religio Medici; but she must apol-
ogise to me for certain disrespectful insinuations, which
she has been pleased to throw out latterly, touching the
intellectuals of a dear favourite of mine, of the last
century but one - the thrice noble, chaste, and virtuous,
- but again somewhat fantastical, and original-brain'd,
generous Margaret Newcastle. (42)

---

(iv) 1821, 1823

---

My First Play was published in the 'London Magazine',
December 1821 and was included by Lamb in the 'Essays'.

---

   I saw these plays in the season 1781-2, when I was from
six to seven years old.   After the intervention of six or
seven other years ... I again entered the doors of a
theatre.   That old Artaxerxes (43) evening had never done
ringing in my fancy.   I expected the same feelings to
come again with the same occasion.   But we differ from
ourselves less at sixty and sixteen than the latter does
from six.   In that interval what had I not lost!   At the

first period I knew nothing, understood nothing, discriminated nothing.  I felt all, loved all, wondered all -

　　Was nourished, I could not tell how - (44)

I had left the temple a devotee, and was returned a
rationalist.  The same things were there materially;  but
the emblem, the reference, was gone! - The green curtain
was no longer a veil, drawn between two worlds, the un-
folding of which was to bring back past ages, to present
"a royal ghost," (45) - but a certain quantity of green
baize, which was to separate the audience for a given time
from certain of their fellow-men who were to come forward
and pretend those parts.  The lights - the orchestra
lights - came up a clumsy machinery.  The first ring, and
the second ring, was now but a trick of the prompter's
bell - which had been, like the note of the cuckoo, a
phantom of a voice, no hand seen or guessed at which mini-
stered to its warning.  The actors were men and women
painted.  I thought the fault was in them;  but it was in
myself.

---

(v) 1823, 1833

---

Lamb's Preface to the 'Last Essays' was originally published in the 'London Magazine', January 1823, and was
probably intended by Lamb to mark the end of his career as
Elia.  It was originally entitled A Character of the late
Elia, and was signed 'Phil-Elia.'  The obituary however,
was premature, and Lamb used it ten years later, with
omissions, as the preface to his second collection of
essays in 1833.

---

　　THIS poor gentleman, who for some months past had been
in a declining way, hath at length paid his final tribute
to nature.
　　To say truth, it is time he were gone.  The humour of
the thing, if there was ever much in it, was pretty well
exhausted;  and a two years' and a half existence has been
a tolerable duration for a phantom.
　　I am now at liberty to confess, that much which I have
heard objected to my late friend's writings was well-
founded.  Crude they are, I grant you - a sort of un-
licked, incondite things - villainously pranked in an affected array of antique modes and phrases.  They had not
been *his*, if they had been other than such;  and better it

is, that a writer should be natural in a self-pleasing quaintness, than to affect a naturalness (so called) that should be strange to him.   Egotistical they have been pronounced by some who did not know, that what he tells us, as of himself, was often true only (historically) of another;   as in a former Essay (to save many instances) - where under the *first person* (his favourite figure) he shadows forth the forlorn estate of a country-boy placed at a London school, (46) far from his friends and connections - in direct opposition to his own early history. If it be egotism to imply and twine with his own identity the griefs and affections of another - making himself many, or reducing many unto himself - then is the skilful novelist, who all along brings in his hero, or heroine, speaking of themselves, the greatest egotist of all;   who yet has never, therefore, been accused of that narrowness. And how shall the intenser dramatist escape being faulty, who doubtless, under cover of passion uttered by another, oftentimes gives blameless vent to his most inward feelings, and expresses his own story modestly?

My late friend was in many respects a singular character.   Those who did not like him, hated him;   and some, who once liked him, afterwards became his bitterest haters.   The truth is, he gave himself too little concern what he uttered, and in whose presence.   He observed neither time nor place, and would e'en out with what came uppermost.   With the severe religionist he would pass for a free-thinker;   while the other faction set him down for a bigot, or persuaded themselves that he belied his sentiments.   Few understood him;   and I am not certain that at all times he quite understood himself.   He too much affected that dangerous figure - irony.   He sowed doubtful speeches, and reaped plain, unequivocal hatred. - He would interrupt the gravest discussion with some light jest;   and yet, perhaps, not quite irrelevant in ears that could understand it.   Your long and much talkers hated him.   The informal habit of his mind, joined to an inveterate impediment of speech, forbade him to be an orator;   and he seemed determined that no one else should play that part when he was present.   He was *petit* and ordinary in his person and appearance.   I have seen him sometimes in what is called good company, but where he has been a stranger, sit silent, and be suspected for an odd fellow;   till some unlucky occasion provoking it, he would stutter out some senseless pun (not altogether senseless perhaps, if rightly taken), which has stamped his character for the evening.   It was hit or miss with him;   but nine times out of ten, he contrived by this device to send away a whole company his enemies.

His conceptions rose kindlier than his utterance, and his
happiest *impromptus* had the appearance of effort.   He has
been accused of trying to be witty, when in truth he was
but struggling to give his poor thoughts articulation.
He chose his companions for some individuality of character which they manifested. - Hence, not many persons of
science and few professed *literati*, were of his councils.
They were, for the most part, persons of an uncertain fortune;   and, as to such people commonly nothing is more obnoxious than a gentleman of settled (though moderate) income, he passed with most of them for a great miser.    To
my knowledge this was a mistake.   His *intimados*, to confess a truth, were in the world's eye a ragged regiment.
He found them floating on the surface of society;   and the
colour, or something else, in the weed pleased him.    The
burrs stuck to him - but they were good and loving burrs
for all that.   He never greatly cared for the society of
what are called good people.   If any of these were scan-
dalised (and offences were sure to arise), he could not
help it.   When he has been remonstrated with for not
making more concessions to the feelings of good people, he
would retort by asking, what one point did these good
people ever concede to him?   He was temperate in his
meals and diversions, but always kept a little on this
side of abstemiousness.   Only in the use of the Indian
weed he might be thought a little excessive.   He took it,
he would say, as a solvent of speech.   Marry - as the
friendly vapour ascended, how his prattle would curl up
sometimes with it! the ligaments, which tongue-tied him,
were loosened, and the stammerer proceeded a statist!
   I do not know whether I ought to bemoan or rejoice that
my old friend is departed.   His jests were beginning to
grow obsolete, and his stories to be found out.   He felt
the approaches of age;   and while he pretended to cling to
life, you saw how slender were the ties left to bind him.
Discoursing with him latterly on this subject, he expressed himself with a pettishness, which I thought unworthy
of him.   In our walks about his suburban retreat (as he
called it) at Shacklewell, some children belonging to a
school of industry had met us, and bowed and curtseyed, as
he thought, in an especial manner to *him*.   "They take me
for a visiting governor," he muttered earnestly.   He had
a horror, which he carried to a foible, of looking like
anything important and parochial.   He thought that he
approached nearer to that stamp daily.   He had a general
aversion from being treated like a grave or respectable
character, and kept a wary eye upon the advances of age
that should so entitle him.   He herded always, while it
was possible, with people younger than himself.   He did

not conform to the march of time, but was dragged along in
the procession.   His manners lagged behind his years.
He was too much of the boy-man.   The *toga virilis* (47)
never sate gracefully on his shoulders.   The impressions
of infancy had burnt into him, and he resented the imper-
tinence of manhood.   These were weaknesses; but such as
they were, they are a key to explicate some of his writings.

---

(vi) 1822, 1833

---

Detached Thoughts on Books and Reading first appeared in
the 'London Magazine', July 1822, and was reprinted in
'Last Essays'.

---

At the hazard of losing some credit on this head, I must
confess that I dedicate no inconsiderable portion of my
time to other people's thoughts.   I dream away my life in
others' speculations.   I love to lose myself in other
men's minds.   When I am not walking, I am reading;  I
cannot sit and think.   Books think for me.

I have no repugnances.   Shaftesbury is not too genteel
for me, nor Jonathan Wild too low.   I can read any thing
which I call a *book*.   There are things in that shape
which I cannot allow for such.

In this catalogue of *books which are no books - biblia
a-biblia* - I reckon Court Calendars, Directories, Pocket
Books, Draught Boards bound and lettered at the back, Scientific Treatises, Almanacks, Statutes at Large;  the
works of Hume, Gibbon, Robertson, Beattie, Soame
Jenyns, (48) and, generally, all those volumes which "no
gentleman's library should be without:"  the Histories of
Flavius Josephus (that learned Jew), and Paley's Moral
Philosophy. (49)   With these exceptions, I can read almost any thing.   I bless my stars for a taste so catholic, so unexcluding.

I confess that it moves my spleen to see these *things
in books' clothing* perched upon shelves, like false
saints, usurpers of true shrines, intruders into the sanctuary, thrusting out the legitimate occupants.   To reach
down a well-bound semblance of a volume, and hope it some
kind-hearted play-book, then, opening what "seem its
leaves," (50) to come bolt upon a withering Population
Essay. (51)   To expect a Steele, or a Farquhar, and find
- Adam Smith.   To view a well-arranged assortment of
blockheaded Encyclopaedias ... when a tithe of that good
leather would comfortably re-clothe my shivering folios....

Books of quick interest, that hurry on for incidents, are for the eye to glide over only. It will not do to read them out. I could never listen to even the better kind of modern novels without extreme irksomeness.

---

(vii) 1797

---

From a letter to Coleridge, 7 January.

---

Priestly, whom I sin in almost adoring, speaks of "such a choice of company, as tends to keep up that right bent, & firmness of mind, which a nec[e]ssary intercourse with the world would otherwise warp & relax. Such fellowship is the true ba[lsam] of life, it[s] cement is infinitely more durable than that of the friendships of the world, & it looks for its proper fruit, & complete gratification, to the life beyond the Grave." (52)   Is there a possible chance for such an one as me to realize in this world, such friendships?   Where am I to look for 'em? what testimonials shall I bring of my being worthy of such friendship?   Alas! the great & good go together in separate Herds, & leave such as me to lag far far behind in all intellectual, & far more grievous to say, in all moral accomplishments - .   Coleridge, I have not one truly elevated character among my acquaintance: not one Christian: not one, but undervalues Christianity -- singly what am I to do....   Wesley has said, "Religion is not a solitary thing." (53)   Alas! it necessarily is so with me, or next to solitary.   Tis true, you write to me.   But correspondence by letter, & personal intimacy, are very widely different.   Do, do write to me, & do some good to my mind, already how much "warped & relaxed" by the world!
   ...Are you yet a Berkleyan?   Make me one.   I rejoyce in being, speculatively, a necessarian. - Would to God, I were habitually a practical one.   Confirm me in the faith of that great & glorious doctrine, & keep me steady in the contemplation of it....   But I must talk.   I love to write to you.   I take a pride in it - .   It makes me think less meanly of myself.   It makes me think myself not totally disconnected from the better part of Mankind. I know, I am too dissatisfied with the beings around me....   I know, I am no ways better in practice than my neighbors - but I have a taste for religion, an occasional earnest aspiration after perfection, which they have not.   I gain nothing by being with such as myself - we encourage one another in mediocrity - I am always longing

to be with men more excellent than myself.... I have just been reading, Priestly on Philosophical necessity, in the thought that I enjoy a kind of Communion, a kind of friendship even, with the great & good. Books are to me instead of friends, - I wish they did not resemble the latter in their scarceness. -

---

## (viii) 1801

---

From a letter to Walter Wilson, 14 August.

---

I know that you think a very important difference in opinion with respect to some more serious subjects between us makes me a dangerous companion; but do not rashly infer, from some slight and light expressions which I may have made use of in a moment of levity in your presence, without sufficient regard to your feelings - do not conclude that I am an inveterate enemy to all religion. I have had a time of seriousness, and I have known the importance and reality of a religious belief. Latterly, I acknowledge, much of my seriousness has gone off, whether from new company or some other new associations; but I still retain at bottom a conviction of the truth, and a certainty of the usefulness of religion. I will not pretend to more gravity or feeling than I at present possess; my intention is not to persuade you that any great alteration is probable in me; sudden converts are superficial and transitory; I only want you to believe that I have *stamina* of seriousness within me, and that I desire nothing more than a return of that friendly intercourse which used to subsist between us, but which my folly has suspended.

---

## (ix) 1804

---

From a letter to Robert Lloyd, 13 March.

---

it is the character of your letters, that you omit facts, dates, names & matter, and describe nothing but feelings, in which as I cannot always partake, as being more intense in degree or different in kind from my own tranquil ones, I cannot always well tell how to reply. Your dishes are too much sauced and spiced and flavored, for me to suppose that you can relish my plain meats and vulgar aliment.

---

(x) 1822

From a letter to John Taylor, 7 December.   Lamb initially
intended this passage to be the preface to the 'Essays' of
1823, published by Taylor and Hessey.   However, in the
same letter he changed his mind and withdrew it on the
grounds that a preface is nothing but a talk with the
reader, and his essays were nothing else.

DEDICATION
TO THE FRIENDLY AND JUDICIOUS READER,
who will take these Papers, as they were meant;   not
understanding every thing perversely in the absolute and
literal sense, but giving fair construction as to an
after-dinner conversation;   allowing for the rashness and
necessary incompleteness of first thoughts;   and not re-
membering, for the purpose of an after taunt, words spoken
peradventure after the fourth glass.   The Author wishes
(what he would will for himself) plenty of good friends to
stand by him, good books to solace him, prosperous events
to all his honest undertakings, and a candid interpretation to his most hasty words and actions.   The other sort
(and he hopes many of them will purchase his book too) he
greets with the curt invitation of Timon, 'Uncover, dogs,
and lap:' (54) or he dismisses them with the confident
security of the philosopher, - 'you beat but on the case
of ELIA.'

(xi) 1824

From a letter to Bernard Barton, 9 January.

    Do you know what it is to succumb under an insurmount-
able day mare - a whoreson lethargy, Falstaff calls
it (55) - an indisposition to do any thing, or to be anything - a total deadness and distaste - a suspension of
vitality - an indifference to locality - a numb soporifi-
cal good for nothingness - an ossification all over - an
oysterlike insensibility to the passing events - a mind-
stupor - a brawny defiance to the needles of a thrusting-
in conscience - did you ever have a very bad cold with a
total irresolution to submit to water gruel processes? -
this has been for many weeks my lot, and my excuse - my
fingers drag heavily over this paper, and to my thinking

it is three and twenty furlongs from here to the end of
this demi-sheet - I have not a thing to say - nothing is
of more importance than another - I am flatter than a denial or a pancake - emptier than Judge Parks wig when the
head is in it (56) - duller than a country stage when the
actors are off it - a cypher - an O - I acknowledge life
at all only by an occasional convulsional cough, and a
permanent phlegmatic pain in the chest - I am weary of
the world - Life is weary of me - My day is gone into Twilight and I dont think it worth the expence of candles -
my wick hath a thief in it, but I c'ant muster courage to
snuff it - I inhale suffocation - I ca'nt distinguish veal
from mutton - nothing interests me - tis 12 o Clock, and
Thurtell is just now coming out upon the New Drop - Jack
Ketch alertly tucking up his greasy sleeves to do the last
office of mortality, yet cannot I elicit a groan or a
moral reflection - if you told me the world will be at end
tomorrow, I should just say, "will it?" - I have not voli-
tion enough to dot my i's - much less to comb my eye brows
- my eyes are set in my head - my brains are gone out to
see a poor relation in Moorfields, and they did not say
when they'd come back again - my Scull is a Grubstreet
Attic, to let - not so much as a joint stool or a crackd
jordan left in it - my hand writes, not I, from habit, as
chickens run about a little when their heads are off - O
for a vigorous fit of gout cholic tooth ache - an earwig
in my auditory, a fly in my visual organs - pain is life -
the sharper, the more evidence of life - but this apathy,
t[his] death....
  Who shall deliver me from the body of this death? (57)

---

(xii) 1824

---

From a letter to Bernard Barton, 23 January.

---

Never mind my dulness, I am used to long intervals of it.
The heavens seem brass to me - then again comes the refreshing shower.   "I have been merry once or twice ere
now." (58)

---

(xiii) 1825

---

From a letter to Bernard Barton, 10 August.   In an earlier letter, 2 July 1825, Lamb had thanked Barton for a

presentation copy of his 'Poems', but had complained that topics of religious consolation are so often repeated that a 'sort of triteness' is inevitable. In particular Barton's friends, he says, lose too many exemplary children.

---

I did not express myself clearly about what I think a false topic insisted on so frequently in consolatory addresses on the death of Infants. I know something like it is in Scripture, but I think humanly spoken. It is a natural thought, a sweet fallacy to the Survivors - but still a fallacy. If it stands on the doctrine of this being a probationary state, it is liable to this dilemma. Omniscience, to whom possibility must be clear as act, must know of the child, what it would hereafter turn out: if good, then the topic is false to say it is secured from falling into future wilfulness, vice &c. If bad, I do not see how its exemption from certain future overt acts by being snatched away at all tells in its favor. You stop the arm of a murderer, or arrest the finger of a pickpurse, but is not the guilt incurred as much by the intent as if never so much acted. Why children are hurried off, and old reprobates of a hundred left, whose trial humanly we may think was complete at fifty, is among the obscurities of providence. The very notion of a state of probation has darkness in it. The all-knower has no need of satisfying his eyes by seeing what we will do, when he knows before what we will do. Methinks we might be condemn'd before commission. In these things we grope and flounder, and if we can pick up a little human comfort that the child taken is snatch'd from vice (no great compliment to it: by the bye) let us take it. And as to where an untried child goes, whether to join the assembly of its elders who have borne the heat of the day - fire-purified martyrs and torment-sifted confessors - what know we? - We promise heaven methinks too cheaply, and assign large revenues to Minors, incompetent to manage them. Epitaphs run upon this topic of consolation, till the very frequency induces a cheapness. Tickets for admission into Paradise are sculptured out at a penny a letter, twopence a syllable &c. It is all a mystery, and the more I try to express my meaning (having none that is clear) the more I founder. Finally write what your own conscience which to you is the unerring judge, seems best, and be careless about the whimsies of such a half-baked notionist as I am.

(xiv) 1827

---

From a letter to Barron Field, 4 October.

---

For Mathews - I know my own utter unfitness for such a
task. (59)   I am no hand at describing costumes, a great
requisite in an account of manner'd pictures.   I have not
the slightest acquaintance with pictorial language even.
An imitator of me, or rather pretender to be *me*, in his
Rejected Articles, (60) has made me minutely describe the
dresses of the Poissards at Calais.   I could as soon resolve Euclid.   I have no eye for forms and fashions.   I
substitute analogies, and get rid of the phenomenon by
slurring in for it its impression.   I am sure you must
have observed this defect, or peculiarity, in my writings.
Else the delight would be incalculable in doing such a
thing for Mathews....   Christ! what a feast 'twould be to
be sitting at the pictures, painting 'em into words, but I
could almost as soon make words into pictures.   I speak
this deliberately, and not out of modesty.   I pretty well
know what I ca'nt do.

---

(xv) 1830

---

From a letter to Sir Anthony Carlisle, possibly August.

---

Much thanks for your Spleen-theory. (61)   I wish I was
more competent to admire it properly.   It *reads like a
work of sense.*   But I have a most unscientific head, and
can only *believe* that we are wonderfully and fearfully
made. (62) - I perfectly agree with the sentiments in your
note.   The March of Intellect, in respect of Science, and
encouragement of the highest Science, is a Dead March....
I am 35 years too old to enter into a proper sympathy with
new French revolutions. (63)   Faustae felices-que
sint (64) - but they affect me little more now than lunary
phases -

---

(xvi) 1830

---

From a letter to George Dyer, 20 December.

---

Can we ring the bells backward?   Can we unlearn the arts
that pretend to civilize, and then burn the world?   There
is a march of Science;  but who shall beat the drums for
its retreat?

---

(xvii) 1831

---

From a letter to P.G. Patmore, possibly 10 or 20 April.

---

I can promise little help if you mean literary, when I
reflect that for 5 years I have been feeling the necessity
of scribbling, but have never found the power.

Lamb's review of the first volume of Hazlitt's 'Table-Talk', 1821, published here for the first time, is reproduced by permission of the New York Public Library where the manuscript is housed in the Berg Collection, No. 220284B.   The bibliographical description, provided by the library, is as follows:  '"Table Talk, or, Original Essays.   By William Hazlitt.   11pp.   folio. being an unpublished review of the first volume of Hazlitt's essays by that name.  *Circa* June 1821.   This was never published.   There are many deletions and corrections in Lamb's hand.   Reference is made to Hazlitt's satire of Leigh Hunt.   Perhaps Lamb did not want to stir up any more ill-feeling now that Hunt had been conciliated.' An account of the manuscript is to be found in G.L. Barnett's An Unpublished Review by Lamb, 'MLQ', XVII, 1956. It is the most important of Lamb's reviews, and cancellations of any critical significance are provided in the notes.

As his Letter of Elia to Robert Southey indicates, Lamb greatly valued Hazlitt's friendship.   In 'Figures of Several Centuries', Arthur Symons described his character of Hazlitt there as 'the finest piece of emotional prose which he ever wrote'.   According to Talfourd in the 1840 edition of the 'Works', Hazlitt's death in 1830

did not so much shock Lamb at the time, as it weighed down his spirits afterwards, when he felt the want of those essays which he had used periodically to look for with eagerness in the magazines and reviews which they alone made tolerable to him;  and when he realised the dismal certainty that he should never again enjoy that rich discourse of old poets and painters with which so many a long winter's night had been gladdened, or taste

life with an additional relish in the keen sense of
enjoyment which endeared it to his companion (Letters,
Pt II, p. 77).

In 1834, just before his own death, Lamb is reported to
have said:  'I can read no prose now, though Hazlitt sometimes, to be sure - but then Hazlitt is worth all modern
prose-writers put together' (Lucas, 'Life', II, 265).

---

A series of Miscellaneous Essays, however well executed
in the parts, if it have not some pervading character to
give a unity to it, is ordinarily as tormenting to get
through as a set of aphorisms, or a jest-book. - The
fathers of Essay writing in ancient and modern times -
Plutarch in a measure, and Montaigne without mercy or
measure - imparted their own personal peculiarities to
their themes.  By this balm are they preserved.  The
Author of the Rambler in a less direct way has attained
the same effect.  Without professing egotism, his work is
as essentially egotistical as theirs.  He deals out
opinion, which he would have you take for argument;  and
is perpetually obtruding his own particular views of life
for universal truths.  This is the charm which binds us
to his writings, and not any steady conviction we have of
the solidity of his thinking.  Possibly some of those
Papers, which are generally understood to be failures in
the Rambler - its ponderous levities for instance, and un-
wieldy efforts at being sprightly - may detract less from
the general effect, than if something better in kind, but
less in keeping, had been substituted in place of them.
If the author had taken his friend Goldsmith into partnership, and they had furnished their quotas for alternate
days, the world had been gainer by the arrangement, but
what a heterogeneous mass the work itself would have presented! (65)
    Another class of Essayists, equally impressed with the
advantages of this sort of appeal to the reader, but more
dextrous at shifting off the invidiousness of a perpetual
self-reference, substituted for themselves an *ideal character*;  which left them a still fuller licence in the delivery of their peculiar humours and opinions, under the
masqued battery of a fictitious appellation.  Truths,
which the world would have startled at from the lips of
the gay Captain Steele, it readily accepted from the pen
of old Isaac Bickerstaff.  But the breed of the Bicker-
staffs, as it began, so alas! it expired with him.  It
shewed indeed a few feeble sparks of revival in Nestor
Ironside, (66) but soon went out.  Addison had stepped in
with his wit, his criticism, his morality - the cold gen-

eralities which extinguish humour - and the Spectator, and
its Successor, were little more than bundles of Essays
(valuable indeed, and elegant reading above our praise)
but hanging together with very slender principles of bond
or union.   In fact we use the word Spectator, and mean a
Book.   At mention of the Tatler we sigh, and think of
Isaac Bickerstaff.   Sir Roger de Coverly, Will Wimble,
Will Honeycomb, live for ever in memory - but who is their
*silent Friend*? - Except that he never opens his mouth, we
know nothing about him.   He writes finely upon all subjects - but himself.   He sets every thing in a proper
light - but we do not see through his spectacles.   He
colours nothing with his own hues.   The Lucubrations come
as from an old man, an old bachelor to boot, and a humour-
ist.   The Spectator too, we are told, *is* all this.   But
a young man, a young married man moreover, or any description of man, or woman, with no sort of character beyond
general shrewdness, and a power of observation, might
have strung together all that discordant assemblage of
Papers, which call the Spectator father.   They describe
indeed with the utmost felicity all ages & conditions of
men, but they themselves smack of no peculiar age or condition.   He writes, we are told, because he cannot bring
himself to speak, but why he cannot bring himself to
speak is the riddle.   He is used to good company.   Why
he should conceal his name, while he lavishly proclaims
that of his companions, is equally a secret.   Was it to
remove him still further from any possibility of our sympathies? - or wherein, we would be informed, lurks the
mystery of his short chin? - As a visitor at the Club (a
sort of *umbra*) he might have shewn to advantage among
those short but masterly sketches - but the mass of
matter, spread through eight volumes, is really somewhat
too miscellaneous and diffuse, to hang together for identity upon such a shade, such a tenuity!
   Since the days of the Spectator and Guardian, Essayists, who have appeared under a fictitious appellation,
have for the most part contented themselves with a brief
description of their character and story in the opening
Paper; after which they dismiss the Phantom of an Editor,
and let the work shift for itself, as wisely and wittily
as it is able, unsupported by any characteristic pretences, or individual colouring. - In one particular indeed
the followers of Addison were long and grievously misled.
For many years after the publication of his celebrated
Vision of Mirza, no book of Essays was thought complete
without a Vision.   It set the world dreaming.   Take up
any one of the volumes of this description, published in
the last century; - you will possibly alight upon two or

three successive papers, depicting, with more or less
gravity, sober views of life *as it is* - when - pop - you
come upon a Vision, which you trembled at beforehand from
a glimpse you caught at certain abstractions in Capitals,
Fame, Riches, Long Life, Loss of Friends, Punishment by
Exile - a set of denominations part simple, part compoun-
ded - existing in single, double, and triple hypostases. -
You cannot think on their fantastic essences without gid-
diness, or describe them short of a solecism. - These
authors seem not to have been content to entertain you
with their day-light fancies, but you *must* share their
vacant slumbers & common-place reveries.   The humour,
thank Heaven, is pretty well past.   These Visions, any
thing but visionary - (for who ever dreamt of Fame, but by
metaphor, some mad Orientalist perhaps excepted?) - so
tamely extravagant, so gothically classical - these in-
spirations by downright malice aforethought - these heartless, bloodless literalities - these "thin consisten-
cies", (67) dependent for their personality upon Great
Letters - for write them small, and the tender essences
fade into abstractions - have at length happily melted
away before the progress of good sense;  or the absurdity
has worn itself out.  We might else have still to lament,
that the purer taste of their inventor should have so
often wandered aside into these caprices;  or to wish, if
he had chosen to indulge in an imitation of Eastern extra-
vagance, that he had confined himself to that least obnoxious specimen of his skill, the Allegory of Mirza. -
     The Author before us is, in this respect at least, no
visionary.  He talks to you in broad day-light.   He
comes in no imaginary character.  He is of the class of
Essayists first mentioned.  He attracts, or repels, by
strong realities of individual observation, humour, and
feeling.
     The title, which Mr Hazlitt has chosen, is characteris-
tic enough of his Essays.  The tone of them is uniformly
conversational;  and they are not the less entertaining,
that they resemble occasionally the *talk* of a very clever
person, when he begins to be animated in a convivial
party.  You fancy that a disputant is always present, and
feel a disposition to take up the cudgels yourself [o]n behalf of the other side of the question.  Table-Talk is
not calculated for cold or squeamish readers.  The average thinker will find his common notions a little too
roughly disturbed.  He must brace up his ears to the re-
ception of some novelties.  Strong traits of character
stand out in the work;  and it is not so much a series of
well argued treatises, as a bold confession, or exposi-
tion, of Mr Hazlitt's own ways of feeling upon the sub-

jects treated of.    It is in fact a piece of Autobiogra-
phy;   and, in our minds, a vigorous & well-executed one.
The Writer almost every where adopts the style of a dis-
contented man.    This assumption of a character, if it be
not truly (as we are inclined to believe) his own, is that
which gives force & life to his writing.    He murmers most
musically through fourteen ample Essays.    He quarrels
with People that have but one idea, and with the Learned
that are oppressed with many;   with the man of Paradox,
and the man of Common-Place;   with the Fashionable, and
with the Vulgar;   with Dying Men that make a Will, and
those who die & leave none behind them;   with Sir Joshua
Reynolds for setting up study above genius, and with the
same person for disparaging study in respect of genius;
lastly, he quarrels with himself, with book-making, with
his friends, with the present time, and future - (the last
he has an especial grudge to, and strives hard to prove
that it has no existence) - in short, with every thing in
the world, *except what he likes* - his past recollections
which he describes in a way to make every one else like
them too;   the Indian Jugglers;   Cavanagh, the Fives-
Player;   the noble art and practice of Painting, which he
contends will make men both healthy and wise;   and the Old
Masters. -
    He thus describes (*con amore*) his first visit to the
Louvre, at its golden period before Taste had cause to
lament the interposition of ruthless Destiny. - [Lamb
quotes the passage from the essay, The Pleasures of Painting beginning 'I had made some progress ... gone a pilgrimage to thee'.]
    With all this enthusiasm for the Art, and the intense
application which at one time he seems to have been disposed to give to it, the wonder is, that Mr. Hazlitt did
not turn out a fine painter, rather than writer.    Did he
lack encouragement? or did his powers of application fail
him from some doubt of ultimate success?    [Lamb quotes
the passage from the same essay beginning 'One of my first
attempts ... of hope, & charity'!]
    There is a *naivete* commingled with pathos in this
little scene, which cannot be enough admired.    The old
dissenting clergyman's pride at his son's getting on in
his profession as an artist, still with a wish rather that
he had taken to his own calling;   and then an under-vanity
of his own in "having his picture drawn" coming in to comfort him;   the preference he would have given to some more
orthodox book, with some sort of satisfaction still that
he was drawn with a book - above all, the tenderness in
the close - make us almost think we are perusing some
strain of Mackenzie;   or some of the better (because the

more pathetic) parts of the Tatler.   Indeed such passages
are not unfrequent in this writer;  and break in upon us,
amidst the spleen and severity of his commoner tone, like
springs bursting out in the desert.   The author's wayward
humour, turning inwards from the contemplation of real or
imagined grievances - or exhausting itself in gall and
bitterness at the things *that be* - reverts for its solace,
with a mournfully contrasting spirit of satisfaction, to
the past.   The corruption of Hope quickens into life
again the perishing flowers of the Memory. - In this
spirit, in the third, and the most valuable of his Essays,
that "On the past and future", - in which he maintains the
reality of the former as a possession in hand, against
those who pretend that the future is every thing and the
past nothing - after some reasoning, rather too subtle and
metaphysical for the general reader - he exclaims with an
eloquence that approximates to the finest poetry - [Lamb
quotes the passage beginning 'Is it nothing to have been
... to bear the thing I am'.]

   The Tenth Essay, On Living to One's-self, has this
singular passage.   [Lamb quotes the passage beginning
'Even in the common affairs ... relish or their wholesome-
ness'.]

   We hope that this is more dramatically than truly written.   We recognise nothing like it in our own circle.
We had always thought that Old Friends, and Old Wine were
the best. - We should conjecture that Mr Hazlitt has been
singularly unfortunate, or injudicious, in the choice of
his acquaintance, did not one phenomenon stagger us.   We
every now & then encounter in his Essays with a *character*,
apparently from the life, too mildly drawn for an enemy,
too sharply for a friend.   We suspect that Mr Hazlitt
does not always play quite fairly with his associates.
There is a class of critics - and he may be of them - who
pry into men with "too respective eyes." (68)   They will
"anatomize Regan",(69) when Cordelia would hardly bear
such dissection.   We are not acquainted with Mr Hazlitts
"familiar faces", (70) but when we see certain Characters
exposed & hung up, not in Satire - for the exaggerations
of *that* cure themselves by their excess, as we make allowance for the over-charged features in a caricature -
but certain poor whole-length figures dangling with all
the *best* & *worst* of humanity about them displayed with
cool and unsparing impartiality - Mr Hazlitt must excuse
us if we cannot help suspecting some of them to be the
shadows of defunct Freindships. (71) - This would be a
recipe indeed, a pretty sure one, for converting friends
"into bitterest enemies or cold, uncomfortable acquaintance". - The most expert at drawing Characters, are the

very persons most likely to be deceived in individual &
home instances.   They will seize an infirmity, which
irritates them deservedly in a companion, and go on piling
up every kindred weakness they have found by experience
apt to coalesce with that failing (gathered from a thousand instances) till they have built up in their fancies
an *Abstract*, widely differing indeed from their poor *concrete friend*!   What blunders Steele, or Sterne, may not
in this way have made *at home*! - But we forget.   Our
business is with books.   We profess not, with Mr Hazlitt,
to be Reviewers of Men. - We are willing to give our readers a specimen of what this writer can do, when the moody
fit is off him.   One of the pleasantest and lightest of
his Essays is "On People with one Idea".   We quote his
first instance.   [Lamb reprints the passage beginning
'There is Major C ... Dulce loquentem!'"]

   This is all extremely clever, and about as true as it
is necessary for such half-imaginary sketches to be.   The
veteran subject of it has had his name bandied to & fro,
for praise & blame, the better part of a century, and has
learned to'stand harder knocks than these.   He will
laugh, we dare say, very heartily at this Chimaera of himself from the pen of a *brother-reformer*.   We would venture a wager that the writer of it, with all his appearance of drawing from the life, never spent a day in company with the Major.   We have passed many, & can assure
the Essayist, that Major C—— has many things in his head,
and in his mouth too, besides Parliamentary Reform.   We
know that he is more solicitous to evade the question,
than to obtrude it, in private company;   and will chuse to
turn the conversation purposely to topics of philology &
polite literature, of which he is no common master.   He
will not shun a metaphysical point even if it come in his
way, though he professes not to enter into that sort of
science so deeply as Mr Hazlitt;   and will discuss any
point "at sight" from history & chronology, his favorite
subjects, down to the merits of his scarcely less darling
Norfolk dumpling.   We suspect that Mr Hazlitt knows nothing of the veteran beyond his political speeches, which
to be sure are pretty monotonous upon one subject, and has
carved the rest out of his own brain.   But to deduce a
man's general conversation from what falls from him in
public meetings, expressly convened to discuss a particular topic, is about as good logic, as it would be in the
case of another sort of *Reformer*, who, like Major C—— ,
but in an humbler sphere, goes about professing to *remove
nuisances* - if we should infer, that the good man's whole
discourse, at bed & board, in the ale-house & by the road-
side, was confined to two cuckoo syllables, because in the

exercise of his public function we had never heard him
utter anything beyond Dust O!

The "Character of Cobbett" (Sixth Essay) comes nearer
the mark.  It has the freedom of a sketch, and the truth
of an elaborated portrait.  Nothing is extenuated, nothing overdone.  It is "without oerflowing full". (72)
It may be read with advantage by the partisans & opponents
of the most extraordinary political personage that has appeared in modern times.  It is too long to quote, too
good for abridgment.  We prefer closing our extracts with
a portion of the Twelfth Essay, both for variety-sake, and
because it seems no inappropriate conclusion to leave off
with *that* which is ordinarily the latest of human actions
- "the last infirmity of common minds" (73) - the making
of a Will.  [Lamb quotes extensively but with omissions
the passage beginning 'Few things shew the human character ... that we came into it!']

We cannot take leave of this agreeable and spirited
volume without bearing our decided testimony to Mr Hazlitt's general merits as a writer.  He is (we have no
hesitation in saying) one of the ablest prose-writers of
the age.  To an extraordinary power of original observation he adds an equal power of familiar and striking expression.  There is a ground-work of patient and curious
thinking in almost every one of these Essays, while the
execution is in a high degree brilliant and animated.
The train of reasoning or line of distinction on which he
insists is often so fine as to escape common observation;
at the same time that the quantity of picturesque and
novel illustration is such as to dazzle and overpower
common attention.  He is however a writer perfectly free
from affectation, and never rises into that tone of rapid
and glowing eloquence of which he is a master, but when
the occasion warrants it.  Hence there is nothing more
directly opposite to his usual style than what is understood by *poetical prose*. - If we were to hazard an analy-
tical conjecture on this point, we should incline to think
that Mr H. as a critic and an Essayist has blended two
very different and opposite lines of study and pursuit, a
life of internal reflection, and a life of external observation, together;  or has, in other words, engrafted the
Painter on the Metaphysician;  and in our minds, the
union, if not complete or in all respects harmonious, presents a result not less singular than delightful.  If Mr
H. criticises an author, he paints him.  If he draws a
character, he dissects it;  and some of his characters
"look a little the worse" (as Swift says) "for having the
skin taken off". (74)  If he describes a feeling, he is
not satisfied till he embodies it as a real sensation in

all its individuality and with all the circumstances that
give it interest.  If he enters upon some distinction too
subtle and recondite to be immediately understood, he re-
lieves it by some palpable and popular illustration.  In
fact, he all along acts as his own interpreter, and is
continually translating his thoughts out of their original
metaphysical obscurity into the language of the senses and
of common observation.  This appears to us to constitute
the excellence and to account for the defects of his writings.  There is a display (to profusion) of various and
striking powers;  but they do not tend to the same object.
The thought and the illustration do not always hang well
together:  the one puzzles, and the other startles.  From
this circumstance it is that to many people Mr Hazlitt
appears an obscure and unconnected and to others a forced
and extravagant writer.  He may be said to paint caricatures on gauze or cobwebs;  to explain the mysteries of
the Cabbala by Egyptian hieroglyphics.  Another fault is
that he draws too entirely on his own resources.  He
never refers to the opinions of other authors (ancient or
modern) or to the common opinions afloat on any subject,
or if he does, it is to treat them with summary or elaborate contempt.  Neither does he consider a subject in
all its possible or most prominent bearings, but merely in
those points (sometimes minute and extraneous, at other
times more broad and general) in which it happens to have
pressed close on his own mind or to have suggested some
ingenious solution.  He follows out his own view of a
question, however, fearlessly and patiently;  and puts the
reader in possession without reserve of all he has thought
upon it.  There is no writer who seems to pay less attention to the common prejudices of the vulgar;  or the com-
mon-places of the learned;  and who has consequently given
greater offence to the bigotted, the self-sufficient, and
the dull.  We have nothing to do with Mr Hazlitt as a
controversial writer;  and even as a critic, he is perhaps
too much of a partisan, he is too eager and exclusive in
his panegyrics or invectives;  but as an Essayist, his
writings can hardly fail to be read with general satisfaction and with the greatest by those who are most able to
appreciate characteristic thought and felicitous expression.

1 More's 'The Confutation of Tyndale's Answer', 1532-3, was in reply to Tyndale's 'An Answer unto Sir Thomas More's Dialoge', 1531.  'A Dialogue of Sir Thomas More' was published in 1529, and 'A Dialogue concerning Heresies' in 1528.

2 Cf. 'Religio Medici', II, i.

3 Coleridge, Ode to Tranquillity, l. 32.

4 Paine's 'Rights of Man', 1791-2, was in reply to Burke's 'Reflections on the Revolution in France', 1790.

5 Cf. Horace, 'Ars Poetica', ll. 15-16:  'More resplendent cloths.'

6 Pope, 'Moral Essays', I, 146-7.  According to Warburton, Pope preferred Charron's 'De La Sagesse', 1601, because he moderated 'everywhere the extravagant Pyrrhonism of his friend'.  Pierre Charron (1541-1603), French moralist and theologian.

7 By Jeremy Taylor, 1650.

8 George Berkeley, 'Alciphron:  or the Minute Philosopher', 1732.

9 Cf. 'Religio Medici', II, i.

10 Thomas Fuller (1608-61), divine and historian.  Lamb quotes from the following works:  'The Holy State', 1642;  'A Pisgah-Sight of Palestine', 1650;  'The Church History of Britain', 1655;  'The History of the Worthies of England', 1662.

11 Bacon, 'Novum Organum', I, 49;  II, 32:  'Dry light.'

12 'The Holy State', III, 8.

13 'Worthies of England', II, Lincolnshire.

14 'Church History', IV, ii.

15 'Hamlet', V, i, 207-10;  cf. 'King Lear', IV, vi, 133-4.

16 Cf. 'Richard II', IV, i, 260-2.

17 Jeremiah 9:1.

18 In the 'Reflector' article the footnote continued:

> We are too apt to indemnify ourselves for some
> characteristic excellence we are kind enough to con-
> cede to a great author, by denying him every thing
> else. Thus Donne and Cowley, by happening to pos-
> sess more wit and faculty of illustration than other
> men, are supposed to have been incapable of nature
> or feeling: they are usually opposed to such wri-
> ters as Shenstone and Parnel; whereas in the very
> thickest of their conceits, - in the bewildering
> maze of their tropes and figures, a warmth of soul
> and generous feeling shines through, the "sum" of
> which "forty thousand" of those natural poets, as
> they are called, "with all their quantity, could not
> make up." - Without any intention of setting Fuller
> on a level with Donne or Cowley, I think the injus-
> tice which has been done him in the denial that he
> possesses any other qualities than those of a quaint
> and conceited writer, is of the same kind as that
> with which those two great Poets have been treated.

19 Cf. 'Othello', III, iii, 144.
20 Cf. 'A Midsummer Night's Dream', II, ii, 11-12, 23.
21 The edition of Bunyan to which Lamb is referring is
that of 1830, with a life of Bunyan by Southey, illustrations by John Martin and W. Harvey, and a prefatory
poem by Bernard Barton, not Mrs Hemans.
22 Pidcock exhibited his lions at Bartholomew Fair.
23 Charles Heath (1785-1848), engraver.
24 Anthony Ashley Cooper, third Earl of Shaftesbury (1671-
1713), author of 'Characteristics', 1711; Sir William
Temple (1628-99), diplomat and man of letters. His
essays, 'Miscellanea', were published in 1680, 1690,
and 1701. In addition to the essays mentioned by
Lamb, there are also references to On Health and Long
Life, On the Cure of the Gout, and Of Gardening.
25 Cowley's 'Several Discourses by way of Essays' was
published in his 'Works', 1668.
26 Abbé Sièyes (1748-1836), French political theorist.
27 Gilbert Burnet (1643-1715). 'Bishop Burnet's History
of His Own Times' was published 1724-34.
28 'High relief.'
29 William Robertson (1721-93), Scottish historian and
author of 'The History of the Reign of the Emperor
Charles V', 1769, and 'The History of America', 1777.
William Roscoe's principal work was his 'Life of Lorenzo de' Medici', 1795.
30 Lamb was mistaken in this.

# VI  Painting

This essay, like that on Shakespeare, first appeared in
Leigh Hunt's 'Reflector', 1811.   It was published in the
third number and was entitled *On the Genius and Character
of Hogarth; with some Remarks on a Passage in the Writings of the late Mr. Barry*.   Lamb reprinted it in his
'Works', 1818.   In his essay on Hogarth in 'The Round
Table', Hazlitt wrote:  'Of the pictures in the *Rake's
Progress* in this collection, we shall not here say any
thing, because ... they have already been criticised by a
writer, to whom we could add nothing, in a paper which
ought to be read by every lover of Hogarth and of English
genius' ('Works', IV, 31).   His final judgment in 'The
Spirit of the Age' was that 'Mr. Lamb is a good judge of
prints and pictures.   His admiration of Hogarth does
credit to both, particularly when it is considered that
Leonardo da Vinci is his next greatest favourite, and that
his love of the *actual* does not proceed from a want of
taste for the *ideal*' (Ibid., XI, 181).   According to
Crabb Robinson, Coleridge 'praised warmly an essay on Hogarth by Charles Lamb' ('Diary', I, 42).   He also noted
in his diary that Lamb had 'no relish for landscape painting.   But his relish for historic painting is exquisite'
(Ibid., I, 145).   When he read the essay to Flaxman, the
artist 'acknowledged the literary merit of the piece, but
he by no means concurred in the opinion Charles Lamb maintains, that Hogarth is a moral painter.   On the contrary
Flaxman asserted that he was a very wicked though most
witty artist' (Ibid., I. 50).   Lamb's friend, Barron
Field, also had reservations:  'In his estimation of
prints and pictures, as well as of actors and actresses,
we think that, like all near-sighted people, he had
"visions of his own," and would not "undo them"' (Lucas,
'Life', I, 358).

ONE of the earliest and noblest enjoyments I had when a
boy was in the contemplation of those capital prints by
Hogarth, the *Harlot's* and *Rake's Progresses*, which, along
with some others, hung upon the walls of a great hall in
an old-fashioned house in ———shire, (1) and seemed the
solitary tenants (with myself) of that antiquated and
life-deserted apartment.

Recollection of the manner in which those prints used
to affect me, has often made me wonder, when I have heard
Hogarth described as a mere comic painter, as one whose
chief ambition was to *raise a laugh*.  To deny that there
are throughout the prints which I have mentioned circumstances introduced of a laughable tendency, would be to
run counter to the common notions of mankind;  but to suppose that in their *ruling character* they appeal chiefly to
the risible faculty, and not first and foremost to the
very heart of man, its best and most serious feelings,
would be to mistake no less grossly their aim and purpose.
A set of severer Satires (for they are not so much Comedies, which they have been likened to, as they are strong
and masculine Satires) less mingled with any thing of mere
fun, were never written upon paper, or graven upon copper.
They resemble Juvenal, or the satiric touches in Timon of
Athens.

I was pleased with the reply of a gentleman, who being
asked which book he esteemed most in his library, answered, - "Shakspeare:"  being asked which he esteemed next
best, replied,- "Hogarth."   His graphic representations
are indeed books:  they have the teeming, fruitful, suggestive meaning of *words*.   Other pictures we look at, -
his prints we read.

In pursuance of this parallel, I have sometimes entertained myself with comparing the *Timon of Athens* of Shakspeare (which I have just mentioned) and Hogarth's *Rake's
Progress* together.   The story, the moral, in both is
nearly the same.   The wild course of riot and extrava-
gance, ending in the one with driving the Prodigal from
the society of men into the solitude of the deserts, and
in the other with conducting the Rake through his several
stages of dissipation into the still more complete desola-
tions of the mad-house, in the play and in the picture are
described with almost equal force and nature.   The levee
of the Rake, which forms the subject of the second plate
in the series, is almost a transcript of Timon's levee in
the opening scene of that play.   We find a dedicating
poet, and other similar characters, in both.

The concluding scene in the *Rake's Progress* is perhaps
superior to the last scenes of *Timon*.   If we seek for
something of kindred excellence in poetry, it must be in

the scenes of Lear's beginning madness, where the King and
the Fool and the Tom-o'-Bedlam conspire to produce such.a
medley of mirth checked by misery, and misery rebuked by
mirth; where the society of those "strange bed-fellows" (2) which misfortunes have brought Lear acquainted
with, so finely sets forth the destitute state of the monarch, while the lunatic bans of the one, and the disjointed sayings and wild but pregnant allusions of the other,
so wonderfully sympathize with that confusion, which they
seem to assist in the production of, in the senses of that
"child-changed father." (3)

In the scene in Bedlam, which terminates the *Rake's
Progress*, we find the same assortment of the ludicrous
with the terrible.  Here is desperate madness, the over-
turning of originally strong thinking faculties, at which
we shudder, as we contemplate the duration and pressure of
affliction which it must have asked to destroy such a
building; - and here is the gradual hurtless lapse into
idiocy, of faculties, which at their best of times never
having been strong, we look upon the consummation of their
decay with no more of pity than is consistent with a
smile.  The mad taylor, the poor driveller that has gone
out of his wits (and truly he appears to have had no great
journey to go to get past their confines) for the love of
*Charming Betty Careless*, (4) - these half-laughable,
scarce-pitiable objects take off from the horror which the
principal figure would of itself raise, at the same time
that they assist the feeling of the scene by contributing
to the general notion of its subject:-

Madness, thou chaos of the brain,
What art, that pleasure giv'st, and pain?
Tyranny of Fancy's reign!
Mechanic Fancy, that can build
Vast labyrinths and mazes wild,
With rule disjointed, shapeless measure,
Fill'd with horror, fill'd with pleasure!
Shapes of horror, that would even
Cast doubts of mercy upon heaven.
Shapes of pleasure, that, but seen,
Would split the shaking sides of spleen.* (5)

Is it carrying the spirit of comparison to excess to
remark, that in the poor kneeling weeping female, who accompanies her seducer in his sad decay, there is something
analogous to Kent, or Caius, as he delights rather to be
called, in *Lear*, - the noblest pattern of virtue which

*Lines inscribed under the plate.

even Shakspeare has conceived, - who follows his royal
master in banishment, that had pronounced *his* banishment,
and forgetful at once of his wrongs and dignities, taking
on himself the disguise of a menial, retains his fidelity
to the figure, his loyalty to the carcass, the shadow, the
shell and empty husk of Lear?

In the perusal of a book, or of a picture, much of the
impression which we receive depends upon the habit of mind
which we bring with us to such perusal.   The same circumstance may make one person laugh, which shall render another very serious;   or in the same person the first impression may be corrected by after-thought.   The misem-
ployed incongruous characters at the *Harlot's Funeral*, on
a superficial inspection, provoke to laughter;   but when
we have sacrificed the first emotion to levity, a very
different frame of mind succeeds, or the painter has lost
half his purpose.   I never look at that wonderful assemblage of depraved beings, who, without a grain of reverence or pity in their perverted minds, are performing the
sacred exteriors of duty to the relics of their departed
partner in folly, but I am as much moved to sympathy from
the very want of it in them, as I should be by the finest
representation of a virtuous death-bed surrounded by real
mourners, pious children, weeping friends, - perhaps more
by the very contrast.   What reflexions does it not awake,
of the dreadful heartless state in which the creature (a
female too) must have lived, who in death wants the accompaniment of one genuine tear.   That wretch who is re-
moving the lid of the coffin to gaze upon the corpse with
a face which indicates a perfect negation of all goodness
or womanhood - the hypocrite parson and his demure partner - all the fiendish group - to a thoughtful mind present a moral emblem more affecting than if the poor
friendless carcass had been depicted as thrown out to the
woods, where wolves had assisted at its obsequies, itself
furnishing forth its own funeral banquet.

It is easy to laugh at such incongruities as are met
together in this picture, - incongruous objects being of
the very essence of laughter, - but surely the laugh is
far different in its kind from that thoughtless species to
which we are moved by mere farce and grotesque.   We laugh
when Ferdinand Count Fathom, at the first sight of the
white cliffs of Britain, feels his heart yearn with filial
fondness towards the land of his progenitors, which he is
coming to fleece and plunder, (6) - we smile at the exquisite irony of the passage, - but if we are not led on by
such passages to some more salutary feeling than laughter,
we are very negligent perusers of them in book or picture.

It is the fashion with those who cry up the great His-

torical School in this country, at the head of which Sir
Joshua Reynolds is placed, to exclude Hogarth from that
school, as an artist of an inferior and vulgar class.
Those persons seem to me to confound the painting of subjects in common or vulgar life with the being a vulgar
artist. (7)  The quantity of thought which Hogarth crowds
into every picture, would alone *unvulgarize* every subject
which he might choose.  Let us take the lowest of his
subjects, the print called *Gin Lane*.  Here is plenty of
poverty and low stuff to disgust upon a superficial view;
and accordingly, a cold spectator feels himself immediately disgusted and repelled.  I have seen many turn away
from it, not being able to bear it.  The same persons
would perhaps have looked with great complacency upon
Poussin's celebrated picture of the *Plague at Athens*.*
Disease and Death and bewildering Terror in *Athenian garments* are endurable, and come, as the delicate critics express it, within the "limits of pleasurable sensation."
But the scenes of their own St. Giles's, delineated by
their own countryman, are too shocking to think of.  Yet
if we could abstract our minds from the fascinating colours of the picture, and forget the coarse execution (in
some respects) of the print, intended as it was to be a
cheap plate, accessible to the poorer sort of people, for
whose instruction it was done, I think we could have no
hesitation in conferring the palm of superior genius upon
Hogarth, comparing this work of his with Poussin's picture.  There is more of imagination in it - that power
which draws all things to one, - which makes things animate and inanimate, beings with their attributes, subjects
and their access[o]ries, take one colour, and serve to one
effect.  Every thing in the print, to use a vulgar expression, *tells*.  Every part is full of "strange images
of death." (8)  It is perfectly amazing and astounding to
look at.  Not only the two prominent figures, the woman
and the half-dead man, which are as terrible as any thing
which Michael Angelo ever drew, but every thing else in
the print contributes to bewilder and stupefy, - the very
houses, as I heard a friend of mine express it, tumbling
all about in various directions, seem drunk - seem absolutely reeling from the effect of that diabolical spirit
of phrenzy which goes forth over the whole composition. -
To shew the poetical and almost prophetical conception in
the artist, one little circumstance may serve.  Not content with the dying and dead figures, which he has strewed
in profusion over the proper scene of the action, he shews
you what (of a kindred nature) is passing beyond it.

*At the late Mr. Hope's, in Cavendish-square.

Close by the shell, in which, by direction of the parish
beadle, a man is depositing his wife, is an old wall,
which, partaking of the universal decay around it, is tumbling to pieces.  Through a gap in this wall are seen
three figures, which appear to make a part in some funeral
procession which is passing by on the other side of the
wall, out of the sphere of the composition.  This extending of the interest beyond the bounds of the subject could
only have been conceived by a great genius.  Shakspeare,
in his description of the painting of the Trojan War, in
his *Tarquin and Lucrece*, has introduced a similar device,
where the painter made a part stand for the whole:-

> For much imaginary work was there,
> Conceit deceitful, so compact, so kind,
> That for Achilles' image stood his spear,
> Grip'd in an armed hand;  himself behind
> Was left unseen, save to the eye of mind:
> A hand, a foot, a face, a leg, a head,
> Stood for the whole to be imagined. (9)

This he well calls *imaginary work*, where the spectator
must meet the artist in his conceptions half way;  and it
is peculiar to the confidence of high genius alone to
trust so much to spectators or readers.  Lesser artists
shew every thing distinct and full, as they require an
object to be made out to themselves before they can comprehend it.

When I think of the power displayed in this (I will not
hesitate to say) sublime print, it seems to me the extreme
narrowness of system alone, and of that rage for classification, by which, in matters of taste at least, we are
perpetually perplexing instead of arranging our ideas,
that would make us concede to the work of Poussin above-
mentioned, and deny to this of Hogarth, the name of a
grand serious composition.

We are for ever deceiving ourselves with names and
theories.  We call one man a great historical painter,
because he has taken for his subjects kings or great men,
or transactions over which time has thrown a grandeur.
We term another the painter of common life, and set him
down in our minds for an artist of an inferior class,
without reflecting whether the quantity of thought shewn
by the latter may not much more than level the distinction
which their mere choice of subjects may seem to place between them;  or whether, in fact, from that very common
life a great artist may not extract as deep an interest as
another man from that which we are pleased to call history.

I entertain the highest respect for the talents and virtues of Reynolds, but I do not like that his reputation should overshadow and stifle the merits of such a man as Hogarth, nor that to mere names and classifications we should be content to sacrifice one of the greatest ornaments of England.

I would ask the most enthusiastic admirer of Reynolds, whether in the countenances of his *Staring* and *Grinning Despair*, which he has given us for the faces of Ugolino and dying Beaufort, there be any thing comparable to the expression which Hogarth has put into the face of his broken-down rake in the last plate but one of the *Rake's Progress*,\* where a letter from the manager is brought to him to say that his play "will not do?"   Here all is easy, natural, undistorted, but withal what a mass of woe is here accumulated! - the long history of a misspent life is compressed into the countenance as plainly as the series of plates before had told it;  here is no attempt at Gorgonian looks which are to freeze the beholder, no grinning at the antique bed-posts, no facemaking, or consciousness of the presence of spectators in or out of the picture, but grief kept to a man's self, a face retiring from notice with the shame which great anguish sometimes brings with it, - a final leave taken of hope, - the coming on of vacancy and stupefaction, - a beginning alienation of mind looking like tranquillity.   Here is matter for the mind of the beholder to feed on for the hour together, - matter to feed and fertilize the mind.   It is too real to admit one thought about the power of the artist who did it. - When we compare the expression in subjects which so fairly admit of comparison, and find the superiority so clearly to remain with Hogarth, shall the mere contemptible difference of the scene of it being laid in the one case in our Fleet or King's Bench Prison, and in the other in the State Prison of Pisa, or the bed-room of a cardinal, - or that the subject of the one has never been authenticated, and the other is matter of history, - so weigh down the real points of the comparison, as to induce us to rank the artist who has chosen the one scene or subject (though confessedly inferior in that which constitutes the soul of his art) in a class from which we ex-

---

\*The first perhaps in all Hogarth for serious expression.   That which comes next to it, I think, is the jaded morning countenance of the debauchée in the second plate of the *Marriage Alamode*, which lectures on the vanity of pleasure as audibly as any thing in Ecclesiastes.

clude the better genius (who has happened to make choice
of the other) with something like disgrace?*

*The Boys under Demoniacal Possession* of Raphael and
Dominichino, (12) by what law of classification are we
bound to assign them to belong to the great style in
painting, and to degrade into an inferior class the Rake
of Hogarth when he is the Madman in the Bedlam scene?   I
am sure he is far more impressive than either.  It is a
face which no one that has seen can easily forget.  There
is the stretch of human suffering to the utmost endurance,
severe bodily pain brought on by strong mental agony, the
frightful obstinate laugh of madness, - yet all so un-
forced and natural, that those who never were witness to
madness in real life, think they see nothing but what is
familiar to them in this face.  Here are no tricks of
distortion, nothing but the natural face of agony.  This
is high tragic painting, and we might as well deny to
Shakspeare the honours of a great tragedian, because he
has interwoven scenes of mirth with the serious business
of his plays, as refuse to Hogarth the same praise for the
two concluding scenes of the *Rake's Progress*, because of
the Comic Lunatics** which he has thrown into the one, or

*Sir Joshua Reynolds, somewhere in his lectures, speaks
of the *presumption* of Hogarth in attempting the grand
style in painting, by which he means his choice of certain
Scripture subjects. (10)   Hogarth's excursions into Holy
Land were not very numerous, but what he has left us in
this kind have at least this merit, that they have expression of *some sort or other* in them, - the *Child Moses
before Pharaoh's Daughter*, for instance:  which is more
than can be said of Sir Joshua Reynolds's *Repose in Egypt*,
painted for Macklin's Bible, (11) where for a Madon[n]a he
has substituted a sleepy, insensible, unmotherly girl, one
so little worthy to have been selected as the Mother of
the Saviour, that she seems to have neither heart nor
feeling to entitle her to become a mother at all.  But
indeed the race of Virgin Mary painters seems to have been
cut up, root and branch, at the Reformation.  Our artists
are too good Protestants to give life to that admirable
commixture of maternal tenderness with reverential awe and
wonder approaching to worship, with which the Virgin
Mothers of L. da Vinci and Raphael (themselves by their
divine countenances inviting men to worship) contemplate
the union of the two natures in the person of their
Heaven-born Infant.

**There are of madmen, as there are of tame,
  All humour'd not alike.  We have here some

the Alchymist that he has introduced in the other, who is
paddling in the coals of his furnace, keeping alive the
flames of vain hope within the very walls of the prison to
which the vanity has conducted him, which have taught the
darker lesson of extinguished hope to the desponding
figure who is the principal person of the scene.

It is the force of these kindly admixtures, which as-
similates the scenes of Hogarth and of Shakspeare to the
drama of real life, where no such thing as pure tragedy is
to be found;  but merriment and infelicity, ponderous
crime and feather-light vanity, like twi-formed births,
disagreeing complexions of one intertexture, perpetually
unite to shew forth motley spectacles to the world.   Then
it is that the poet or painter shews his art, when in the
selection of these comic adjuncts he chooses such circumstances as shall relieve, contrast with, or fall into,
without forming a violent opposition to, his principal
object.   Who sees not that the Grave-digger in *Hamlet*,
the Fool in *Lear*, have a kind of correspondency to, and
fall in with, the subjects which they seem to interrupt,
while the comic stuff in *Venice Preserved*, and the doggrel
nonsense of the Cook and his poisoning associates in the
*Rollo* of Beaumont and Fletcher, are pure, irrelevant, impertinent discords, - as bad as the quarrelling dog and
cat under the table of the *Lord and the Disciples at
Emmaus* of Titian?

Not to tire the reader with perpetual reference to
prints which he may not be fortunate enough to possess, it
may be sufficient to remark, that the same tragic cast of
expression and incident, blended in some instances with a
greater alloy of comedy, characterizes his other great
work, the *Marriage Alamode*, as well as those less elaborate exertions of his genius, the prints called *Industry*
and *Idleness*, the *Distrest Poet*, &c. forming, with the
*Harlot's* and *Rake's Progresses*, the most considerable if
not the largest class of his productions, - enough surely
to rescue Hogarth from the imputation of being a mere
buffoon, or one whose general aim was only to *shake the
sides*.

There remains a very numerous class of his performan-

> So apish and fantastic, play with a feather;
> And though 'twould grieve a soul to see God's image
> So blemish'd and defac'd, yet do they act
> Such antick and such pretty lunacies,
> That, spite of sorrow, they will make you smile.
> Others again we have, like angry lions,
> Fierce as wild bulls, untameable as flies.
> 
> *Honest Whore*. (13)

ces, the object of which must be confessed to be principally comic.   But in all of them will be found something
to distinguish them from the droll productions of Bunbury
and others. (14)   They have this difference, that we do
not merely laugh at, we are led into long trains of reflection by them.   In this respect they resemble the
characters of Chaucer's *Pilgrims*, which have strokes of
humour in them enough to designate them for the most part
as comic, but our strongest feeling still is wonder at the
comprehensiveness of genius which could crowd, as poet and
painter have done, into one small canvas so many diverse
yet co-operating materials.

The faces of Hogarth have not a mere momentary interest, as in caricatures, or those grotesque physiognomies
which we sometimes catch a glance of in the street, and,
struck with their whimsicality, wish for a pencil and the
power to sketch them down;  and forget them again as
rapidly, - but they are permanent abiding ideas.   Not the
sports of nature, but her necessary eternal classes. (15)
We feel that we cannot part with any of them, lest a link
should be broken.

It is worthy of observation, that he has seldom drawn
a mean or insignificant countenance.*   Hogarth's mind was
eminently reflective;  and, as it has been well observed
of Shakspeare, that he has transfused his own poetical
character into the persons of his drama (they are all more
or less *poets*) Hogarth has impressed a *thinking character*
upon the persons of his canvas.   This remark must not be
taken universally.   The exquisite idiotism of the little
gentleman in the bag and sword beating his drum in the
print of the *Enraged Musician*, would of itself rise up
against so sweeping an assertion.   But I think it will be
found to be true of the generality of his countenances.
The knife-grinder and Jew flute-player in the plate just
mentioned may serve as instances instead of a thousand.
They have intense thinking faces, though the purpose to
which they are subservient by no means required it;  but
indeed it seems as if it was painful to Hogarth to contemplate mere vacancy or insignificance.

This reflection of the artist's own intellect from the

*If there are any of that description, they are in his
*Strolling Players*, a print which has been cried up by Lord
Orford as the richest of his productions, (16) and it may
be, for what I know, in the mere lumber, the properties,
and dead furniture of the scene, but in living character
and expression it is (for Hogarth) lamentably poor and
wanting;  it is perhaps the only one of his performances
at which we have a right to feel disgusted.

faces of his characters, is one reason why the works of
Hogarth, so much more than those of any other artist are
objects of meditation.   Our intellectual natures love the
mirror which gives them back their own likenesses.   The
mental eye will not bend long with delight upon vacancy.
   Another line of eternal separation between Hogarth and
the common painters of droll or burlesque subjects, with
whom he is often confounded, is the sense of beauty, which
in the most unpromising subjects seems never wholly to
have deserted him.   "Hogarth himself," says Mr. Coleridge,* from whom I have borrowed this observation, speaking of a scene which took place at Ratzeburg, "never drew
a more ludicrous distortion, both of attitude and physiognomy, than this effect occasioned: nor was there wanting
beside it one of those beautiful female faces which the
same Hogarth, *in whom the satirist never extinguished that
love of beauty which belonged to him as a poet*, so often
and so gladly introduces as the central figure in a crowd
of humourous deformities, which figure (such is the power
of true genius) neither acts nor is meant to act as a contrast;  but diffuses through all, and over each of the
group, a spirit of reconciliation and human kindness;  and
even when the attention is no longer consciously directed
to the cause of this feeling, still blends its tenderness
with our laughter:  and *thus prevents the instructive merriment at the whims of nature, or the foibles or humours
of our fellow-men, from degenerating into the heart-poison
of contempt or hatred*." (17)   To the beautiful females in
Hogarth, which Mr. C. has pointed out, might be added, the
frequent introduction of children (which Hogarth seems to
have taken a particular delight in) into his pieces.
They have a singular effect in giving tranquillity and a
portion of their own innocence to the subject.   The baby
riding in its mother's lap in the *March to Finchley*,(its
careless innocent face placed directly behind the intri-
guing time-furrowed countenance of the treason-plotting
French priest) perfectly sobers the whole of that tumultuous scene.   The boy mourner winding up his top with so
much unpretending insensibility in the plate of the *Harlot's Funeral*, (the only thing in that assembly that is
not a hypocrite) quiets and soothes the mind that has been
disturbed at the sight of so much depraved man and woman
kind.
   I had written thus far, when I met with a passage in
the writings of the late Mr. Barry, (18) which, as it
falls in with the *vulgar notion* respecting Hogarth, which
this Essay has been employed in combating, I shall take

*The Friend*, No. XVI.

the liberty to transcribe, with such remarks as may suggest themselves to me in the transcription;   referring the
reader for a full answer to that which has gone before.

"Notwithstanding Hogarth's merit does undoubtedly entitle him to an honourable place among the artists, and
that his little compositions, considered as so many dramatic representations, abounding with humour, character, and
extensive observations on the various incidents of low,
faulty, and vicious life, are very ingeniously brought together, and frequently tell their own story with more facility than is often found in many of the elevated and more
noble inventions of Rafaelle, and other great men;   yet it
must be honestly confessed, that in what is called knowledge of the figure, foreigners have justly observed, that
Hogarth is often so raw and unformed, as hardly to deserve
the name of an artist.   But this capital defect is not
often perceivable, as examples of the naked and of elevated nature but rarely occur in his subjects, which are for
the most part filled with characters, that in their nature
tend to deformity;   besides, his figures are small, and
the jonctures, and other difficulties of drawing that
might occur in their limbs, are artfully concealed with
their clothes, rags, &c.   But what would atone for all
his defects, even if they were twice told, is his admirable fund of invention, ever inexhaustible in its resources;   and his satyr, which is always sharp and pertinent,
and often highly moral, was (except in a few instances,
where he weakly and meanly suffered his integrity to give
way to his envy) seldom or never employed in a dishonest
or unmanly way.   Hogarth has been often imitated in his
satirical vein, sometimes in his humourous;   but very few
have attempted to rival him in his moral walk.   The line
of art pursued by my very ingenious predecessor and
brother academician, Mr. Penny, is quite distinct from
that of Hogarth, and is of a much more delicate and superior relish;   he attempts the heart, and reaches it, whilst
Hogarth's general aim is only to shake the sides;   in
other respects no comparison can be thought of, as Mr.
Penny has all that knowledge of the figure and academical
skill, which the other wanted.   As to Mr. Bunbury, who
had so happily succeeded in the vein of humour and caricatura, he has for some time past altogether relinquished
it, for the more amiable pursuit of beautiful nature:
this, indeed, is not to be wondered at, when we recollect
that he has, in Mrs. Bunbury, so admirable an exemplar of
the most finished grace and beauty continually at his
elbow.   But (to say all that occurs to me on this subject) perhaps it may be reasonably doubted, whether the
being much conversant with Hogarth's method of exposing

meanness, deformity, and vice, in many of his works, is
not rather a dangerous, or, at least, a worthless pursuit;
which, if it does not find a false relish and a love of
and search after satyr and buffoonery in the spectator, is
at least not unlikely to give him one.   Life is short;
and the little leisure of it is much better laid out upon
that species of art which is employed about the amiable
and the admirable, as it is more likely to be attended
with better and nobler consequences to ourselves.   These
two pursuits in art may be compared with two sets of
people with whom we might associate;   if we give ourselves
up to the Foot[e]s, the Kenricks, &c. we shall be continually busied and paddling in whatever is ridiculous,
faulty, and vicious in life;   whereas there are those to
be found, with whom we should be in the constant pursuit
and study of all that gives a value and a dignity to human
nature."   [Account of a Series of Pictures in the Great
Room of the Society of Arts, Manufactures, and Commerce,
at the Adelphi, by James Barry, R.A. Professor of Painting
to the Royal Academy;   reprinted in the last quarto edition of his works.] (19)

"——— it must be honestly confessed, that in what is
called knowledge of the figure, foreigners have justly observed," &c.

It is a secret well known to the professors of the art
and mystery of criticism, to insist upon what they do not
find in a man's works, and to pass over in silence what
they do.   That Hogarth did not draw the naked figure so
well as Michael Angelo might be allowed, especially as
"examples of the naked," as Mr. Barry acknowledges, "rarely (he might almost have said never) occur in his subjects;"   and that his figures under their draperies do not
discover all the fine graces of an Antinous or an Apollo,
may be conceded likewise;   perhaps it was more suitable to
his purpose to represent the average forms of mankind in
the mediocrity (as Mr. Burke expresses it) (20) of the age
in which he lived:  but that his figures in general, and
in his best subjects, are so glaringly incorrect as is
here insinuated, I dare trust my own eye so far as positively to deny the fact.   And there is one part of the
figure in which Hogarth is allowed to have excelled, which
these foreigners seem to have overlooked, or perhaps calculating from its proportion to the whole (a seventh or an
eighth, I forget which) deemed it of trifling importance;
I mean the human face;   a small part, reckoning by geo-
graphical inches, in the map of man's body, but here it is
that the painter of expression must condense the wonders

of his skill, even at the expense of neglecting the "jonctures and other difficulties of drawing in the limbs,"
which it must be a cold eye that in the interest so
strongly demanded by Hogarth's countenances has leisure to
survey and censure.

"The line of art pursued by my very ingenious predecessor and brother academician, Mr. Penny."

The first impression caused in me by reading this passage, was an eager desire to know who this Mr. Penny
was. (21)   This great surpasser of Hogarth in the "delicacy of his relish," and the "line which he pursued,"
where is he, what are his works, what has he to shew?   In
vain I tried to recollect, till by happily putting the
question to a friend who is more conversant in the works
of the illustrious obscure than myself, I learnt that he
was the painter of a *Death of Wolfe* which missed the prize
the year that the celebrated picture of West on the same
subject obtained it; (22)   that he also made a picture of
the *Marquis of Granby relieving a Sick Soldier;* moreover,
that he was the inventor of two pictures of *Suspended and
Restored Animation*, which I now remember to have seen in
the Exhibition some years since, and the prints from which
are still extant in good men's houses.   This then I suppose is the line of subjects in which Mr. Penny was so
much superior to Hogarth.   I confess I am not of that
opinion.   The relieving of poverty by the purse, and the
restoring a young man to his parents by using the methods
prescribed by the Humane Society, are doubtless very amiable subjects, pretty things to teach the first rudiments
of humanity;   they amount to about as much instruction as
the stories of good boys that give away their custards to
poor beggar-boys in children's books.   But, good God! is
this *milk for babes* to be set up in opposition to Hogarth's moral scenes, his *strong meat for men?*   As well
might we prefer the fulsome verses upon their own goodness, to which the gentlemen of the Literary Fund annually
sit still with such shameless patience to listen, to the
satires of Juvenal and Persius;   because the former are
full of tender images of Worth relieved by Charity, and
Charity stretching out her hand to rescue sinking Genius,
and the theme of the latter is men's crimes and follies
with their black consequences - forgetful meanwhile of
those strains of moral pathos, those sublime heart-
touches, which these poets (in *them* chiefly shewing themselves poets) are perpetually darting across the otherwise
appalling gloom of their subject - consolatory remembran-
cers, when their pictures of guilty mankind have made us

even to despair for our species, that there is such a
thing as virtue and moral dignity in the world, that her
unquenchable spark is not utterly out - refreshing admonitions, to which we turn for shelter from the too great
heat and asperity of the general satire.

And is there nothing analogous to this in Hogarth?
nothing which "attempts and reaches the heart?" - no aim
beyond that of "shaking the sides?" - If the kneeling
ministering female in the last scene of the *Rake's Progress*, the Bedlam scene, of which I have spoken before,
and have dared almost to parallel it with the most absolute idea of Virtue which Shakspeare has left us, be not
enough to disprove the assertion;  if the sad endings of
the Harlot and the Rake, the passionate heart-bleeding
entreaties for forgiveness which the adulterous wife is
pouring forth to her assassinated and dying lord in the
last scene but one of the *Marriage Alamode*, - if these be
not things to touch the heart, and dispose the mind to a
meditative tenderness:  is there nothing sweetly concilia-
tory in the mild, patient face and gesture with which the
wife seems to allay and ventilate the feverish irritated
feelings of her poor poverty-distracted mate (the true
copy of the *genus irritabile*) (23) in the print of the
*Distrest Poet*? or if an image of maternal love be required, where shall we find a sublimer view of it than in
that aged woman in *Industry and Idleness* (plate V.) who is
clinging with the fondness of hope not quite extinguished
to her brutal vice-hardened child, whom she is accompany-
ing to the ship which is to bear him away from his native
soil, of which he has been adjudged unworthy:  in whose
shocking face every trace of the human countenance seems
obliterated, and a brute beast's to be left instead,
shocking and repulsive to all but her who watched over it
in its cradle before it was so sadly altered, and feels
it must belong to her while a pulse by the vindictive
laws of his country shall be suffered to continue to beat
in it.   Compared with such things, what is Mr. Penny's
"knowledge of the figure and academical skill which Hogarth wanted?"

With respect to what follows concerning another gentleman, with the congratulations to him on his escape out of
the regions of "humour and caricatura," in which it appears he was in danger of travelling side by side with Hogarth, I can only congratulate my country, that Mrs. Hogarth knew *her* province better than by disturbing her husband at his pallet to divert him from that universality of
subject, which has stamped him perhaps, next to Shakspeare, the most inventive genius which this island has
produced, into the "amiable pursuit of beautiful nature,"

*i.e.* copying ad infinitum the individual charms and graces
of Mrs. H——.

> "Hogarth's method of exposing meanness, deformity,
>     and vice,
> paddling in whatever is ridiculous, faulty, and vicious."

A person unacquainted with the works thus stigmatised,
would be apt to imagine, that in Hogarth there was nothing
else to be found but subjects of the coarsest and most repulsive nature.  That his imagination was naturally un-
sweet, and that he delighted in raking into every species
of moral filth.  That he preyed upon sore places only,
and took a pleasure in exposing the unsound and rotten
parts of human nature;- whereas, with the exception of
some of the plates of the *Harlot's Progress*, which are
harder in their character than any of the rest of his productions, (the *Stages of Cruelty* I omit as mere worthless
caricaturas, foreign to his general habits, the offspring
of his fancy in some wayward humour), there is scarce one
of his pieces where vice is most strongly satirised, in
which some figure is not introduced upon which the moral
eye may rest satisfied;  a face that indicates goodness,
or perhaps mere good humouredness and carelessness of mind
(negation of evil) only, yet enough to give a relaxation
to the frowning brow of satire, and keep the general air
from tainting.  Take the mild, supplicating posture of
patient Poverty in the poor woman that is persuading the
pawnbroker to accept her clothes in pledge, in the plate
of *Gin Lane*, for an instance.  A little does it, a little
of the *good* nature overpowers a world of *bad*.  One cordial honest laugh of a Tom Jones absolutely clears the atmosphere that was reeking with the black putrifying
breathings of a hypocrite Blifil.  One homely expostulat-
ing shrug from Strap, warms the whole air which the sug-
gestions of a gentlemanly ingratitude from his friend
Random had begun to freeze.  One "Lord bless us!" of
Parson Adams upon the wickedness of the times, exorcises
and purges off the mass of iniquity which the world-know-
ledge of even a Fielding could cull out and rake together.
But of the severer class of Hogarth's performances,
enough, I trust, has been said to shew that they do not
merely shock and repulse;  that there is in them the
"scorn of vice" and the "pity" too;  something to touch
the heart, and keep alive the sense of moral beauty;  the
"lacrymae rerum,"(24) and the sorrowing by which the heart
is made better.  If they be bad things, then is satire
and tragedy a bad thing;  let us proclaim at once an age
of gold, and sink the existence of vice and misery in our
speculations;  let us

———— wink, and shut our apprehensions up
From common sense of what men were and are: (25)

let us *make believe* with the children that every body is
good and happy;  and, with Dr. Swift, write panegyrics
upon the world.

But that larger half of Hogarth's works which were
painted more for entertainment than instruction (though
such was the suggestiveness of his mind, that there is
always something to be learnt from them) his humourous
scenes, - are they such as merely to disgust and set us
against our species?

The confident assertions of such a man as I consider
the late Mr. Barry to have been, have that weight of authority in them which staggers, at first hearing, even a
long preconceived opinion.  When I read his pathetic ad-
monition concerning the shortness of life, and how much
better the little leisure of it were laid out upon "that
species of art which is employed about the amiable and the
admirable;"  and Hogarth's "method" proscribed as a "dangerous or worthless pursuit," I began to think there was
something in it;  that I might have been indulging all my
life a passion for the works of this artist, to the utter
prejudice of my taste and moral sense;  but my first convictions gradually returned, a world of good-natured English faces came up one by one to my recollection, and a
glance at the matchless *Election Entertainment*, which I
have the happiness to have hanging up in my parlour, sub-
verted Mr. Barry's whole theory in an instant.

In that inimitable print, (which in my judgment as far
exceeds the more known and celebrated *March to Finchley*,
as the best comedy exceeds the best farce that ever was
written,) let a person look till he be saturated, and when
he has done wondering at the inventiveness of genius which
could bring so many characters (more than thirty distinct
classes of face) into a room, and set them down at table
together, or otherwise dispose them about, in so natural a
manner, engage them in so many easy sets and occupations,
yet all partaking of the spirit of the occasion which
brought them together, so that we feel that nothing but an
election time could have assembled them;  having no central figure or principal group, (for the hero of the
piece, the Candidate, is properly set aside in the levelling indistinction of the day, one must look for him to
find him) nothing to detain the eye from passing from part
to part, where every part is alike instinct with life, -
for here are no furniture-faces, no figures brought in to
fill up the scene like stage choruses, but all dramatis
personae:  when he shall have done wondering at all these

faces so strongly charactered, yet finished with the accu-
racy of the finest miniature; when he shall have done admiring the numberless appendages of the scene, those gratuitous doles which rich genius flings into the heap when
it has already done enough, the over-measure which it delights in giving, as if it felt its stores were exhaust-
less; the dumb rhetoric of the scenery - for tables, and
chairs, and joint-stools in Hogarth, are living and significant things; the witticisms that are expressed by
words, (all artists but Hogarth have failed when they have
endeavoured to combine two mediums of expression, and have
introduced words into their pictures), and the unwritten
numberless little allusive pleasantries that are scattered
about; the work that is going on in the scene, and beyond
it, as is made visible to the "eye of mind," by the mob
which choaks up the door-way, and the sword that has
forced an entrance before its master: when he shall have
sufficiently admired this wealth of genius, let him fairly
say what is the *result* left on his mind.   Is it an impression of the vileness and worthlessness of his species?
or is not the general feeling which remains, after the
individual faces have ceased to act sensibly on his mind,
a *kindly one in favour of his species?* was not the general
air of the scene wholesome? did it do the heart hurt to be
among it?   Something of a riotous spirit to be sure is
there, some worldly-mindedness in some of the faces, a
Doddingtonian (26) smoothness which does not promise any
superfluous degree of sincerity in the fine gentleman who
has been the occasion of calling so much good company together:  but is not the general cast of expression in the
faces, of the good sort? do they not seem cut out of the
*good old rock*, substantial English honesty? would one fear
treachery among characters of their expression? or shall
we call their honest mirth and seldom-returning relaxation
by the hard names of vice and profligacy?   That poor
country fellow, that is grasping his staff (which, from
that difficulty of feeling themselves at home which poor
men experience at a feast, he has never parted with since
he came into the room), and is enjoying with a relish that
seems to fit all the capacities of his soul the slender
joke, which that facetious wag his neighbour is practising
upon the gouty gentleman, whose eyes the effort to sup-
press pain has made as round as rings - does it shock the
"dignity of human nature" to look at that man, and to sympathise with him in the seldom-heard joke which has unbent
his care-worn hard-working visage, and drawn iron smiles
from it? or with that full-hearted cob[b]ler, who is hon-
ouring with the grasp of an honest fist the unused palm of
that annoyed patrician, whom the licence of the time has
seated next him[?]

I can see nothing "dangerous" in the contemplation of
such scenes as this, or the *Enraged Musician*, or the
*Southwark Fair*, or twenty other pleasant prints which come
crowding in upon my recollection, in which the restless
activities, the diversified bents and humours, the blameless peculiarities of men, as they deserve to be called,
rather than their "vices and follies," are held up in a
laughable point of view.   All laughter is not of a dangerous or soul-hardening tendency.   There is the petrify-
ing sneer of a demon which excludes and kills Love, and
there is the cordial laughter of a man which implies and
cherishes it.   What heart was ever made the worse by
joining in a hearty laugh at the simplicities of Sir Hugh
Evans or Parson Adams, where a sense of the ridiculous
mutually kindles and is kindled by a perception of the
amiable?   That tumultuous harmony of singers that are
roaring out the words, "The world shall bow to the Assyrian throne," from the opera of *Judith*, (27) in the third
plate of the series, called the *Four Groups of Heads;*
which the quick eye of Hogarth must have struck off in the
very infancy of the rage for sacred oratorios in this
country, while "Music yet was young;" (28)  when we have
done smiling at the deafening distortions, which these
tearers of devotion to rags and tatters, these takers of
Heaven by storm, in their boisterous mimicry of the occupation of angels, are making, – what unkindly impression
is left behind, or what more of harsh or contemptuous
feeling, than when we quietly leave Uncle Toby and Mr.
Shandy riding their hobby-horses about the room?   The
conceited, long-backed Sign-painter, that with all the
self-applause of a Raphael or Corregio (the twist of body
which his conceit has thrown him into has something of the
Corregiesque in it) is contemplating the picture of a
bottle which he is drawing from an actual bottle that
hangs beside him, in the print of *Beer Street*, – while we
smile at the enormity of the self delusion, can we help
loving the good humour and self-complacency of the fellow?
would we willingly wake him from his dream?
I say not that all the ridiculous subjects of Hogarth
have necessarily something in them to make us like them;
some are indifferent to us, some in their natures repulsive, and only made interesting by the wonderful skill and
truth to nature in the painter;  but I contend that there
is in most of them that sprinkling of the better nature,
which, like holy water, chases away and disperses the contagion of the bad.   They have this in them besides, that
they bring us acquainted with the every-day human face, –
they give us skill to detect those gradations of sense and
virtue (which escape the careless or fastidious observer)

in the countenances of the world about us;   and prevent
that disgust at common life, that *taedium quotidianarum
formarum*, (29) which an unrestricted passion for ideal
forms and beauties is in danger of producing.   In this,
as in many other things, they are analogous to the best
novels of Smollett or Fielding.

---

Lamb's review of the Reynolds Exhibition held at the
Shakespeare Gallery in Pall Mall was one of a series of
articles contributed to the 'Examiner' under the general
heading of Table-Talk.  It appeared anonymously in the
issue of 6 June 1813 and was never reprinted by Lamb.

---

The Reynolds' Gallery has upon the whole disappointed
me.  Some of the portraits are interesting.  They are
faces of characters whom we (middle-aged gentlemen) were
born a little too late to remember, but about whom we have
heard our fathers tell stories, till we almost fancy to
have seen them.  There is a charm in the portrait of a
Rodney, or a Keppel, which even a picture of Nelson must
want for me.  I should turn away after a slight inspection from the best likeness that could be made of Mrs.
Anne Clark;  but Kitty Fisher is a considerable personage.
Then the dresses of some of the women so exactly remind us
of modes which we can just recall;  of the forms under
which the venerable relationships of aunt or mother first
presented themselves to our young eyes;  the aprons, the
coifs, the lappets, the hoods.  Mercy on us, what a load
of head-ornaments seem to have conspired to bury a pretty
face in the picture of Mrs. Long, *yet could not!*  Beauty
must have some "charmed life" (30) to have been able to
surmount the conspiracy of fashion in those days to destroy it.  The portraits which least pleased me were those
of boys as infant Bacchuses, Jupiters, &c.  But the
Artist is not to be blamed for the disguise.  No doubt
the parents wished to see their children deified in their
lifetime.  It was but putting a thunderbolt (instead of a
squib) into young master's hands, and a whey-faced chit
was transformed into the infant Ruler of Olympus, him who
was afterward to shake heaven and earth with his black

brow.   Another good boy pleased his grandmama with saying
his prayers so well, and the blameless dotage of the good
old woman imagined in him an adequate representative of
the infancy of the awful prophet Samuel.   *But the great
historical compositions, where the Artist was at liberty
to paint from his own idea - the Beaufort and the Ugolino;*
- why then, I must confess, pleading the liberty of Table-
Talk for my presumption, that they have not left any very
elevating impressions upon my mind.   Pardon a ludicrous
comparison, I know, Madam, you admire them both;  but
placed opposite to each other as they are at the Gallery,
as if to set the one work in competition with the other,
they did remind me of the famous contention for the prize
of deformity, mentioned in the 173d number of the *Spectator*. (31)   The one stares and the other grins;  but is
there common dignity in their countenances?   Does any
thing of the history of their life gone by peep through
the ruins of the mind in the face, like the unconquerable
grandeur that surmounts the distortions of the Laocoon? -
The figures which stand by the bed of Beaufort are indeed
happy representations of the plain unmannered old Nobility
of the English Historical Plays of Shakspeare;  but for
any thing else, - give me leave to recommend these Maca-
roons.

    After leaving the Reynolds' Gallery, where, upon the
whole, I received a good deal of pleasure, not feeling
that I had quite had my fill of paintings, I stumbled upon
a picture in Piccadilly (No. 22, I think), which purports
to be a portrait of Francis the First by Leonardo da
Vinci. (32)   Heavens, what a difference!   It is but a
portrait as most of those I had been seeing;  but placed
by them it would kill them, swallow them up as Moses's rod
the other rods.   Where did those old painters get their
models?   I see no such figures, not in my dreams, as this
Francis, in the character, or rather with the attributes
of John the Baptist.   A more than mortal majesty in the
brow and upon the eyelid - an arm muscular, beautifully
formed ; the long graceful massy fingers compressing, yet
so as not to hurt, a lamb more lovely, more sweetly
shrinking, than we can conceive that milk-white one which
followed Una.   The picture altogether looking as if it
were eternal - combining the truth of flesh with a promise
of permanence like marble.

    Leonardo, from the one or two specimens we have of him
in England, must have been a stupendous genius.   I scarce
can think he has had his full fame - he who could paint
that wonderful personification of the Logos or third
person of the Trinity, grasping a globe, late in the possession of Mr. Troward of Pall-Mall, (33) where the hand

was by the boldest licence twice as big as the truth of
drawing warranted, yet the effect to every one that saw
it, by some magic of genius, was confessed to be not *monstrous*, but *miraculous* and *silencing*.   It could not be
gainsaid.

---

Lamb entitled this essay Barrenness of the Imaginative
Faculty in the Productions of Modern Art.  It was originally intended to appear in the November issue of the
'Englishman's Magazine', 1831, but when that ceased publication in the October it was transferred in the following
year to another of Moxon's short-lived periodicals, the
'Reflector'.  Only a partial publication was secured,
however, and the essay eventually appeared in full for the
first time in the 'Athenaeum', 12, 19, 26 January, 2 February 1833.  Lamb included it in the 'Last Essays' which
appeared later the same year.

---

HOGARTH excepted, can we produce any one painter within
the last fifty years, or since the humour of exhibiting
began, that has treated a story *imaginatively?*  By this
we mean, upon whom his subject has so acted, that it has
seemed to direct *him* - not to be arranged by him?  Any
upon whom its leading or collateral points have impressed
themselves so tyrannically, that he dared not treat it
otherwise, lest he should falsify a revelation?  Any that
has imparted to his compositions, not merely so much truth
as is enough to convey a story with clearness, but that
individualising property, which should keep the subject so
treated distinct in feature from every other subject, however similar, and to common apprehensions almost identical;  so as that we might say, this and this part could
have found an appropriate place in no other picture in the
world but this?  Is there anything in modern art - we
will not demand that it should be equal - but in any way
analogous to what Titian has effected, in that wonderful
bringing together of two times in the "Ariadne," in the
National Gallery? (34)  Precipitous, with his reeling
Satyr rout about him, re-peopling and re-illuming suddenly

the waste places, drunk with a new fury beyond the grape,
Bacchus, born in fire, fire-like flings himself at the
Cretan.  This is the time present.  With this telling of
the story an artist, and no ordinary one, might remain
richly proud.  Guido, in his harmonious version of it,
saw no further.  But from the depths of the imaginative
spirit Titian has recalled past time, and laid it contri-
butory with the present to one simultaneous effect.  With
the desert all ringing with the mad cymbals of his followers, made lucid with the presence and new offers of a god,
- as if unconscious of Bacchus, or but idly casting her
eyes as upon some unconcerning pageant - her soul undis-
tracted from Theseus - Ariadne is still pacing the solitary shore, in as much heart-silence, and in almost the
same local solitude, with which she awoke at day-break to
catch the forlorn last glances of the sail that bore away
the Athenian.

Here are two points miraculously co-uniting;  fierce
society, with the feeling of solitude still absolute;
noon-day revelations, with the accidents of the dull grey
dawn unquenched and lingering;  the *present* Bacchus, with
the *past* Ariadne;  two stories, with double Time;  separate, and harmonising.  Had the artist made the woman
one shade less indifferent to the God;  still more, had
she expressed a rapture at his advent, where would have
been the story of the mighty desolation of the heart previous? merged in the insipid accident of a flattering
offer met with a welcome acceptance.  The broken heart
for Theseus was not lightly to be pieced up by a God.

We have before us a fine rough print, from a picture by
Raphael in the Vatican.  It is the Presentation of the
new-born Eve to Adam by the Almighty.  A fairer mother of
mankind we might imagine, and a goodlier sire perhaps of
men since born.  But these are matters subordinate to the
conception of the *situation*, displayed in this extraordinary production.  A tolerably modern artist would have
been satisfied with tempering certain raptures of connu-
bial anticipation, with a suitable acknowledgment to the
Giver of the blessing, in the countenance of the first
bridegroom;  something like the divided attention of the
child (Adam was here a child man) between the given toy,
and the mother who had just blest it with the bauble.
This is the obvious, the first-sight view, the superficial.  An artist of a higher grade, considering the awful
presence they were in, would have taken care to subtract
something from the expression of the more human passion,
and to heighten the more spiritual one.  This would be as
much as an exhibition-goer, from the opening of Somerset
House to last year's show, has been encouraged to look

for. (35)   It is obvious to hint at a lower expression,
yet in a picture, that for respects of drawing and colouring, might be deemed not wholly inadmissible within these
art-fostering walls, in which the raptures should be as
ninety-nine, the gratitude as one, or perhaps Zero!   By
neither the one passion nor the other has Raphael expoun-
ded the situation of Adam.   Singly upon his brow sits the
absorbing sense of wonder at the created miracle.   The
*moment* is seized by the intuitive artist, perhaps not
self-conscious of his art, in which neither of the con-
flicting emotions - a moment how abstracted - have had
time to spring up, or to battle for indecorous mastery. -
We have seen a landscape of a justly admired neoteric, in
which he aimed at delineating a fiction, one of the most
severely beautiful in antiquity - the gardens of the Hesperides. (36)   To do Mr. ——— justice, he had painted a
laudable orchard, with fitting seclusion, and a veritable
dragon (of which a Polypheme by Poussin is somehow a fac-
simile for the situation), looking over into the world shut
out backwards, so that none but a "still-climbing Hercules" (37) could hope to catch a peep at the admired Ter-
nary of Recluses.   No conventual porter could keep his
keys better than this custos with the "lidless eyes." (38)
He not only sees that none *do* intrude into that privacy,
but, as clear as daylight, that none but *Hercules aut Diabolus* (39) by any manner of means *can*.   So far all is
well.   We have absolute solitude here or nowhere.   *Ab
extra*(40) the damsels are snug enough.   But here the artist's courage seems to have failed him.   He began to
pity his pretty charge, and, to comfort the irksomeness,
has peopled their solitude with a bevy of fair attendants,
maids of honour, or ladies of the bed-chamber, according
to the approved etiquette at a court of the nineteenth
century;   giving to the whole scene the air of a *fête
champêtre*, if we will but excuse the absence of the gentlemen.   This is well, and Watteauish.   But what is
become of the solitary mystery - the

>      Daughters three,
> That sing around the golden tree? (41)

This is not the way in which Poussin would have treated
this subject.
   The paintings, or rather the stupendous architectural
designs, of a modern artist, have been urged as objections
to the theory of our motto. (42)   They are of a character, we confess, to stagger it.   His towered structures
are of the highest order of the material sublime.   Whether they were dreams, or transcripts of some elder work-

manship - Assyrian ruins old - restored by this mighty
artist, they satisfy our most stretched and craving conceptions of the glories of the antique world.   It is a
pity that they were ever peopled.   On that side, the imagination of the artist halts, and appears defective.
Let us examine the point of the story in the "Belshazzar's
Feast."   We will introduce it by an apposite anecdote.

The court historians of the day record, that at the
first dinner given by the late King (then Prince Regent)
at the Pavilion, the following characteristic frolic was
played off.   The guests were select and admiring;   the
banquet profuse and admirable;   the lights lustrous and
oriental;   the eye was perfectly dazzled with the display
of plate, among which the great gold salt-cellar, brought
from the regalia in the Tower for this especial purpose,
itself a tower! stood conspicuous for its magnitude.   And
now the Rev. * * * * the then admired court Chaplain, was
proceeding with the grace, when, at a signal given, the
lights were suddenly overcast, and a huge transparency was
discovered, in which glittered in golden letters -
      "BRIGHTON - EARTHQUAKE - SWALLOW-UP-ALIVE!"
Imagine the confusion of the guests;   the Georges and gar-
ters, jewels, bracelets, moulted upon the occasion!   The
fans dropt, and picked up the next morning by the sly
court pages!   Mrs. Fitz-what's-her-name fainting, and the
Countess of * * * * holding the smelling bottle, till the
good humoured Prince caused harmony to be restored by
calling in fresh candles, and declaring that the whole was
nothing but a pantomime *hoax*, got up by the ingenious Mr.
Farley, of Covent Garden, from hints which his Royal High-
ness himself had furnished!   Then imagine the infinite
applause that followed, the mutual rallyings, the declara-
tions that "they were not much frightened," of the assembled galaxy.

The point of time in the picture exactly answers to the
appearance of the transparency in the anecdote.   The
huddle, the flutter, the bustle, the escape, the alarm,
and the mock alarm;   the prettinesses heightened by consternation;   the courtier's fear which was flattery, and
the lady's which was affectation;   all that we may conceive to have taken place in a mob of Brighton courtiers,
sympathising with the well-acted surprise of their sovereign;   all this, and no more, is exhibited by the well-
dressed lords and ladies in the Hall of Belus. (43)   Just
this sort of consternation we have seen among a flock of
disquieted wild geese at the report only of a gun having
gone off!

But is this vulgar fright, this mere animal anxiety for
the preservation of their persons, - such as we have wit-

nessed at a theatre, when a slight alarm of fire has been
given - an adequate exponent of a supernatural terror? the
way in which the finger of God, writing judgments, would
have been met by the withered conscience?    There is a
human fear, and a divine fear.    The one is disturbed,
restless, and bent upon escape.    The other is bowed down,
effortless, passive.    When the spirit appeared before
Eliphaz in the visions of the night, and the hair of his
flesh stood up, was it in the thoughts of the Temanite to
ring the bell of his chamber, or to call up the servants?
But let us see in the text what there is to justify all
this huddle of vulgar consternation.

From the words of Daniel it appears that Belshazzar had
made a great feast to a thousand of his lords, and drank
wine before the thousand.    The golden and silver vessels
are gorgeously enumerated, with the princes, the king's
concubines, and his wives.    Then follows -

"In the same hour came forth fingers of a man's hand,
and wrote over against the candlestick upon the plaster of
the wall of the king's palace;  and the *king* saw the part
of the hand that wrote.    Then the *king's* countenance was
changed, and his thoughts troubled him, so that the joints
of his loins were loosened, and his knees smote one
against another." (44)

This is the plain text.    By no hint can it be otherwise inferred, but that the appearance was solely confined
to the fancy of Belshazzar, that his single brain was
troubled.    Not a word is spoken of its being seen by any
else there present, not even by the queen herself, who
merely undertakes for the interpretation of the phenomenon, as related to her, doubtless, by her husband.    The
lords are simply said to be astonished; *i.e.* at the
trouble and the change of countenance in their sovereign.
Even the prophet does not appear to have seen the scroll,
which the king saw.    He recals it only, as Joseph did the
Dream to the King of Egypt.    "Then was the part of the
hand sent from him [the Lord], and this writing was written."    He speaks of the phantasm as past.

Then what becomes of this needless multiplication of
the miracle? this message to a royal conscience, singly
expressed - for it was said, "thy kingdom is divided," -
simultaneously impressed upon the fancies of a thousand
courtiers, who were implied in it neither directly nor
grammatically?

But admitting the artist's own version of the story,
and that the sight was seen also by the thousand courtiers
- let it have been visible to all Babylon - as the knees
of Belshazzar were shaken, and his countenance troubled,
even so would the knees of every man in Babylon, and their

countenances, as of an individual man, been troubled;
bowed, bent down, so would they have remained, stupor-
fixed, with no thought of struggling with that inevitable
judgment.

Not all that is optically possible to be seen, is to
be shown in every picture.  The eye delightedly dwells
upon the brilliant individualities in a "Marriage at
Cana," by Veronese, or Titian, to the very texture and
colour of the wedding garments, the ring glittering upon
the bride's fingers, the metal and fashion of the wine
pots;  for at such seasons there is leisure and luxury to
be curious.  But in a "day of judgment," or in a "day of
lesser horrors, yet divine," as at the impious feast of
Belshazzar, the eye should see, as the actual eye of an
agent or patient in the immediate scene would see, only in
masses and indistinction.  Not only the female attire and
jewelry exposed to the critical eye of the fashion, as
minutely as the dresses in a lady's magazine, in the criticised picture, - but perhaps the curiosities of anatomi-
cal science, and studied diversities of posture in the
falling angels and sinners of Michael Angelo, - have no
business in their great subjects.  There was no leisure
of them.

By a wise falsification, the great masters of painting
got at their true conclusions;  by not showing the actual
appearances, that is, all that was to be seen at any given
moment by an indifferent eye, but only what the eye might
be supposed to see in the doing or suffering of some portentous action.  Suppose the moment of the swallowing up
of Pompeii.  There they were to be seen - houses, col-
umns, architectural proportions, differences of public and
private buildings, men and women at their standing occupations, the diversified thousand postures, attitudes,
dresses, in some confusion truly, but physically they were
visible.  But what eye saw them at that eclipsing moment,
which reduces confusion to a kind of unity, and when the
senses are upturned from their proprieties, when sight and
hearing are a feeling only?  A thousand years have
passed, and we are at leisure to contemplate the weaver
fixed standing at his shuttle, the baker at his oven, and
to turn over with antiquarian coolness the pots and pans
of Pompeii.

"Sun, stand thou still upon Gibeah, and thou, Moon, in
the valley of Ajalon." (45)  Who, in reading this magnificent Hebraism, in his conception, sees aught but the
heroic sun of Nun, with the outstretched arm, and the
greater and lesser light obsequious?  Doubtless there
were to be seen hill and dale, and chariots and horsemen,
on open plain, or winding by secret defiles, and all the

circumstances and stratagems of war.   But whose eyes
would have been conscious of this array at the interposition of the synchronic miracle?   Yet in the picture of
this subject by the artist of the 'Belshazzar's Feast' -
no ignoble work either - the marshalling and landscape of
the war is everything, the miracle sinks into an anecdote
of the day;   and the eye may "dart through rank and file
traverse" (46) for some minutes, before it shall discover,
among his armed followers, *which is Joshua!*   Not modern
art alone, but ancient, where only it is to be found if
anywhere, can be detected erring, from defect of this imaginative faculty.   The world has nothing to show of the
preternatural in painting, transcending the figure of
Lazarus bursting his grave-clothes, in the great picture
at Angerstein's. (47)   It seems a thing between two
beings.   A ghastly horror at itself struggles with newly-
apprehending gratitude at second life bestowed.   It cannot forget that it was a ghost.   It has hardly felt that
it is a body.   It has to tell of the world of spirits. -
Was it from a feeling, that the crowd of half-impassioned
by-standers, and the still more irrelevant herd of passers-by at a distance, who have not heard or but faintly
have been told of the passing miracle, admirable as they
are in design and hue - for it is a glorified work - do
not respond adequately to the action - that the single
figure of the Lazarus has been attributed to Michael
Angelo, and the mighty Sebastian unfairly robbed of the
fame of the greater half of the interest?   Now that there
were not indifferent passers-by within actual scope of the
eyes of those present at the miracle, to whom the sound of
it had but faintly, or not at all, reached, it would be
hardihood to deny;   but would they see them? or can the
mind in the conception of it admit of such unconcerning
objects? can it think of them at all? or what associating
league to the imagination can there be between the seers,
and the seers not, of a presential miracle?
     Were an artist to paint upon demand a picture of a
Dryad, we will ask whether, in the present low state of
expectation, the patron would not, or ought not to be
fully satisfied with a beautiful naked figure recumbent
under wide-stretched oaks?   Disseat those woods, and
place the same figure among fountains, and falls of pellu-
cid water, and you have a - Naiad!   Not so in a rough
print we have seen after Julio Romano, we think - for it
is long since - *there*, by no process, with mere change of
scene, could the figure have reciprocated characters.
Long, grotesque, fantastic, yet with a grace of her own,
beautiful in convolution and distortion, linked to her
connatural tree, co-twisting with its limbs her own, till

both seemed either - these, animated branches;  those,
disanimated members - yet the animal and vegetable lives
sufficiently kept distinct - *his* Dryad lay - an approxima-
tion of two natures, which to conceive, it must be seen;
analogous to, not the same with, the delicacies of Ovidian
transformations.

To the lowest subjects, and, to a superficial compre-
hension, the most barren, the Great Masters gave loftiness
and fruitfulness.   The large eye of genius saw in the
meanness of present objects their capabilities of treatment from their relations to some grand Past or Future.
How has Raphael - we must still linger about the Vatican -
treated the humble craft of the ship-builder, in *his*
"Building of the Ark?"   It is in that scriptural series,
to which we have referred, and which, judging from some
fine rough old graphic sketches of them which we possess,
seem to be of a higher and more poetic grade than even the
Cartoons.   The dim of sight are the timid and the shrinking.   There is a cowardice in modern art.   As the
Frenchmen, of whom Coleridge's friend made the prophetic
guess at Rome, from the beard and horns of the Moses of
Michael Angelo collected no inferences beyond that of a He
Goat and a Cornuto; (48)  so from this subject, of mere
mechanic promise, it would instinctively turn away, as
from one incapable of investiture with any grandeur.   The
dock-yards at Woolwich would object derogatory associations.   The depôt at Chatham would be the mote and the
beam in its intellectual eye.   But not to the nautical
preparations in the ship-yards of Civita Vecchia did
Raphael look for instructions, when he imagined the Building of the Vessel that was to be conservatory of the
wrecks of the species of drowned mankind.   In the intensity of the action, he keeps ever out of sight the meanness of the operation.   There is the Patriarch, in calm
forethought, and with holy prescience, giving directions.
And there are his agents - the solitary but sufficient
Three - hewing, sawing, every one with the might and earnestness of a Demiurgus;  under some instinctive rather
than technical guidance;  giant-muscled;  every one a Hercules, or liker to those Vulcanian Three, that in sounding
caverns under Mongibello wrought in fire - Brontes, and
black Steropes, and Pyracmon. (49)  So work the workmen
that should repair a world!

Artists again err in the confounding of *poetic* with
*pictorial subjects*.   In the latter, the exterior accidents are nearly everything, the unseen qualities as nothing.   Othello's colour - the infirmities and corpulence
of a Sir John Falstaff - do they haunt us perpetually in
the reading? or are they obtruded upon our conceptions one

time for ninety-nine that we are lost in admiration at the
respective moral or intellectual attributes of the character?   But in a picture Othello is *always* a Blackamoor;
and the other only Plump Jack.   Deeply corporealised, and
enchained hopelessly in the grovelling fetters of externality, must be the mind, to which, in its better moments,
the image of the high-souled, high-intelligenced Quixote -
the errant Star of Knighthood, made more tender by eclipse
- has never presented itself, divested from the unhallowed
accompaniment of a Sancho, or a rabblement at the heels of
Rosinante.   That man has read his book by halves;   he has
laughed, mistaking his author's purport, which was -
tears.   The artist that pictures Quixote (and it is in
this degrading point that he is every season held up at
our Exhibitions) in the shallow hope of exciting mirth,
would have joined the rabble at the heels of his starved
steed.   We wish not to see *that* counterfeited, which we
would not have wished to see in the reality.   Conscious
of the heroic inside of the noble Quixote, who, on hearing
that his withered person was passing, would have stepped
over his threshold to gaze upon his forlorn habiliments,
and the "strange bed-fellows which misery brings a man acquainted with?" (50)   Shade of Cervantes! who in thy
Second Part could put into the mouth of thy Quixote those
high aspirations of a super-chivalrous gallantry, where he
replies to one of the shepherdesses, apprehensive that he
would spoil their pretty net-works, and inviting him to be
a guest with them, in accents like these:   "Truly, fairest
Lady, Actaeon was not more astonished when he saw Diana
bathing herself at the fountain, than I have been in be-
holding your beauty:   I commend the manner of your pastime, and thank you for your kind offers;   and, if I may
serve you, so I may be sure you will be obeyed, you may
command me:   for my profession is this, To shew myself
thankful, and a doer of good to all sorts of people, especially of the rank that your person shows you to be;
and if those nets,as they take up but a little piece of
ground, should take up the whole world, I would seek out
new worlds to pass through, rather than break them:   and
(he adds,) that you may give credit to this my exaggeration, behold at least he that promiseth you this, is Don
Quixote de la Mancha, if haply this name hath come to your
hearing." (51)   Illustrious Romancer! were the "fine
frenzies," (52) which possessed the brain of thy own
Quixote, a fit subject, as in this Second Part, to be exposed to the jeers of Duennas and Serving Men? to be mon-
stered, and shown up at the heartless banquets of great
men?   Was that pitiable infirmity, which in thy First
Part misleads him, *always from within*, into half-

ludicrous, but more than half-compassionable and admirable errors, not infliction enough from heaven, that men by studied artifices must devise and practise upon the humour, to inflame where they should soothe it? Why, Goneril would have blushed to practise upon the abdicated king at this rate, and the she-wolf Regan not have endured to play the pranks upon his fled wits, which thou hast made thy Quixote suffer in Duchesses' halls, and at the hands of that unworthy nobleman.*

In the First Adventures, even, it needed all the art of the most consummate artist in the Book way that the world hath yet seen, to keep up in the mind of the reader the heroic attributes of the character without relaxing; so as absolutely that they shall suffer no alloy from the debasing fellowship of the clown. If it ever obtrudes itself as a disharmony, are we inclined to laugh; or not, rather, to indulge a contrary emotion? - Cervantes, stung, perchance, by the relish with which *his* Reading Public had received the fooleries of the man, more to their palates than the generosities of the master, in the sequel let his pen run riot, lost the harmony and the balance, and sacrificed a great idea to the taste of his contemporaries. We know that in the present day the Knight has fewer admirers than the Squire. Anticipating, what did actually happen to him - as afterwards it did to his scarce inferior follower, the Author of "Guzman de Alfarache" (53) - that some less knowing hand would prevent him by a spurious Second Part: and judging, that it would be easier for his competitor to out-bid him in the comicalities, than in the *romance*, of his work, he abandoned his Knight, and has fairly set up the Squire for his Hero. For what else has he unsealed the eyes of Sancho; and instead of that twilight state of semi-insanity - the madness at second-hand - the contagion, caught from a stronger mind infected - that war between native cunning, and hereditary deference, with which he has hitherto accompanied his master - two for a pair almost - does he substitute a downright Knave, with open eyes, for his own ends only following a confessed Madman; and offering at one time to lay, if not actually laying, hands upon him! From the moment that Sancho loses his reverence, Don Quixote is become a - treatable lunatic. Our artists handle him accordingly.

*Yet from this Second Part, our cried-up pictures are mostly selected; the waiting-women with beards, &c.

53  *Ut Poesis Pictura*
    1833

---

From a letter to Samuel Rogers, 21 December.

---

But I am jealous of the combination of the Sister Arts.
Let them sparkle apart.   What injury (short of the
Theatres) did not Boydell's Shakspeare Gallery (54) do me
with Shakspeare? to have Opie's Shakspeare, Northcote's
Shakspeare, light-headed Fuselis' Shakspeare, heavy-headed
Romney's Shakspeare, wooden-headed West's Shakspeare (tho'
he did the best in Lear) deaf-headed Reynolds's Shakspeare, instead of my, and every body's Shakspeare, To be
tied down to an authentic face of Juliet!   To have Imogen's portrait! to confine the illimitable!

1 Blakesware, Hertfordshire, where Lamb's grandmother, Mary Field, had been housekeeper.
2 'The Tempest', II, ii, 37.
3 'King Lear', IV, vii, 17.
4 A famous London courtesan (d. 1752).
5 The inscriptions for the 'Rake's Progress' were by the Rev. John Hoadley (1711-76), poet and dramatist.
6 Smollett, 'Ferdinand Count Fathom', chapter 27.
7 This passage is ambiguous. Reynolds was, of course, a portrait painter. Lamb's views were shared by Hazlitt, 'Works', xvi, 206.
8 'Macbeth', I, iii, 97.
9 'The Rape of Lucrece', 11. 1422-8.
10 Reynolds, 'Discourses on Art', lecture 14.
11 Macklin's Bible, 1790.
12 E.V. Lucas suggests that the paintings in question are Raphael's 'Transfiguration', and Domenichino's 'St. Nil delivering the Son of Polyeucte of a Devil'.
13 Dekker, 'The Honest Whore', V, ii, 155-63.
14 Henry William Bunbury (1750-1811), painter and caricaturist.
15 An unconscious echo of Blake's note on the Canterbury pilgrims in the 'Descriptive Catalogue', 1809.
16 Horace Walpole, 'Anecdotes of Painting', chapter 20.
17 'The Friend', ii, 213. For 'effect' read 'effort'. The italics are Lamb's.
18 James Barry, RA (1741-1806), Irish historical painter and Professor of Painting at the Royal Academy, 1783-99.
19 First published in 1783.
20 Burke, 'A Philosophical Enquiry into the Origin of our Ideas of the Sublime and Beautiful', III, v.
21 Edward Penny (1714-91), portrait and historical painter, first Professor of Painting at the Royal Academy of which he was a founder member.

22 Benjamin West (1738-1820), American historical painter
   who became President of the Royal Academy on the death
   of Reynolds in 1792.   'The Death of Wolfe' was exhibited at the Academy in 1771.
23 Horace, 'Epistles', II, ii, 102:   'Sensitive breed.'
24 Virgil, 'Aeneid', I, 462:   'The sense of tears in
   mortal things.'   See Arnold's Geist's Grave, 1. 16.
25 Cf. Marston's prologue to 'Antonio's Revenge', 11. 17-
   18.
26 George Bubb Doddington, Lord Melcome (1691-1762), politician, wit and dandy.
27 By Thomas Augustus Arne (1710-78).   First produced in
   1764.
28 Cf. Collins, Ode on the Passions, 1. 1.
29 Cf. Terence, 'Eunuchus', 1. 297:   'The weariness with
   everyday forms.'
30 'Macbeth', V, viii, 12.
31 Addison's account of the Ugly Club is to be found in
   the 17th number of the 'Spectator' (20 March 1711);
   the 173rd number (18 September 1711) describes the
   grinning match.
32 This painting, which Lamb attributes to Leonardo, has
   not been traced.
33 The Logos/Creator Mundi, School of Leonardo, was sold
   in 1925 at the Fermor-Hesketh sale for 85 guineas.
34 Writing to Wordsworth in May 1833, Lamb confessed that
   Titian's 'Bacchus and Ariadne' was not one of his favourite paintings, and that he had used it only as an
   illustration.
35 The exhibitions of the Royal Academy were held at
   Somerset House from 1780 until 1837.
36 Probably J.M.W. Turner's 'Garden of the Hesperides'
   (1806), now in the National Gallery.
37 Cf. 'Love's Labour's Lost', IV, iii, 336-7.
38 Cf. Coleridge, Ode to the Departing Year, 1. 145.
39 'Hercules or the devil.'
40 'From the outside.'
41 Cf. 'Comus', 11. 982-3.
42 John Martin (1789-1854), English painter of large visionary and apocalyptic landscapes.   'Belshazzar's
   Feast' was painted in 1821.
43 Belshazzar.
44 Daniel 5.   Lamb's italics.   His reference to Eliphaz
   is from Job 4:15.
45 Joshua 10:12.   Martin's painting, 'Joshua commanding
   the Sun to stand still', was executed in 1816.
46 Cf. 'Paradise Lost', I, 567-8.
47 John Julius Angerstein (1735-1823), merchant and art
   collector, the greater part of whose collection was

bought by the nation in 1824 for £60,000 and formed the nucleus of the newly founded National Gallery.  Sebastiano del Piombo's 'Raising of Lazarus' is still owned by the National Gallery.

48 'Biographia Literaria', chapter 21.
49 The Vulcanian Cyclops had their workshops below the volcanoes of Sicily, of which Mongibello, a vent of Mt Etna, is one.
50 Cf. 'The Tempest', II, ii, 36-7.
51 'Don Quixote', II, chapter 58.
52 Cf. 'A Midsummer Night's Dream', V, i, 12.
53 See p. 123, n., p. 130.
54 This was a series of 170 works of art, of which 162 were oil paintings by leading artists of the day, projected by John Boydell, engraver and print publisher. Begun in 1786, they were published as engravings in 1802.

# Bibliography

TEXTS AND BIBLIOGRAPHIES

LUCAS, E.V. (ed.), 'The Works of Charles and Mary Lamb'
(London, 1903-5), 7 vols.
LUCAS, E.V. (ed.), 'The Letters of Charles and Mary Lamb'
(London, 1935), 3 vols.
LUCAS, E.V., 'The Life of Charles Lamb' (London, 1905), 2
vols.
MARRS, E.W. (ed.), 'The Letters of Charles and Mary Anne
Lamb' (Ithaca, NY, 1975), 3 vols published.
'The New Cambridge Bibliography of English Literature',
ed. George Watson (Cambridge, 1969), iii, 1223-30.
BARNETT, G.L. and TAVE, S.M., in 'The English Romantic
Poets & Essayists:  A Review of Research and Criticism',
ed. C.W. and L.H. Houtchens (New York, rev. edn, 1966),
pp. 37-74.
JACK, Ian, 'English Literature 1815-1832' (Oxford, 1963),
pp. 567-72.


CRITICISM

The best criticism of Lamb is still that by his contem-
poraries - Hazlitt, Coleridge, De Quincey, Leigh Hunt,
B.W. Proctor, P.G. Patmore, Talfourd and Crabb Robinson.
An excellent selection from these and other contemporary
sources was made by Edmund Blunden in 'Charles Lamb:  His
Life Recorded by his Contemporaries' (London, 1934).
ADES, J., Charles Lamb, Shakespeare, and Early Nineteenth-
Century Theatre, 'Publications of the Modern Language As-
sociation', 85, 1970.
BARNET, S., Lamb's Contributions to the Theory of Dramatic
Illusion, 'Publications of the Modern Language Associa-
tion', 69, 1954.

BARNET, S., Lamb and the Tragic Malvolio, 'Philological Quarterly', 33, 1954.

BARNETT, G.L., 'Lamb: The Evolution of Elia' (Bloomington, Ind., 1964).

HAVEN, R., The Romantic Art of Lamb, 'Journal of English Literary History', 30, 1963.

HOUGHTON, W.E., Lamb's Criticism of Restoration Comedy, 'Journal of English Literary History', 10, 1943.

JESSUP, B., The Mind of Elia, 'Journal of the History of Ideas', 15, 1954.

McKENNA, W., 'Lamb and the Theatre' (Gerrards Cross, 1978).

MULCAHY, D.J., Lamb: The Antithetical Manner and the Two Planes, 'Studies in English Literature', 3, 1963.

ORAGE, A.R., in his 'Selected Essays and Critical Writings', ed. H. Read and D. Saurat (London, 1935).

PARK, R., Lamb and Restoration Comedy, 'Essays in Criticism', 29, 1979.

PATER, W., in his 'Appreciations' (London, 1889).

POWYS, J.C., in his 'Visions and Revisions' (London, 1955).

RANDEL, F.V., 'The World of Elia' (Port Washington, NY, 1975).

REIMAN, D.H., Thematic Unity in Lamb's Familiar Essays, 'Journal of English and Germanic Philology', 64, 1965.

SAINTSBURY, G., 'A History of English Criticism' (Edinburgh, 1911).

SCOGGINS, J., Images of Eden in the Essays of Elia, 'Journal of English and Germanic Philology', 71, 1972.

SWINBURNE, A., in his 'Miscellanies' (London, 1886).

SYMONS, A., in his 'Figures of Several Centuries' (London, 1916).

THOMPSON, D., in 'Determinations', ed. F.R. Leavis (London, 1934).

WHALLEY, G., Coleridge's Debt to Lamb, 'Essays and Studies', 11, 1958.

The more recent issues of 'The Charles Lamb Bulletin' contain interesting historical and critical articles by John Ades, G.L. Barnett, John Beer, Hugh Sykes Davies, R.A. Foakes, Basil Willey and others.

# Index